Contents

Introduction

This book is a user-friendly, accessible guide to the Early Years care and education of children from birth to 16 years. It has been written for learners of the Council for Awards in Children's Care and Education (CACHE) Level 2 Award/Certificate/Diploma in Child Care and Education. It also covers the requirements for underpinning knowledge for National Vocational Qualifications (NVQs) in Children's Care, Learning and Development at Level 2. Learners on any of the many other courses that require a knowledge and understanding of Early Years care and education will also find this book useful. Child care settings may find it a valuable addition to their reference shelves and helpful in supporting in-service training.

Contents of the book

The book is divided into eleven units which match the units of the CACHE Level 2 qualification. The mandatory units and all of the optional units are covered. CACHE learners complete differing units depending on whether they're undertaking the Award, Certificate or Diploma. The units in this book are colour coded to reflect this, so learners will easily be able to see which units apply to them.

Throughout the book, information is given in a straight-forward style ideal for Level 2 learners. The role and responsibilities of practitioners are emphasised, and good practice is highlighted. Practical examples help readers to relate theory to real-life situations, and questions and tasks help readers to recall knowledge and develop understanding. You can read more about the text features on pages vii-viii.

About the authors

Miranda Walker has worked with children from birth to 16 years in a range of settings, including her own day nursery and out of school clubs. She has inspected nursery provision for Ofsted, and worked at East Devon College as an Early Years and Playwork lecturer and NVQ assessor and internal verifier. She is a regular contributor to industry magazines and an established author.

Marian Beaver has worked in social work, teaching and Early Years care and education. She taught for many years in FE at New College Nottingham and was an external verifier for CACHE. She inspected nursery provision for Ofsted, as well as writing. Prior to her recent retirement, she worked in Early Years and Childcare for Nottinghamshire County Council.

Jo Brewster has practised as a nurse, midwife and health visitor. She has taught for many years on Childcare courses in FE at New College Nottingham. She has inspected nursery provision for Ofsted and has worked as an internal and external verifier for CACHE.

Sally Neaum has taught in nursery classes and across the infant age range. She has also taught on a range of FE courses and has been an Ofsted inspector for nursery provision.

Jill Tallack has worked in schools across the whole primary age range, in a college of further education, training childcare students and as a registered nursery inspector. She is currently working as a local authority advisory teacher and area SENCo, supporting under-fives provision in the private, voluntary and independent sector.

Acknowledgements

Miranda Walker: Love and thanks to Nick Walker for his endless support and assistance with photography.

Every effort has been made to contact copyright holders and we apologise if anyone has been overlooked.

How to use this book

Welcome to CACHE Level 2 Childcare and Education. This section explains the features of this book and how to use them as a tool for learning. **It's important that you read this section.**

CACHE Level 2 learners complete different units depending on whether they're undertaking the CACHE Award, Certificate or Diploma. This book is divided into colour coded units, so you will easily be able to see which Units apply to you.

Learners registered for the CACHE Level 2 Award will follow Units 1 and 2. Learners registered for the CACHE Level 2 Certificate will follow Units 1 to 5. Learners registered for the CACHE Level 2 Diploma will follow Units 1 to 6, and will also undertake an optional unit. All of the optional units available are covered in this book, but Diploma learners will only need to choose **one** optional unit to study.

Learning Outcomes

In this Unit you'll learn about:

1. The types of settings and local provision for children
2. How to prepare for your placements
3. Your role and responsibilities in placements
4. Children's individual needs and the need for fairness and inclusive practice
5. Your own preferred learning style and relevant study skills

Learning outcomes

All units are divided into 'learning outcomes'. The first page of each unit lists the relevant learning outcomes.

FOCUS ON...

In this section you'll learn about the main types of settings available for children to attend and you'll find out about some local settings.

This links with Assessment Criteria 1.1, 1.2

FOCUS ON...
your learning

In this section you've learnt about the types of provision that are available to children. You've also learnt how to find out about the provision in your own local area.

Questions:

1 What does "statutory" mean?
2 How can you find out about provision in your local area?

Focus on...

This feature appears at the beginning of each learning outcome and again at the end. At the beginning it explains the focus of the outcome and makes a link to the CACHE Assessment Criteria.

At the end of each learning outcome the 'Focus on...' feature reminds you what you have learnt. It includes two questions to help you test your own learning. Answering these will confirm that you have understood what you have read.

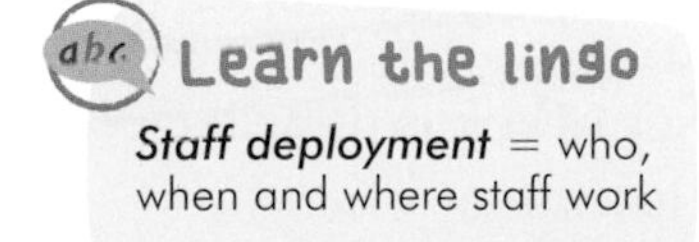

Learn the lingo

During your course you'll come across new words and terms that you may not have heard before. When these words and terms are first used in the book the 'Learn the lingo' feature appears. This gives you a clear, simple definition of the word or term.

Practical examples

Practical examples (case studies) are included to help you understand how theory links with practical work in real settings. After each case study a question or two is provided to help you think about how you can use your learning in real situations.

Practical example

Shopping with Millie

Four year old Millie is 'playing up' at the supermarket because she wants some sweets. Her Mum has told her 'no', but Millie continues to whine and cry. Mum tells her 'no' again. Millie throws herself on the floor, crying loudly. Other shoppers have noticed. Feeling embarrassed, Mum says, '"Alright, have the sweets! Just stop making such a fuss!" Millie chooses her sweets and puts them in the trolley.

1. *What has Millie learnt she should do to get what she wants when her Mum says "no"?*
2. *How would you respond to Millie in the same situation?*

Have a go

'Have a go' sections ask you to do small tasks based on the text you have read. The tasks will help you to understand and remember the information. Some tasks are linked to your placement. These will help you to apply your learning to your practical work.

Have a go!

The next time you want to attract a group of children over to an activity, try out this technique. Let children see you notice the activity and make your way over. Get busy! Become engaged in doing the activity, whatever it is. Be intent. Concentrate. Being interested is interesting! You will probably find that children are soon coming over. They'll be curious about the activity. They'll want to see what you're doing, and hopefully they'll be motivated to try it for themselves.

Good practice

It's important that you always work to high standards and do your best for the children in your care. This feature highlights good practice.

GOOD

Most settings will use a fever scan thermometer (placed on a child's forehead) or a digital thermometer (either placed in the mouth or the ear). These come with directions for use.

Fast facts

The 'fast fact' feature gives you bite-sized nuggets of information.

FAST FACT

Your setting may provide an identity badge for you to wear, giving your name and role.

Rapid recap

This feature appears towards the end of each unit. It gives a brief summary of what you have learnt. This will help you to recap quickly, and can be used as a revision tool.

FAQs

FAQs stands for 'frequently asked questions'. This feature appears towards the end of each unit, giving information on how the unit will be assessed.

Weblinks

Each unit ends with the addresses of relevant websites you may like to visit to further your learning.

Weblinks

You can read more about this online at:

- www.cache.org.uk

New legislation

Some new legislation affecting childcare and education will be introduced in England from September 2008. Please turn to the appendix on page 411 for details. It's important that you are aware of this development.

Language

This book is user-friendly. Information is given in a straightforward way that is appropriate for Level 2 learners. The term 'childcarer' is used to describe professional child care workers who work with children in a broad range of settings.

CACHE statement of values

CACHE has developed a set of values that underpin their courses. These values are promoted within this book. The CACHE statement of values are:

You must ensure that you:

1. Put children first by
    - Ensuring the child's welfare and safety
    - Showing compassion and sensitivity
    - Respecting the child as an individual
    - Upholding the child's rights and dignity
    - Enabling the child to achieve their full learning potential
2. Never use physical punishment
3. Respect the parent as the primary carer and educator of their child
4. Respect the contribution and expertise of staff in the care and education field, and other professionals who may be involved
5. Respect the customs, values and spiritual beliefs of the child and their family
6. Uphold the Council's Equal Opportunity Policy
7. Honour the confidentiality of information relating to the child and their family, unless its disclosure is required by law or is in the best interests of the child.

You can read more about this online at www.cache.org.uk

Unit 1

An introduction to working with children

Learning Outcomes

In this unit you'll learn about:

1. The types of settings and local provision for children.
2. How to prepare for your placements.
3. The responsibilities and limits of your role in placements.
4. Children's individual needs and the necessity for fairness and inclusive practice.
5. Your own preferred learning style and relevant study skills.

Learning Outcome 1

FOCUS ON...

the types of settings and local provision for children

In this section you'll learn about the main types of settings available for children to attend, and find out about some of the settings within local provision.

This links with Assessment Criteria **1.1, 1.2**

Learn the lingo

Statutory service = exists because parliament has passed a law to say that the service either must or can be provided.

Private provision = owned by an individual person or a company, and aims to make a profit.

Independent schools = run independently of the government and do not receive government funding, sometimes referred to as 'private schools'.

Voluntary provision = run by organisations such as charities and committees, does not make a profit.

FAST FACT

In England, settings that provide the Early Years Foundation Stage for children will receive some government funding. In return, the setting must provide high-quality education. The provision will be regularly inspected by **Ofsted**.

Services and facilities for children and families

There are many different services and facilities for children and their families in the UK. They can be divided into three categories:

- Statutory.
- Voluntary.
- Private/independent sectors.

Statutory settings are provided by the state, and funded by either central government or local government. A **statutory service** is one that exists because parliament has passed a law to say that the service either must or can be provided. Schools are statutory services. They exist because legally education must be provided free of charge by the government for all children aged between five and 16 years.

Private provision is owned by an individual person or a company and aims to make a profit. Families pay fees for their children to attend. Some families may receive funding to help them pay. Private providers of childcare must still meet the requirements and standards laid down by government. Examples of private provision include day nurseries, crèches and out-of-school clubs. Some schools run independently of the government and do not receive government funding. These are called **Independent schools** (although they're sometimes referred to as 'private schools').

Voluntary provision doesn't make a profit. Voluntary settings are run by organisations such as charities and committees. They may raise funds themselves and apply for grants. Users of the service may also pay a fee to attend

Learn the lingo

Ofsted = The Office for Standards in Education, Children's Services and Skills that inspects and regulates care and education for children and young people.

(usually a small amount). Examples of voluntary provision include parent and toddler groups and some pre-schools and out-of-school clubs.

The table below shows a range of provision. Providers generally offer childcare (which allows parents to work or do other things), education for children, or a mixture of both. Some settings (such as **Children's centres**) also offer additional services.

Provision offered

Setting/Provider	* Provision offered
Day nurseries	Provide childcare throughout the day to suit the needs of working parents. Usually open from 8am–6pm, Monday to Friday, closing only during the Christmas period. Nurseries often care for babies and children from 12 weeks to five years. There will usually be a separate baby room. The Early Years Foundation Stage is generally available to children aged three to five years. Some workplaces set up their own nursery for the children of their staff.
Pre-schools	Pre-schools can vary greatly in terms of opening times. Many open the same hours as school, closing for holidays. Some have hours similar to day nurseries. Some open every weekday, others just on two or three days a week. Most cater for children aged three to five years. The Early Years Foundation Stage is generally available.
Childminders	Provide childcare in their own home, caring for children of any age. The Early Years Foundation Stage may be available to children aged three to five years.
Nannies	Provide childcare in the child's home, caring for children of any age. A nanny may live-in or live-out of the family home.
Crèches	Provide childcare for a period of time (often only up to two hours) while parents do another activity such as shopping, attending a short course or going to a leisure centre.
Children's centres	(Including Sure Start Centres). These are known as multi-agency settings because professionals from different sectors will work there. Provision may include a combination of: childcare for children of all ages, Early Years Foundation Stage for children aged three to five years, health services, family support services, drop-in sessions and special events.
Nursery schools	Provide education for children from age two upwards during term time. Children may follow the Early Years Foundation Stage from age three.

Setting/Provider	* Provision offered
Infant schools	Provide education for children aged five to seven years during term time. Children follow the Early Years Foundation Stage and the National Curriculum. A nursery class for children aged three upwards may be attached to the school.
Primary schools	Provide education for children aged five to 11 years during term time. Children follow the Early Years Foundation Stage and the National Curriculum.
Out-of-school clubs	These may include before school, after school and school holiday provision. Childcare is combined with a safe place to play for children of school age. Breakfast clubs usually open at 8am. Staff look after children until it's time to escort them to school. After school clubs collect children from school, usually staying open until 6pm. Holiday clubs often open all day from 8am–6pm. Clubs may be attached to another setting such as a school, day nursery or leisure centre.
*The provision of the Early Years Foundation Stage and the National Curriculum applies to settings in England.	

Out-of-school clubs provide a safe place to play for older children

To find out about providers in your local area you can:

- Contact your local authority, which will provide a **Children's Information Service** holding details of all the providers in your area. You will probably find a link to the Children's Information Service on your local authority's website.
- Look in the local telephone directory.
- Ask at the library. Most libraries keep a directory of local clubs and organisations.

- Keep an eye on your local newspaper. New provision opening in the area is likely to be mentioned. Some settings may place adverts. Children's special events and open days may be listed in the 'What's on' pages.

The diagram below shows some of the additional provision you may find in your local area.

Learn the lingo

Children's Information Service = Each council has a CIS that provides information on childcare and related services for children aged from birth to 14 (up to aged 16 for children with special needs).

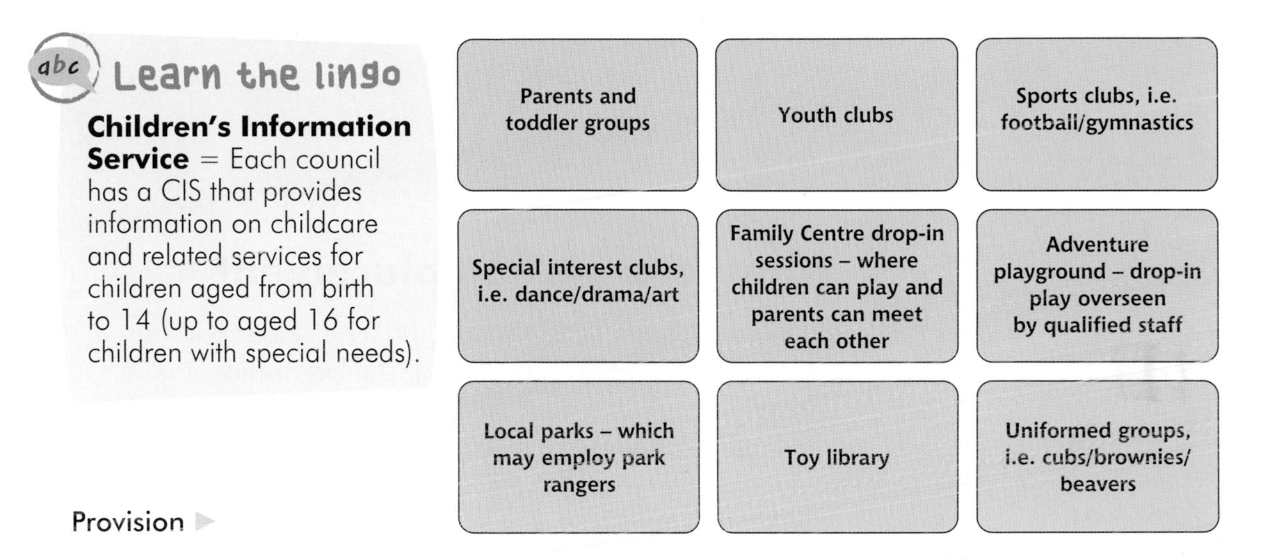

Provision ▶

FOCUS ON...
your learning

In this section you've learnt about the types of provision that are available to children. You've also learnt how to find out about the provision in your own local area.

Questions:

1. What does 'statutory' mean?
2. How can you find out about provision in your local area?

Learning Outcome 2

FOCUS ON...

how to prepare for your placements

In this section you'll learn how to prepare yourself for placements. You'll find out what to wear, how to behave and what to expect. This will help you to feel more confident and to fit in at the setting.

This links with Assessment Criterion **2.1**

What to expect on placement

It's normal to feel both excited and a bit nervous about starting a placement, especially at the beginning of your course. Most people feel this way, so don't worry! There are some steps you can take to prepare and they'll help you to feel more confident.

Settings are used to having learners working with them. The staff won't expect you to know everything already – you wouldn't need a placement if you did! Settings are happy to help you learn and to introduce you to new practical experiences.

Your placement supervisor

Learners usually go to their setting for a visit before starting the actual placement. This gives you an opportunity to meet the person who will be your placement supervisor. This might not be the actual supervisor of the setting, but it will be a senior member of staff. Your placement supervisor will be the key person for you to go to when you need guidance and support throughout your placement. Your supervisor will liaise (be in contact) with your tutor. They will also be involved in closely monitoring your PERS tasks and signing your placement documents. You will want to make a good first impression by showing that you're responsible and keen to learn. You'll learn how to do this in this section.

On your visit, your placement supervisor will generally show you around and introduce you to the staff and the children. They'll tell you everything you need to know before your placement starts. This is likely to include:

- When you're expected to attend the setting.
- Where you will be working (if there's more than facility, such as baby room and a nursery room).
- What you're expected to do.
- How you're expected to behave.
- The limits of your responsibilities.

Your placement supervisor will be a busy person. While they'll be keen to support you, their main priority will be working with children and families. So make good use of the time they devote to you. Always listen carefully to what you're told and take notes when necessary. Be on time to meetings. Make sure you have organised any paperwork you need them to look at or sign. If you need to ask your supervisor a question or for some help, ask when would be a good time to do so. Always thank you supervisor for their time at the end of meetings.

What to wear

While schools may require a formal look, most settings ask staff to dress in a smart, casual style. Your supervisor will tell you about the dress code. Make a point of noticing what the staff are wearing on your visit. Even if they have a uniform it will give you an idea. For instance, if staff members wear a t-shirt with the name of their pre-school printed on, you'll know it's acceptable to wear a t-shirt rather than a blouse or shirt. The following guidelines will also help you:

- Make sure clothes are clean, tidy and ironed.
- Wear clothes that are practical for getting down on the floor, bending down and stretching up.
- Short skirts and belly tops are best avoided. Your underwear should not show!
- Choose clothes that can be washed easily. Expect to get dirty from paint and so on from time to time.
- Avoid clothing with large logos or messages.
- Some settings (i.e. where babies are cared for) will ask you to bring indoor shoes or slippers to change into to help keep the environment hygienic.
- Many settings don't allow jeans or trainers.
- Wear comfortable shoes as you'll be on your feet a lot of the time. Avoid high heels and heavy shoes that can hurt

children if you tread on them. High heels are also a trip hazard – you don't want to increase the risk of falling as you may be carrying babies and young children.

- Keep jewellery to a minimum. Children may pull on and break necklaces, bracelets and dangly earrings (which is painful and can tear an earlobe). The broken small parts are potentially dangerous to children.

Personal hygiene

Your setting will expect you to arrive for work looking clean and tidy. Personal hygiene is important to prevent the spread of infection, so your body must be clean. This includes your hands and nails. Avoid wearing nail polish and false nails as you're likely to be preparing food and drink. It is best to keep natural nails short as long nails can scratch and harbour germs. Hair should be clean. Many settings prefer long hair to be tied back, particularly if you'll be working with babies.

Your setting may provide an identity badge for you to wear, giving your name and role.

A learner in smart/casual dress, hair tied back, wearing an identity badge

Timekeeping

Being on time is a matter of respect for other people. It's also part of being a professional. Being punctual from the first day of your placement will stand you in good stead for the rest of your career. Settings need staff they can rely on to be there when they're supposed to be so that the setting can open on time. Be ready to start work on time in the morning and return promptly from your breaks. You should ideally plan to arrive at your placement at least 10 minutes before you're due to start work. Then you'll have time to put away your belongings and be in the room a few minutes early. This shows that you're responsible and keen to work. You'll also have a few minutes to spare if you're delayed on your way in. Being late is unprofessional, but very occasionally it's unavoidable. If you are delayed, call the setting and let them know that you're on your way if possible.

You should attend your placement on the days agreed unless you're ill or have another very good reason not to attend. You must call the setting as soon as possible to let them know. You should also call your Centre to tell them you're absent from placement. You must complete the practical aspect of your course to gain your qualification.

Have a go!

Keep the phone number of your setting and Centre with you in case you need to call them at short notice. Enter the numbers into your mobile phone or write them in your diary. Having no credit on your phone is not a good reason for not ringing in. Keep a phone card handy for work purposes. It's your responsibility to call the setting and your Centre yourself.

Behaviour

Learn the lingo

Professional conduct = behaving in a way that is appropriate in the workplace.

Professional conduct is an important part of your role, so it's important to behave responsibly. You are a role-model for children, who learn how to behave by watching those around them. Always be polite and friendly. Be patient with other people and show them respect. Be considerate of other people's feelings. Your supervisor will explain key policies of the setting to you over time. These will influence how you behave and respond to various situations – when children are behaving inappropriately for instance. Your increasing knowledge and understanding will also inform the way you behave as you progress through your course.

Attitude

You need to demonstrate a positive attitude whenever you're working professionally.

The diagram below shows signs of a positive attitude. Your placement supervisor will be looking out for them. Compare these to the list you've made.

Have a go!

Try this brief task before reading on. Think about someone you know who generally has a positive attitude. What is it about their manner that makes you see them as positive? Make a short list of the main factors. Now think of someone displaying a negative attitude and list what makes you think of them as being negative.

Positive attitude

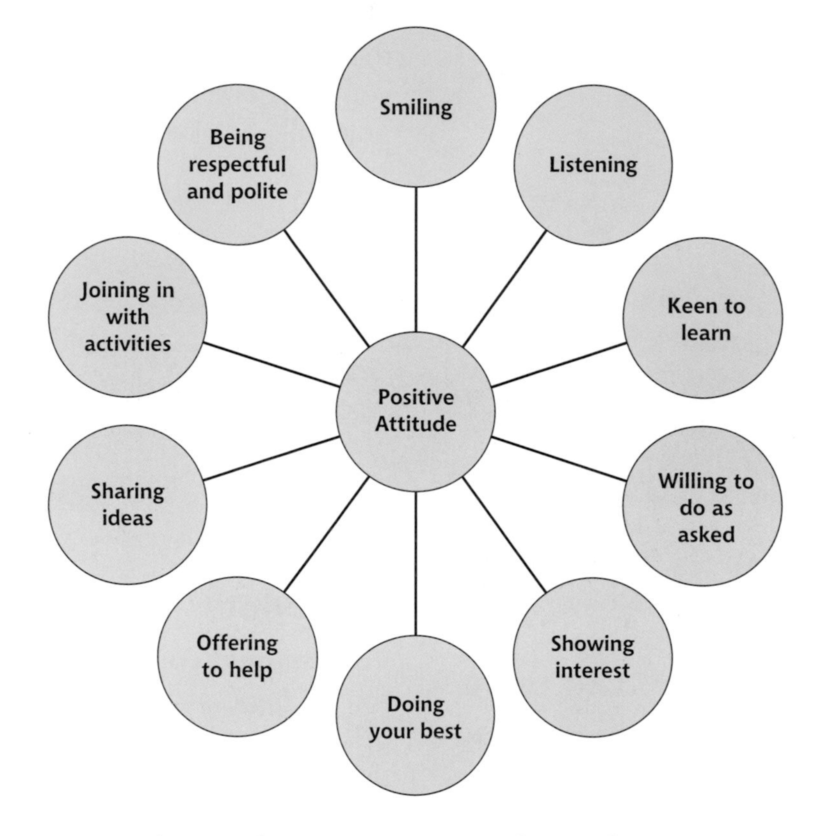

As you've learnt, dressing appropriately, good time keeping and behaviour also contribute to a positive attitude.

Do join in with activities in placement, even if you feel a little shy at first. During activities such as dancing and singing it really doesn't matter what you look or sound like. It's the experience that the children have that counts. Remember you're a **role-model** and get stuck in! The other adults in the room will all do exactly the same things themselves anyway. You'll only be out if place if you *don't* join in.

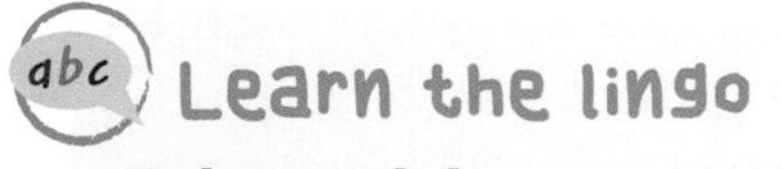

Role-model
= person who serves as an example.

Childcarers carry out some activities that don't involve contact with the children but are a necessary part of the role. This includes duties such as mixing paint, preparing snacks, setting up activities, tidying up, organising resources and some cleaning. You should approach these jobs with the same positive attitude that you bring to working directly with children.

Join in with singing

Have a go!

Read the list of negative factors you made earlier. Wouldn't you rather work with someone with a positive attitude than a negative one? Give your colleagues that chance by displaying a positive attitude yourself. Your tutor will appreciate a positive attitude to learning and carrying out assignments too.

There's one fantastic phrase that's always good to hear from a learner on placement, 'Is there anything I can do to help?' You only get one chance to make a first impression, but if you prepare well you'll be set to make it a good one.

FOCUS ON...
your learning

In this section you've learnt how to prepare for your placement by considering your dress, behaviour, time-keeping and attitude.

Questions:

1 Can you name four indicators of a positive attitude?

2 What can you do to prepare for a meeting with your workplace supervisor?

Learning Outcome 3

FOCUS ON...
the responsibilities and limits of your role in placements

In this section you'll learn about your responsibilities, the importance of meeting them and when to refer to someone else.

This links with Assessment Criterion **3.1**

Your role and responsibilities

All adults who work with children have a duty to act responsibly, to be a good role-model and to protect children from harm. As a learner on placement, this applies to you. Part of acting responsibly is remembering that you're not a member of staff and that there are limits to your role. As mentioned in Learning Outcome 2, your workplace supervisor will give you specific guidance about your role and responsibilities within your own placement. You should always work in line with this. Some general guidance is given here.

Professional relationships

You will want to get on well with the staff at your setting and developing good relationships is important. But professional relationships are not the same as friendships. While staff will generally go out of their way to get to know you a little bit and help you to settle in, they won't have time to get to know you all that well. Some members of staff are likely to have become friends over time. During working hours it's inappropriate for staff to talk about their personal lives. So it's understandable that friends may spend time talking to each other during their breaks. Other staff may want a few minutes of peace and quiet in their break. Don't take offence if someone in the staff room doesn't talk with you. Learners often like to take a book or magazine with them to read in their breaks. But make sure you chat politely if a member of staff strikes up a conversation with you. A positive attitude is required at all times, including during breaks. If you have a problem connected to your placement, arrange a time to talk it over with your workplace supervisor, rather than telling everyone about it.

As a learner you will have limited contact with parents and carers. Although you may greet them with a 'hello' and a smile, the staff will be responsible for receiving the children when they arrive and seeing them out when they leave. This handover time gives the staff and parents a chance to catch up with each other and share important information. When you are in contact with parents you should be professional and friendly. But if you're asked for information or given any information to pass on, explain that you're a learner and so you must fetch a member of staff for them. These situations do arise, especially if your setting doesn't have a badge for you to wear that makes it clear you're not a member of staff. Even once qualified, you should avoid becoming overfamiliar with parents. A relationship outside of the setting can lead to difficulties within the setting. It's best to politely turn down offers of babysitting work and so on.

Confidentiality

Full information about confidentiality can be found on page 228. It's a good idea to read this before you go on placement.

But briefly, you should treat all personal information you learn about children, families and staff as confidential. Don't talk about children, families and staff outside of the setting. Breaking confidentiality is serious and it can get you into trouble. The staff at your setting may need to discuss some confidential matters out of your earshot, so you may be asked to leave a room occasionally.

Health and safety

There's more information about this on page 112.

Your setting will have a health and safety policy in place. You must follow your setting's procedures to keep children safe. Some basic safety measures you should follow are shown in the diagram on page 14.

Managing children's behaviour

You'll find detailed information about how to manage children's behaviour on pages 167–173.

Learn the lingo

Behaviour management policy = procedure for dealing with inappropriate behaviour.

Every setting will have a **behaviour management policy**, and it's important that you work in line with it. Brief guidelines are given here.

Children can sometimes get over-excited when playing with learners. This is partly because children can get excitable when someone new plays with them and gives them attention, and partly because learners may not yet know how to have fun with children without overexciting them. When children are over excited they can become silly, have difficulty calming down and they may get into trouble. Watch how the staff interact and play with children and follow their lead. Notice how staff can be playful with children in a low-key way. Chasing children, tickling them, rough and tumble play, laughing wildly and talking loudly may all contribute to over-excited children. It is not advisable and would be considered inappropriate in many settings.

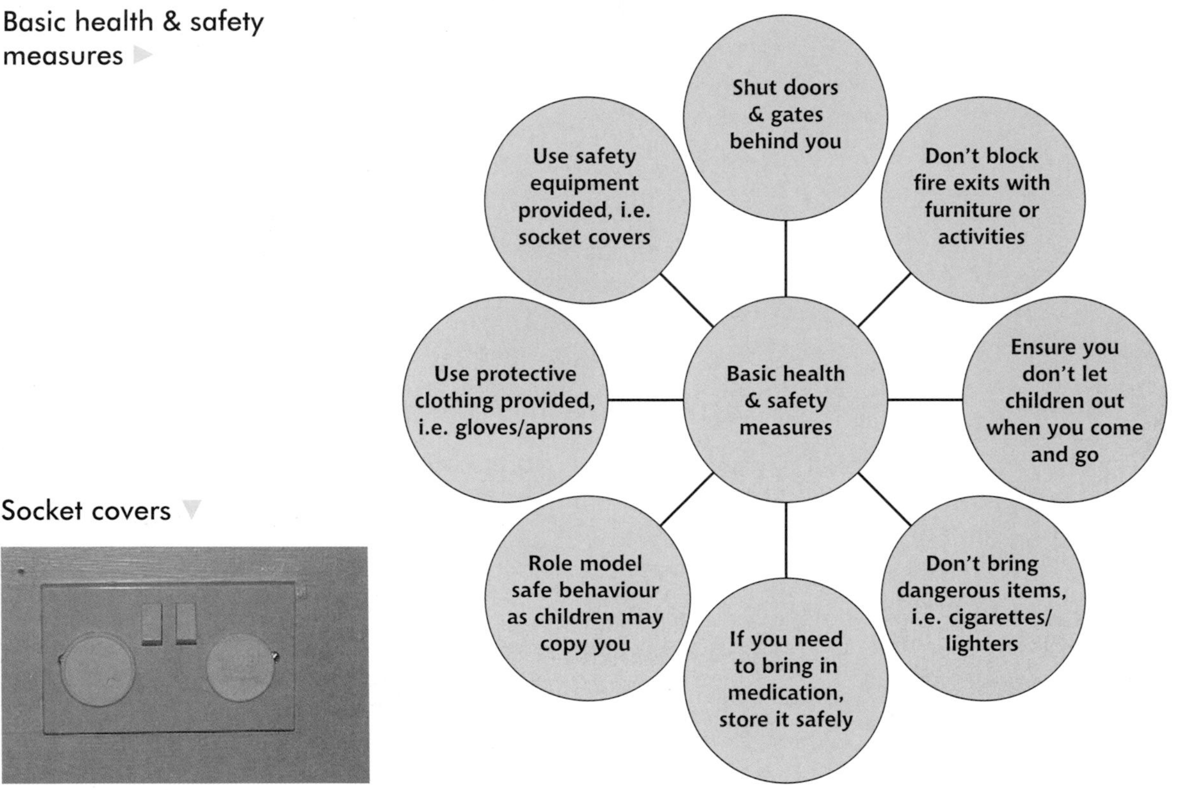

Basic health & safety measures ▶

Socket covers ▼

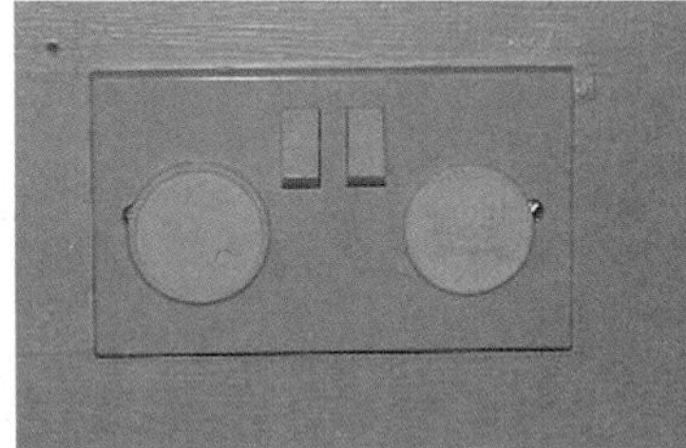

Also take note of the way staff handle **inappropriate behaviour**. It takes time and experience to know how to intervene and to have the confidence to do so. Your placement supervisor will understand this, and will probably tell you to take a back seat when inappropriate behaviour occurs and let staff deal with it at first. You should not be left to supervise children alone, so this shouldn't be a problem.

YOU MUST NEVER PHYSICALLY PUNISH, THREATEN OR HUMILATE A CHILD IN ANY WAY.

When you do start to handle inappropriate behaviour yourself, remember you can go to staff for assistance if necessary at any point.

abc **Learn the lingo**

Inappropriate behaviour
= behaviour that is considered unacceptable.

It takes time and experience to know how to intervene

Practical example

Shanice asks for help

New learner Shanice is playing a board game with three four-year olds. Josiah is losing and he's feeling frustrated. He throws the dice on the floor. Shanice picks it up and encourages him to keep playing. He tips the board game onto the floor and walks away. The other children are annoyed. Unsure what to do, Shanice calls to a free member of staff, who comes over. The staff member asks Shanice to settle the other children while she deals with Josiah. They pick up the pieces and start a new game. Later, Shanice asks the staff member how she dealt with Josiah, so she'll know what to do if a similar situation occurs again.

1. *Why did Shanice do the right things in the circumstances?*

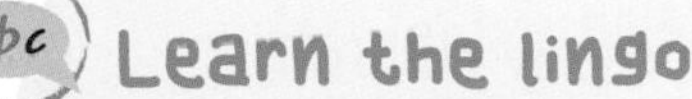

Child protection
= protecting children from physical, emotional or sexual abuse or neglect.

Child protection

Child protection is about keeping children safe from abuse. Every setting will have a child protection policy and it's important that you work in line with it. Brief guidelines are given here.

You'll find detailed information on child protection on pages 140–159.

It's a sad fact that some people abuse children. But because they do it's important for children to increasingly learn safe behaviour as they grow up. Young children need touch and hugs from their carers and they will often initiate them. But settings generally do not encourage this as children grow up. It can be difficult at first to judge how to behave with children of different ages and needs. Pay attention to experienced staff and follow their lead.

Your setting has to keep records about who works with the children when, so it's likely that your supervisor will show you how to sign in when you arrive and sign out when you leave. It's usual for settings not to allow learners to be left alone with a child at any time. As well as protecting children, this protects you from allegations of abuse. Always stick strictly to the rules. If anything concerns you in regards to child protection, speak confidentially to your supervisor.

Read page 141 for further information on safe ways to work.

The golden rule

Probably the most important piece of advice to remember when it comes to the responsibilities and limits of your role is IF YOU'RE NOT SURE, ASK! If you're in doubt about what you should or shouldn't do, it's always best to check. No one will mind and it's much better than making a mistake.

FOCUS ON...
your learning

In this section you've learnt about the responsibilities and limits of your role as a learner in placement. You've learnt how important it is to meet these and when you should refer to other staff.

Questions:

1 Name three basic things you can do to show an awareness of health and safety.

2 Why are learners usually not allowed to be left alone with any child?

Learning Outcome 4

FOCUS ON...

children's individual needs and the necessity for fairness and inclusive practice

In this section you'll learn about children's differing individual needs and ways of working that promote diversity and inclusive practice.

This links with Assessment Criterion **4.1**

Prejudice

The word **prejudice** means to pre-judge. People who are prejudice make unfair judgements about others based on a 'group' they believe the person to 'belong to'. They already have a negative view before they even meet the person or find out anything about them.

Learn the lingo

Bias = having a preference for one particular view or perspective over others.

Discrimination = choosing certain qualities as desirable and others as undesirable and rejecting those that have the undesirable qualities.

Equal opportunities policy = the practice of offering equal opportunities to those that may be at risk of discrimination.

Prejudice = preconceived preference or idea.

You'll learn more about equal opportunities in Unit 7. A brief overview is given here.

Discrimination

Discrimination occurs when people act on prejudice. For example, a prejudiced person might believe that playing with dolls is only for girls. They will be discriminating if they don't allow boys to play with dolls in the setting.

Anti-bias practice

Anti-bias practice describes the ways settings work and the steps they take in order to challenge and overcome prejudice and discrimination.

Equal opportunities

Some children and families have traditionally experienced discrimination. To ensure that this does not happen in settings, all providers are required to have an **Equal Opportunities policy**, which you must work in line with. There are also laws about discrimination.

Meeting everyone's needs

The aim of childcarers is to ensure that all children and families have equal opportunities within the setting. But this doesn't mean that everyone should be treated the same. It means that we should meet the needs of all children and families. Their needs will be different, so we will need to work in different ways with different children and families to give them equal opportunities. Although some children may need to be given more time and attention than others, everyone should be equally valued and treated with the same concern.

All children are equal and important

You should always treat the children you work with fairly, so:

- Get to know all the children.
- Don't have favourites.
- Resolve conflict between children fairly.
- Find reasons to praise all children.
- Notice when and how individual children need your help.

Identifying needs

You'll learn about children's individual needs in Unit 9.

But when you start your placement, your supervisor may tell you confidentially about the individual needs of some children. This might include:

- A disability
- A medical condition
- A communication need
- A dietary requirement

Listen carefully to what you're told about meeting individual children's needs. You may need to adapt the way you work. For instance, if a child uses a wheelchair, the setting may do some extra things to make sure she can join in with all the activities offered, such as adjusting the height of the water tray.

In Unit 3 you'll learn how to make formal observation of children, which will help you assess how to support them.

When you're working with children, observe how they're coping with the activity or experience. Think of ways you can offer them support if appropriate. Children's needs change all the time, so it's important to be observant.

Make a point of paying attention to the way experienced staff meet children's individual needs and take your cue from them. Ask for guidance if you need it.

FOCUS ON...
your learning

In this section you've learnt the importance of fairness and anti-bias practice. You've learnt that you must adapt the ways in which you work with individual children and families in order to provide equal opportunities for all.

Questions:

1. What is discrimination?
2. What is meant by anti-bias practice?

Learning Outcome 5

FOCUS ON...

your own preferred learning style and relevant study skills

In this section you'll learn how to identify your own preferred learning style and develop relevant study skills.

This links with Assessment Criteria **5.1, 5.2**

Learning styles

People (adults and children) have different preferred styles of learning, or in other words, ways of learning that are particularly effective for them. The styles are known as:

- Visual.
- Auditory.
- Kinaesthetic.

Styles of learning are about the way people:

- Perceive information.
- Learn information.
- Process information.
- Think and interpret information.
- Organise and present information.
- Remember and pass on information.

Most people use a mixture of styles to learn. But it's likely that one of the styles works particularly well for you. It makes sense to spend some time thinking about this so you can study in the ways that suit you best when you're revising or preparing for tests.

Visual learners prefer to learn by seeing. They may:

- Often prefer an orderly environment.
- Become distracted by untidiness or movement.
- Be good at imagining.
- Be good at reading.
- Particularly enjoy looking at pictures.

Learn the lingo

Visual learners
= people who prefer to learn by seeing.

If you're a **visual learner** you could try:

- Writing key points you need to learn on pieces of paper and sticking them up somewhere you'll see them often (don't do too many at once).
- Recording information in diagrams or mind maps to look at.

Auditory learners prefer to learn by hearing. They may:

- Learn things well through discussion.
- Think things through well when asked questions.
- Enjoy listening to stories, radio, podcasts.
- Like reciting information.
- Be good at remembering what they're told.

Learn the lingo

Auditory learners
= people who prefer to learn by hearing.

If you're an **auditory learner** you could try:

- Reading your revision notes into a recorder so you can play them back.
- Writing a list of questions on index cards. Answer each one by talking out loud.

Kinaesthetic learners learn through doing, movement and action. They may:

- Learn well when they are moving around.
- Learn best when they have the opportunity to do a task rather than listen to theory.
- Be good at constructing things.
- Use expressive movements.
- Become distracted by activities around them.
- Prefer to jump right in rather than being shown what to do.
- Prefer action plots in stories, film and television programmes.

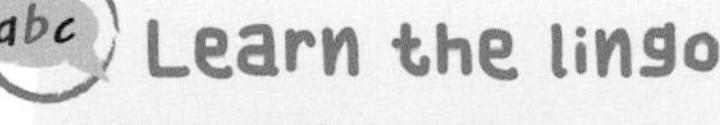

Kinaesthetic learners
= people who prefer to learn through doing, movement and action.

If you're a **kinaesthetic learner** you could try:

- Moving as you revise. You might walk slowly around the room, or use actions to help you remember certain things. For instance, to remember what the word 'auditory' means, you might touch your ear when you say or read the word.
- Practicing skills as often as possible.

Have a go!

Go through the bullet points above for each of the styles of learning. In pencil, tick the bullet points that apply to you. Can you recognise yourself as a particular type of learner? You probably can, although it's likely that you have traits that fit into more than one style. Read on to find out how you can use the information you've gathered about yourself to help you learn effectively.

Different styles for different tasks

While it's helpful to know your preferred style of learning, you'll find you still need to use a range of learning methods. This is because learning some skills or information suits a particular style. For instance, even if you're mainly an auditory learner, you'll probably learn some things best when someone shows you what to do. Learning to fold a terry towelling nappy is a good example. You'll probably learn to do this visually by watching someone else fold a nappy. You'll follow this up by learning kinaesthetically as you have a go at folding a nappy yourself. It would be very difficult to learn to fold a nappy just by hearing the technique explained.

FAST FACT

Children have preferred learning styles too. When you're working with children it's helpful to provide a balance of activities that appeal to different styles of learner.

Study skills

You will also need some general study skills throughout your course as you'll be required to:

- Write assignments.
- Take tests, for which you'll need to prepare.
- Plan activities for children.
- Make observations of children and write them up.
- Keep your placement diary.

Taking notes

Taking notes is important. It helps you to focus on key bits of information. The act of writing key information down often helps people to learn and remember and you can refer to your notes later. People develop their own ways of taking notes and some will write down more than others. Some people like to use bullet points or diagrams, while others just write freely. Whichever method you use there are some tips that will help you organise your notes.

Taking notes is important

Get into the habit of writing the date on your notes and use headings. If you're taking notes in a class, write down the name of the subject and tutor. If you're taking notes as you learn from a book, start by writing down the title of the book and the name of the author. As you work your way through the book, write down the page number you're working from (also see the information on working with books below). If you need more information when you refer to your notes later, these techniques will ensure you'll know just where to find it. Dates will help you to put notes from class into the right order.

Working with books and written material

If you want to take a piece of text or an idea from a book or any other source and put it in your assignment, you must reference it. Copying from a book and failing to reference means you're passing someone else's work off as your own. This is called plagiarism. It is not allowed, so you will fail your assignment.

(see page 25).

When you're taking notes from books and other materials, make sure you use your own words to summarise the information you've read. That way you'll avoid accidently using the author's words when you use your notes to write an assignment. If you want to make a note of something the author has said word for word, write clearly in your notes that this section is a direct quote. You'll learn how to use quotes below.

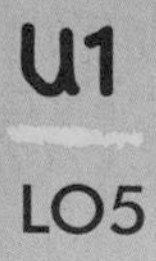

Books will be a great help to you throughout your career. If you're not already a member of your local library, it's a good idea to join. To help you find the information you're looking for in books, make use of the contents page of the front and the index page at the back.

When you're reading written information, stop regularly to think about what you've read and make notes of key points if necessary. If you're finding information hard to take in, try stopping more often so you just read and think about a small section at a time. If you're given handouts in class, it's a good idea to read them through again and highlight key points with a highlighter pen. These methods will help to make written information more meaningful to you. The process of taking key points from written materials is called 'reading and summarising information'.

Bibliography and reference lists

By including references and a bibliography in your assignments you can achieve higher grades. It's worth getting into the habit of writing these early on as it's easy to do. A bibliography is simply a list of resources you've used to help you complete your assignment. For a book you would record:

- The title
- Author's name
- Publisher
- Date of publication
- Edition number, if relevant.

You can read about referencing on page 27.

You'll find the date of publication and the edition number at the beginning of a book just inside the cover. You may also list magazines, journals and websites. When you're using materials to help you with an assignment, make a note of the information you'll need for the bibliography and reference list as you go. Your bibliography and reference list should go at the end of your assignment on a separate sheet, under the heading 'bibliography and reference list'.

When you're writing up your bibliography, put the material you've used in alphabetical order according to the author's last names, as shown in the example below. Write the author's last name in full, followed by their initial as shown. Write the year of publication in brackets. If you've used the internet, just state the website address and the date you visited the site. This book is the first one listed below:

Example bibliography

Beaver, M., Brewster, J., Jones, P., Neaum, S., Tallack, J. and Walker, M. (2008), *Cache Level 2 Child Care and Education*, Nelson Thornes.

Walker, M. (2007) 'A Healthy Child', *Practical Professional Childcare*, January 2007.

Have a go!

Turn to the beginning of this book to see where the date of publication and the edition number are to be found.

Assignments

Before you start an assignment you need to have a clear idea of what the assignment is asking you to do and what you need to include in it. It's normal to feel a bit anxious about a new assignment at first. But your tutor will explain each step to you and you can ask them questions. It's helpful to spend some extra time on your own:

- reading the assignment task
- reading the guidance beneath the task that tells you what your work should include
- reading the assignment criteria that tells you what you must do to achieve different grades.

Research

Once you're clear about what you have to include in your assignment, you can start to get some information together. The diagram on page 25 shows some sources of information:

Look at your chosen sources of information and write some notes from them. Give yourself time to think about what you've read. Think again about what the assignment is asking you to do. By now you should be developing some ideas.

Writing assignments

You will need to write your assignments. If you have difficulties with writing, don't worry. There will be free, confidential help available for you at your Centre. Your Centre will help people with their writing all the time in a range of ways, so there's no need to be embarrassed. You needn't tell other people on your course that you're receiving help unless you want to. You can have a quiet word with your tutor to ask for the help you need. Writing is a skill that childcarers use all the time, so it makes sense to get some help now at the start of your career.

Sources of information ▼

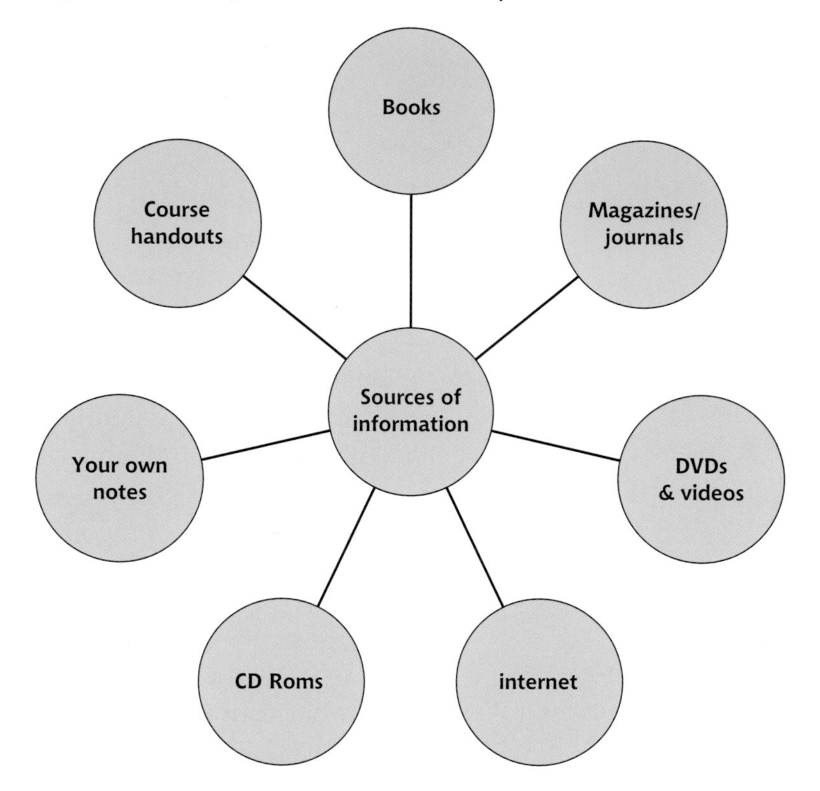

Many learners aren't confident about their grammar, punctuation and spelling. Using a computer to word process work can help because there are features to help you check and correct these types of errors. You should do your best with your written work, but as long as you meet the grading criteria of each assignment, errors in writing won't hold you back.

Structuring assignments

Follow the instructions for the assignment carefully. It helps to give some thought to how you will structure (lay out) your work. If there are different sections to the assignment, you can give them numbered headings (i.e. Section 1). Your tutor will explain this to you when you're given your first assignment. Think about the word limit too. Have a rough idea of how many words you'll allocate to each part of the assignment. This will help you not to run out of words as you get to the end.

Remember to list the materials you've referenced on your bibliography and reference list, as explained on page 24.

Using references

There are two types of references, **direct** and **indirect**.

A direct reference is when you take a short piece of text, copy it word for word and place it in your assignment. After the quote, you reference the text by writing in brackets:

- The author's last name.
- The date the book was published.
- The page of the book on which the quote appears.

The reader can then turn to your bibliography and reference list to see the title of the book if they want to. An example of a direct quote:

Example of direct reference ▶

I asked the children to suggest activities they would like to do during the summer holidays. Walker tells us that, 'The process of consultation can help children to feel listened to, valued and included' (Walker, 2007, p203).

An indirect reference is when you refer to an author's ideas or something they've said without copying their actual words, as the example below shows.

Example of an indirect reference ▶

After conducting research, Siraj Blatchford suggested that name-calling is the most common form of racism (Blatchford, 1994).

Writing different documents

During your course you'll be asked to produce various written documents, such as a leaflet, poster or brochure. It will help you to:

- Look at documents of that type first so you're clear about the style of them, i.e. have a good look at a few leaflets to see how much writing there is, etc.
- Make a list of the key points you need to include in your document.
- Do a rough draft first.
- Ask someone to check your grammar, spelling and punctuation if you're concerned about it.
- Produce the actual document.

GOOD PRACTICE

Make sure you complete any necessary additional paperwork before you hand in your assignment. Your tutor will tell you what you need to do.

Time management

You need to manage your time well to make sure you get your work done by the deadlines given to you by your tutor. It helps to break the work down into smaller tasks. Think about how long it will take you to do each task. Plan to start your work early, then if you're ill or something takes you longer than expected you won't feel under pressure. Getting hold of books and other information can take a while if other learners are using them too. So it's best to start researching as soon as possible.

During your course, you'll also need to plan time to revise before tests.

Revising

One way to revise is to read your notes or relevant books. This is definitely worthwhile, but you may find you remember more easily when you use a range of revision methods. You can also try:

- Working with other learners, taking it in turn to test each other.
- Reading information out loud.
- Going through your notes and handouts and highlighting key points.
- Using practice papers to test yourself, writing down the answers.
- Writing key points on index cards and sticking them up somewhere you'll see them often.
- Carrying the index cards with you and reviewing them in spare time, i.e. on the bus.
- Using other methods that suit your preferred style of learning.

(see page 20).

Giving presentations

Tutors sometimes ask learners to report to the group about something they've learned or experienced. This is good practice, as you'll need to present information to colleagues in team meetings if you're employed in a group setting later on. There's no need to be self-conscious, as everyone in the group will be taking their turn. These guidelines will help:

1. Think about the key points the others need to know.
2. Think about the best way to tell them clearly. Make notes. You might like to write each point on a separate card.
3. Put the notes into an order that makes sense. Refer to them during your presentation.
4. Have a practice to yourself.

Talking about things helps you to understand

Group discussion

Your tutor will sometimes ask you to discuss an aspect of childcare either within a small group or a large group. This is a good opportunity to listen to what other people have to say and put across your own point of view. You get the most out of discussions when you actively join in. Talking about things helps you to understand and to form opinions. You shouldn't worry too much about saying the wrong thing. The idea is to learn. Your tutors will want to get an idea of everyone's level of understanding so they know what to teach you next. So speak up! Make sure you remember to listen too. Group discussion in class is good practice for giving your point of view in workplace meetings.

FOCUS ON...
your learning

In this section you've learnt how to identify your own preferred learning style. You've also learnt about study skills that will help you throughout your course.

Questions:

1 What are the advantages of knowing your own preferred learning style?

2 What strategies can you use to help you time manage effectively?

RAPID RECAP

Learning Outcome 1

There are a range of settings available for children. They can be divided into three categories – statutory, volunteer, private/independent. They generally offer childcare, education or a mixture of both. Your local Children's Information Service will hold details of all the providers in your local area.

Learning Outcome 2

Take the time to prepare yourself properly for placement. It's important to appear clean and tidy and to dress appropriately. Be punctual. Ring the setting and your Centre if you are absent (you must have a very good reason). Display a positive attitude – be willing to help and keen to learn. You're a role-model for children, so behave appropriately at all times.

Learning Outcome 3

As a learner you have responsibilities in placement to behave responsibly, be a good role-model and to protect children from harm. Your role also has limits as you are not a member of staff. You must refer to others in certain situations. You must make sure you understand how to behave in connection to health and safety, child protection, behaviour management, confidentiality and relationships.

Learning Outcome 4

Settings must promote fairness and anti-bias practice. They must meet the needs of all children in order to provide them with equal opportunities. Because different children have different needs, you must adapt the ways in which you work with them. Some children may need more time and attention than others. But everyone should be valued equally and you should have the same level of concern for each and every child.

Learning Outcome 5

It's worth understanding your own preferred learning style (either visual, auditory or kinaesthetic) as it can help you to choose ways of studying that suit you. It's important to develop good study skills including note-taking, researching, writing, revising and time management.

FAQ

Q How will I be assessed on this Unit?

A *You will be required to complete an assignment entitled 'An introduction to working with children'.*

Q What will I have to do?

A *Your tutor or Centre will help you to understand the task. It involves writing about your role within settings. See Learning Outcome 5 of this unit for more information on study skills.*

Weblinks

You may like to visit the following websites:

The following sites give information and advice on providing high quality childcare and education:

- www.ofsted.gov.uk
  The site of Ofsted.
- www.ndna.org.uk
  The site of the National Day Nurseries Association
- www.pre-school.org.uk
  The site of the Pre-School Learning Alliance
- www.ncma.org.uk
  The site of the National Childminding Association
- www.4children.org.uk
  The site of 4Children

Unit 2

The developing child

Learning Outcomes

In this unit you'll learn about:

1. The expected pattern of children's development.
2. The importance of careful observations and how they support development.
3. How to identify influences that affect children's development.
4. How to use everyday care routines and activities to support development.
5. How to support children through transitions in their lives.

Have a go!

See primitive reflexes for yourself by stimulating a neonate in the following ways and watching her respond:

Rooting reflex

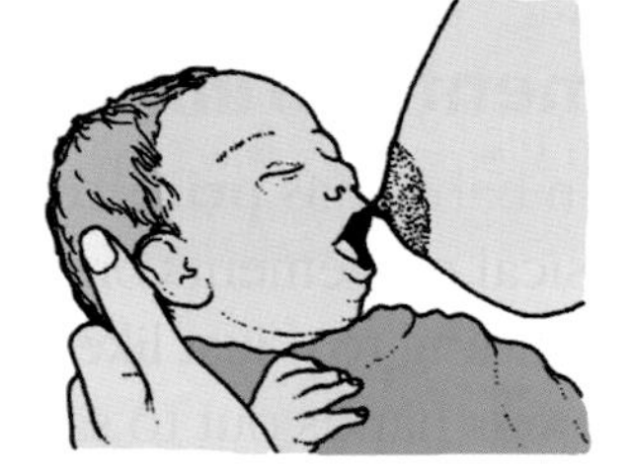

Stimulus: Brush the baby's cheek with your finger

Response: The baby turns to the side brushed in search of the mother's nipple for a feed

Sucking reflex

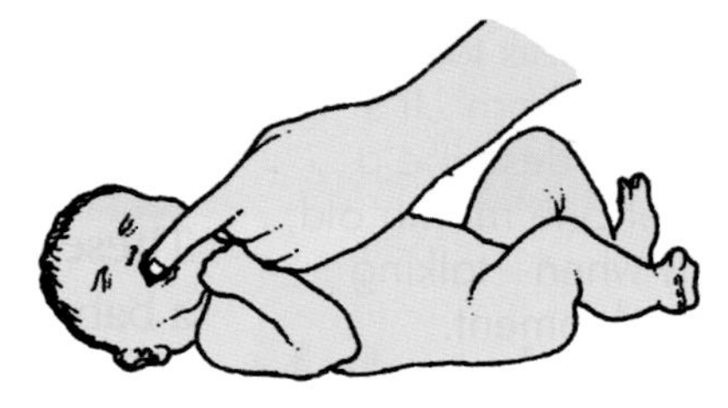

Stimulus: Place a teat in the baby's mouth

Response: The baby sucks to feed

Grasping reflex

Stimulus: Place an object in the baby's palm

Response: The baby's fingers close tightly around the object

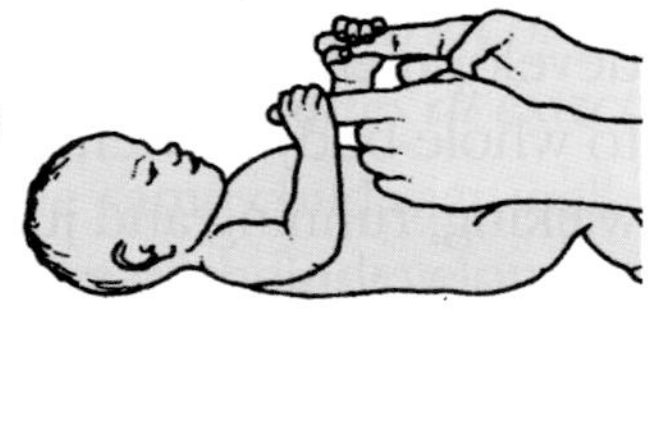

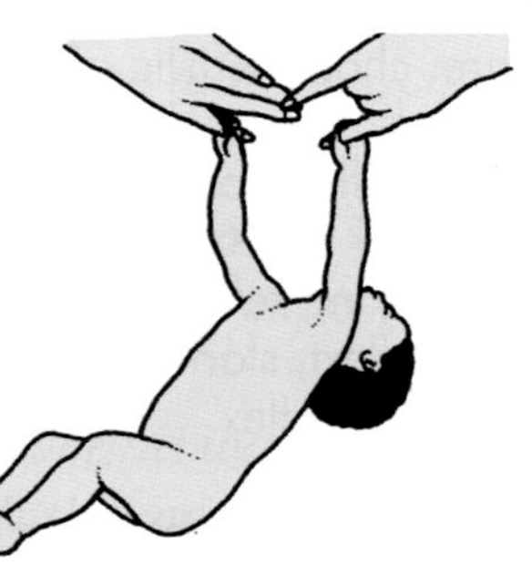

Walking reflex

Stimulus: Hold the baby in a standing position, feet touching a hard surface

Response: The baby's legs move forward alternatively as if walking

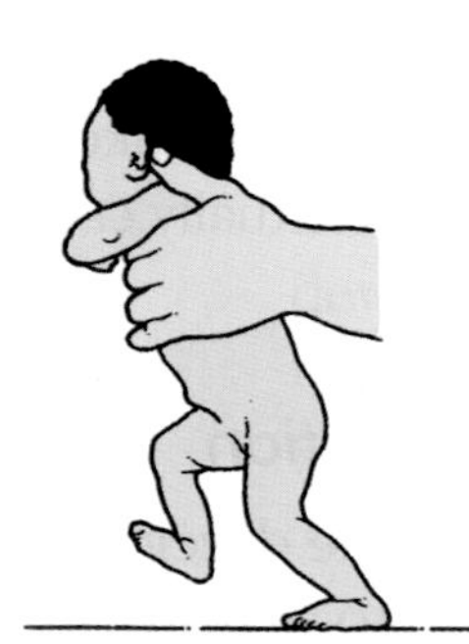

Placing reflex

Stimulus: Brush the top of the baby's foot against a table top

Response: The baby lifts her foot and places it on the table

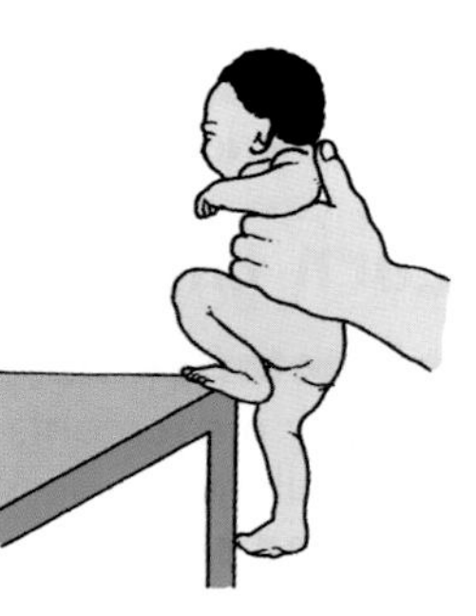

Fine motor skills involved in the development of manipulation

Holding and exploring objects

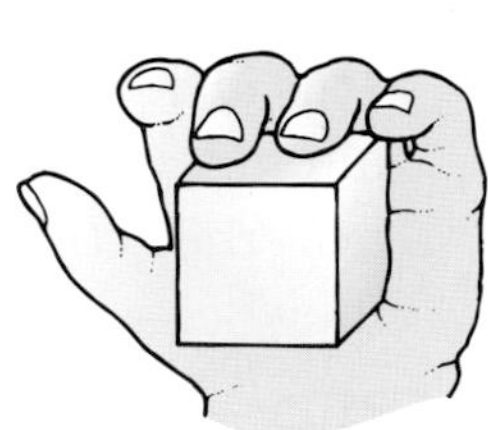

Palmar grasp using whole hand

More delicate palmar grasp involving the thumb

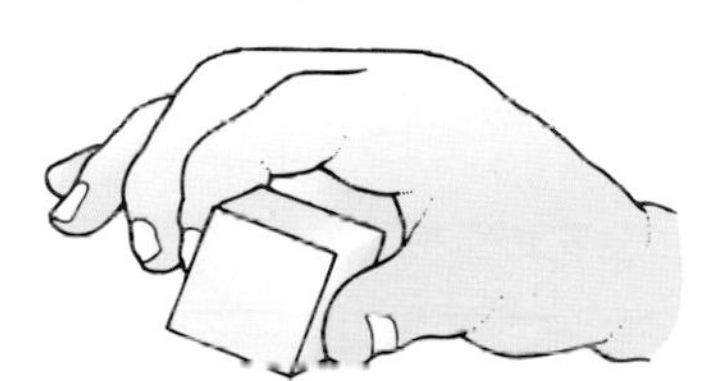

Inferior pincer grasp

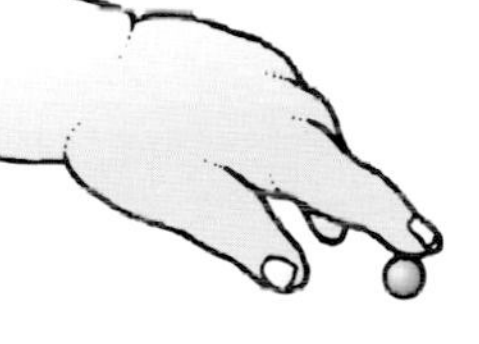

Exploring with the Index finger

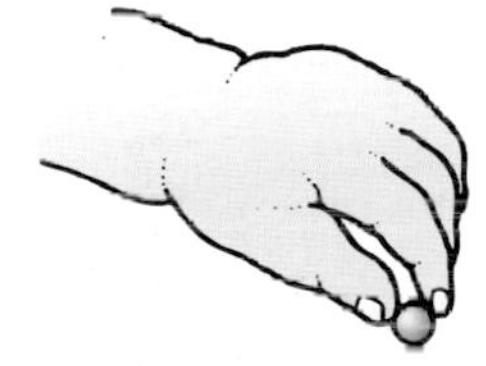

Delicate/mature pincer grasp

You can follow the sequence of this development in the tables starting on page 38

Learn the lingo

Intellectual development = the development of thinking and understanding.

Communication and intellectual development

You can follow the sequence of communication and **intellectual development** in the development tables. You'll already know that babies, children and young people communicate in a range of ways, from crying and babbling to talking and writing. We also use language to think and so intellectual development (the development of thinking and understanding) is linked to communication.

Have a go!

Spend a moment thinking about the things you have to do tomorrow.

You'll almost certainly have thought to yourself in language, perhaps something along the lines of, 'I have to remember to post that letter on the way to college...' It would be very unusual for someone to simply picture themselves posting a letter without using the language of thought, because communication and intellect are so closely linked.

You'll learn more about communication in Unit 5. You can find out more about children's learning in Unit 10.

GOOD PRACTICE

Parents and carers can sometimes feel competitive about when their children reach milestones. But child development isn't a race! Remember that it's normal for all children to develop at different rates.

Social, emotional and behavioural development

This includes how babies, children and young people interact with others at different stages of development, how they cope with and control their feelings and how they behave.

You can also follow the sequence of social, emotional and behavioural development in the development tables, starting below.

Stages of development

Rates of development for 1 month

Physical development – gross motor skills

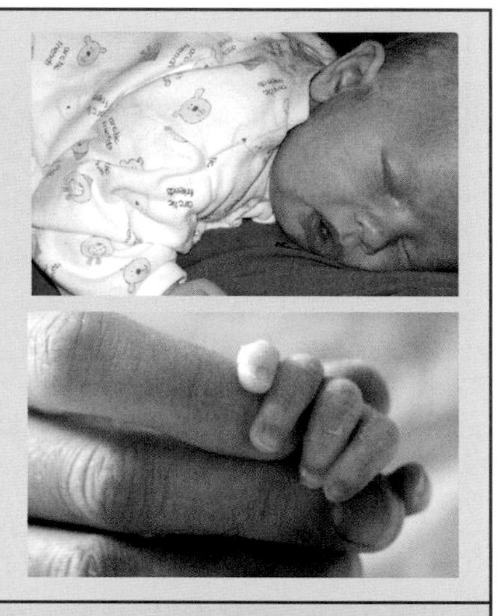

In supine: head is on one side

In prone: head is on one side, can be lifted

When sitting: head falls forwards (known as head lag), and the back curves

Head will turn towards light and noise

Hands are closed tighlty

Reflexes help a baby to survive

Physical development – fine motor skills

Gazes attentively at faces, particularly when fed and talked to

Social and emotional development

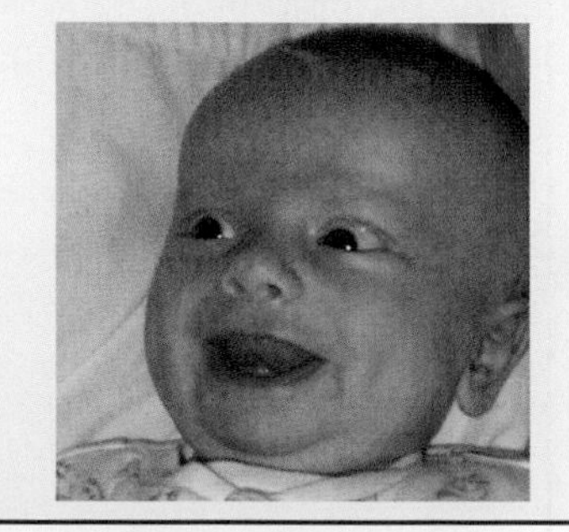

Totally dependent on others

Smiles from about 5 weeks

Senses are used for exploration

Begins to respond to sounds heard in the environment by making own sounds

Communication and intellectual development

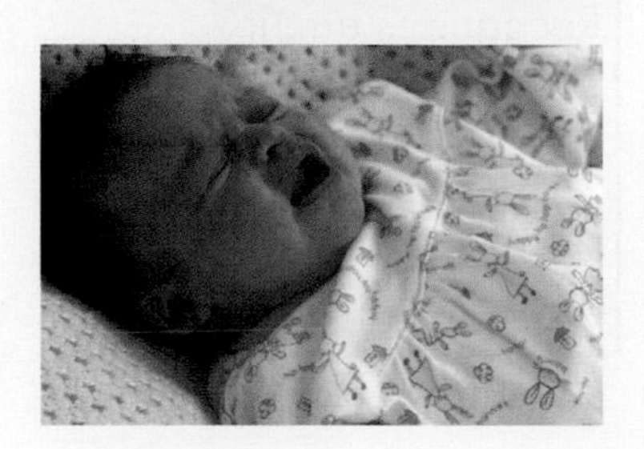

Communicates needs through sounds

Communicates needs through crying

Communication occurs through the physical closeness

Begins to coo and gurgle in response to interaction from carers

Rates of development for 3 months

Physical development – gross motor skills

Turns from side to back

In supine: head in central position

In prone: head and chest can be lifted from the floor, supported by the forearms

When sitting: little head lag remains, back is straighter

Arms can be waved and brought together

Legs can be kicked separately and together

Physical development – fine motor skills

Alert, the baby moves her head to watch others

Engages in hand and finger play

Holds rattle briefly before dropping

Social and emotional development

Through use of senses, a baby begins to understand she is a separate person

Baby begins to discover what she can do, and this creates a sense of self

May cry if a primary carer leaves the room, not yet understanding that they still exist and will return

Shows feelings such as excitement and fear

Reacts positively when a carer is caring, kind and soothing. If a carer does not respond to a baby, she may stop trying to interact

Communication and intellectual development

Recognises and links familiar sounds such as the face and voice of a carer

Will hold 'conversations' with carer when talked to, making sounds and waiting for a response

Can imitate high and low sounds

Rates of development for 6 months

Physical development – gross motor skills

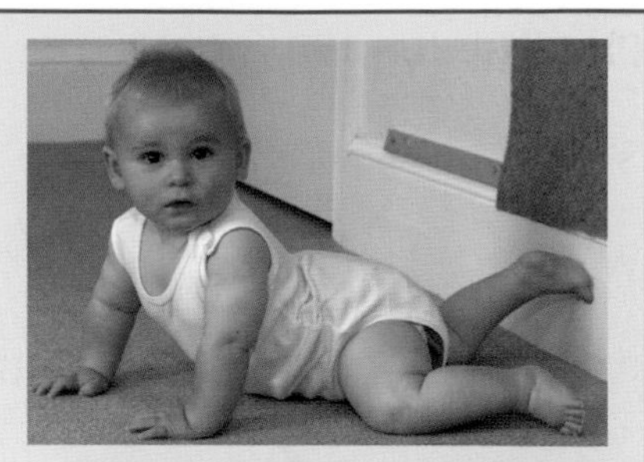

Turns from front to back, and may do the reverse

In supine: head can be lifted and controlled when pulled to sitting position

In prone: head and chest can be fully extended supported by arms, with the hands flat on the floor

Sits unsupported for some time, with back straight, and plays in this position

Uses hands to play with feet, and may take them to the mouth

Weight-bears when held in standing position

Physical development – fine motor skills

Interested in bright, shiny objects

Watches events keenly

Uses palmar grasp to pick up objects. Takes them to the mouth for exploration

Passes objects from hand to hand

Social and emotional development

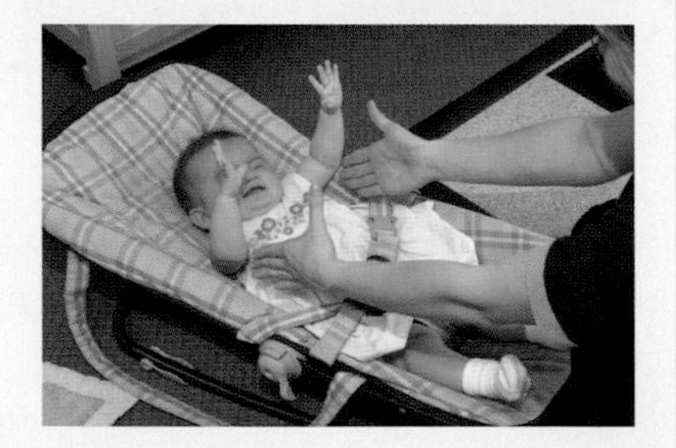

Shows a wider range of feelings more clearly and vocally. May laugh and screech with delight, but cry with fear at the sight of a stranger

Clearly tells people apart, showing a preference for primary carers/siblings

Reaches out to be held, and may stop crying when talked to

Enjoys looking at self in the mirror

Enjoys attention and being with others

Communication and intellectual development

Sounds are used intentionally to call for a carer's attention

Babbling is frequent. The baby plays tunefully with the sounds they can make

Rhythm and volume are explored vocally

Enjoys rhymes and accompanying actions

Rates of development for 9 months

Physical development – gross motor skills

Sits unsupported on the floor

Will go on hands and knees, and may crawl

Pulls self to standing position using furniture for support

Cruises around the room (side-stepping, holding furniture for support)

Takes steps if both hands are held by carer

Physical development – fine motor skills

Uses an inferior pincer grasp to pick up objects

Explores objects with the eyes

Points to and pokes at objects of interest with index finger

Social and emotional development

Enjoys playing with carers, e.g. peek-a-boo games and pat-a-cake.

Offers objects, but does not yet let go

Increasing mobility allows baby to approach people

Begins to feed self with support

Communication and intellectual development

Initiates a wider range of sounds, and recognises a few familiar words. Understands 'no', and knows own name

Greatly enjoys playing with carers and holding conversations

Makes longer strings of babbling sounds

Intentionally uses volume vocally

Rates of development for 12 months

Physical development – gross motor skills

Sits down from standing position

Stands alone briefly and may walk a few steps alone

Throws toys intentionally

Physical development – fine motor skills

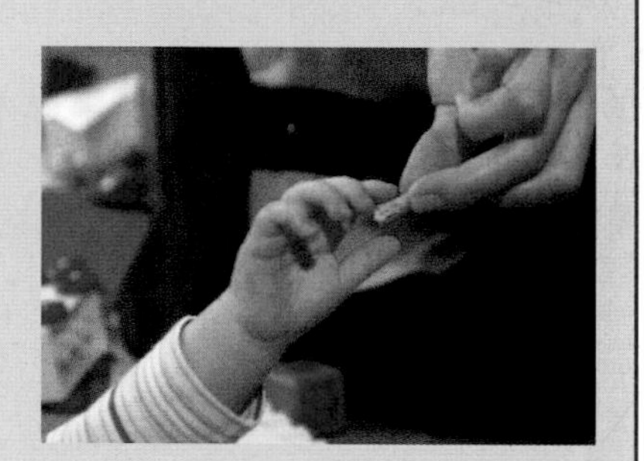

Clasps hands together

Uses sophisticated pincer grasp, and releases hold intentionally

Looks for objects that fall out of sight, understanding they still exist although they can't be seen

Feeds self with spoon and finger foods

Social and emotional development

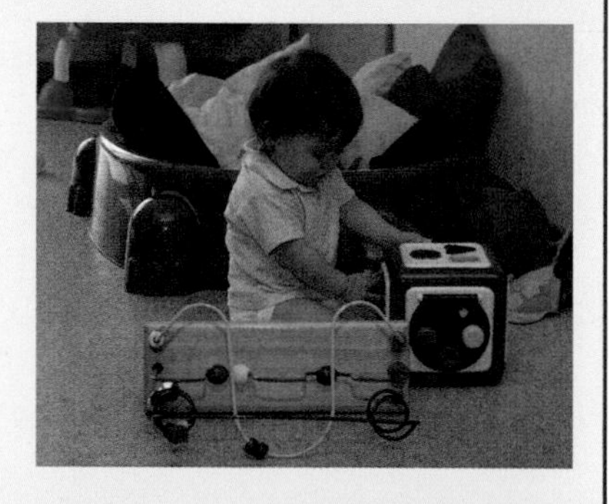

The sense of self-identity increases, as self-esteem and self-confidence develop

Waves goodbye, when prompted at first, and then spontaneously

Content to play alone or alongside other children for increasing periods of time

Communication and intellectual development

Increasingly understands the basic messages communicated by carers and older siblings

Can respond to basic instructions

Babbling sounds increasingly like speech, and leads to the first single words being spoken

Shows understanding that particular words are associated with people and objects, by using a few single words in context

Rates of development for 15 months

Physical development – gross motor skills

Walks independently

Crawls upstairs. Crawls downstairs feet first

Sits in a child-sized chair independently

Physical development – fine motor skills

Tries to turn the pages of a book

Makes a tower of two blocks

Makes marks on paper with crayons

Holds own cup when drinking

Social and emotional development

Curious. Wants to explore the world, as long as carers are close by

May show signs of separation anxiety (i.e. upset when left at nursery)

May 'show off' to entertain carers

Shows a keener interest in the activities of peers

Can be jealous of the attention/toys given to another child

Changeable emotionally. Quickly alternates between wanting to do things alone and being dependent on carers

Communication and intellectual development

Will put away/look for very familiar objects in the right place

Uses toys for their purpose, e.g. puts a doll in a pram

Understands the concepts of labels such as 'you', 'me', 'mine', 'yours'

The use of single words increases, and more words are learnt

Behavioural development

May respond with anger when told off or thwarted. May throw toys or have a tantrum

Can be distracted from inappropriate behaviour

Possessive of toys and carers. Reluctant to share

Child 'is busy' or 'into everything'

Rates of development for 18 months

Physical development – gross motor skills
Walks confidently. Attempts to run Walks up and down stairs if hand is held by carer Bends from the waist without falling forwards Balances in the squatting position Pushes and pulls wheeled toys Rolls and throws balls, attempts to kick them 
Physical development – fine motor skills
Uses delicate pincer grasp to thread cotton reels Makes a tower of three blocks Makes large scribbles with crayons Can use door handles 
Social and emotional development
Has a better understanding of being an individual Very curious, and more confident to explore Becomes frustrated easily if incapable of doing something Follows carers, keen to join in with their activities Plays alongside peers more often (parallel play), and may imitate them Still very changeable emotionally May show sympathy for others (e.g. putting their arm around a crying child) 
Communication and intellectual development
Understands a great deal of what carers say More words spoken. Uses people's names Uses trial and error in exploration (tries to post several shapes in the hole of a shape sorter)
Behavioural development
Can be restless and very determined, quickly growing irritated or angry May assert will strongly, showing angry defiance and resistance to adults Can still be distracted from inappropriate behaviour

Rates of development for 2 years

Physical development – gross motor skills

Runs confidently

Walks up and down stairs alone holding hand rail

Rides large wheeled toys (without peddles)

Kicks stationary balls

Physical development – fine motor skills

Makes a tower of six blocks

Joins and separates interlocking toys

Draws circles, lines and dots with a pencil

Puts on shoes

Social and emotional development

Beginning to understand own feelings. Identifies sad and happy faces

Experiences a range of changeable feelings that are expressed in behaviour

More responsive to the feelings of others

Often responds to carers lovingly, and may initiate loving gestures (a cuddle)

Communication and intellectual development

Completes simple jigsaw puzzles (or 'play-trays')

Understands that actions have consequences

Will often name objects on sight (e.g. may point and say 'chair' or 'dog')

Vocabulary increases. Joins two words together, e.g. 'shoes on'

Short sentences are used by 30 months. Some words are used incorrectly, e.g. 'I goed in'

Behavioural development

May use growing language ability to protest verbally

May get angry with peers, and lash out on occasion (e.g. pushing or even biting them)

Rates of development for 3 years

Physical development – gross motor skills

Walks and runs on tip-toes

Walks up and downstairs confidently

Rides large wheeled toys using peddles and steering

Kicks moving balls forwards

Enjoys climbing and sliding on small apparatus

Physical development – fine motor skills

Makes a tower of nine blocks

Turns the pages of a book reliably

Draws a face with a pencil, using the preferred hand. Attempts to write letters

Puts on and removes coat. Fastens large, easy zippers

Social and emotional development

Child can tell carers how she is feeling. Empathises with the feelings of others

Uses the toilet and washes own hands. Can put on clothes

Imaginary and creative play is enjoyed

Enjoys company of peers and makes friends. Wants adult approval. Is affected by mood of carers/peers

Communication and intellectual development

Child is enquiring. Frequently asks 'what' and 'why' questions

Use of language for thinking and reporting. Enjoys stories and rhymes

Vocabulary increases quickly. Use of plurals, pronouns, adjectives, possessives and tenses

Longer sentences are used. By 42 months, most language is used correctly

Can name colours. Can match and sort items into simple sets (e.g. colour sets)

Can count to ten by rote. Can only count out three or four objects

Begins to recognise own name when seen written down

Behavioural development

Increasingly able to understand consequence of behaviour and the concept of 'getting in trouble'

Understands the concept of saying sorry and 'making up'

Less rebellious. Less likely to physically express anger as words can be used

Rates of development for 4 years

Physical development – gross motor skills

Changes direction while running

Walks in a straight line successfully

Confidently climbs and slides on apparatus

Hops safely

Can bounce and catch balls, and take aim

Physical development – fine motor skills

Makes a tower of ten blocks

Learning to fasten most buttons and zips

Learning to use scissors. Cuts out basic shapes

Draws people with heads, bodies and limbs. Writes names and letters in play as the awareness that print carries meaning develops

Social and emotional development

May be confident socially. Self-esteem is apparent. Awareness of gender roles

Friendship with peers is increasingly valued. Enjoys playing with groups of children

Control over emotions increases. Can wait to have needs met by carers

As imagination increases child may become fearful (e.g. of the dark or monsters)

Communication and intellectual development

Completes puzzles of 12 pieces

Memory develops. Child recalls many songs and stories. Fantasy and reality may be confused

Problem solves (I wonder what will happen if), and makes hypothesis (I think this will happen if)

Sorts objects into more complex sets. Number correspondence improves

As an understanding of language increases so does enjoyment of rhymes, stories and nonsense

Behavioural development

If exposed to swearing child is likely to use these words in her own language

Learning to negotiate and get along with others through experimenting with behaviour

Experiences being in/out of control, feeling power, having quarrels with peers, being blamed, blaming

Has a good understanding of familiar, basic rules

Distraction works less often, but child increasingly understands reasoning

Rates of development for 5 years

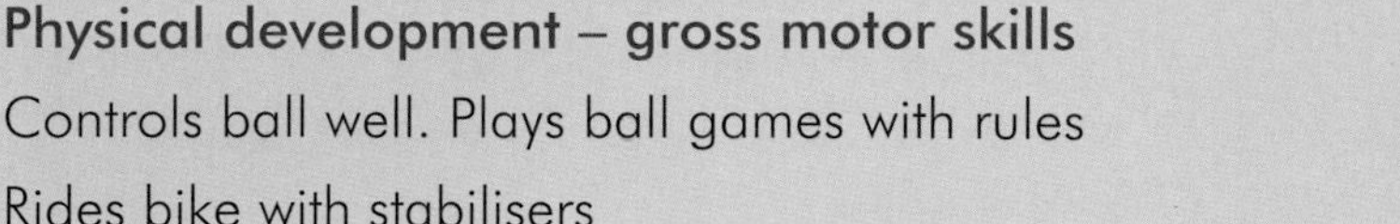

Physical development – gross motor skills

Controls ball well. Plays ball games with rules

Rides bike with stabilisers

Balance is good, uses low stilts confidently

Sense of rhythm has developed. Enjoys dance and movement activities

Physical development – fine motor skills

Controls mark-making materials well (e.g. pencils). Writing more legible

Writes letters and short, familiar words

Learns to sew

Social and emotional development

Child will have started school. This transition may be unsettling

Enjoys group play and co-operative activities

Increasingly understands rules of social conduct and rules of games, but may have difficulty accepting losing

Increasing sense of own personality and gender

Keen to 'fit in' with others. Approval from adults and peers desired

Friends are important. Many are made at school

Many children will have new experiences out of school (e.g. play clubs, friends coming for tea)

Increasingly independent, undertaking most physical care needs for themselves

Communication and intellectual development

Options/knowledge of subjects are shared using language for thinking

Enjoys books. Learning to read. Recognises some words

Thinking skills and memory increase as vocabulary grows

Spends longer periods at activities when engaged. Shows persistence

Children learn from new experiences at school. Learning style preferences may become apparent

Behavioural development

Feels shame/guilt when adults disapprove of behaviour

May seek attention, 'showing off' in front of peers

Keen to win and be 'right'. Adults need to meditate in squabbles

Often responds to 'time out' method of managing behaviour

Rates of development for 6–7 years

Physical development – gross motor skills

Can hop on either leg, skip and play hopscotch

Rides bicycle without stabilisers

Confidently climbs and slides on larger apparatus in school and in parks

Physical development – fine motor skills

Can catch a ball with one hand only

Writing is legible

Sews confidently and may tie shoe laces

Social and emotional development

Enjoys team games and activities

Towards age 7, a child may doubt their learning ability ('I can't do it')

May be reluctant to try or persevere, becoming frustrated easily

Personality is established. Attitudes to life are developed

Solid friendships are formed. The relationship with 'best friends' is important

More susceptible to peer pressure. Cultural identity also established

Has learnt how to behave in various settings and social situations (e.g. at school, play club, a friend's house)

Communication and intellectual development

Imagination skills are developed. Fantasy games are complex and dramatic

Language refined and more adult-like. Enjoys jokes and word play

Many children read and write basic text by age 7, but this varies widely

Ability to predict and to plan ahead has developed. Understands cause and effect well

Can conserve number. Does simple calculations. Understands measurement and weighing

Behavioural development

May sulk or be miserable at times (when under pressure or when conflict arises)

May be over-excitable at times, leading to 'silly' behaviour

May still rebel, but more capable of intentionally choosing behavioural response to conflict

Increasingly able to settle minor disputes and conflict independently

May argue over carrying out tasks (e.g. tidying up or doing homework)

Has a strong sense of right and wrong. May tell adults when another child has broken a rule

Rates of development for 8–12 years

Physical development – gross motor skills

Physical growth slows at first, so there are fewer physical milestones reached

Puberty generally begins between 11–13 years (see 13–16 years table)

Co-ordination and speed of movement develops

Muscles and bones develop. Has more physical strength

Begins to run around less in play

Interest in TV, computers, console games, DVDs may mean child is less active. A balanced, active lifestyle should be encouraged

Physical development – fine motor skills

Does joined-up writing, which becomes increasingly adult-like

Has computer skills. May type well and control the mouse as an adult would

Can sew well, and may be adept at delicate craft activities such as braiding threads

Social and emotional development

May feel unsettled when making the transition from primary school to secondary school, and as puberty approaches

Stable friendships are relied upon. These are generally same-sex, although children play in mixed groups/teams

May be reluctant to go to a play club or event unless a friend will be there too

More independent. Makes more decisions. May play unsupervised at times. May travel to school alone by end of age band

Communication and intellectual development

May read for enjoyment in leisure time

Can make-up and tell stories that have been plotted out

Verbal and written communication is fluent, often with correct grammar usage. Enjoys chatting to friends/adults

Range of new subjects may be learnt at secondary school

Child may follow their interests, learning outside of school

Sense of logic develops. Thinking in abstract by 10 (can consider beliefs, morals and world events)

Behavioural development

Mood swings may be experienced during puberty (see 13–16 years table)

Conflict with parents due to desire for increasing independence ('Why can't I stay home alone?')

May feel rules are unfair ('But all my friends are allowed to do it!')

May refuse to go along with some decisions made by parents (e.g. refusing to wear certain clothes purchased for them)

Rates of development for 13–16 years

Physical development – gross motor skills

The bodies of both boys and girls change throughout puberty.
There is variation in the age at which this occurs
Girls generally enter puberty by 13 years, becoming women physically by 16 years
Boys generally enter puberty by 14 years, becoming men physically by 16 or 17 years
Sporting talents may become apparent

Physical development – fine motor skills

May learn/refine new manipulative skills (such as drawing, stitching, carpentry, woodwork, playing an instrument)
Talent in arts or crafts may become apparent

Social and emotional development

Desire to express individuality, but also a strong desire to fit in with peers
Becomes romantically/sexually interested in others, and in own sexuality
May express self creatively through art/music/dance or creative writing
May worry about aspects of physical appearance
May express self/experiment with identity through appearance (e.g. dress, hairstyles, piercings)
Pressure at school mounts as exam curriculum is followed
Young people may feel overwhelmed or anxious
A balance of school work/leisure time is important, especially if young people take on part-time jobs
Developing own morals, beliefs and values outside of parents' influence
Likely to communicate innermost thoughts and feelings more frequently to friends than to adults
May prefer to spend more time with friends than with family. May stay in bedroom more at home

Communication and intellectual development

Academic knowledge increases as exam curriculum is followed
Towards age 16, decisions are made about the future (college course/career)
Young people may be reluctant to directly ask adults for the advice or information they need. They may prefer to access it anonymously

Behavioural development

May swing between acting maturely, and saying/doing 'childish' things (e.g. may watch a young children's TV programme, or sit on a swing in the park)
May experiment with smoking, alcohol, drugs or early promiscuity. This behaviour is linked with low self-esteem
May experience mood swings. Tense atmospheres are lightened when adults remain in good humour
May disregard the opinions/values of parents if they conflict with those of the peer group
Acting on own values may cause conflict at home (e.g becoming a vegetarian)

FOCUS ON...
your learning

In this section you've learnt about the expected pattern of children's development. You've learnt how to identify the main areas of development and to relate the stages and sequence of development to children aged from birth to 16 years.

Questions:

1 What are the three main areas of development?

2 What does the term 'expected pattern of development' mean?

Learning Outcome 2

FOCUS ON...

the importance of careful observation and how they support development

In this section you'll learn why we make observations of children and how to carry out your own observations. You'll also learn how observations can be used to support children's development.

This links with Assessment Criteria **2.1, 2.2**

Learn the lingo

Observation – watching and recording what a child does.

Why we observe children

We observe children all the time in our work. We watch them to make sure they're safe and to ensure all their needs are met. But when we talk about making **observations**, we mean setting aside some time to specifically watch and record what a child does.

We observe children in this way for the following reasons:

- To understand the pattern of child development.
  The expected pattern of development you learnt about in Learning Outcome 1 was devised by experts who studied children's development through observation. In the same way, observing children regularly over a period of time will help you to understand the pattern of development. It's a special experience to witness children reaching for and achieving milestones.
- To assess a child's current stage of development.
  When a child first attends a setting, it's usual to observe them to see which milestones they have already met. This is called 'baseline' or 'formative' assessment. From then on, progress can be monitored.
- To ensure appropriate activities are provided to support development.
  When you're aware of a child's stage of development, you can provide appropriate activities. For instance, you might do 12-piece jigsaws with a child close to four years, because they are expected to be able to complete one at around four years old. If a child isn't given a 12-piece puzzle, they can't achieve the milestone.

- To monitor ongoing development and plan for the next stage.
  It's important to check that development is progressing steadily. With a good understanding of development patterns, you can plan for the next stage. For instance, you might arrange to get a push-along baby walker for a baby who's just learnt to stand up and will soon be ready to learn to walk alone.

You can find out more about this in Unit 9.

- To identify any particular difficulties a child may have.
  Because observation helps us to focus closely on all aspects of development, we can detect if a child is having difficulties in any area. We can then plan how to help them.
- To know and understand an individual child better.
  We can learn about an individual child's likes and dislikes, how they interact with others and how they behave in different situations. We can share the observations with the child's parents and carers, using them as a starting point for discussion about development.

You'll learn more about this in Units 3 and 7.

- To record any behaviour that causes concern.
  It's helpful to observe worrying behaviour so that it can be analysed later. Observing also provides written details of when and how the behaviour occurs.

You can find out more about this in Unit 10.

- To monitor progress towards national targets that apply to the setting.
  Such as the Early Years Foundation Stage
- To evaluate the standard of the provision.
  How well children are progressing can indicate how well the setting is meeting children's needs. This includes how good the quality of the learning experiences are and how well the staff support and care for the children.

The reasons for observing children are summarised in the diagram on page 55.

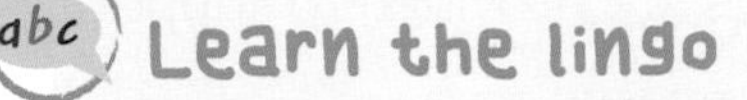

Baseline or formative assessment
= the first assessment of a child's current stage of development.

The observation cycle

Observation is carried out in a cycle. Firstly, baseline information is collected to tell us about a child's current stage of development. From then on, observations are carried out regularly. These help us to monitor the progress made since the **baseline assessment** information was collected. Over time, an ongoing record of children's development is built up. The observations are also used to help us plan how to support the next stage of children's development.

Reasons for observing

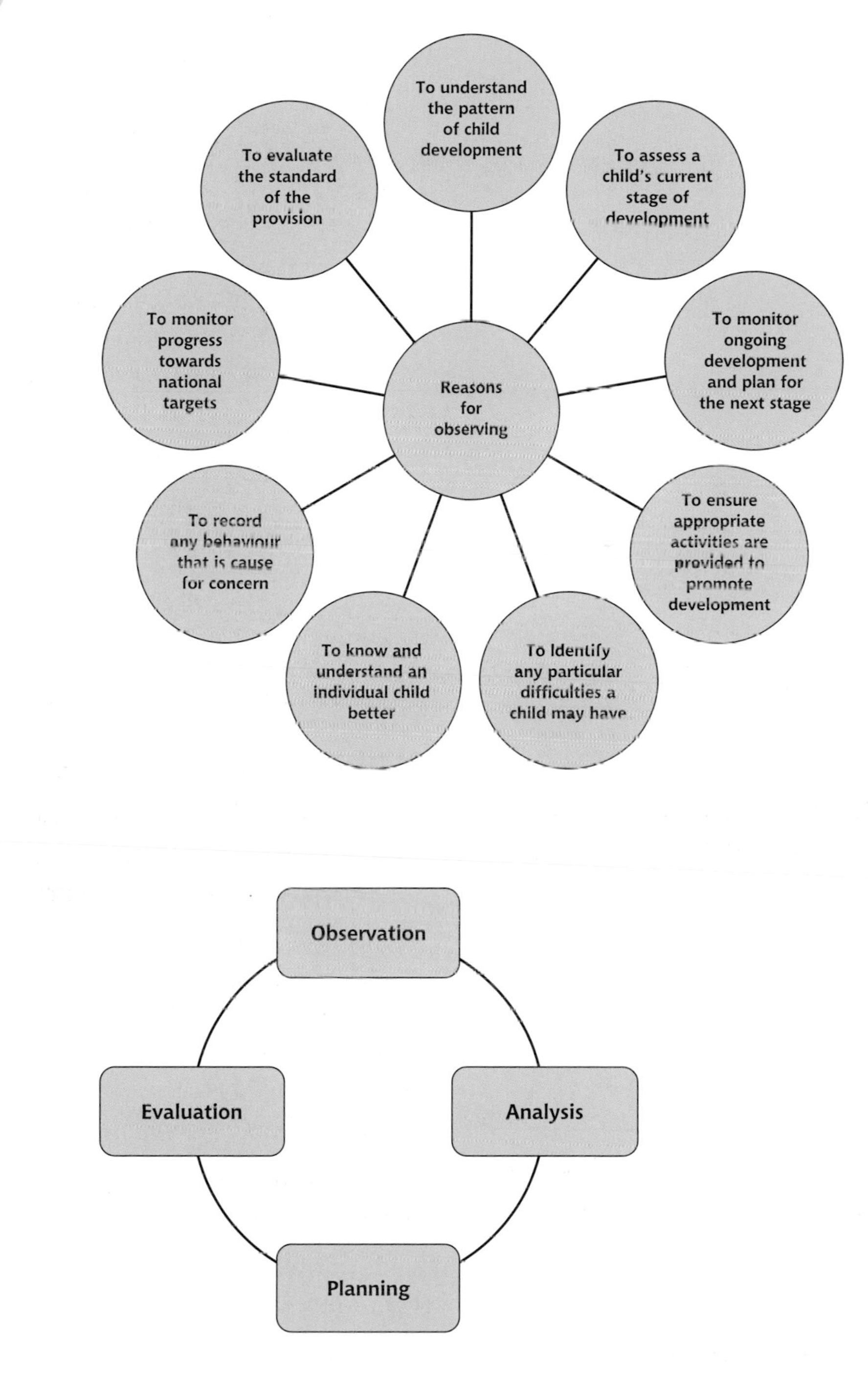

The observation cycle

Being objective

When observing, it's important to be as objective as you can. You should note down just the facts of what you see and hear during the observation and nothing else. You might write, 'Kierra snatched Toby's teddy from his hand and walked away.' You shouldn't write 'Kierra was jealous of Toby's new toy, so she snatched it and walked away.' This is because you can't be sure she was jealous. It's your opinion, not a fact.

Later on, after the observation notes have been completed, you can start to analyse the observation and make educated guesses about what you've seen and heard. Then you can record your opinions separately to your factual observation record. It's important for other people reading the observation to know what is fact and what is your opinion. You may find you change your mind about the reasons for the behaviour you see as you learn more about the child and patterns of development. This won't affect the observation itself if you record your opinions separately. You may start by using the phrase, 'In my opinion...' or 'I suspect that...'

Permission

Settings must obtain written permission from parents to carry out observations and to keep them on record. Many settings ask for parental permission on the registration form that parents complete when they enrol their child at the setting.

Every setting has to store personal information about families correctly to comply with the Data Protection Act 1994/1998.

You must get permission from workplace supervisors before carrying out any observations. Supervisors will probably ask to see your completed observation. The child's family may also want to have a copy.

Confidentiality

See page 228 for further information about confidentiality.

Details of observations should be kept confidential unless withholding information would affect the well-being of the child.

GOOD PRACTICE

- Make sure you fully understand your setting's confidentiality policy and work in line with it at all times.

Focus

Sometimes childcarers will carry out general observations of whatever children happen to be doing. But other observations are focused. For instance, you may decide to observe a child playing outside with his friends because you want to focus on observing his gross motor skills and his social skills.

GOOD PRACTICE

Settings will have their own policies and procedures about the way observations are carried out. Ask your supervisor to explain these to you and to show you any observation forms the setting completes.

Choosing an observation technique

There are several methods of recording observations. It's good practice for you to become familiar with all of the methods over time. Aim to select the most appropriate method to suit your focus and the age of the child and work in line with the requirements of your setting.

During observations the behaviour of children can change. If they are aware of being watched, some children may feel anxious or excited, or they may try harder than usual. To overcome this, childcarers often try to be as unobtrusive as possible by settling themselves somewhere suitable to watch the child, without alerting them to the fact they're being observed. The childcarer won't interact with the children during this time. They won't speak, so there's no need to make a record of their own actions or words during the observation. If you use this method you're known as a **non-participant observer**.

Learn the lingo

Non-participant observer = an observer who doesn't interact with the child being observed

This technique is well suited to the 'free-description' and 'target child' methods of observation, which are explained on page 58 and page 61.

It's easier to be objective and to record what's happening when you are not involved in events. There can be drawbacks though – it can be hard to find somewhere unobtrusive that still allows you to see and hear everything. Also, if you're looking to observe certain aspects of development or behaviour, you may not see them if you don't encourage children to carry out particular activities or tasks.

You may choose to be a **participant observer**. The participant observer can directly ask or encourage children to do things.

Learn the lingo

Participant observer = an observer who does interact with the child being observed

This technique works well with the 'checklist method' of observation described on page 59, which is often used with babies and young children.

You might ask a child to build a tower for instance, to see how many bricks they can stack. Participant observers can also ask questions to find out the reason for a child's behaviour – 'Why are you doing that?' A drawback of this method is that the childcarer can influence the child, affecting the result. For instance, a participant observer may ask a child to fetch a particular object. Subtle clues such as where the observer is looking at can help to tip off the child. Obvious clues, such as pointing to the object, are easier to avoid! Keep any instructions to the bare minimum.

GOOD PRACTICE

- You must plan observation time with your supervisor to ensure that it fits in with the overall plans of the setting.

Whatever method of observation is used, the following key pieces of information are always needed on the observation record:

- The name of child (or alternate method of identifying them – initials perhaps).
- Date and timing of the observation.
- Where the observation was carried out.
- Name of the observer.
- Activity observed/focus of observation.
- Other children present.
- Other adults present.

Have a go!

The key techniques of observation are outlined below. Try one or two out for yourself. (Remember to get permission from your supervisor.)

FAST FACT

Sometimes you might need to abandon an observation, for example, if you see something unsafe about to happen or if a child in search of assistance cannot be redirected to another adult.

Free description (also known as narrative description)

The observer focuses on the activity of the child, writing down everything seen during the allotted time. Free-description observations are generally short, lasting for perhaps five minutes or less. They are helpful for focusing on areas of difficulty for children, for instance working out exactly what's happening when a child struggles to feed herself. These observations are often recorded in a notebook and written up afterwards.

You will need:

- A notepad.
- A pen.

What to do

Write a detailed description of how the child carries out the activity being observed. Note their actions and behaviour, including their facial expressions. Record what the child says and any non-verbal communication such as gestures. This is intensive work, which is why this type of observation is usually used for just a few minutes. Observations are recorded in the present tense.

Example

Ben is sitting at the painting table next to Jessica. He picks up his paintbrush and looks at her. She looks back. He smiles and holds his brush out to her. Jessica takes it and smiles back. Ben says, 'Thank you.'

Checklists (also known as tick lists)

A form prompts the observer to look for particular skills or reflexes that a child has. The observer ticks them off as they are seen. This method is often used for assessing a child's stage of development. It's good for observing the development of babies, whose physical development progresses quickly. The observations may be done over time, or older babies and children may be asked to carry out specific tasks.

You will need:

- A prepared checklist (these can be bought or developed by childcarers/settings).
- A pen.

What to do

The checklist tells you what to observe and record. As a participant observer, encourage children to carry out the necessary tasks, ticking the relevant boxes to record the child's response – generally whether they could carry out the task competently. As a non-participant observer, tick the boxes as you see evidence of children's competence naturally occurring.

Example

Example checklist ▼

Activity	Yes	No	Date	Observer's comments
Rolls from back to front				
Rolls from front to back				

Time samples

The observer decides on a period of time for the observation, such as two hours or the length of a session. The child's activity is recorded on a form at set intervals

– perhaps every 10 or 15 minutes. This tracks the child's activity over the period of time. However, significant behaviours may occur between the intervals and these will not be recorded.

You will need:

- A prepared form giving the times for the observations.
- A pen.
- A watch.

What to do

Keep an eye on the time to ensure you observe at regular intervals. At each allotted time, observe the child and record their activity in the same way as in the 'free-description' method.

Example

10.00 a.m.

Ben is sitting at the painting table next to Jessica. He picks up his paintbrush and looks at her. She looks back. He smiles and holds his brush out to her. Jessica takes it and smiles back. Ben says 'thank you.'

10.15 a.m.

Ben gets down from the table. He goes to the nursery nurse. He looks at her and says, 'Wash hands.'

Event samples

This method is used when there's reason to record how often an aspect of a child's behaviour or development occurs. A form is prepared identifying the aspect being tracked. Each time the behaviour or development occurs, a note of the time and circumstance is recorded. Samples may take place over a session, a week or even longer. Practitioners may want to observe how frequently a child is physically aggressive for instance.

You will need:

- A prepared form adapted for the objective of the observation.
- A pen.

What to do

Watch a child, and each time the aspect of behaviour or development being observed occurs, record the circumstances along with the time.

Example

Example observation ▼

Event no.	Time	Event	Circumstances
1	2.30 p.m.	Joshua pushed Daisy over	Joshua had left his teddy on the floor. He saw Daisy pick it up. He went over to Daisy and tried to take the teddy. She did not let go. Joshua pushed her over. Daisy gave Joshua the toy and started to cry. Joshua walked away quickly with the teddy.

Target child

The observer will record a child's activity over a long period of time, but unlike the time-sample method, the aim is not to have any gaps in the duration of the observation. To achieve this the observer uses a range of codes to record, in shorthand on a ready-prepared form, what is happening.

You will need:

- A prepared form with a key to the abbreviations that will be used.
- A pen.
- A watch.

What to do

With this type of observation the observer has to make decisions about which things are important and should be recorded, because it's impossible to record every detail over a long period. Language and activity are recorded in separate columns for ease. It takes practice to get used to using the codes, so don't worry if you find it tricky at first.

Example activities

Example

Time	Activity	Language	Social grouping	Involvement level
11.30	TC goes to the box of blocks. Uses both hands to tip the box up and get the blocks out	_TC_ 'Out'	SOL	1
11.31	TC sits down. Using right hand he places one block on top of another. He repeats this, building a tower of four blocks		SOL	1

Key:
TC = target child
_TC_ = target child talking to self
SOL = solitary grouping
1= target child absorbed in their activity
Additional codes will be used. Codes vary within settings. Refer to your organisational procedures.
Further information is given in A Practical Guide to Observation and Assessment 3rd Edition (Hobart, C. and Frankel, J. (2004) Nelson Thornes Ltd, Cheltenham)

FAST FACT

It's interesting for two people to observe the same target child over the same period and then compare notes. They're likely to have recorded different things.

Sharing observations

Childcarers share information gained through observation with colleagues who work directly with the child in question and with senior staff. Talking about observations with colleagues helps to build up a well-rounded picture of a child. Most settings will set aside time for colleagues to meet and talk about their observations.

Have a go!

When you have the opportunity to discuss an observation with a colleague, make a note of your colleague's opinions. Add these to the observation record. It's also important to contribute to colleagues observations when you can. An example of this is given in the case study below.

Discuss observations with colleagues

Practical example

Kyle contributes to observation

In a meeting, childcarer Amy shares her observation with her colleagues. Kyle listens carefully as Amy describes the way her Target Child struggled to put on a dressing up outfit and became frustrated and upset. Kyle then tells Amy that he has noticed that the Target Child often says he's too hot to wear his coat outside and tries to avoid putting it on.

This helps to build up a picture of a child having difficulties dressing himself. The staff can now plan how to help the Target Child overcome this difficulty.

1 *Suggest a way the staff could help the Target Child?*

Settings also share information about the development and progress of children with their parents and carers. This should be done in an open, positive way. Keyworkers often arrange a meeting with families to talk about a child's progress. It's important to remember that the parents generally know their child best. Families have much to contribute to a discussion about the progress of their child and this information should be valued. It can also be recorded in the child's records.

In many settings more than one childcarer carries out observations on the same child over time. This helps to ensure that the development records that build up are objective.

Reporting concerns

If you become concerned about a child following observation, tell your supervisor as soon as you can. This means that children can get the help and support they may need as soon as possible.

Interpreting observations

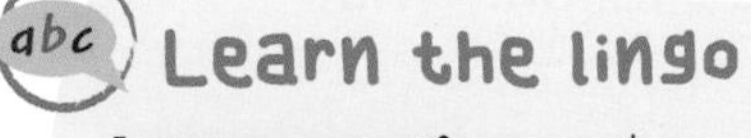

Interpretation = the process of assessing and evaluating an observation or series of observations.

Once an observation (or series of observations) has been completed, childcarers consider the observation carefully and then draw conclusions. This process is known as 'assessment' and the conclusions drawn are known as the 'evaluation' or the 'outcome'. The whole process of assessing and evaluating is called the **interpretation**.

Settings will have developed their own techniques for interpretation and for writing the interpretation up. You should follow your setting's guidelines. They are likely to follow the steps outlined in this chart:

- Go through the whole observation, noting sections that seem important in terms of behaviour and development
- Reflect on each important section, drawing conclusions related to behaviour and development, i.e. how does it compare with the expected pattern of development?
- Think about what is known about the child from previous observations and/or baseline assessment. Are they making progress? If not, is there cause for concern? Should you consult with colleagues at this stage?
- Write up the interpretation
- File the observation until it is required/share with colleagues, parents/carers

Guidelines for interpreting observations ▲

FOCUS ON...
your learning

In this section you've learnt why observations are important to support development. You've learnt about observation techniques, confidentiality and objectivity. You've also learnt how to share observations with colleagues, and how observations can be used to support the development of children.

Questions:

1. How does observing support children's development?
2. The name of the observer should be given on every observation. What other basic information should always be recorded?

Learning Outcome 3

FOCUS ON...

how to identify influences that affect children's development

In this section you'll learn about factors that can affect children's development, including their background, health and environment.

This links with Assessment Criterion **3.1**

Influences that affect development

There are influences (factors) that affect children's development. These fall into two key categories:

- Nature.
- Nurture.

Nature

We use the word **nature** to describe the aspects of child development that happen naturally at certain times in a child's life, without any outside influences. Some aspects of development that are down to nature include the primitive reflexes we see in newborn babies and increasing physical abilities, such as the ability to roll over and sit up. Nature continues to play a part in development as children grow. The onset of puberty is another example of this. Development from nature happens because children are genetically programmed from birth to be able to do certain things at certain times.

Learn the lingo

Nature = describes the way children are genetically programmed from birth to be able to do certain things at certain times.

see page 51.

Nurture

The aspects of development that aren't down to nature are down to nurture. **Nurture** is the word we use to describe the development that happens in response to the experiences that individual children have from the time they are born onwards. For instance, children won't learn to read unless they are exposed to written letters and words. They aren't genetically programmed by nature to just begin reading at a certain age without outside influences.

Learn the lingo

Nurture = describes the development that happens in response to the experiences that individual children have from the time they are born onwards.

Nature and nurture

It's generally accepted that children develop as they do because of a combination of the two key influences – nature and nurture. Language is a good example of this. Studies have shown that babies all over the world make coos, gurgles and other sounds that are very similar. The potential to speak and the ability to make pre-language sounds would seem to be down to nature. But children only learn to speak the languages they are exposed to in their lives. This is down to nurture.

Because of the nurture factor, individual children's development and levels of maturity will depend partly on the experiences they have had. All children have different experiences at different times, so it's normal for them to develop at different rates.

Children can't be expected to achieve aspects of development that are largely down to nurture if they haven't yet been exposed to experiences that encourage this development. For instance, if a child isn't talked to very much, the lack of exposure to language will affect their communication development.

Influences that affect development

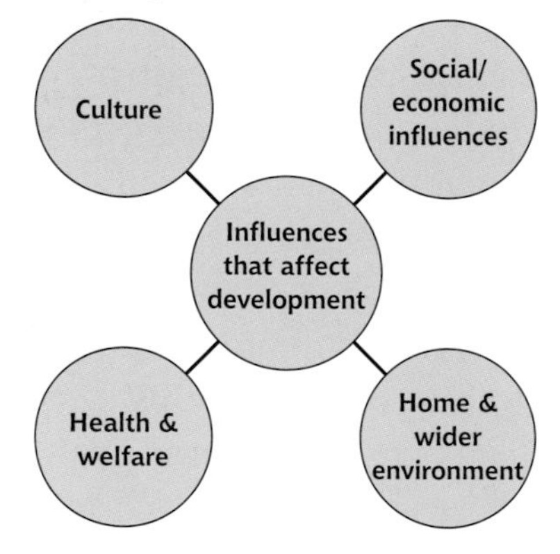

The influence of background

A child's background affects the experiences a child has and this affects their development. Children grow up within unique families – every family is different. Different families influence children in widely different ways, depending on their culture, beliefs, lifestyles and their own experiences.

The circumstances children live in also affects their development. The way life unfolds around a child impacts greatly on the experiences they have. Children of the same age growing up in different places can experience daily life in very different ways. This applies to children living not just in different countries, but in different parts of the UK and even in different parts of the same city or town.

Economics (or money matters) play a part too. If a child lives in **poverty** they may not have access to many of the experiences that other children benefit from. Children may 'fail to thrive' if poverty or lack of care affects their health and welfare. Also, any child who is unwell may

You'll find out more about this in Units 3 and 9.

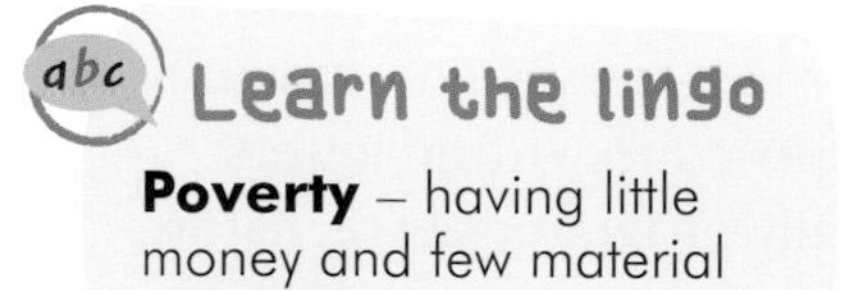

Learn the lingo

Poverty – having little money and few material possessions.

miss out on certain activities and experiences and in some cases, periods of education. Children may also have additional needs that affect their development.

Different families will influence children in different ways ▶

GOOD PRACTICE

To ensure your expectations about a child's development are realistic, you should take their background into account.

The diagram on page 66 summarises the key elements of a child's background that can influence development.

FOCUS ON...
your learning

In this section you've learnt about nature and nurture. You've learnt about how some of the influences within a child's background can affect development.

Questions:

1 What is meant by the terms 'nature' and 'nurture'?

2 Why is it normal for children to develop at different rates?

Learning Outcome 4

FOCUS ON...

everyday care routines and activities to support development

In this section you'll learn how to use everyday care routines to promote **hygiene**, support children's welfare and meet children's care needs.

This links with Assessment Criteria **4.1, 4.2**

Care routines

When we care for young babies and children repetitive tasks are carried out, such as:

- Washing.
- Dressing.
- Feeding.
- Changing nappies.
- Toileting.

The ways in which children's care needs are met are part of children's daily routines. Because these routines are repeated so frequently when children are young, they're an important part of their overall experience of life. It's important to always meet children's care needs sensitively and to interact with them gently. Good care routines support children's health and **welfare**.

During care routines you can:

- Make the most of one-to-one time
  Care routines are a great time to bond and play with babies and children on a one-to-one basis. Approaching care routines playfully also helps children to enjoy them. For instance, while babies are changed or fed, they are lying or sitting in front of their carer. It's an ideal time to make eye contact and to talk.
- Let children know they are cared for and respected
  By attending to care needs at a child's pace and by using respectful, affectionate touch, speech and gesture.
- Use the experience as a learning opportunity
  For instance, it's never too soon to talk with babies and children about care routines. While washing a

Learn the lingo

Hygiene – things we do to ensure good health and cleanliness.
Welfare – well-being.

Also see Physical and health needs on page 282.

GOOD PRACTICE

- For children to have a positive experience, it's important that you don't rush when attending to care needs. Childcarers working in busy group settings with several children to attend to must remember to take their time with each child, avoiding the 'treadmill approach' of simply dealing with one task after another without engaging with the individual babies or children concerned.

Looking after their own care needs ▼

child's hands for instance, you can say, 'We'll rub some soap in to make your hands nice and clean.'

- Encourage independence
  Because children will take responsibility for all of their own care needs eventually.

Key attachments

Babies begin to emotionally bond with their parents after birth. This gives them a sense of safety, security and love. To feel settled and secure, babies and young children also need to make attachments with other adults that care for them.

Attachments are made when familiar adults spend time with babies and children, interacting with them frequently and sensitively. The attachment felt by the child is strengthened when a familiar adult attends to their care needs. A young child will come to trust and depend on the adult to support them, both emotionally and in a practical sense. Good care routines help children to feel cared for.

For instance, when a baby is fed a bottle, they'll be held securely against the body of the adult feeding them. They receive undivided time and attention. The adult and baby will often gaze into one another's eyes. The baby may hold the fingers of the adult around the warm bottle. A feeling of closeness is shared by the adult and the baby.

Learn the lingo

Key attachment = the special emotional bond that forms between a child and her closest carers.

There is further information about the role of keyworkers in Unit 7.

Learn the lingo

Keyworker – a childcarer appointed to form a key attachment with a child, and to take a special interest in her welfare and development

GOOD PRACTICE

So attachments form and thrive between babies, young children and adults, it is good practice for group settings to appoint a **keyworker** for each child. The role of a keyworker is to take special interest in the well-being of their key children and to form attachments with them. Attending to children's care needs is an important part of forming such an attachment.

Personal hygiene

Children need adult help and supervision to ensure their bodies are kept clean and hygienic. Good hygiene practices are important because they:

- Help to prevent disease and the spread of infection.
- Prepare children for life by teaching them how to care for themselves.
- Play a part in children being socially accepted by other people.

You'll find out more about cross-infection in Unit 3.

Skin

The skin performs the following jobs:

- Protects the body, preventing germs from entering.
- Feels sensations of hot, cold, soft and hard.
- Secretes (produces and discharges) an oily substance called 'sebum'.

  This keeps the skin supple and waterproof
- Excretes (discharges) sweat.

  Which helps to regulate temperature when the body is hot.
- Makes vitamin D when exposed to sunlight.

Care of the skin

Children's skin can be kept clean and hygienic by following these guidelines:

- Wash the hands and face first thing in the morning.
- Wash hands after going to the toilet and after messy play, and before eating, drinking or touching food.
- Keep the nails short: this will prevent dirt collecting under them.
- A daily bath or shower is necessary with young children who play outside and become dirty, hot and sweaty. Dry them thoroughly, especially between the toes and in the skin creases to prevent soreness and cracking.
- If a daily bath is not possible, a thorough wash will do instead. Remember to encourage children to wash their bottoms after the face, neck, hands, armpits and feet. A separate flannel should be used for the hands, face and neck.
- Observe the skin for rashes and soreness.
- Black skin and other dry skin types need moisturising. Putting oil in the bath water and massaging oil or moisturisers into the skin afterwards helps to prevent dryness.
- Wash hair two or three times a week, or more often if parents prefer. Rinse shampoo out thoroughly in clean water. Conditioners may be useful for hair that is difficult to comb. Use a mild shampoo if hair is washed more frequently.
- Black hair may need hair oil applying daily to prevent dryness and hair breakage, particularly if it's curly.

- All skin types need protecting from the sun. Use a sun block or high factor sun cream and keep a close eye on the length of time children spend in the sun. Children should wear a legionnaire style hat that covers their neck and head on sunny days. You can now buy special clothing that prevents strong sunlight from penetrating children's skin when they're covered up. Sunglasses are also beneficial.

Bathing and washing babies

Some families will give their baby a bath each day. Others may bath their baby less often, but 'top and tail' the baby daily. This term describes the process of washing a baby's face, neck, hands and bottom without putting them in a bath of water. Some families make bath-time part of the getting-ready-for-bed routine. Others prefer to wash babies in the morning so they start the day feeling fresh.

Most daycare settings don't bath babies. But childminders and nannies working in the home may give baths. It's best for you to watch an experienced childcarer bathing a baby so you can see how to securely hold a slippery baby for yourself. You need to change the way you support babies according to their age. You must NEVER LEAVE A BABY UNATTENDED IN OR NEAR WATER, and you must NEVER LOOK AWAY, EVEN FOR A SECOND. If you do have to leave the bathing area YOU MUST TAKE THE BABY WITH YOU.

Bathing a baby ▼

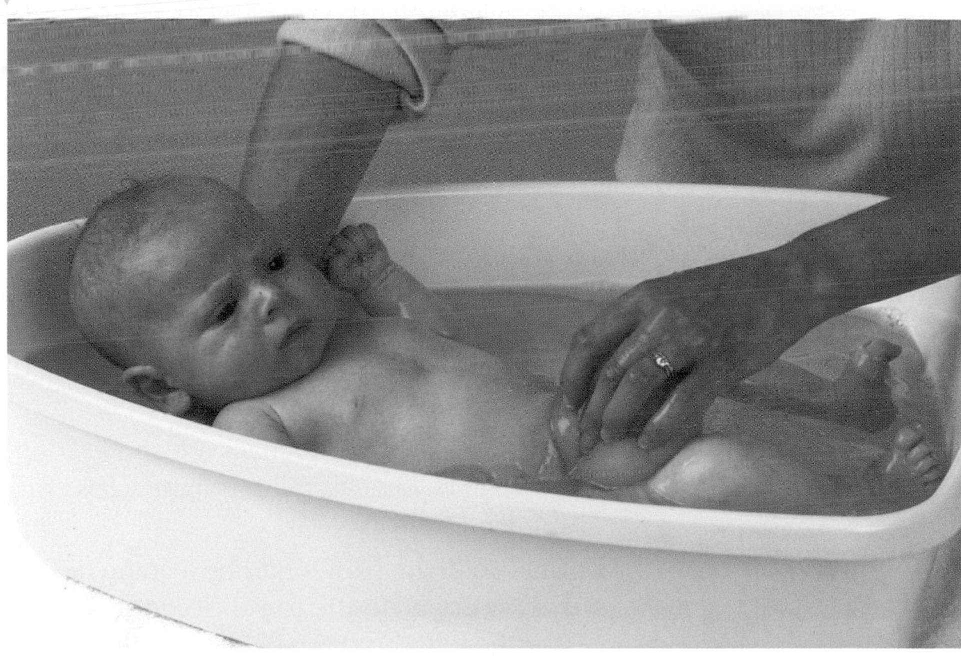

How to bath a baby

Here are some basic guidelines for bathing a baby of approximately five to seven weeks:

1. Make preparations: Gather together all the equipment you will need – bath, changing mat, nappy changing equipment, clean clothes, baby toiletries, such as bathing lotion and other lotions/oils if necessary, cotton wool, a soft warm towel and blunt-ended nail scissors. Make sure the baby bath is securely placed on a flat surface. Close windows and doors to ensure there isn't a draught and ensure the room is sufficiently warm, as babies lose heat quickly. Look for and remove any risks – taps that are hot to the touch can be covered by a cold wet flannel for instance, and soap should be placed out of reach. Wash your hands thoroughly and make sure your nails are clean and not too long, or they may dig into the baby. Remove jewellery on your hands and wrists and any jewellery that may dangle down, and tie long hair back if appropriate. Wear protective clothing such as an apron and latex gloves. You should also wear flat shoes as the floor may become slippery.
2. Using a bath thermometer, fill the bath with water of the correct temperature – approximately 38°C. Mix the water with your hand to ensure there are no 'hot spots'. You should also prepare a small bowl of boiled warm water to be used for the baby's face.
3. Undress the baby, but leave the nappy on for now. Wrap the baby securely in a warm towel (from below the neck) and lay her on the mat.
4. Wash the baby's face first, using cooled boiled water to dampen cotton wool. Using a different piece of cotton wool for each eye, gently wipe across each eye in one movement, beginning at the inside corner and moving to the outside edge (nose to ear). The cotton wool should only be used once for hygiene reasons. Use more dampened cotton wool to wipe around the rest of the baby's face and ears. Avoiding the eye area, dry carefully with clean cotton wool.
5. Check the baby's nails are short. Long or jagged nails can be cut carefully straight across with blunt-ended nail scissors.
6. Wash the baby's hair by leaning her over the bath, still wrapped in the towel. To do this you need to use one hand to hold the baby and the other for washing the

Wash the baby's hair by leaning her over the bath

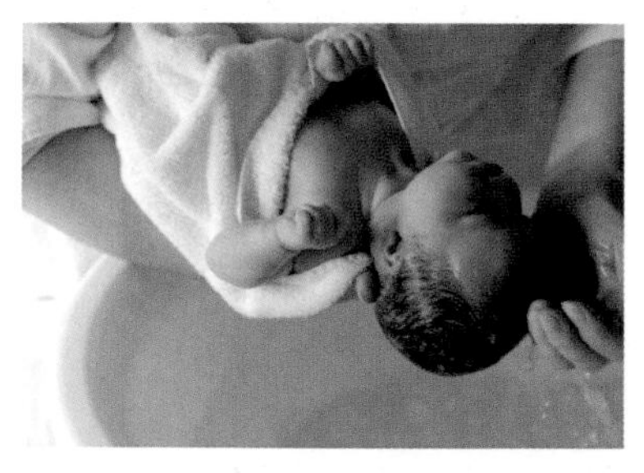

hair. Support the baby's head and shoulders in your hand, tucking their legs securely under your arm. Using your other hand, gently cup water over the head – you don't generally need shampoo for young babies. Dry the head gently by patting with a towel. A baby's head must not be left wet as the baby will quickly become cold. Place the baby back on the mat.

7. Remove the towel and the nappy. Clean the nappy area, as you usually would when changing a nappy, and dispose of the nappy and soiled toiletries as usual. (See page 78.) Lay a towel out ready for after the bath.
8. Lay the baby in the crook of your arm so that the head and neck are supported. Use your hand to hold the arm and shoulder furthest from you. Use your other hand to support the baby's bottom as you lower her into the bath. You can then let go of the bottom half of the baby – you now have a hand free for washing. Ensure you still have a secure grasp with your remaining hand.
9. Gently cup water over the baby with your hand, using stroking movements to massage the skin clean. You can gently use a flannel or sponge, but avoid rubbing. Pay close attention to skin creases in the thighs, neck, arms and under arms that can trap sweat and bacteria leading to soreness.
10. Some babies enjoy bathing more than others. If a baby is happy, let them to splash and kick for a short while before ending the bath. Don't do this for too long as young babies get cold quickly.
11. Support the bottom half of the baby as before. Ensure you have a secure hold as the baby will be slippery. Lift the baby out and lay them on the mat. Wrap them in a warm towel straight away.
12. Pat the baby's delicate skin dry (don't rub), paying close attention to the skin creases as before.
13. Apply any lotions necessary and put on a clean nappy. Dress the baby and gently brush the hair with a baby brush if appropriate (use a wide toothed comb for African-Caribbean hair). Settle the baby somewhere safe before cleaning up.
14. Put everything away. Drain the water away first, as this can be a safety hazard. Clean the baby bath out, ready for next time. Put clothes in the appropriate place ready to be washed. Wash your hands, even if you have been wearing gloves.

How to top and tail

As with bathing a baby, you should watch an experienced childcarer top and tail a baby before you do it yourself. The process of topping and tailing requires the same skills as bathing a baby, but you don't need to follow all of the same steps. Basic guidelines are:

- Make preparations following steps 1 and 2 of how to bath a baby.
- Undress the baby and clean her eyes, face and ears, following steps 3 and 4.
- Use additional dampened cotton wool to wash the baby's hands, cleaning in between the fingers. Pat the hands dry gently with a towel. Check the baby's nails, following step 5.
- Following step 7, remove the baby's nappy and clean the nappy area.
- Follow step 13, put on a clean nappy, dress the baby, brush her hair and settle her safely.
- Clear up and wash your hands, following step 14.

FAST FACT

There are products especially designed for the delicate skin and hair of babies, including soft, baby hairbrushes and toothbrushes.

GOOD PRACTICE

You can encourage children to brush their teeth from the time they are babies. Provide a soft toothbrush for a baby to become familiar with. They will naturally take the brush to their mouths. You can also give them the opportunity to watch adults and older children cleaning their teeth.

FAST FACT

Looking after teeth well in childhood helps them to last a lifetime.

Toiletries

Each child needs to have their own flannel and toothbrush and a clean towel. When it comes to using soaps, lotions, oils, toothpaste, sun screens and so on, it is important to ensure that the products selected meet children's individual needs. (Some children may be allergic to some products and families will have their own preferences.)

Teeth

Teeth appear at any time during a child's first two years of life. They usually come through in the order as shown on page 75. By the age of three, most children have their first set of 20 teeth, known as the milk teeth. From five to six years, these teeth begin to fall out as the permanent adult teeth come through. There are 32 permanent teeth.

Brushing teeth

When the first tooth does appear, try to clean it gently with a small, soft brush. Ensure that cleaning the teeth becomes a habit: in the morning after breakfast and after the last drink or snack before bed. Cleaning the teeth after meals should be encouraged, but this may not always be possible.

Cleaning teeth should be a daily habit

Teeth

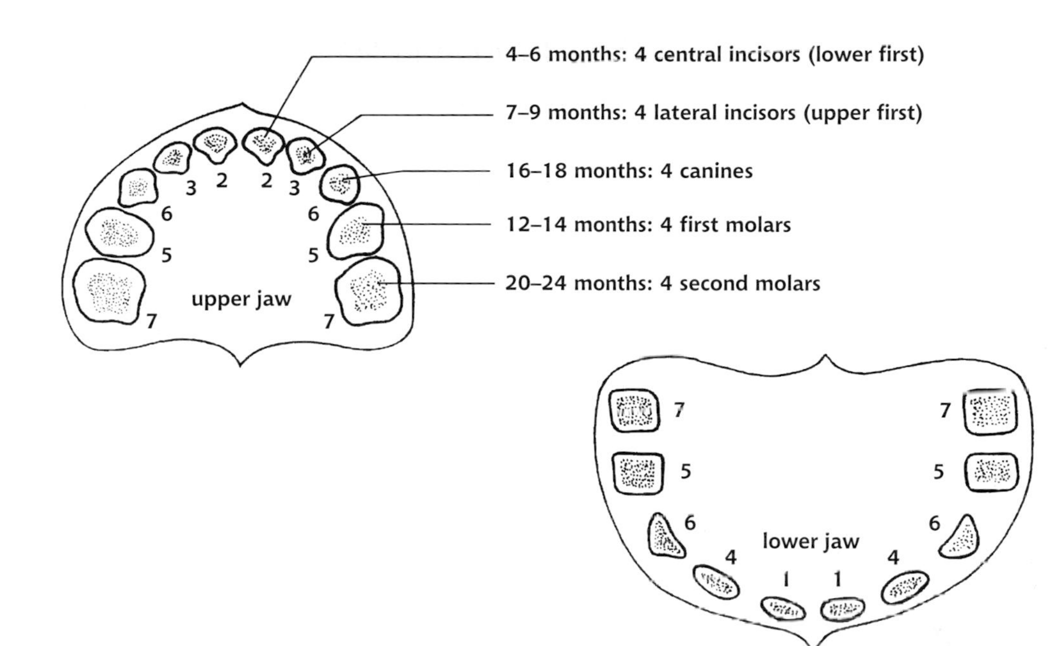

Diagram to show the usual order in which the milk teeth appear

GOOD PRACTICE

Avoid giving sweet drinks to babies and children, especially in a bottle, as this coats the gums and teeth in sugar and encourages decay.

FAST FACT

Sugar can penetrate the gum and cause decay to teeth before they have even come through.

A healthy diet that's high in calcium and vitamins and low in sugar encourages healthy teeth and helps to prevents decay. It's also important to visit the dentist regularly. A baby who attends with an adult, and then has their own appointments, will feel more confident about the procedure later on. Settings often help to prepare children for their dental appointments by talking about what happens and reading stories about visits to the dentists. Some set up a dentist surgery imaginary area, where children can role-play going to an appointment. It's important never to pass on any feelings of anxiety about the dentist that you may have yourself.

Nappies

Wet and dirty nappies are uncomfortable for babies. They can cause a baby's skin to become sore and inflamed. To avoid this, you should change a baby's nappy as often as necessary. It's usual to change nappies every three to four hours to coincide with mealtimes and in between if the baby is awake and uncomfortable. Babies should always be settled down to sleep in a clean nappy.

Many settings have a routine of changing nappies at regular times to make sure no child is left feeling uncomfortable. In addition, childcarers will change a nappy whenever they notice a baby is wet or dirty. Settings also keep a record of nappy changes and the information is given to parents and carers at the end of the session.

Nappy changing

Baby changing areas must:

- Be separate from food preparation and eating areas.
- Be warm and draught free.
- Be stocked with the necessary equipment/toiletries.
- Have hygienic facilities for the safe disposal of used nappies.
- Have a container for the storage of soiled clothes.
- Have facilities for cleaning changing mats and washing your hands after each baby has been changed.

Reusable nappies are folded to fit individual babies

Nappy types

There are two types of nappies, both listed below.

Reusable nappies

Although shaped nappies are available, reusable nappies are generally made from a rectangle of absorbent terry towelling. These are folded to fit individual babies and fastened with nappy pins. There are a range of nappy-folding techniques to suit babies of different sizes and some methods are more suited to boys or girls. It's best to learn how to fold nappies from an experienced childcarer who can demonstrate on one nappy whilst you follow along using another.

A disposable nappy liner may be used inside of the terry nappy. Plastic pants are placed over the nappy. For reuse, terry nappies must be thoroughly rinsed out. They should then be placed in a nappy pail (a bucket with a close fitting lid) filled with sterilising solution and be left to soak. They can then be washed in a washing machine.

Disposable nappies

Disposable nappies are available in a range of sizes and especially shaped to be suitable for boys or girls. Used nappies must always be hygienically disposed of. Some settings have a nappy unit that automatically seals a nappy into a plastic wrapping as it is placed inside. In other settings, staff place soiled nappies in plastic bag and tie the bag closed. The bag will then be disposed of in the appropriate bin and the bin lid will be replaced.

In some cultures a cloth may be placed under young babies in place of a nappy.

Cause for concern

Changing nappies gives practitioners the opportunity to detect any cause for concern in the nappy area of a baby's body. Details of some such concerns, along with concerns about infection and irregular bowel movements or urination, are given in the table below.

Cause for concern ▼

Cause for concern	Possible explanation and what to do
Baby passing stools very frequently. Stools are loose in consistency, and may be watery.	The baby may have diarrhoea caused by infection. In a group setting, a child with diarrhoea should be sent home as soon as possible. Parents and carers will need to seek medical advice if diarrhoea persists.
Baby passing hard stools which may be green in colour, or failing to pass stools regularly.	The baby may be constipated. It is important to make parents and carers aware of this. Initially, giving a weaned baby fruit may be sufficient to solve the problem.
Blood can be seen in stools or streaks of blood are on the nappy.	The baby may have an injury. Or, sometimes a small amount of blood is passed with hard stools when a baby is constipated. This information should be passed on to parents and carers who can seek medical advice.
Bruising or other marks on the skin of the nappy area.	The baby may have been injured in an accident, or they may have been injured intentionally. If you do not know how the marks occurred, you may need to ask parents or carers, and/or log the incident. See page 000 for further details.
Soreness/redness, a rash, blisters. This is very painful, and a baby may cry when her nappy is changed. Untreated soreness can quickly progress to a rash/blistering.	The baby may have nappy rash or an allergy to the nappy/nappy liner, or in the case of reusable nappies, the detergent used for laundering. Or, the baby may have an infection such as thrush. Report to parents and carers, and ensure nappies are changed frequently – at least every two hours and when necessary in between. Make sure the baby's bottom is thoroughly dried after cleaning. Creams should be used sparingly (if appropriate). Sometimes special creams are prescribed by a doctor.
Failure to urinate regularly.	The baby may not be drinking enough liquid. Offer frequent drinks and report to parents and carers.
Strong-smelling urine, which may be dark in colour.	The baby may have a urine infection. Offer plenty of fluids, and report to parents and carers who will need to seek medical advice.

How to change a nappy

Always have all the nappy changing equipment ready so you won't need to leave the area. To keep babies safe, you must NEVER LEAVE A BABY UNATTENDED ON A CHANGING MAT. You MUST NOT LOOK AWAY, EVEN FOR A MOMENT. If you do need to leave the area for any reason, YOU MUST TAKE THE BABY WITH YOU.

1. Wash your hands and put on protective clothing – latex gloves and an apron.
2. Place the baby on the changing surface. If the changing mat is not on the floor, it's safest to keep one hand on the baby throughout the changing process. If the baby is happy, talk to her playfully and make eye contact. Soothe the baby with your voice if she is unhappy.
3. Undress the bottom half of the baby, gently pulling her clothes well out of the way before you remove the nappy. Sometimes a nappy leaks a little, so check that clothes have not become wet or dirty. If they have, remove them.
4. Clean the nappy area thoroughly but gently. The method chosen for this will depend on the baby's requirements – you may use wet wipes or other lotions, or water and cotton wool. Make sure the skin is left dry to prevent soreness. Then apply any lotions in line with parents or carer's wishes.
5. Give the baby time to move her legs around while the nappy is off, sometimes called 'kicking free'. This helps to make nappy changing an enjoyable experience. But if the baby is distressed, finish the changing process so that you can comfort her.
6. Put a clean nappy on the baby and redress her, using fresh clothing if necessary. Settle the baby safely elsewhere before clearing away.
7. Dispose of the nappy correctly, according to your setting's facilities. Place any soiled clothes into the correct container ready for washing.
8. Don't remove your gloves yet. Wash your hands.
9. Clean the changing area, including the mat, following your setting's procedures.
10. Dispose of your protective clothing (including gloves) in the correct bin, then wash your hands again.
11. Make a record of the nappy change if required, in line with your setting's procedures.

Changing nappies ▼

GOOD PRACTICE

When toilet training:

- The approach to training must be agreed with parents and carers.
- Be relaxed. Don't rush children.
- Give praise for success.
- Don't show displeasure or disapproval about accidents. Deal with them without fuss, and in private, getting children into clean clothes as soon as possible.
- Provide good role-models. Seeing other children use the toilet will help the child to understand the process.
- Read stories about using the toilet or potty.
- Give opportunities to visit the toilet or potty regularly. Children will need reminding, especially when they're absorbed in an activity.
- Avoid sitting children on the toilet or potty for long periods of time.
- Always promote good hygiene practices – read on to find out more about these.

You'll learn more about this in Unit 3.

Toilet training

Children can only become clean and dry, or 'toilet trained', when they have control over their bowels and bladder. There's no point in trying to toilet train a child until this time.

Bowel and bladder control develops at different times in different children. It often occurs between the age of about 18 months and three years. Most children are dry and clean during the daytime by the time they are three. Frequent accidents can be expected at first as children may not notice until the last minute that they need to go to the toilet. Or children may wait too long to go, particularly if they're absorbed in an activity. Adults need to remind children to go to the toilet at first.

Night-time control takes longer to develop. Many children still have accidents at night until the age of six or seven, and some beyond this age. Some disabled children or those with special educational needs may develop bowel and bladder control much later and may continue to use nappies. Some may never develop control.

Wait until a child is showing definite signs of being ready for training before attempting the process. Most children aren't ready until the age of two or over. Signs that a child is ready include telling a carer when they're about to soil or wet their nappy, telling a carer that their nappy needs changing and showing reluctance to wear a nappy. Children must be able to tell their carer, verbally or with actions, that they need to go.

Good hygiene practices

To keep children safe you must always promote good hygiene practices. It's important for you to understand:

- The principles of cross-infection.
- How to dispose of different types of waste safely.
- How to handle food safely.
- How to handle body fluids safely.
- The issues concerning the spread of blood-borne viruses such as hepatitis, HIV and AIDS.

Practical example

Toilet training

Cheryl is a nanny. She cares for two-year old Toby while his parents are working. Toby is a happy little boy who is still wearing disposable nappies all the time. Toby's Dad is keen that he should become toilet trained and has asked Cheryl for her advice and help.

1. *How will Cheryl know if Toby is ready to be trained?*

Clothing must be comfortable ▼

Clothing

Clothing must be washable, comfortable and loose enough to allow easy movement. Young children should have fasteners that a child can manage, for example large buttons, toggles, Velcro and zips. Encourage children to help with dressing until they can manage independently.

Underwear

- Cotton is best as it absorbs sweat.
- All-in-one vests prevent cold spots.

General clothing

- Trousers are best for both sexes when a child is crawling as dresses can get in the way of active play.
- Track-suits, T-shirts and cotton jumpers are ideal.
- Add extra, light layers when it's cold.
- A shower-proof coat with a hood that is warm and easily washed.
- Waterproof trousers and wellingtons allow happy puddle splashing.

Pyjamas

- All-in-one suits without feet, with correctly sized socks.

FAST FACT

Some children may dress in a particular way for cultural reasons. For instance, a girl may not wear trousers, or a boy may keep his head covered. You must always respect a family's wishes.

Footwear

Shoes don't need to be worn until a child needs them to protect the feet and keep them warm when they walk outside. Young children can walk without shoes in the house. This is good for them as they use their toes to balance.

The bones of the feet may be easily deformed if they're pushed into badly fitting shoes or socks. Feet grow two or three sizes each year until the age of four years. The rate of growth then slows down. Footwear should fit correctly and a trained fitter should check the growth of the feet every three months when children are young. Both the length and width should be checked. Shoes should:

- Protect the feet.
- Have no rough areas to rub or chafe the feet.
- Leave room for growth, but not slip from the foot.
- Have an adjustable fastener, i.e. a buckle or Velcro.
- Be flexible and allow free movement.
- Fit around the heel.
- Support the foot and prevent it from sliding forwards.

Socks should also be the correct size. Stretchy socks should be avoided when children are young.

Encouraging hygiene independence

Children will be able to become increasingly responsible for their own personal hygiene as they grow up and develop. You can encourage young children to develop independence by:

- Establishing routines that encourage hygiene from babyhood.
- Showing children how to carry out tasks such as washing, dressing and cleaning their teeth.
- Providing positive role-models.
- Encouraging children to help as you wash them, dress them and so on.
- Encouraging children to take care of the environment as they care for themselves by keeping areas tidy and safe (e.g. by cleaning up water spillages in the bathroom).
- Praising children for their attempts at self-care.
- Making care routines fun (by providing bath toys for example).

GOOD PRACTICE

You should pay close attention to which aspects of self-care children are comfortable with. Respect their wishes when it comes to the assistance they need. However, you may need to step in sometimes to ensure hygiene standards are met. The practical example below gives an example of this.

- Allowing children to choose their own flannel, toothbrush, towel, hairbrush, etc.
- Providing a step so children can reach the basin to wash and their clean teeth independently.

Practical example

Mark encourages independence

Three-year old Ruby has been painting at her crèche. Childcarer Mark is in charge of supervising the children as they wash their hands before lunch. Ruby has confidently washed her hands by herself, but when she has finished, they still have some paint on them.

Mark gently points out the missed paint and directs Ruby back to the sink. He asks her if she would like some help. She says yes, and they wash her hands together.

1. *What did Mark do to prevent damaging Ruby's confidence in hand-washing?*

Learn the lingo

Nutrition – ensuring you eat the right foods for a healthy and well-balanced diet.

Healthy eating and nutrition

Food and water is the body's fuel. Human beings die without it. Large quantities of the following four nutrients are found in our food and drink:

- Protein.
- Fat.
- Carbohydrates.
- Water.

But only small quantities of the following are present:

- Vitamins.
- Minerals.
- Fibre.

Getting the right balance of nutrients is especially important during childhood when the body is growing and developing.

Vitamins and minerals are needed for healthy growth, development and normal functioning of the body. Water maintains fluid in the cells of the body and in the

The charts and tables below explain the sources and functions of nutrients.

bloodstream, and also contains some minerals. Fibre adds roughage to food. This encourages the body to pass out the waste products of food after it's been digested, by stimulating the bowel muscles.

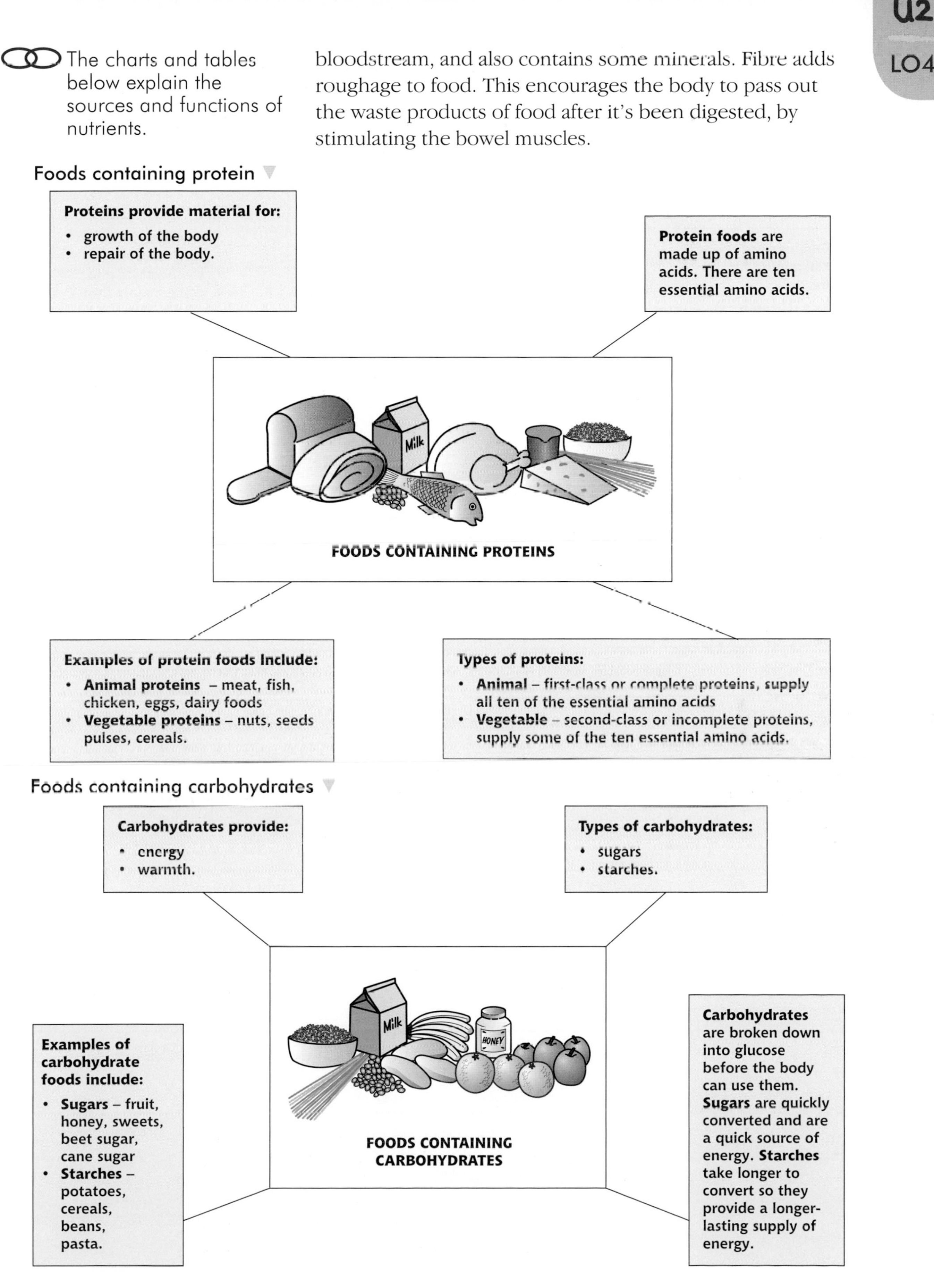

Foods containing protein

Proteins provide material for:

- growth of the body
- repair of the body.

Protein foods are made up of amino acids. There are ten essential amino acids.

FOODS CONTAINING PROTEINS

Examples of protein foods include:

- **Animal proteins** – meat, fish, chicken, eggs, dairy foods
- **Vegetable proteins** – nuts, seeds pulses, cereals.

Types of proteins:

- **Animal** – first-class or complete proteins, supply all ten of the essential amino acids
- **Vegetable** – second-class or incomplete proteins, supply some of the ten essential amino acids.

Foods containing carbohydrates

Carbohydrates provide:

- energy
- warmth.

Types of carbohydrates:

- sugars
- starches.

Examples of carbohydrate foods include:

- **Sugars** – fruit, honey, sweets, beet sugar, cane sugar
- **Starches** – potatoes, cereals, beans, pasta.

FOODS CONTAINING CARBOHYDRATES

Carbohydrates are broken down into glucose before the body can use them. **Sugars** are quickly converted and are a quick source of energy. **Starches** take longer to convert so they provide a longer-lasting supply of energy.

Foods containing fat

Fats:

- provide energy and warmth
- store fat-soluble vitamins
- make food pleasant to eat.

Types of fats:

- saturated
- unsaturated
- polyunsaturates.

Examples of foods containing fat include:

- **Saturated fat** – butter, cheese, meat, palm oil
- **Unsaturated** – olive oil, peanut oil
- **Polyunsaturated** – oily fish, corn oil, sunflower oil.

Saturated fats are solid at room temperature and come mainly from animal fats. **Unsaturated and polyunsaturated fats** are liquid at room temperature and come mainly from vegetable and fish oils.

The main vitamins

Vitamin	Purpose	Foods
A Fat-soluble Pregnant woman must avoid too much vitamin A	Maintenance of good vision and healthy skin. Promotes normal growth and development. Deficiency may lead to skin and vision problems	Carrots, tomatoes, eggs, butter, cheese
B Water-soluble Very regular intake required	Promotes healthy functioning of the nerves and the muscles. Deficiency may lead to anaemia and wasting of the muscles	Meat, fish, green vegetables. Some breakfast cereals are fortified with vitamin B (it is added to them)
C Water-soluble Daily intake required	Maintenance of healthy tissue and skin. Deficiency leads to a decreased resistance to infection, and can result in scurvy	Fruit. Oranges and blackcurrants have a high vitamin C content
D Fat-soluble	Maintenance of bones and teeth. Assists body growth. Deficiency in children may lead to bones that do not harden sufficiently (skeletal condition known as rickets). Also leads to tooth decay	Oily fish and fish oil, egg yolk. Milk and margarines are fortified with vitamin D. Sunlight on the skin can cause the body to produce vitamin D
E Fat-soluble	Promotes blood clotting, healing and metabolism. Deficiency may result in delayed blood clotting	Cereals, egg yolk, seeds, nuts, vegetable oils
K Fat-soluble	Promotes healing. Necessary for blood clotting. Deficiency may lead to excessive bleeding due to delayed blood clotting. Vitamin K is normally given to babies after birth as deficiency is sometimes seen in newborns, although rare in adults	Whole grains, green

FAST FACT

The Government has produced guidelines on healthy eating and nutrition for children.

GOOD PRACTICE

Too much salt is bad for children. It's good practice not to add salt to children's food before, during or after preparation.

See the weblinks section on page 108 for further details.

The main minerals

Mineral	Purpose	Foods
Calcium	Required for growth of teeth and bones. Also necessary for nerve and muscle function. Works with vitamin D. Deficiency may lead to rickets and tooth decay	Milk, cheese, eggs, fish, pulses, whole grain cereals. White and brown flour are fortified with calcium
Fluoride	Maintenance of healthy bones and protection from tooth decay	Present in water in varying quantities. May be added to water. Many toothpastes contain fluoride
Iodine	Used to make the thyroid hormone. Also required for normal neurological development. Deficiency may lead to thyroid problems	Dairy products, sea-foods, vegetables, water. Salt is fortified with iodine
Iron	Essential for the formation of haemoglobin in the red blood cells, which transport oxygen around the body. Deficiency may lead to anaemia. Vitamin C helps the absorption of iron	Meat, eggs, green vegetables, dried fruits
Phosphorus Babies must not have a high intake as can be harmful	Promotes the formation of teeth and bones	Meat, fish, vegetables, eggs, fruit
Potassium	Essential for water balance in the body. Also promotes functioning of cells, including the nerves	A wide range of foods
Sodium chloride Salt must not be added to food for babies or young children during food preparation or at the table	Essential for water balance in the body. Involved in energy utilisation and nerve function	Salt, meat, fish, bread, processed food

Feeding routines

From birth to three months, babies are fed entirely on milk. Somewhere between three and six months babies are gradually introduced to pureed, smooth foods. This process is called weaning.

From nine months most babies are able to sit up straight in a high chair. From about 12 months most children are eating a normal diet rather than baby food. By two years old most children can eat within a social group at the table since they are fairly independent with a spoon and beaker. Now is the time to introduce a fork and, when that is mastered, a knife. Most children can use a knife and fork by the time they are four and can cut most food themselves at five. (Some cultural practices associated with feeding differ from the process described above.) Once they are fully weaned, children generally need three main meals each day, plus a small snack mid-morning and mid-afternoon. Drinks should be supplied with meals, snacks and whenever children are thirsty. Remember to offer extra drinks in hot weather and after physical exercise.

GOOD PRACTICE

Encourage children to drink plenty of water. It keeps them hydrated and even helps concentration.

Breast-feeding

Breast milk naturally contains all the nutrients that babies need in the correct proportions at the right stage. It's considered to be the best milk for babies.

Colostrum is the name given to the first milk that is produced. This contains maternal antibodies produced within the mother's body. They're passed on to the baby through the milk and can protect them against some infections. There's less risk of infection occurring in the feeding process when babies are breast-fed. The milk itself doesn't contain any germs.

Some mums express their breast milk and supply it in a feeding bottle so childcarers can bottle feed their baby with breast milk. In this case:

- All equipment must be sterilised as described on page 87.
- Bottles should be clearly labelled with the date and the baby's name.
- Expressed breast milk must be stored in the fridge and used within 24 hours.
- Expressed breast milk may be kept in the freezer for up to three months by parents and carers at home. It must be thoroughly defrosted before use.

GOOD PRACTICE

At a workplace crèche, a mum may be able to come and breast feed her baby when necessary. Settings can provide a comfortable, private area where mums can breast feed or express milk.

Preparing formula feeds

Some families feed their baby formula milk (milk made up from a powder). This may be a personal choice, or the mum may have difficulties breast feeding. Whatever the reason, the family's choice should be respected and supported.

There are two stages to preparing a formula feed for babies – the cleaning and sterilising of equipment and making up the formula.

Sterilising equipment

Before making up formula for babies under one year old, all of the equipment that will be used must be thoroughly cleaned and sterilised. This kills germs that may still remain after the usual washing and drying of dishes. All feeding equipment (such as bowls and spoons) used for this age group must also be sterilised. The equipment used includes:

- Bottles.
- Teats.
- Bottle caps.
- Measuring spoons.
- Plastic knife.
- Plastic jug.
- Bottle brush.
- Teat cleaner.
- Sterilising unit with sterilising tablets or liquid OR
- a steam sterilising unit.

Cleaning and sterilising feeding equipment ▼

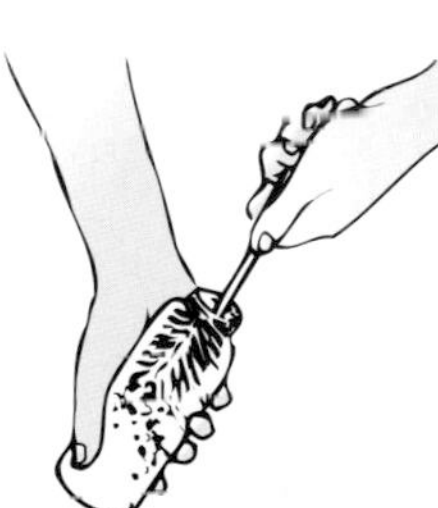

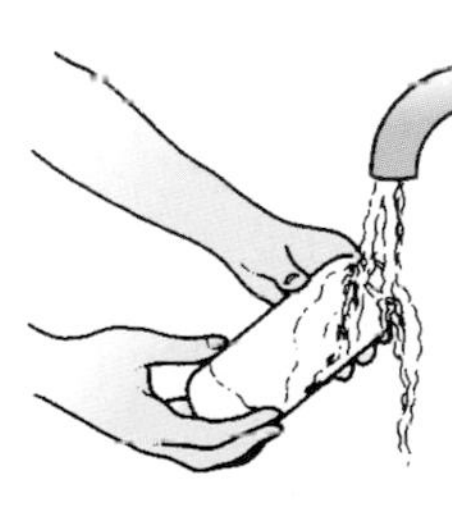

1. Before sterilising, the equipment must be cleaned. It must be rinsed, washed and rinsed again (see the diagram below). A bottle brush must be used to clean the bottles. A much smaller version of this, known as a teat cleaner, should be used on the teat. At one time salt was used to clean teats, but this is no longer considered good practice as there is a risk of increasing

the salt intake of a baby if residue remains in the teat. **Never use this method**.

2. The equipment can now be sterilised. There are different methods of sterilising. The traditional method is to make-up a sterile solution by mixing either sterilising tablets or sterilising solution with water, according to the manufacturer's instructions. The equipment is then submerged in a sterilising unit for a specified time (see below). Steam sterilising units are also available. They come with manufacturers' instructions for use.

The diagram on page 89 shows the procedure that should be followed.

Making up formula

It's very important to make-up formula correctly otherwise babies could become ill.

There are some important things to remember:

- Use the brand of formula milk agreed with the parents unless a doctor or health visitor advises otherwise.
- Only use boiled water to make-up feeds.
- Always measure the formula powder out carefully. Formula that's too strong can make babies ill. Formula that's too weak means that babies won't get the nutrients they need.

Don't:

- Pack the powder down into the scoop.
- Use heaped scoops.
- Add extra scoops of powder.

Do:

- Level the scoop off with a sterilised knife, as shown in the diagram.

Once a feed is made:

- It should either be used immediately or cooled and stored in the fridge.
- Once taken from the fridge and warmed in preparation for a feed, formula must be used within 45 minutes. Otherwise it must be thrown away.
- After 24 hours any unused feeds must be taken from the fridge and thrown away.

1 Check that the formula has not passed its sell-by date. Read the instructions on the tin. Ensure the tin has been kept in a cool, dry cupboard.

2 Boil some fresh water and allow to cool.

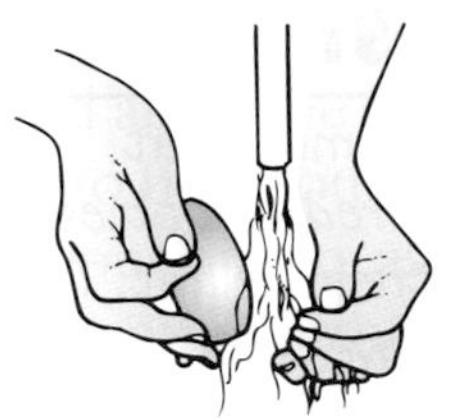

3 Wash hands and nails thoroughly.

4 Take required equipment from sterilising tank and rinse with cool, boiled water.

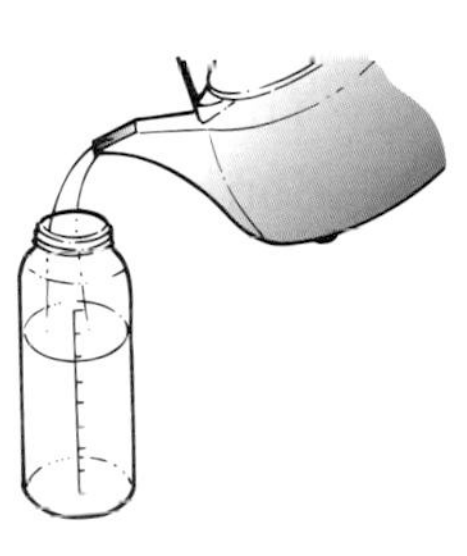

5 Fill bottle, or a jug if making a large quantity, to the required level with water.

6 Measure the exact amount of powder using the scoop provided. Level with a knife. Do not pack down.

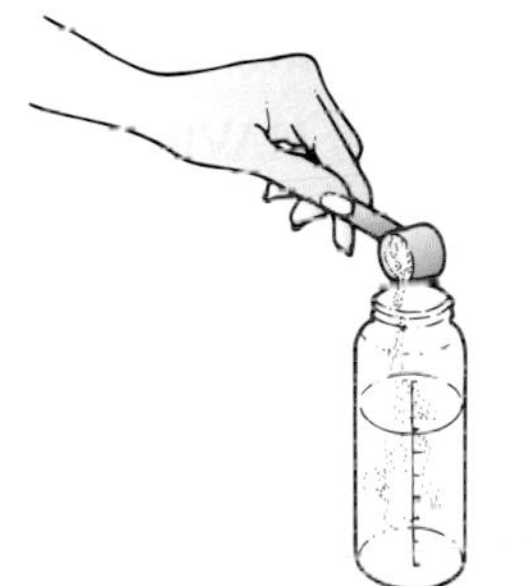

7 Add the powder to the measured water in the bottle or jug.

8 Screw cap on bottle and shake, or mix well in the jug and pour into sterilised bottles.

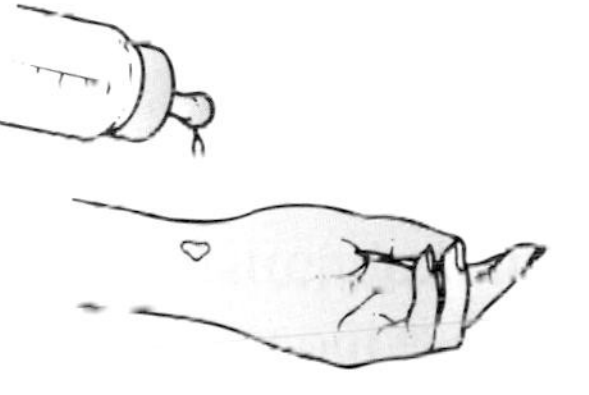

9 If not using immediately, cool quickly and store in the fridge. If using immediately, test temperature on the inside of your wrist.

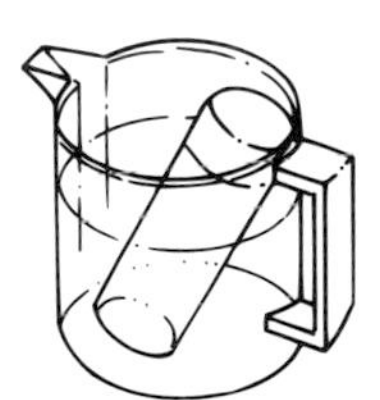

10 Babies will take cold milk but they prefer warm food (as from the breast). If you wish to warm the milk, place bottle in a jug of hot water. Never keep feeds warm for longer than 45 minutes, to reduce the chance of bacteria breeding.

Note: whenever the bottle is left for short periods, or stored in the fridge, cover with the cap provided.

Preparing a feed ▲

To warm a feed:

- Shake the bottle well as some of the powder may have settled in the bottom.
- Place the bottle in a jug of hot water to heat it through. This will take a few minutes.

- At first babies should be offered a small amount of bland, warm food of a sloppy consistency. The food should be free from salt, gluten and sugar. Baby rice and banana are both ideal, and they can be mixed with warm milk from the baby's bottle. Half to a full teaspoon of food is enough to start with.
- Babies may refuse the food at first because the experience is new. But the same food can be offered again the following day. It's good practice to give babies the opportunity to get used to one taste over two or three days before a new taste is introduced. This also means that adults can easily identify a food that may upset a baby's stomach.
- Pureed fruits, vegetables and bland baby cereals are all good foods for early weaning. Gradually babies will begin to take more spoonfuls of food. As the amount of solids taken increases, the amount of milk given should decrease. By about the fifth week of weaning, one of the baby's milk feeds should be replaced entirely by solid food. Cooled boiled water can be offered to drink at this mealtime.
- Babies gradually learn to manage lumps, and by seven months they can be offered harder foods such as peeled apple cubes and bread crusts. Babies can chew these with their hard back gums. They are ideal 'finger foods' for babies to feed to themselves.
- As babies become interested in their feeding spoon, have an extra one for them to hold at feeding times, and allow them to help. This is the first step towards independence at mealtimes. Protect clothing and flooring well so that you can relax about this as learning to feed is a messy affair!

GOOD PRACTICE

Remember that mealtimes should be a positive social experience. Always supervise young children's eating in case of choking, and be particularly aware when new textures and lumps are introduced.

Younger children need to practise feeding themselves

GOOD PRACTICE

It's good practice for settings to display a list of children's dietary requirements in the kitchen and eating area to remind all staff. You must always check the list before giving a child:

- Food or drink to consume.
- Raw cooking ingredients.
- Food to be used in play (e.g. jelly).

FAST FACT

Nuts are a choking hazard for young children and they are a common cause of food allergy. So many settings have introduced a 'no nut policy'. They don't use nuts or nut products and children aren't allowed to bring them into the setting.

GOOD PRACTICE

It's generally considered appropriate to let children know that no foods are completely unacceptable, but that sugary foods (such as sweets and fizzy drinks) and those that are high in saturated fats (such as cakes) should be thought of as occasional treats.

Specific dietary requirements

When a child is first registered with a setting, the parents or carers will be asked about any dietary requirements the child may have. It's important for childcarers to know about, and understand, any specific dietary requirements. This allows them to meet the child's needs whilst still promoting a healthy diet.

Food has a spiritual significance within some cultures, religions and ethnic groups. This may mean that certain foods cannot be eaten by some children, or that food should be prepared in a particular way. Other families make decisions about food based on personal beliefs. They might choose to be vegetarian for instance.

Childcarers must respect and comply with parental wishes. You should never assume that you will be able to tell what a child may or may not eat from their religion – always find out directly from the family.

Some children have food allergies, intolerances or medical conditions that mean their diets have to be restricted. This can be caused by an allergic response, diabetes or an enzyme deficiency. Common allergens (causes of allergic reactions) include nuts and milk.

Some children may need to eat at certain times of the day and may take medication for their condition. Some children need to be given medication if they show symptoms of their condition or if they have eaten (or in some cases even touched) a food they should not have. Childcarers must be absolutely clear about what to do for a child in their care with an allergy, intolerance or medical condition. Doing the right thing quickly can save a child's life.

It's VERY IMPORTANT that you fully understand children's dietary requirements so you can meet their needs without making mistakes. Settings record full details of dietary requirements on children's registration forms. Settings must make sure children's requirements are explained to everyone involved in caring for the child.

Planning menus

When planning menus, including snacks and drinks, it's important to consider:

GOOD PRACTICE

If children are reluctant to try something new, or they don't like new food, simply remove it and offer an alternative. Do offer the food again at another time though. Some children change their mind once a food is familiar to them. If not, don't make a fuss. Our tastes for food change throughout our lives – we go off things, or suddenly start to enjoy a taste. The child may enjoy the food at some point in the future.

FAST FACT

If a setting becomes concerned about a child's eating habits, the keyworker will generally talk to their parents or carers to agree a way forward. Dieticians will give advice if necessary.

– see page 108.

- The nutritional balance needed by children for a healthy diet – what have children eaten for their previous meal/snack and what will they have next?
- The current government guidelines.
- The time of day the food will be eaten.
- Children's individual dietary requirements and allergies.
- Children's likes and dislikes.
- Variety.
- Offering children new and interesting foods to try.
- How older children can be involved in choosing and preparing food.
- How food will be presented to add interest.
- How families can be consulted.

Not making a fuss about food is a good general rule – battling with children over food is unproductive and the child may come to dread mealtimes. If children regularly refuse food, not offering food outside of mealtimes can be the solution.

Unsuitable foods

The following table explains which foods are unsuitable for babies and children at different ages and the reason for this. Information about suitable and unsuitable foods for weaning and general weaning guidance can be found on the Food Standards Agency website

Unsuitable foods

Details of food	Details of age restriction	Reason
Salt Must not be added to babies' food. It is not allowed to be added to baby foods on sale in the UK. Limit the intake of food high in salt, such as cheese, bacon, sausages. Do not give processed foods not intended for babies (such as breakfast cereals) as these may be high in salt	Up to six months babies should have less that 1g of salt. From seven months to one year they should have no more than 1g. (Formula and breast milks contain the right amount of salt)	A baby's immature kidneys cannot cope with more than the recommended amount of salt

Details of food	Details of age restriction	Reason
Sugar Do not add it to food or drinks. Sour fruit such as rhubarb can be sweetened with alternatives such as mashed banana or formula/breast milk	This is advisable for all babies and young children	Sugar can encourage an unhealthy sweet tooth and cause tooth decay as teeth come through
Honey	Do not give honey until babies are at least one year old	Honey can contain a bacteria that produces toxins in immature intestines, causing serious illness
1. Wheat-based foods and other foods containing gluten, including bread, wheat flour, breakfast cereals and rusks 2. Nut and seeds 3. Eggs 4. Fish and shellfish 5. Citrus fruit and citrus fruit juice	Avoid these five foods until a baby is six months old. Only ground or flaked nuts should be given to children under five. Many settings have a no nut policy due to the commonality of nut allergies among children. Egg white and yolk must always be cooked to a solid consistency to prevent food poisoning	These foods can cause allergic reactions, so it is advised that they are not introduced before the age of six months. GPs may advise introducing certain foods even later if food allergies run in the family
Full-fat cow's milk Goat's and sheep's milk	Avoid until the baby is one year old. (All milk must be pasteurised)	It does not contain enough iron and nutrients to meet the needs of younger babies
Semi-skimmed milk	Avoid until the age of two years	Can be introduced then if a child is a good eater with a varied diet
Skimmed milk	Unsuitable for children under five	It does not contain sufficient nutrients
Squash, fizzy drinks, flavoured milk, herbal drinks, diet drinks, tea and coffee	These are unsuitable for babies and toddlers	These are not recommended for one or more of the following reasons: they may contain sugar or caffeine, they may cause tooth decay or fill babies up, leading to a poor appetite and poor weight gain

Learning opportunities

We've looked at how everyday routines such as eating, drinking, personal hygiene and dressing give opportunities for children to learn about independent self care. But there are also opportunities for children to learn and develop in other areas. Some examples of learning opportunities are:

Using cutlery

- When dressing, children can practise the fine motor skills required to fasten buttons, Velcro, toggles and zips.
- Children can help each other with putting on outside clothes, developing their social skills.
- When eating, children can practise the hand/eye co-ordination needed to pick up food with cutlery.
- When pouring out their own drinks from a jug children can learn about capacity and volume.
- While sitting at the table at mealtimes, children can learn about manners and social skills as they interact with one another.
- Children can count out the right number of cups or plates at snack time, learning about numbers.
- Babies and young children can communicate with their carers, practising their early language. Adults and children may also share rhymes or songs.

Safeguarding children

It's essential that all settings adopt 'safe working practices'. These are procedures that make sure:

- Children are safeguarded (protected) from abuse and exploitation whenever they are at the setting, including during personal care routines such as toileting, bathing and nappy changing.
- Childcarers who may become vulnerable to accusations of behaving improperly are protected.

You'll find out more about this in Unit 3.

Exercise and physical activities

Exercise is a necessary and natural part of life for everyone. It's especially important for young children who need to develop and practise their physical skills. Encouraging exercise from an early age will help children to develop healthy exercise habits. Children who don't get enough

exercise will be at increased risk of heart disease and other health problems later in life. It's also important for children to have fresh air and opportunities to play outside.

Exercise and physical activities must be supervised as appropriate to children's individual needs. For instance, many babies are mobile by the time they reach their first birthday. But they have little concept of danger. They need a watchful adult to ensure their safety as they explore and investigate the world. As children grow, their gross motor skills develop, and they are ready to tackle a range of physical activities that give them exercise.

Have a go!

Turn to the development tables in this Unit. Make a list of physical activities you could provide to promote exercise, under the following headings:

- 12 months
- 2 years
- 4 years
- 6 years
- 8–12 years
- 13–16 years

Follow the gross motor section from 12 months (page 42) to 16 years (page 51).

Rest and sleep

GOOD PRACTICE

Childcarers can set up relaxing or quiet areas in their settings without too much difficulty. A cosy book area or home corner, with soft cushions, bean bags or soft furniture is ideal. This can easily be provided in most settings, including nurseries, schools, homes and out-of-school clubs. These areas should be away from noisy activities.

Children should exercise regularly but they must be allowed to rest – this may be relaxation, sleep or just doing a calmer activity. Children don't need to be stimulated all the time. It's sometimes useful for them to be given toys or activities that are relatively easy to do, particularly after a challenging activity or at the end of a busy day. For instance, after-school clubs find that many children like to have time to sit and chat with their friends when they first arrive, perhaps while doing something simple such as colouring.

It's important to take this into account when you're planning children's routines. Make sure there's a good mix of active and calm activities, and indoor and outdoor activities. For instance, you may plan to have storytime indoors after children have been playing running games outside.

Sleep routines

Different babies and children need different amounts of sleep, just like adults. But much depends on their age, stage of development and the amount of exercise taken. Some babies may only seem to sleep and feed for the first few months, while others sleep very little. Toddlers vary too. Some need a nap in the morning, some need a nap in the afternoon, and some need both! Some children wake often at night, even after settling late, while others sleep through from an early age.

Following a sensible routine helps children to settle into regular sleeping patterns that give them the rest they need. It's important for childcarers to plan a child's sleep routine with their parents or carers. The following guidelines are helpful:

- Plan a bedtime routine and follow it sensibly.
  Don't make unnecessary changes to the routine, but be flexible enough to allow for a child's changing sleep requirements. Children will sleep less as they grow up, but may need more sleep if they're feeling unwell or have had a particularly disturbed night.
- Don't stimulate a child just before bedtime.
  Instead, plan a quiet activity such as story time. It helps children to have a nightly getting-ready-for-bed routine, such as a bath, a story then bedtime.
- Encourage daily exercise.
- Make sure the bedroom is comfortable.
- Avoid loud noises.
- Be patient.

FOCUS ON...
your learning

In this section you've learnt about care routines. You've found out about washing, dressing, feeding, changing nappies, toileting, exercise, rest and sleep. You've learn how to meet children's care needs and support the welfare of children.

Questions:

How can care routines support children's development?

How can you show a child respect when attending to their care needs?

Learning Outcome 5

FOCUS ON...

how to support children through transitions in their lives

In this section you'll learn about some of the transitions children experience in their lives and the effects they can have on social and emotional development. You'll also learn ways to support children through periods of transition.

This links with Assessment Criteria **5.1, 5.2, 5.3**

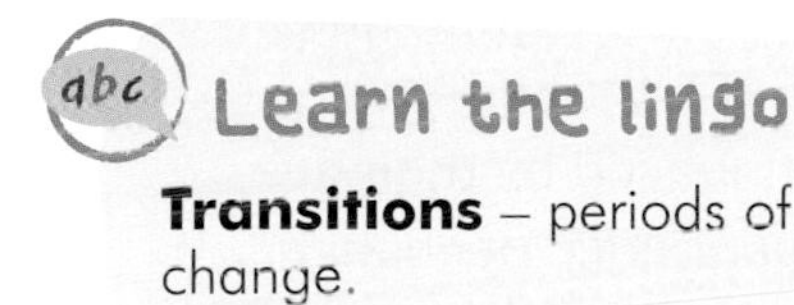

Learn the lingo

Transitions – periods of change.

Common transitions

The word transition means change. In childcare terms, a transition occurs when a child moves from one care situation to another. Children of all ages experience **transitions**.

Common transitions include:

- Attending a setting for the first time.
  Such as a nursery, pre-school, crèche, childminder's home, primary school, out-of-school club or secondary school.
- Moving within a setting.
  From the baby room to the toddler room, or from class to class.
- New living arrangements.
  Moving house, a new addition to the family (such as a new baby or a step-parent), the loss of a family member from the home, young people preparing to leave home, a stay in hospital.
- Young people leaving school to start work/college.

The effect on social and emotional development

Transitional periods generally involve a change of familiar people in a child's life. As an adult you will have experienced feeling unsettled and under pressure yourself at times of transition in your own life, perhaps when you started a new job, placement or college. At these times we tend to be comforted by consistency – knowing a friend will be going to the same college for instance, or by arranging

to meet or call a family member at lunchtime. We also seek reassurance – we might be glad to hear the placement supervisor say we're settling in well. But it still might take us a little while to adjust and get used to interacting with new people, particularly if we miss old classmates or colleagues. A permanent loss, such as a bereavement, can be expected to hit us harder and the affects of the loss may be experienced for a long time to come.

Children experience the same unsettled feelings and they may find them hard to cope with. Most children have less experience of dealing with transitions than adults, and their social and emotional stage of development will affect how they react.

Different children respond differently to transitions. One three-year old may wave their dad goodbye on their first day at pre-school and settle into an activity quite quickly. Another may cling to their mum and cry. Children's responses to transitions will be influenced by their age, ability, personality and previous experience of change. So it's important for you to adjust the way you support individual children to suit their needs.

Pre-school children visiting a school

Have a go!

Close your eyes and think back to a transition you remember from childhood – starting a new school perhaps, or moving to a new area. How did you feel? What were you worried about? Make a note of these feelings – we'll come back to them later.

Supporting children through transitions

You can support the children in your care by helping them to prepare for transitions. Getting used to the idea of a transition gradually helps children not to feel overwhelmed. Some transitions, such as starting school, are known about a long time in advance. This makes them easier to prepare for than an unpredictable transition, such as the need for a stay in hospital or a sudden bereavement.

Settings often have their own policies and procedures in place outlining how children will be supported through transitions, particularly starting new schools. Most early years settings work together with local primary schools to prepare four- and five-year olds. Primary schools work with local secondary schools to prepare older children for the next phase in their education. The case study below gives an example of how one child will be introduced carefully to his new school. This approach successfully promotes consistency and reassurance.

Practical example

Jamal prepares for school

Four-year old Jamal will be leaving nursery in July and starting primary school in September. In May, his new teacher has been invited to the nursery to read stories to the children and Jamal's dad will attend a school meeting for new parents. The teacher will visit Jamal's family at home in June.

In July, the nursery is visiting the school to join in with music activities. Jamal will also attend a school story session with his dad. In September, Jamal will only attend school in the morning for the first week. From the second week onwards, he'll attend full time.

1 *How will these arrangements help Jamal?*

Preparing for transitions

The following strategies help to prepare children for a variety of transitions:

GOOD PRACTICE

Ask your placement supervisor to explain the setting's procedures for supporting children and their families through transitions in their lives.

- Communicating about the transition.
  It's helpful to talk positively about what will happen when the opportunity naturally comes up, and to listen to children's concerns. It's important to be honest and open as well as reassuring. It can be helpful to teach children strategies to deal with their biggest concerns. For instance, if a child is worried about getting lost at secondary school, you can talk about what they should do if they actually become lost.
- Arranging visits to a new setting.
- Reading books, leaflets/brochures, hearing stories, watching videos/DVDs or CD-ROMs that deal with the subject of their future transition.
  Familiarising children with the transition process helps to minimise a fear of the unknown.
- Allowing plenty of opportunities for children to express their feelings through imaginative and expressive play.
- Giving children and young people opportunities to experience increasing independence in line with their needs and abilities.
- Ensuring that all documentation about a child is organised and ready to be passed on to parents/carers or other professionals as appropriate to the situation.
  For instance, a keyworker may hand on a child's development records.

The diagram on page 103 summarises these strategies.

When the transition takes place

There's more childcarers can do to support children at the time of transition (on the actual first day at a new setting for instance). It helps to:

- Encourage children and parents/carers to say goodbye to one another (if parents are present).
  If parents try to slip away unnoticed a child is likely to be confused and may keep looking for them. Trust may also be damaged. Next time they're in a similar situation the child may be clingy and more anxious as they're worried about their parent disappearing.
- Provide honest reassurance for children.
  Never lie about when a child will be reunited with their family. It's important for children to feel they can trust you. Lying only leads to disappointment.

Transition preparation strategies ▶

- When appropriate, families should ideally have access to children.
  If children are away from home overnight (perhaps during a stay in hospital), personal reminders of families, such as photographs, are helpful. In between visits, phone calls, letters, text messages and emails can help children and young people to stay in touch.
- If children have comfort objects brought from home, ensure the child has easy access to them.
  Objects might include a toy or a special blanket.
- Show children around so the environment becomes familiar, and help children to understand routines and/or timetables.
- Provide interesting activities, appropriate to the child's age, needs and abilities.
  Include an activity the child particularly enjoys if possible. The provision of imaginative/creative activities can encourage children to express their feelings.
- Provide positive images of people.
  Reminders of the child's home culture should also be promoted.

There's more about this on page 300.

- Remain supportive while allowing children time to adjust to their new situation.
  Make sure children know who they can go to if they need help. Even if there's a keyworker designated, children should know who to go to if the keyworker is not available.
- Advise families that children may experience unsettled feelings while they adjust to the transition.
  This is completely normal.
- Provide ways to involve families in the child's experience, to assist the transition from the setting to home.
  This is as important for children starting nursery or school as it is for children away from home for longer periods. Daily reports or home-to-setting diaries are helpful.

Practical example

Meera offers support

Meera is an assistant at a pre-school. When four-year old Joseph attended the setting for his first visit, his keyworker greeted him and his Mum. His Mum played in the imaginary area with Joseph for a while, then said goodbye, explaining she would be back in an hour.

Joseph's keyworker reassured him and played with him. Once he had settled down, Joseph came to play near Meera. Meera said hello to Joseph, using his name, and told Joseph her own name. She talked with Joseph briefly about the toy car he had brought with him.

Later, Meera made a point of saying goodbye to Joseph by name when he left the setting.

1. *How did Meera's approach help to support Joseph during the transition?*

Have a go!

Revisit the notes you made earlier about how you felt as a child at a time of transition in your life. Imagine you can go back in time as the childcarer you are now. As a childcarer, how would you support the young you through the transition? Why would it help?

Older children and young people

Older children and young people often experience some of the worries shown in the diagrams below at times of transition in their lives:

Starting secondary school

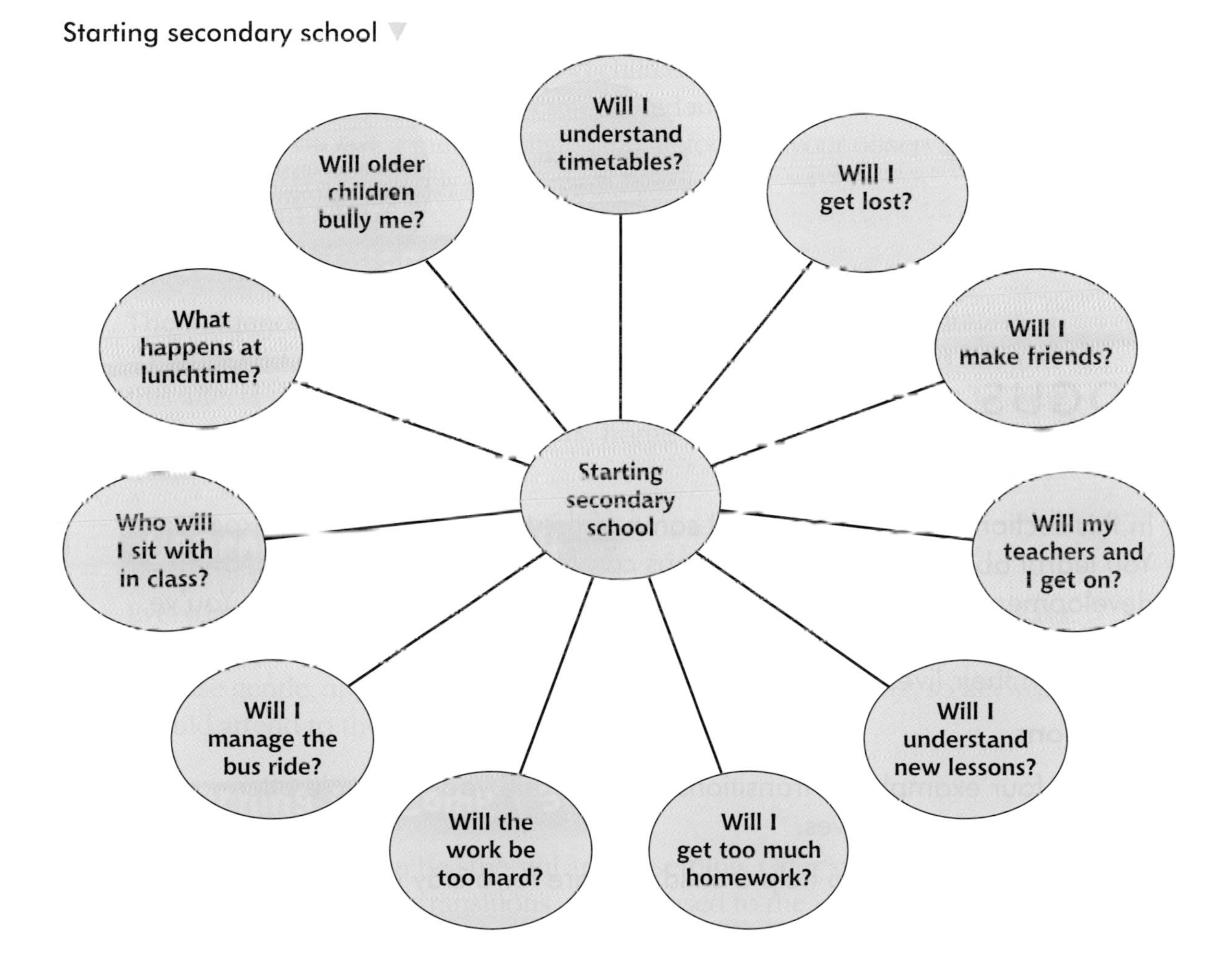

FAQ

Q How will I be assessed on this Unit?

A *You'll complete a multiple choice paper given to your Centre by CACHE. Your tutor will give you plenty of notice so you can prepare. You won't see the paper until the test.*

Q How can I prepare for the test?

A *Studying this Unit will help. Your tutor will also help you to prepare.*

See Unit 1 Learning Outcome 5 for more information on study skills.

Q How is the test graded?

A *Pass or Refer. If you're referred, your Centre can re-enter you to take the test again until you get enough marks to pass.*

Weblinks

You may like to visit te followng websites:

- www.eatwell.gov.uk
  The government's nutrition site, features important, regularly updated advice on all aspects of nutrition for everyone, from babies to adults.

Safe, healthy and nurturing environments for children

Learning Outcomes

In this unit you'll learn about:

1. How to prepare and maintain a safe environment, following policies and procedures.
2. How to implement working practices that safeguard children and the adults who work with them.
3. The role of adults in working with children to manage conflict.

Learning Outcome 1

FOCUS ON...
how to prepare and maintain a safe environment following relevant policies and procedures

This links with Assessment Criteria **1.1, 1.2**

Regulations and requirements

There are several regulations and requirements that normally apply to environments for children. Settings have to comply with these by law. Regulations and requirements tell settings what they must do and what standards they must meet. For instance, the Health and Safety at Work Act 1974 and 1992 says that employers must ensure that the workplace and equipment within it are in a safe condition. But it doesn't tell settings how to achieve this. So that everyone involved knows how to keep the workplace and equipment safe, settings draw up their own policies and procedures explaining what should be done. It's likely the policy will explain when and how equipment should be cleaned for instance and what to do if equipment becomes damaged.

There's more information about policies and procedures on page 164.

You don't need to know all the details of all the regulations off by heart. But you must be aware of them so you can understand your own responsibilities. You DO need to know about and understand all of the policies and procedures at your setting. As long as settings have good policies and procedures in place, you should find that you're meeting regulations and requirements by working in line with them.

The main regulations and requirements that settings must meet are outlined below:

Care Standards Act 2000

Requirements of the Care Standards Act 2000 are expressed in the National Daycare Standards. These standards represent the baseline of quality below that no registered provider may fall. The Act sets out 14 quality outcomes that all daycare settings registered with Ofsted must comply

GOOD PRACTICE

Your setting will have a copy of the relevant Daycare Standards. It's good practice for everyone involved in the setting to be familiar with the standards.

with. These are known as the 14 'standards'. They are shown in the diagram below. Standard 6 is concerned with safety and standard 7 is concerned with health. The Office for Standards in Education (Ofsted), the body that regulates childcare, inspects settings to ensure that all 14 standards are maintained. The National Daycare Standards are matched to each of five different types of provision:

- Full daycare settings.
- Sessional daycare settings.
- Out-of-school settings.
- Crèches.
- Childminding.

Care standards ▼

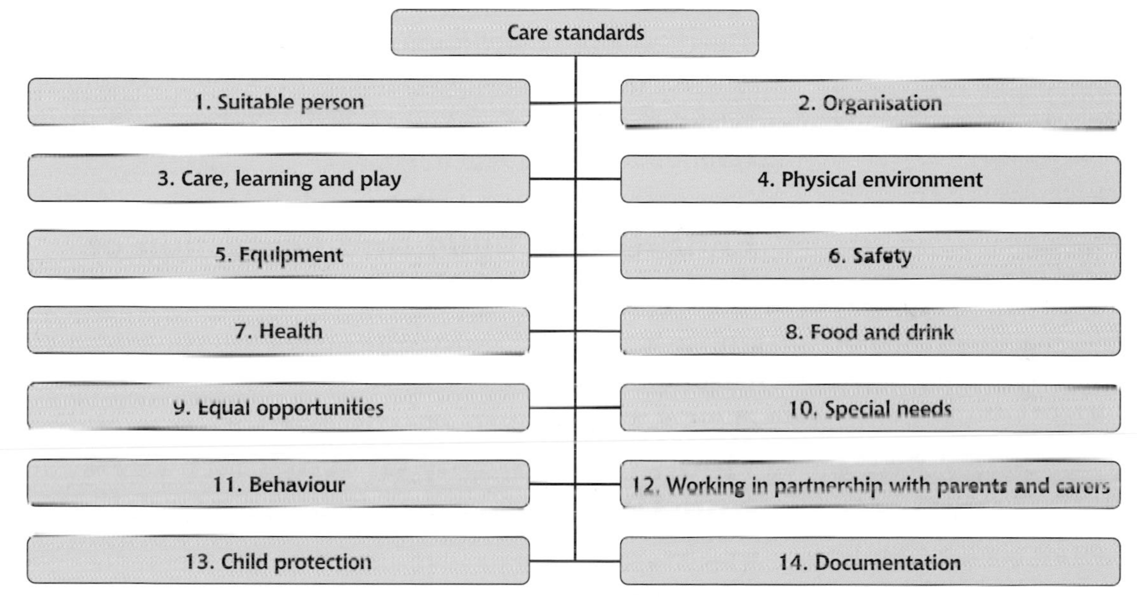

Have a go!

If you haven't yet seen your setting's written policies and procedures:
Ask your workplace supervisor to show and explain them to you. If there's anything you don't understand, ask questions until you're confident that you do fully understand.

If you have seen your setting's written policies and procedures:
Read through them again. Do you fully understand everything? If not, ask your supervisor to explain things to you until you're confident that you do fully understand everything.

There's more about this in Learning Outcome 2.

Children Act 1989

This law covers health and safety and child protection. The Act introduced rules about how many children could be cared for on daycare premises, depending on the size of the rooms. It also set out minimum standards for how many children can be cared for by adults. The current ratios that apply to most daycare setting are:

- 1 adult for every three children aged from birth to one year (Often written as 1:3).
- 1 adult for every four children aged two to three years (1:4).
- 1 adult for every eight children aged three to eight years (1:8).

There are no ratio regulations for children over eight. The regulations differ for nursery classes and schools where a qualified teacher is in charge. From Reception class onwards, there are no regulations about how many children may be taught in a class.

You'll learn more about this in Learning Outcome 2.

Children Act 2004 and Protection of Children Act 1999

These Acts are concerned with child protection (keeping children safe from abuse).

When taking children from Reception class upwards on an outing, it's recommended that schools have a ratio of one adult to six children.

You'll find out more about this on page 116.

Health and Safety at Work Act 1974 and 1992

This Act is relevant to all places of employment, not just children's settings. Employers must ensure that the workplace and equipment within it are in a safe condition. Employees (and volunteers) have a responsibility to take care of themselves and others in co-operation with the employer. The Act also requires employers to use the basic principles of risk management, which are risk assessment, balanced control measures and training.

Health and Safety (First Aid) Regulations 1981

While most childcare settings will have several members of staff qualified to carry out first aid (and must have at least one trained first-aider), these regulations set a minimum standard that applies to all workplaces. Under

them, employers must appoint at least one person to be a designated first-aider, responsible for first aid if an accident occurs. Employers must also keep a stocked first-aid box.

Food Safety Act 1990 and Food Handling Regulations 1995

There's more about this on page 138.

This Act and the regulations cover how food should be prepared and stored, how food areas must be maintained and how staff who prepare food must be trained.

The Control of Substances Hazardous to Health Regulations 1994 (COSHH)

Under these regulations, settings must assess which substances used on the premises are potentially hazardous to health (bleach, for instance). Settings must have recorded procedures in place to manage and store these substances safely.

Fire Precautions (Workplace) Regulations 1997

Fire fighting equipment ▼

These regulations apply to all workplaces and must be considered alongside the National Daycare Standards, which also cover fire safety. Under these regulations, settings must carry out a fire risk assessment addressing seven key areas:

- Fire ignition sources and risk from the spread of fire.
- Escape routes and exits.
- Fire detection and early warning of fire.
- Fire-fighting equipment.
- Fire routine training for staff.
- Emergency plans and arrangements for calling the fire service.
- General maintenance and testing of fire protection equipment.

Reporting of Injuries, Diseases and Dangerous Occurrences Regulations 1995 (RIDDOR)

Under RIDDOR regulations, workplaces must have an accident book. All accidents that occur at the workplace should be recorded in the book. In addition, some types of

accidents that occur at work – serious ones, or those that result in an employee being absent from work for more than three days – must be reported to the Health and Safety Executive. Some diseases that may be contracted by employees must also be reported. Most settings keep one accident book for employees and another for children. Settings must also take out relevant insurance policies.

Personal Protective Equipment at Work Regulations 1992

Under these regulations, employers must provide all protective equipment their employees need to do their job safely. For instance, settings will provide disposable gloves and aprons to be used when dealing with bodily fluids and waste, when changing nappies or cleaning up blood or vomit.

There are pieces of legislation that cover not only children, but families, visitors and staff.

Health and Safety (Young Persons) Regulations 1997

These regulations require employers to conduct special risk assessments for employees or volunteers under the age of 18, as they may be less aware of health and safety issues than more experienced workers.

GOOD PRACTICE

Settings should review policies regularly, checking that they're effective and that they still reflect current regulations. It's also important to assess whether the setting is working in line with its policies in practice.

Policies and procedures

We've learnt that settings devise policies that explain how the setting will work in line with regulations and requirements. Sometimes, extra information is needed to explain how areas of a policy will work in action. So settings may devise additional written procedures that explain what to do in more detail.

Good, clear policies and procedures are important because they communicate how the staff must work. Policies also let other professionals, parents, carers and children know how your setting works. You must make sure that you understand all of your setting's policies and you must work within them.

The following table shows some of the key issues that will usually be covered within an early years setting's health and safety policy. This shows some of the common procedures settings use to maintain a safe physical environment and to safeguard and protect children.

Key health and safety issues covered in a health and safety policy ▼

Issue	General details likely to be given
Registration	• Registration forms That all families must complete forms, giving children's personal and medical details, before children can attend the setting • Daily registers That all children and adults attending a session must be registered on arrival and signed out on their departure
Safeguarding procedures	What the setting does to safeguard children. For instance, the use of safety equipment such as high-chair harnesses and procedures for ensuring young children cannot wander off the premises/older children cannot leave undetected
Risk assessment	When risk assessment will be carried out and how often assessments will be reviewed. What staff training is given on risk assessment
Emergency procedures	• Drills Where the details of drills are displayed on the premises (who does what, where the meeting points are, who will call 999, etc.), and how often drills are carried out • Maintenance of equipment When equipment such as fire extinguishers and alarms are tested, and who by. Where records/certificates of testing are displayed • First aid Who the qualified first-aider is, how they were trained and where their certificate is displayed. How first-aid supplies are checked and replenished. The procedures for calling an ambulance and the family should a child need medical treatment urgently • Care of sick children How sick children cannot be cared for at a group setting. How arrangements will be made for the collection of sick children. The procedure for calling an ambulance and the family should a child need medical treatment urgently
Substances harmful to health	How the setting will identify substances harmful to health and ensure their safe use and storage
Food and drink	• Drinking water How the setting makes water constantly available to children • Dietary requirements How children's dietary requirements are met with regard to families' beliefs/religions/preferences, and regard to individual children's allergies or medical requirements • Healthy foods How the setting will provide healthy meals and/or snacks for children • Hygiene How hygiene will be ensured with regard to food and drink preparation areas. How staff preparing food will have a Food Hygiene Certificate

Hygiene	• Cleaning arrangements How the setting will be kept clean and hygienic. Procedures for each room and the outdoor space may be referenced • Waste disposal How all waste is handled and disposed of safely
Child protection	Settings will have a separate Child Protection Policy, but it may be referenced in the Health and Safety Policy

Practical example

Stars After School Club interprets regulations

Stars After School Club mentions in its health and safety policy that suitable toys are sterilised once a month. This is one of the ways in which the club complies with legislation about health and hygiene.

A separate set of procedures includes a timetable of sterilising, showing when each of the toys should be cleaned. The sterilising process is explained, from how to make-up the sterilising solution to how to dry the toys.

1. *Why is it important for settings to interpret regulations in written policies and procedures?*

Risk

No setting or activity can be completely safe. Children need to be able to take acceptable levels of risk in play, or their development will be stifled. Think of a child who is just starting to walk. They will fall down many times before they master the skill and they might hurt themselves occasionally. But we wouldn't dream of stopping them from walking. It would be overreacting. The risk of injury from a fall is acceptable when a child is learning to walk. But we may decide to take some steps to reduce the chance of injury – perhaps we will remove a rug that they may slip on and make sure there is plenty of clear floor space. Risk assessment is simply a formal version of this process that helps make settings safer places for children.

Settings must carry out risk assessments of their premises (indoors and outdoors) and their activities. Outings must also be risk assessed.

Risk assessment

Settings have their own ways of carrying out and recording risk assessments. But they will involve the following six steps:

1. Identify hazards.
   A HAZARD is the actual item or situation that may cause harm – a stack of chairs for instance.
2. Decide on the level of risk posed by the hazards – low, medium or high.
   The RISK is the likelihood of the hazard causing harm. How risky would you rate the stack of chairs? It would all depend on the circumstances. A stack of chairs in a baby and toddler room would be high risk. It's likely that a child will pull themselves up on the chairs causing them to tumble. A young child could be badly injured. But the same stack of chairs at a holiday club for older children wouldn't be so risky.
3. Evaluate the risks.
   What measures, if any, could/should be taken to minimise or remove the risk? Are there any safety precautions already in place? If so, are they adequate? Is the risk acceptable given the ages, needs and abilities of the children? What levels of supervision will be required? Consider the benefits of activities against the potential for harm. Finally, decide if the risk can be taken.
4. If measures are to be taken to minimise or remove the risk, they should be carried out at this stage.
   In our example, we can either remove the chairs from the room altogether, or simply unstack them. The risk is then removed.
5. Record the assessment.
   Record the whole process and note your findings on your setting's risk assessment forms. Detail any measures you have taken, and enter the date.
6. Review the risk assessment at a later date.
   How effective have your measures been? Take further measures if necessary.

GOOD PRACTICE

- Ask your placement supervisor to show you your setting's risk assessments, and to explain how they were carried out.

Have a go!

Ask your placement supervisor for a blank assessment form. Choose an activity to risk assess. Record the process and your findings. Ask your supervisor to look at your assessment and give you feedback on how you've done.

Considering stages of development

A good understanding of child development will help you to risk assess. You need to be able to consider how aware children are of danger at various ages, their skill levels and the things they are likely to do (pulling themselves up on a chair, for example).

Levels of supervision

Daycare settings must supervise children safely at all times and maintain the minimum staff to child ratios. Many settings aim to exceed these ratios in the interests of quality. The person in charge should normally hold an appropriate qualification to level 3 and at least 50 per cent of staff should normally be qualified to at least level 2. Everyone must be checked by the Criminal Records Bureau.

(given on page 112)

How, when and where staff work (known as **staff deployment**) should be considered carefully throughout each session. Generally, the younger children are, or the more challenging an activity, the closer the supervision will need to be. For some activities, it's safe for children to work on their own as long as there are adults in the room keeping a general eye on things – children can approach them if they need assistance. Other activities would be unsafe without one-to-one support from an adult, for example when a child is learning to use woodworking tools. Levels of supervision required can change as problems occur, the mood of children changes, or children master skills.

Staff deployment
= how, when and where staff work.

FAST FACT

Childcarers learn through experience to adjust the supervision they give to fit changing circumstances.

Adjust levels of supervision when necessary ▼

Practical example

A group of children that would not normally require close supervision during a board game attract the attention of playworker Vicky. The children are squabbling and tempers are becoming frayed. The children temporarily resolve their issue and carry on with the game. But Vicky notices that one child still looks quite angry. Another says she no longer wants to play. Vicky goes over to the group and sits with them. 'This game looks like fun,' she says casually. Her presence seems to diffuse the tension. Vicky watches the game with interest and chats to the group for a while. When the children have settled down, Vicky moves away again, keeping an eye on the game from across the room.

1. *How did Vicky adjust her level of supervision to fit changing circumstances?*

Reporting hazards

If you notice any hazards in the setting, do what you can to minimize risk straight away, then report the hazard to the person in charge as soon as possible. You may need to remove the hazard yourself (in the case of a broken toy for instance). Or you may need to remove children from the hazard (in the case of a water leak in the bathroom for instance).

▲ Safety marks

Safety equipment

There are various pieces of safety equipment that can minimise the risk of accident or injury to children. The table below explains why common pieces of safety equipment are used.

Always check that safety equipment is in good working order and only use it according to the manufacturer's instructions. Only buy safety equipment and toys that have a safety mark (see below). Follow any guidelines given alongside the safety mark. For instance, on a toy car it may say, 'Not suitable for use by children under 36 months due to small parts.'

Safety equipment use ▼

Safety equipment	Use
Harnesses, reins	Prevent falls from prams, push-chairs and high-chairs, and children escaping and running into the road; these should be purchased with the pram, etc.
Safety gates	Prevent access to kitchens, stairways, outdoors; always guard the top and bottom of stairways
Locks for cupboards and windows	Prevent children getting hold of dangerous substances or falling from windows
Safety glass/safety film	Prevents glass from breaking into pieces, causing injuries
Socket covers	Prevents children poking their fingers or other objects into electric sockets
Play pens	Create a safe area for babies
Smoke alarm	Detects smoke and sounds the alarm
Cooker guard	Prevents children pulling pans from the cooker
Corner covers	Protects children from sharp edges on furniture
Fire-fighting equipment, such as a fire extinguisher or fire blanket	May be used to tackle minor fires

There's more about this in Unit 9.

Sometimes you need to take extra precautions though. For instance, imagine you work with a five-year old who has a substantial developmental delay. He still takes toys to his mouth in the manner of a much younger child. You need to think carefully about the toys that can be given to him safely. The toy car wouldn't be suitable for him because, despite his age, he hasn't yet developed sufficiently to play safely with small parts. You must always consider the needs and abilities of children when selecting toys, equipment and materials.

GOOD PRACTICE

Toys, equipment and resources must be kept in a hygienic condition. Settings will have a schedule for washing or sterilising them. Cleaning provides a good opportunity to check that equipment is in a safe condition. Feeding equipment and toys used by babies should be cleaned and sterilised each time they are used. Any toys that are regularly handled should be cleaned each day using soapy water or a disinfectant solution. Surfaces also need to be cleaned at least daily using a suitable anti-bacterial cleaner.

Bodily waste

Bodily waste is potentially harmful substance since infections such as HIV and hepatitis could be passed on. Settings will have procedures in place for handling used nappies, vomit and blood and for clearing up after toileting accidents. Always follow your setting's procedures to ensure the environment is kept safe and hygienic.

Daily checks

Even when risk assessments are in place, childcarers need to make daily checks to ensure that good standards of health, safety and security are maintained. The following must be checked:

- The setting.
- Each activity.

Many settings design their own daily checklist to ensure that the setting is fully assessed indoors and outdoors, and nothing is forgotten. One person will usually take responsibility for completing the checklist before each session starts. During the session, all adults share responsibility for keeping the setting to the appropriate standards. At the end of the session, the setting should be checked again to ensure that it's left in good order.

Many organisations meet in a venue that's also used by other community groups (e.g. a village hall). These groups may well have different standards to your own group, so the premises may need attention before your session begins.

Checks will vary from setting to setting, but are likely to include the following.

Ensure that play equipment is in good order ▼

The outside area:

- Are gates locked and boundary fences secure?
- Can strangers come into contact with the children?
- Are there any problems caused by weather – slippery surfaces, water-logged areas? Is there adequate shelter from the sun? Will children need their sun protection?
- Are there any other risks from water?
- If there are litter bins or drains, are they covered and secure?
- Is the area free of litter, glass, poisonous plants and animal faeces? (Cats in particular are attracted to sand trays – keep them covered when not in use. Even if poisonous plants are not grown, birds sometimes drop berries, or plant matter can be scattered on the wind.)
- Have any items or equipment that could cause harm been left out?
- Is play equipment assembled safely and is it in good order?
- Is play safety flooring in good order? If mats are needed, are they present?

The inside area:

- Are all doors (that should be locked) secured?
- Are all fire exits unobstructed?
- Are all fire doors closed?
- Is fire-fighting equipment in place and intact?
- Are windows intact and safe?
- Are all safety equipment items in place? (Socket covers, cupboard catches, radiator covers, etc.)
- Is the first-aid kit present?
- Are safety notices and all documentation required under legislation fully displayed?
- Is the setting at the correct temperature?
- Are the premises clean and hygienic?
- Are the kitchen and bathroom areas scrupulously clean?
- Are there enough consumables such as toilet rolls, tissues, soap, disposable towels, wet wipes, nappy bags and anti-bacterial cleaning sprays?

- Are equipment and resources safe, clean and assembled correctly?
- Has equipment in storage been put away safely, so that it won't fall or otherwise cause harm?
- Are activities planned and prepared in line with risk assessments?

During the session:

It's important that:

- Appropriate levels of supervision are maintained for children's ages, needs and abilities.
- When equipment and resources are packed away, they are stored safely.
- When new equipment and resources are introduced during the session, they too are assessed as before.
- The activities are being carried out in line with risk assessments and that measures taken to reduce or remove risk are working effectively.
- The activities are given sufficient space.
- No one obstructs the fire exits.
- Toilet and kitchen areas are kept hygienically clean throughout.
- Any documentation necessary is carried out – marking the register for example, filling in medication logs, accident or incident books.
- The movement of children is safely supervised. For instance, before children go outside, a childcarer should check that the gate hasn't been left open. There should be room to move safely between activities. Toys shouldn't be allowed to litter the entire floor space. Consider the needs of disabled children and adults, making sure they can move freely around the setting.

Outings

On outings, settings need to take extra care. Because increased supervision is needed to keep children safe, it's important that the staff to child ratio is high enough. The children's ages, needs and abilities must be taken into consideration, as well as regulations.

Settings usually split the children into small groups or pairs, with each assigned one or more adults to take care of them. This is particularly useful when children

are walking around in a public place, from one location to another, even though the whole group may join in activities together on arrival. Whenever you change location, enter a building or get on or off transport, the children should be counted TWICE, in case of a miscount. It's good practice for more than one member of staff to count in order to double-check that everyone is present before the group moves off.

Before going on a trip, settings generally talk with children and staff about security. It's reassuring to know that safety information is fresh in everyone's minds. Children may be very excited when they arrive at their destination, so it's best to talk with them before leaving the setting. You don't want to dampen good spirits, but if you're responsible for a group of children, do insist they listen carefully so they will stay safe and enjoy the day.

Childcarers will remind children that they must stay in their small groups when asked to do so and that they must not wander off at any time. Procedures for crossing roads will be discussed too, if this is applicable. If using transport, children will be reminded about the importance of wearing their seatbelts and not leaving the vehicle until instructed. Children should know what to do if they do get separated from the group. This will depend on where you're going and the age of the children. Children should know that you expect them to pay attention quickly should you need to give the group further instruction while you are out. This is important in case of an emergency.

Close supervision is needed on outings ▶

GOOD PRACTICE

It's good practice not to have children's names displayed on badges and so on. This is because young children may think they know a stranger who uses their name. They may think it's safe to talk to a stranger or to go off with them.

Prior to a trip, settings must carry out a risk assessment. The person in charge will tell you about any measures necessary to minimise risk. For instance, if children are visiting a park, one member of staff may be posted at each exit to ensure children don't wander out. Frequent toilet stops throughout the trip should also be planned. Staff should always enter public toilets with the children to keep them safe from harm.

Children's role in safety

Children won't always be under the close supervision of adults. As they grow older they will become increasingly independent. So it's essential that children learn to recognise and manage risk for themselves. Experience of doing this should increase as children mature. Involve children in thinking about safety, and encourage them to tell an adult if they see something unsafe. Remember you're a role model, and always follow the safety rules yourself. This is especially important where road safety is involved. Talk to children about road safety, use the Green Cross Code and use controlled crossings where possible. Don't cross at a red light, even if the road is clear.

Security measures

Settings must have measures in place to keep children secure. These may include:

- Name badges for all staff and students.
- Door entry phones and bells.
  To give staff the opportunity to enquire who visitors are and why they are there before allowing them to enter the building.
- Well-supervised outdoor play times.
- Arrival and collection policy.
  Children must be marked in on the register as soon as they arrive, and marked out as soon as they leave. They must be collected by a named adult. Parents should inform staff who will be collecting the child if they cannot do so themselves.
- Missing child policy.
  Explaining what staff must do if a child is discovered missing.

Emergency procedures

All establishments should have:

- Written emergency procedures.
- Staff who have been trained in first-aid.
- A fully stocked first-aid box.
- An accident book for recording incidents requiring first aid.
- A regular review of accidents to reveal any areas of concern – perhaps a certain activity has resulted in several accidents for instance.

Evacuation procedures

It may be necessary to evacuate a setting for a number of reasons, including:

- Fire.
- Flood.
- Gas leak.
- Identification of a dangerous substance.

To ensure that premises can be evacuated effectively in an emergency, it's essential that:

- All staff know how to raise the alarm, where the exit points are, and where the assembly point is.
- All staff are aware of their individual roles, such as taking the register, dialling 999, checking that rooms are empty.
- There are regular opportunities to practice evacuation drills (the sound of the alarm may upset some children, so be sensitive, and help children to settle after the drill).
- Evacuation drill notices should be displayed, giving details of where the fire-extinguishing equipment is kept.
- Fire alarms, smoke detectors and emergency lighting should be checked regularly and maintained, and staff should be trained to use them.
- Emergency exits must not be obstructed.

FAST FACT

Settings must record details of checks and drills in a log book. One person often takes responsibility for overseeing evacuation procedures and fire safety.

GOOD PRACTICE

Make sure that you know how to raise the alarm at your setting in an emergency. You should also be certain about what to do if you hear the alarm raised. If you are at all unsure, ask your supervisor to go over the details with you as soon as possible.

Care of sick children

All children experience illness from time to time. It's important for childcarers to recognise the signs and symptoms of illness in a child. When you notice that a

child is feeling unwell, you should promptly take the appropriate action in line with your setting's policies and procedures. It's a legal requirement that all registered settings have written guidelines for the management of illness within the setting.

It's not the job of childcarers to diagnose diseases or illnesses – that's the role of health professionals such as doctors. It's also not your job to care for sick children and children who are ill should not attend the setting. But there will be times when a child's illness develops whilst they are in your care. Then it's the job of childcarers to:

See the diagram on page 129.

- Recognise promptly when a child is ill.
- Respond to symptoms, if appropriate, in line with policies – cooling down a child with a temperature for instance, or administering a child's asthma inhaler. OFTEN THE MOST QUALIFIED PERSON AT THE SETTING WILL TAKE RESPONSIBILITY FOR A SICK CHILD, SO YOU MAY JUST BE REQUIRED TO REPORT THE SYMPTOMS TO THEM.
- Monitor a child's condition in case it becomes worse. Record appropriate details such as temperature readings or inhalers given.
- Arrange for children to be collected as soon as possible in the case of minor illness.
  The child's parent, carer or alternative contact person (as stated on the registration form) should be called. Be calm and supply the facts. A parent may initially become very anxious about their child, even if symptoms seem minor. If symptoms are more serious, a parent may understandably panic. You must stay in control. Sometimes a parent may need to call you back to confirm collection arrangements. They may need a few minutes to organise things, such as leaving work, or seeing if an alternate contact person is free to come in their place. Parents or carers may ask you what they should do for their child. You are not a doctor and so you should simply advise them to seek medical attention if they are unsure what to do or if they are worried by any symptoms.
- Get emergency assistance urgently if necessary and know which signs and symptoms indicate that immediate medical help is needed.
  Do not wait for parents or carers if it's an emergency. Dial 999 and request an ambulance. If the child needs

Arrange for a child to be collected as soon as possible ▼

to go to hospital before a parent or carer arrives, a childcarer should accompany the child and meet parents at the hospital.

- Do all you can to make a child comfortable until they leave your care.
  Children who are ill may be upset or embarrassed. Be sensitive and caring to soothe them. Stay with a child in a quiet area, and carry out a quiet activity, such as sharing a book, if the child is interested.
- Record the illness, following your setting's procedures.
- Do what you can to stop the spread of infection.
- Reassure other children who may be fearful that a child is ill.

See 'Good hygiene practices' on page 137.

Signs and symptoms of illness

Children who become ill at the setting may display the common signs and symptoms of illness given in the diagram on page 129.

The following signs and symptoms of illness indicate that you may need to call for urgent medical attention:

- Breathing difficulties.
- Convulsions.
- Child seems to be in significant pain.
- Child cannot easily or fully be roused from sleep or a state of drowsiness.
- Baby becomes unresponsive and/or their body seems to be floppy.
- Severe headache that may be accompanied by a stiff neck or a dislike of light.
- Rash that remains (does not fade) when pressed with a glass.
- Vomiting that persists for more than 24 hours.
- Unusual, high-pitched crying in babies.
- High temperature that cannot be lowered.
- Child will not drink fluids – this is most worrying in babies.

High temperatures

The normal temperature reading for a child is between 36.5°C and 37.4°C. Children may have a higher temperature when they're ill. Temperature may also be

higher after physical activity (such as running around) or after taking hot food or fluids. Taking a child's temperature with a thermometer helps you to monitor their illness.

Signs and symptoms of illness ▼

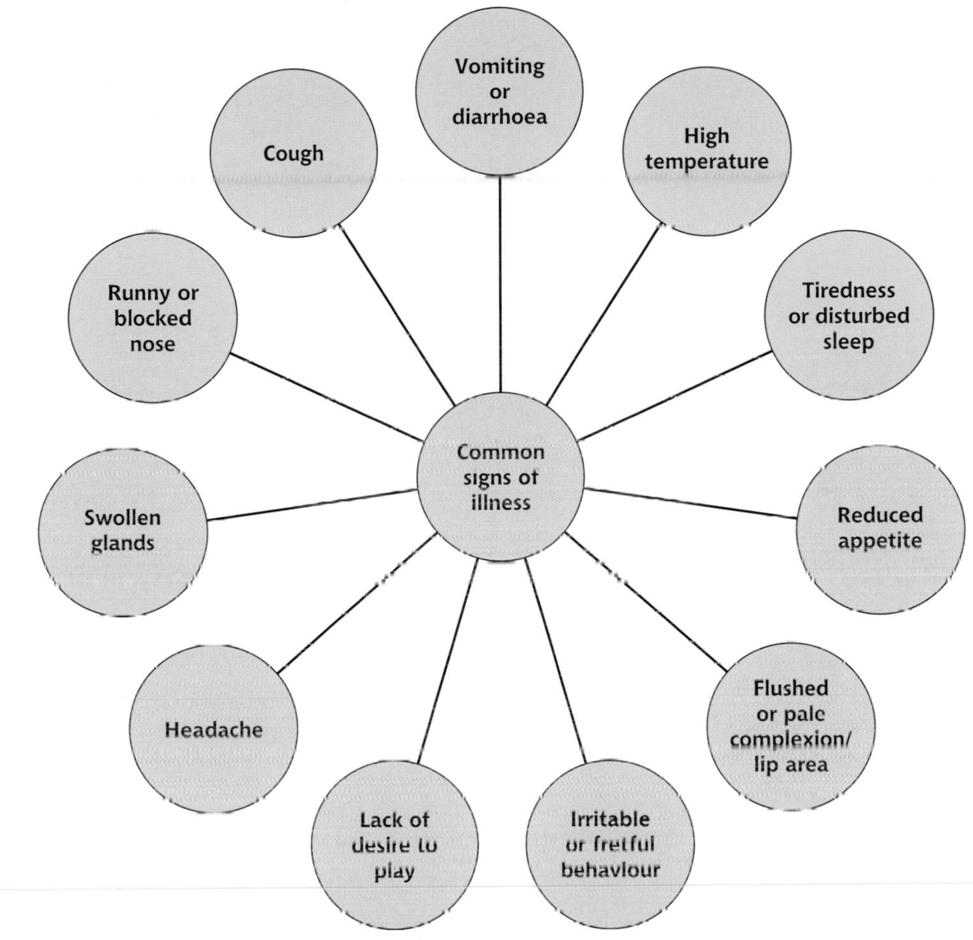

GOOD PRACTICE

Most settings will use a fever scan thermometer (placed on a child's forehead) or a digital thermometer (either placed in the mouth or the ear). These come with directions for use. They are safer than clinical thermometers, which are made of glass and contain mercury.

You should take steps to lower a child's temperature by:

- Seeing that warm clothing is removed so that the child wears just a cool layer.
- Providing a cool drink either of water or diluted by water.
- Cooling the environment (opening windows, turning off heating, using a fan).
- Providing a cool wipe for the face and forehead.

Some children may be given paracetamol syrup by parents or carers, or with parental consent, but this depends on the circumstances and the policy of the setting. For instance, a child may be prone to febrile convulsions brought on by a high temperature. Parents may therefore bring paracetamol syrup to the setting, giving written permission for it to be administered if their child runs a temperature, in the hope that convulsions may be avoided.

First aid in emergencies

Accidents will happen however carefully you carry out risk assessment and supervise children. That's why it is recommended that practitioners take a first-aid course. There has to be at least one first-aider present at all registered settings. CACHE anticipates that employers would expect you to undertake specialised training to gain a qualification in first aid. Your centre and setting can tell you about first-aid training in your local area.

The aims of first aid are often remembered as 'the three p's', that is to:

- Preserve life.
- Prevent the condition worsening.
- Promote recovery.

Sometimes first aid is all that is necessary – for instance, when common minor injuries such as grazes occur. But it's important to recognise when medical assistance is required urgently. Whenever you are dealing with an accident, incident or illness you must stay calm. You should reassure casualties, and children who are bystanders, as they may be very frightened. You should ensure that you and others are not put at unnecessary risk. Think through your actions carefully, and make safety your priority. OFTEN THE MOST QUALIFIED PERSON AT THE SETTING WILL TAKE RESPONSIBILITY FOR ADMINISTERING FIRST AID, SO YOU MAY JUST BE REQUIRED TO INFORM THEM, DEPENDING ON THE CIRCUMSTANCES.

The information given in this book is not intended as first-aid training or instruction. A first-aid course will teach you how to examine and treat a casualty. But essentially, when examining a casualty it's important to:

- Check for a response – call the child's name, pinch their skin.
- Open the airway and check for breathing.
- Check the pulse.

Managing an unconscious child who is breathing

An unconscious child who is breathing and has a pulse should be put into the recovery position. This will keep the airway clear. Keep checking the airway and pulse until help arrives.

Responding to an emergency ▼

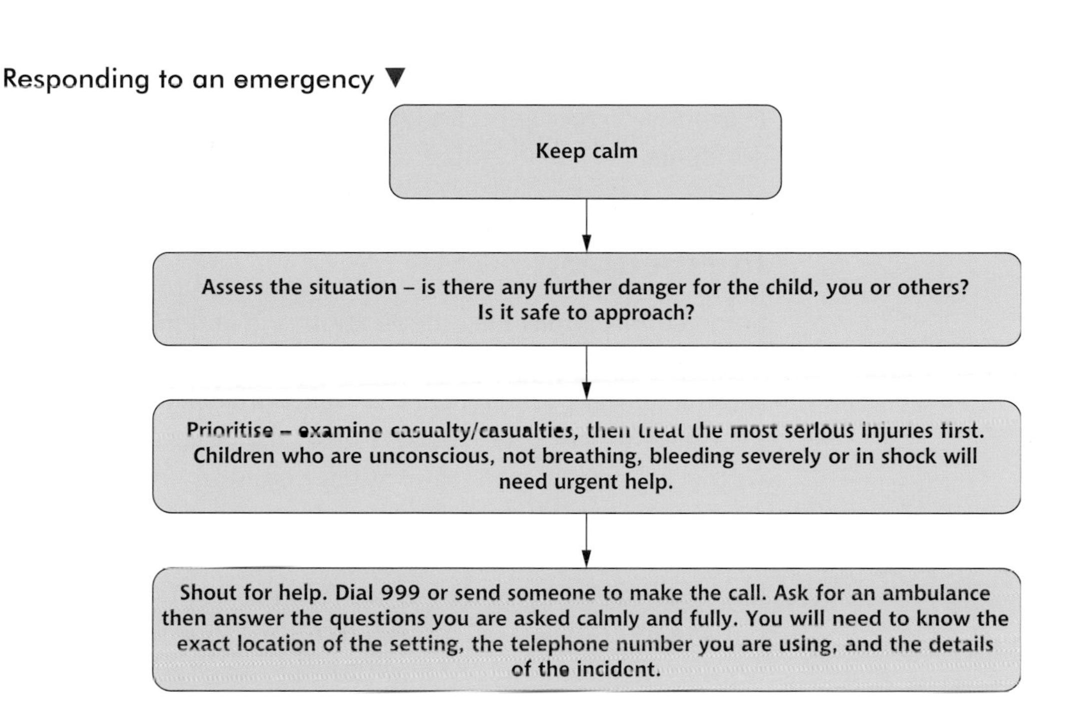

Managing the unconscious child ▼

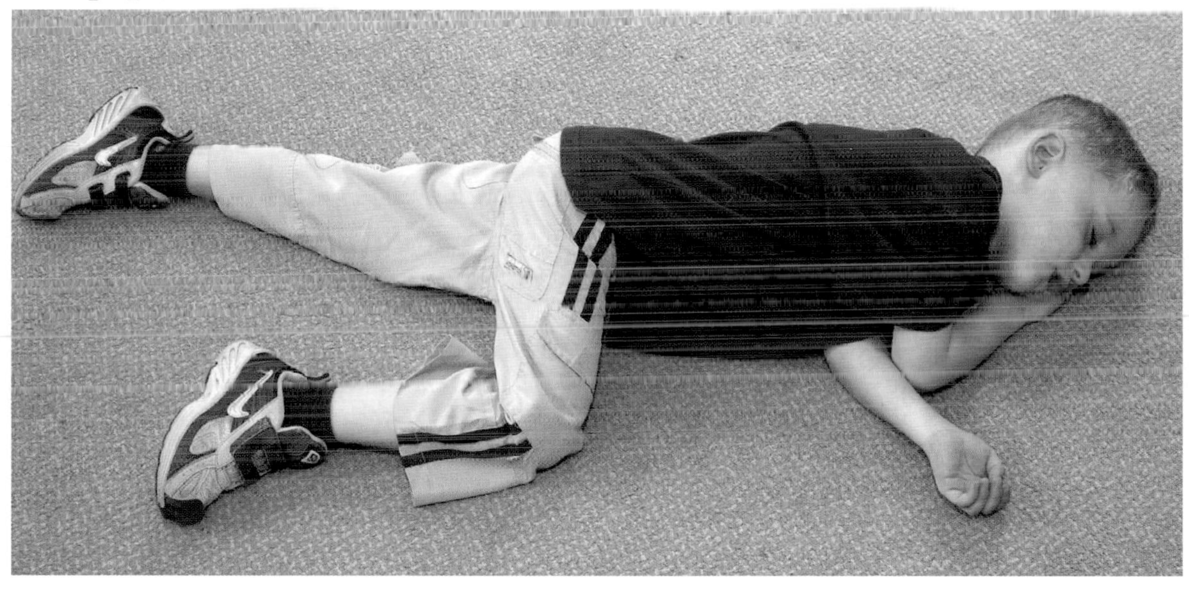

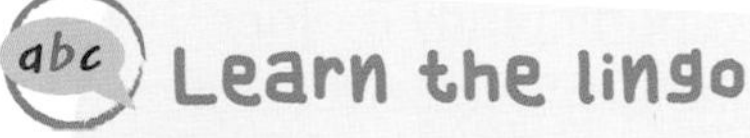

CPR = cardiopulmonary resuscitation. A combination of rescue breaths and chest compressions to stimulate blood circulation (work of the heart) and breathing.

Managing an unconscious child who is not breathing

If a child is unconscious and not breathing, the heartbeat will slow down and eventually stop. They need someone to breathe for them. You will need to have done a registered first-aid course in order to do this. If you are not trained to do this, you must get help as quickly as possible. If you are trained, send someone to dial 999 for an ambulance while you give **CPR**.

But a brief overview of key conditions is given in the table below.

To summarise, you should attend a first-aid course to learn how to recognise and deal with various illnesses and accidents.

Medication

Some children may take medication regularly to treat conditions that they suffer from. For instance, a child with asthma may use inhalers, and a child with attention deficit hyperactivity disorder (ADHD) may take tablets, or a child with eczema may use creams. Other children may need to take medication that was prescribed to treat an illness from which they have since recovered. For instance, a child may have been ill for several days, and absent from the setting, but when they are well enough to return they may still need to finish a course of anti-biotics.

How to recognise and deal with emergencies ▼

Type of emergency	Response required
Anaphylactic shock A severe allergic reaction that can be fatal. Blood pressure falls and breathing is impaired. Tongue and throat may swell	Dial 999 – the casualty needs to be given an adrenaline injection. A child with a known allergy may have adrenaline to be administered. A sitting position helps breathing. Watch for shock, lie casualty down and raise legs if you suspect it. The casualty may need to be resuscitated if they become unconscious: signs of shock may include pale, cold, clammy skin, sweating, weakness, dizziness, feeling sick/vomiting, thirst, rapid shallow breathing
Asthma The airways go into spasm making breathing difficult. This may occur after contact with allergens such as dust, pollen or pet hair. Severity of attacks varies, but they can be serious. Severe attacks are frightening for the child concerned and can also frighten children witnessing the attack. The child wheezes and becomes breathless. Prompt action is needed	Reassure. Give bronchodilator inhaler as instructed if child is a known asthmatic. These inhalers should always be immediately available – they deliver medication to the lungs to relieve affected airways. Children may also have another type of inhaler used to prevent attacks. Make sure you know which to use in an emergency, particularly if older children generally use their inhalers themselves. Sit child upright and leaning forwards in comfortable position. Stay with them. If this is the first attack or the condition persists or worsens call for an ambulance

▶▶

Type of emergency	Response required
Electric shock	Do not touch casualty while he/she is in contact with an electrical current as he/she will be 'live' and you may be electrocuted. Break the electrical contact by turning off the power supply if possible or pulling out the plug or wrenching the cable free. If you cannot reach these, stand on dry insulating material (such as a telephone directory) and use something made of wood (such as a broom handle) to push the appliance aside. You can then check the casualty. They may need to be resuscitated. Dial 999
Bleeding: 1. Minor cuts and grazes 2. Severe 3. Severe with an object embedded in wound (e.g. glass)	1. Clean with water and apply a clean dressing 2. Lay casualty down and cover the wound with a dressing. Apply direct pressure with your hand. If a limb is bleeding, raise and support it. Raise and support legs if you suspect shock may develop. Dial 999 3. As before, but apply direct pressure to either side of the wound. Build padding up around the object, then bandage over the top of it without pressing on the object
Burns and scalds	Cool immediately with cold water. Place body part under running tap, if possible, for at least 10 minutes. Otherwise, lie casualty down and douse the injury, through any clothes, by pouring on cold water if possible, or applying wet cloths. Remove any restricting clothes or jewellery as long as clothes are not stuck to the burn. Cover with a clean, non-fluffy dressing. Watch for shock, and raise and support legs if you suspect it. Dial 999, take or send to hospital, depending on severity Do not cover burns to the face – you could block an airway or cause distress. Do not over-cool or the body temperature may lower dangerously – this applies particularly to babies
Suspected fractures	Keep the casualty as still as possible. Immobilise the affected part of the body and support it. If possible, bandage it to an unaffected part of the body (e.g. bandage a fractured leg to the unaffected leg for support). Depending on the circumstances, take or remove to hospital or dial 999

Type of emergency	Response required
Neck and back injuries	Steady and support the head, and tell the casualty to keep still, with head, neck and back in alignment. Keep holding the head, but get a helper to place rolled up towels or other padding either side of the neck and shoulders. Send the helper to dial 999, and remain holding the head until help arrives
Poisoning – swallowed poisons (e.g. tablets, chemicals, berries)	Dial 999. Take a sample of poison to hospital for analysis if possible. If the child is sick, keep a sample, but never try to make a child sick intentionally. Watch for signs of unconsciousness
Bites and stings – minor 1. General insect 2. To mouth and throat For allergic reactions to bites and stings, see Anaphylactic shock	1. Brush sting away with fingernail if it is visible. Do not use tweezers (if tweezers do need to be used, it is a job for a health professional and medical help should be sought). Raise the affected part and apply an ice-pack or cold compress. The casualty should see a doctor if the pain and swelling persist 2. Give the casualty an ice cube to suck or a cold drink. If swelling starts, dial 999
Effects of extreme heat and cold: 1. Heatstroke Body becomes dangerously overheated, generally due to high fever or overexposure to heat. There may be dizziness, headache, restlessness, hot flushed skin and rapid deterioration in casualty's level of response. Can cause unconsciousness 2. Hypothermia in infants May develop over several days in poorly heated homes or be due to prolonged exposure to the cold outdoors. Babies are particularly vulnerable. Signs are shivering; cold, pale skin; body may feel limp or there may be impaired consciousness; slow, shallow breathing; slow, weak pulse; refusal to feed; unusually quiet	1. Remove casualty to a cool place and remove as much clothing as possible. Dial 999. Wrap the casualty in a cold, wet sheet. Keep the sheet wet until temperature falls to below 38 °C. Then replace the sheet with a dry one. Watch for signs of unconsciousness 2. Re-warm the baby gradually by warming the room and wrapping the infant in blankets. You should call a doctor or take or send a baby to hospital if you suspect hypothermia

Type of emergency	Response required
Meningitis 1. In children: There may be high temperature or fever, vomiting, severe headache, stiff neck, drowsiness, confusion, dislike of brightlight, seizures, skin rash of red/purple 'pin prick' spots. If the spots spread they may resemble fresh bruising, but this is difficult to see on black skin. The rash does not fade when the side of a glass is pressed against it 2. In babies: There may also be restlessness and high-pitched crying or screaming, a limp or floppy body, swelling of the soft fontanelle area of the skull, and refusal to feed	For children and babies: If a doctor cannot be contacted or will be delayed, dial 999. Do not wait for all of the signs and symptoms to appear. If a casualty has already seen a doctor but is becoming worse, seek urgent medical attention again. Reassure the child and keep them cool until help arrives
Foreign bodies stuck (not penetrating) in the: 1. Eyes 2. Ears 3. Nose This may cause swelling and breathing difficulties	1. Sit the casualty down, facing the light, and tip their head back. Stand behind them, and open their eye with your finger and thumb. Pour clean water from a glass gently into the inner corner of the eye. The water will run out of the outer corner of the eye, hopefully flushing the eye clean. If this does not work, take or send to the doctors/hospital 2. Sit the casualty down and have them tip their head to the side. Pour clean water into the ear gently, hopefully flushing the ear clean. If this does not work, take or send to the doctor/ hospital 3. Do not try to remove the object, even if you can see it. Take or send to hospital. Watch for breathing difficulties

Type of emergency	Response required
Choking: 1. Children 2. Babies	1. If the child is conscious, encourage them to cough. If this does not work, bend the child forwards and give up to five back slaps between the shoulder blades with the heel of your hand. Check the mouth. If this has failed, try five chest thrusts, one every three seconds – stand behind the child and make a fist against the lower breastbone (between the ribs and underneath the breastbone). Grasp the fist with your other hand. Pull sharply inwards and upwards. If this does not work, dial 999. Continue alternating between back slaps and thrusts until help arrives or the child becomes unconscious 2. Lay the baby along your forearm, with its head low, supporting the head and back. Give five back slaps. If this fails, do chest thrusts. Turn the baby on its back. Using two fingers push upwards and inwards towards the baby's breastbone (towards the head). This is one finger's width below the nipple line. Dial 999 and continue until help arrives or the infant becomes unconscious
Febrile convulsions May be due to epilepsy or a high temperature. Violent muscle twitching, clenched fists, arched back. May lead to unconsciousness	Do not try to restrain the child. Instead, clear the immediate area and surround the child with pillows or padding for protection. Cool the environment and the child gradually (as for a temperature), sponging skin if necessary. When seizure stops, place child in recovery position. Dial 999
Head injuries There may be dizziness, disorientation, headache, vomiting. May lead to unconsciousness	Treat any bleeding by covering with a dressing and applying direct pressure. Take or send to hospital. If injury is severe, dial 999

FAST FACT

Parents need to give written consent for their child's medication to be administered by the setting. The dosage, when medication should be given and by whom, should all be recorded. The medication should be labelled clearly with the child's name, and it should be kept in a safe, appropriate place. Some medicine needs to be kept in a fridge.

GOOD PRACTICE

Settings will have strict, but differing policies about the way in which medicine is stored and administered. You should be shown how to administer medication such as inhalers. Make sure you are confident about how to administer medication. Rather than make a mistake, always ask for help or advice if you are in any doubt at all. As with first aid, one person at the setting may take responsibility for all medication.

- Overly upset by making a mistake.
- Behaviour associated with comfort seeking in children over five – sucking thumb, rocking, masturbation.

But when children experience an emotional upheaval in their life, such as bereavement, divorce or a new baby in the family, they can also show some of the same signs of stress for a period of time. Childcarers can record instances and share the information with parents and carers. They will then have notes in case the signs persist.

Sexual abuse

Sexual abuse is defined as the involvement of dependant and developmentally immature children in sexual activities. It also includes behaviour that may not involve any physical contact – exposing children to pornography via any media, for instance photographs, videos, DVDs and the internet, or having them witness the sexual acts of others.

Sexual abuse happens to both girls and boys, and to babies. Both men and women sexually abuse children. The majority of children who are sexually abused are abused by someone they know who is in a position of trust, such as a family member or family friend. A minority of sexually abused children go on to become abusers. Sexual abuse often causes lifelong emotional damage and serious difficulties in forming relationships. Sometimes children don't show signs of abuse until much later, when they have reached puberty for instance. It may be that the child had not previously realised that what was happening to them was wrong and abusive.

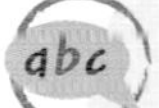

Learn the lingo

Over-sexualised behaviour
= when children act in sexual ways that are inappropriate for their age – they may say or know things you would not expect, or role-play or act out sexual situations.

Signs

The possible physical signs and behavioural indicators are given in the diagrams on page 146. There are few physical signs that are likely to be noticed after a child is independent in terms of caring for their own body, so the behaviour signs are particularly important.

Neglect

Neglect occurs when a family doesn't provide for a child's basic, everyday, essential needs. This can include lack of supervision (such as leaving the child home alone), supervising a child whilst the adult is under the influence

of alcohol or drugs, not protecting a child from danger and not providing stimulation. Children who have been neglected are often said to be 'failing to thrive'. Because of a lack of care and attention to their most basic needs, they may not be able to grow and develop as they should. These children are deprived.

Physical signs of sexual abuse ▼

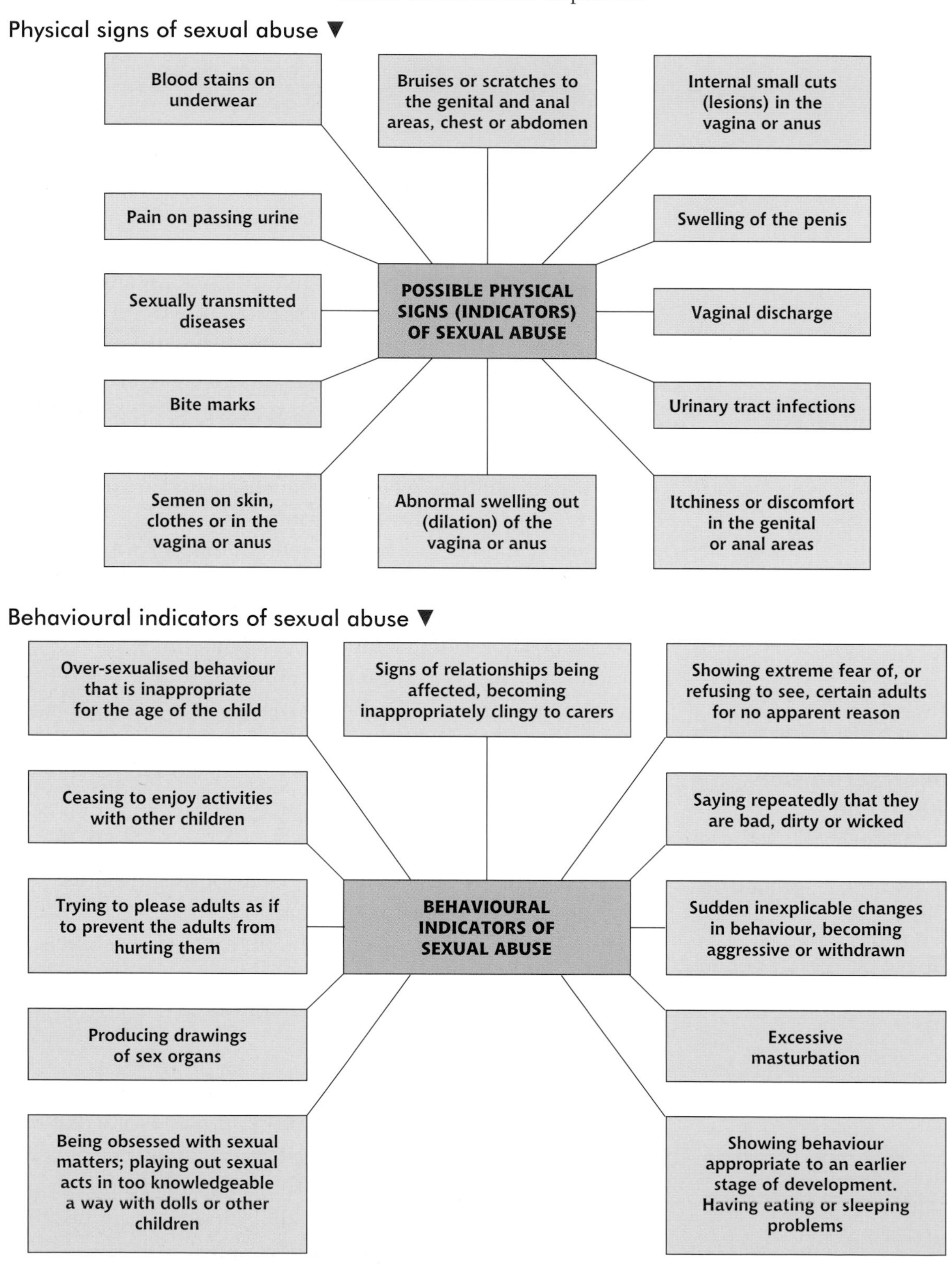

Behavioural indicators of sexual abuse ▼

Signs

Signs may include:

- Lack of food, or lack of healthy food leading to malnourishment, obesity (being overweight), hunger.
- Clothes uncared for, may be dirty, smelly, worn. This can lead to bullying.
- Child may not be cared for hygienically. They may be dirty and they may smell. They may have skin infections and infestations that go untreated (such as head lice). This is also likely to lead to bullying. The child may live in an unhygienic environment and frequently be unwell. Food poisoning is common. There may not be adequate heating at home.
- Inadequate supervision and lack of safety features at home may lead to frequent accidents, the child having too much freedom (they may be out alone in the street or garden late at night for instance, or a younger child may be out unsupervised). The child may be truant from school, leading to a lack of stimulation and education. There may not be a child's safety seat in the car.
- Poor medical care. Illnesses and injuries may go untreated; impairments may go unchecked; developmental check ups, immunisations and dental appointments may be missed, possibly leading to serious or prolonged health problems and disability.
- Lack of love, care, affection and moral guidance leading to isolation and possible early smoking, drinking and substance abuse and promiscuity.

Children may appear to be:

- Nervous, attention seeking or clingy.
- Sad, unpopular with peers.
- Caring for siblings or other family members, including parents.
- Streetwise – they look after themselves.

Disclosure

'Disclosure' is the term used to refer to a child revealing to an adult that they have been abused. This may be in the form of:

- A full disclosure.
  When the child says who has abused them and goes into the history and nature of the abuse.

- A partial disclosure.
  A child may begin to tell of abuse, and then shy away and not continue. Or they may reveal only some details, leaving out what exactly has happened, or the name of the abuser.
- An indirect disclosure.
  This occurs when a child indicates abuse indirectly, through their play (often in a role-play or imaginary situation), their artwork or, in the case of older children, through letters, stories or school work. Children may choose to disclose in this way if they're too afraid to tell directly, too embarrassed or ashamed, or if they find it too painful to discuss. They may be afraid that they won't be believed, or fear they will be punished or sent away from home. They may not know the right words to explain what has happened to them. Children sometimes disclose in this way unintentionally – they may not be aware that what is happening to them is wrong, or they may have tried to block out or disguise the abuse, but have accidently revealed it in their play or conversation.

When a child discloses abuse, it can be quite a shocking experience for a childcarer. But your response is very important in terms of the welfare of the child. You must stay calm, let the child see you are in control of yourself and follow these guidelines for dealing with the situation.

When a child is disclosing:

- Look at the child, maintaining eye contact if the child is choosing to look directly at you. Don't look away from the child or they may think you're disapproving of them. Don't show any signs of disgust on your face, whatever the child says, or they're likely to feel that they disgust you because they were involved in the abuse.
- Let the child do the talking; allow them to tell you in their own way.
- Listen and follow carefully. Try to remember exactly what the child is saying and the language they're using, rather than working out what it all means.
- Don't ask the child questions or prompt them for more information. This may confuse things. It's not helpful for the child to have been 'led' should evidence be needed legally later on. If appropriate, a trained specialist will interview the child at another time.

What to say to the child:

- Let the child know that telling you was the right thing to do ('I'm so glad you've told me').
- Tell them the abuse was not their fault.
- Praise them for having told you and for surviving their ordeal.
- If the child asks if you believe them, say yes.

All allegations of abuse must be reported and taken seriously. Children do not often lie about abuse. Even if the story seems confused or improbable, you must let the child see that you accept it. Your role is not to investigate, but to record and report. Never ask questions such as, 'Are you telling me the truth?' or, 'Are you sure that's what happened?'

- If the child asks you to comment on the abuser, tread carefully. Don't be judgemental. Remember the child may love the abuser. Simply say that the abuser was wrong to do the things they have done.
- If a child asks you what will happen to the abuser, say they will need some help.
- Tell them you have to tell someone else. You should never promise not to tell. It's your duty to report suspicions and disclosures of abuse, and the child will lose their trust in you when you do report it if you haven't explained this.
- Tell them what you're going to do next.
- Say you will talk to them again to let them know what's happened. Reassure them that they can speak to you again about the abuse if they want to talk about it.

You should record and report a disclosure as soon as possible. See below.

You should read this section alongside the information on avoiding premature judgements on page 151.

FAST FACT

Always date your observations. This is good practice in any case, but it's also important if the information is required as evidence.

Recognising and recording signs and symptoms

By recognising signs of abuse, settings can take the first steps that may stop the abuse happening to a child. Having a good knowledge of children's development patterns and behaviour is key. It means you're more likely to spot behaviour that's inappropriate for a child's age – tantrums or wetting themselves in children generally too old for this, or overly sexualised behaviour in children generally too young. This is informed by the regular observations and assessment that settings make on children in their care. Observations can reveal and record how the child forms relationships, how their behaviour or mood may change over time and recurring themes in their play or conversation.

Childcarers may observe any major changes in a child's behaviour or physical appearance ▼

If you suspect a child may be being abused you should write down all the information as soon as you can, while it's still fresh in your mind. It's easy to forget details later. You must record your observations, and you must inform your supervisor of your concerns, following your setting's procedures. Make sure you know and understand these. Your setting will have a Child Protection policy that sets out how you should report concerns and what will happen next. But broadly, you will need to include the following information:

- The date the report is made.
- Child's name, address and date of birth.
- Name of the child's parents or carers.
- Your name and job title.

- Whether you are reporting your own concerns or those that have been reported to you by someone else.
- Concise description of your concerns.
- Incidents leading to your concerns, if applicable (for instance, you may have noticed bruising before, but did not record it until now because you weren't concerned until you saw similar bruising again).
- Accurate description of physical signs, if seen, recorded on a body map.
- Accurate description of behaviour signs if seen.
- If concern has been caused by something a child has said, or if disclosure has taken place, again record only facts, using their exact words as much as possible, not your interpretation of them. You must also record what you said to the child, even if you're concerned that you may not have handled the situation effectively. It is all important detail.
- If a parent or carer has given you any explanations for the signs or symptoms you are concerned about, record the facts, again using their exact words as much as you can.
- Sign the record and store it safely and confidentially in a locked filing cabinet or cupboard. Only appropriate staff members should have access. Only those who need to know, that is your superiors and those who work closely with the child, should be able to access such files. Under the Data Protection Act 1998, parents and carers have a right to see records kept about them and their children if they ask to do so.

Avoiding premature judgements

If you notice signs and symptoms that cause you to suspect abuse, it's very important that you remain objective. Remember that there could be other reasons for the child's behaviour or physical signs.

You must follow procedures without making judgements – you'll find out more about this below. Many settings will require Level 2 qualified childcarers to report their concerns to a more senior colleague, who will take the lead in handling the situation from then on. They will generally ask parents or carers if they've noticed the signs and symptoms and ask them why they think they have occurred. There may be a simple explanation and they will

note what they are told. If necessary, the setting will report concerns to Social Services or another outside agency.

Have a go!

Write an imaginary report and complete any relevant body map drawings describing a child who has come to nursery with a bruised eye. He also has fingertip bruises on the cheek, forehead and upper arms. His mother says this happened while he was playing in the garden.

The policies and procedures of work settings

Every setting in which children are cared for has policies and procedures that aim to protect children from abuse. It's very important that all workers follow these. Policies are guidelines for ways of working. Procedures are steps that must be followed if abuse is suspected. Policies and procedures ensure that all workers know what their duties are and provide clear instructions about what to do. They make clear the steps that must be taken to protect children.

Policies may include the following guidelines:

- How observations and assessments of children's behaviour and development will be carried out.
- That possible signs of abuse should be discussed with a senior colleague, who will be a specifically named person in the organisation. Childcarers who work alone can contact a health visitor for discussion.

Procedures will include the following guidelines:

- Reporting concerns to a specific person.
- Maintaining confidentiality, by only discussing concerns with those who '**need to know**' and storing any reports confidentially.
- Recording specific observations of what has been observed, signing and dating them.
- Decision by a specific person as to whether there are grounds to refer suspicions to the Social Services Department. The police and the National Society for the Prevention of Cruelty to Children may also receive referrals, which they then pass on to social services.

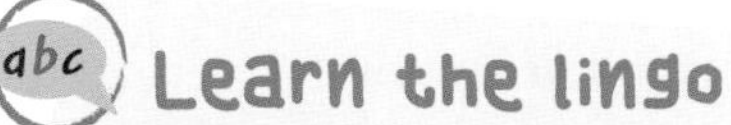

Need-to-know basis
= term used to refer to only revealing confidential information to those who need to know.

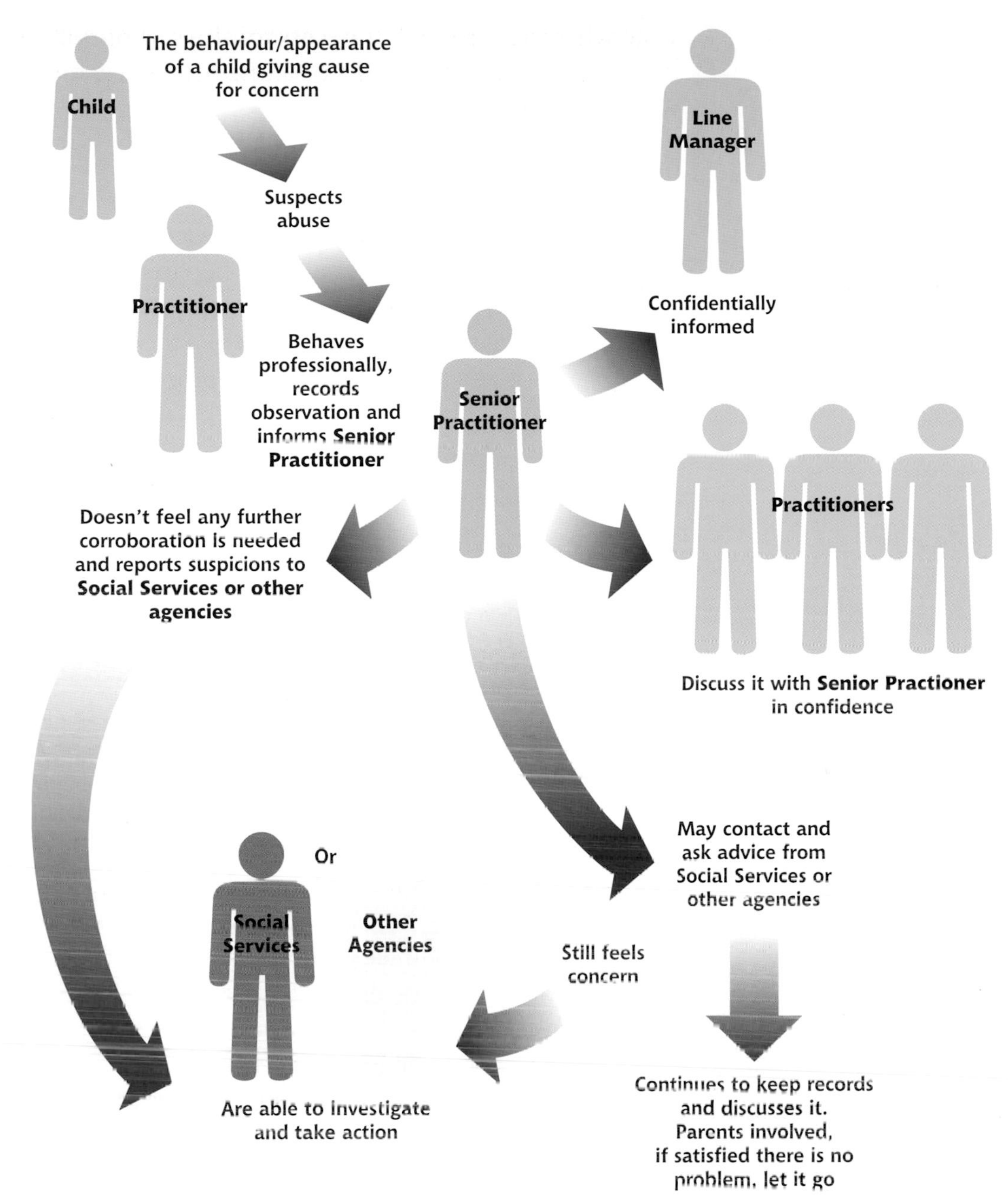

The chain of reporting ▲

- After an investigation, social workers will decide if there are grounds to call a Case Conference with a view to placing the child on the Child Protection Register, or even going to court to remove a child from home. A childcarer may be asked to go to a Case Conference and present a report based on their observations.

Involving parents

One of the principles of the Children Acts is that people who work with children must also work in **partnership with their parents.** Parents should be involved in the

early stages of any enquiry into possible child abuse (with the exception of suspected sexual abuse). This is for the following reasons:

- Parents may be able to provide a clear and satisfactory explanation.
- Or, the way parents respond may give a clear sign that all is not well. This is particularly so if parents give an unsatisfactory explanation, are vague or inconsistent, or delay seeking medical attention. Also if they lack concern or blame others (including the child) for an injury.
- Positive partnerships with parents are the best way to create good, constructive relationships with families.
- If abuse is occurring, the best outcome is to work positively with a family to prevent further abuse and, where possible, to keep the child within the family.
- Enquiries that are not carried out sensitively and respectfully, involving parents, can bring unnecessary distress both to children and their parents.

Childcarers must not make judgements even if actual abuse is confirmed. In the case of either suspected or actual abuse, it can be hard for someone who cares about children not to become upset or feel angry. But as a professional you will want to help the child by doing what's best for them. In the past, children who were being abused were often removed from their families. But it's been found that this is often not the best thing for the child. Some children who were removed have felt that they were being sent away as punishment for 'telling on' their families. The threat that children will be sent away if they tell is often used by abusers – it's often an effective threat because children may desperately want to stay within their family.

The Children Act 1989 says that what is best for children should be paramount.

The modern approach is often to keep children within the family, whilst helping them by preventing further abuse. Families need support if this is to happen. That requires professionals from different agencies to work together (see the diagram on page 155). You must continue to treat the parent as you would any other, and work in partnership with them. If parents feel as though they're being judged or treated differently, they may stop bringing the child, which would have a negative impact on the child and the family.

Professionals are also there to support you. If you're feeling distressed after or during involvement in a case of suspected or actual abuse, you will need to talk through

your feelings. Because of strict confidentiality, you mustn't talk to anyone who doesn't 'need to know'. But you can talk to your supervisor, or ask your supervisor for the name of the outside professional you should contact to talk things over. This is generally a social worker, or a worker from the organisation NSPCC (National Society for the Prevention of Cruelty to Children).

Helping children to protect themselves from abuse

Empowerment, confidence and resilience are factors that help children to protect themselves from abuse and from the effects of abuse. General activities that promote confidence, self-esteem and assertiveness are good for all children.

Multi-professional/agency approach ▼

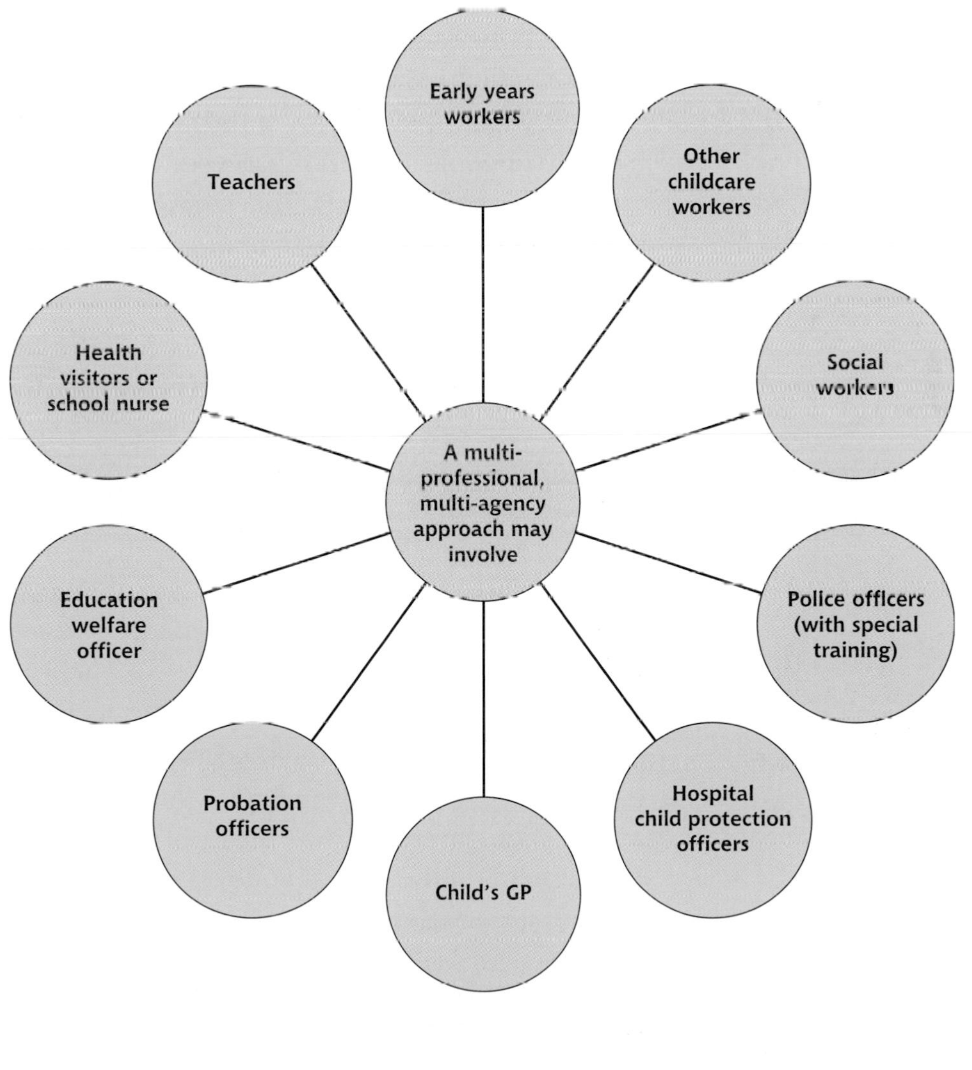

Children should know how to protect themselves ▼

Children should know how to protect themselves, and should be aware of the ways in which they should and should not be treated. This empowers them to act to stop abuse by disclosing it to an appropriate adult. You can help children by teaching them about their rights in respect of their bodies, what to do in emergency situations when they are vulnerable, how to identify and express their feelings, and what to do if they are bullied.

Childcarers should support children in learning about the following:

Children's bodies:

- Their bodies are their own.
- They don't have to show physical affection if they don't want to, including kissing, hugging or sitting on people's laps.
- They can have help if they need it when toileting, but they have a right to privacy if they want it. For older children the same applies to bathing/showering and dressing/undressing.
- Adults should ask children if they would like some help before opening a toilet or bathroom door.
- It's wrong for them to be touched in a way that hurts them, frightens them or feels rude.

Emergency situations:

- What to do if they're lost.
  Stop, look around carefully for the adult they were with. If they can't see them, approach a safe person – a police officer, crossing-patrol guard (lollipop person), cashier at a till in a shop, or lastly a parent with children. They should wait outside until their adult, their parent or a police officer comes to look after them. They shouldn't go anywhere with strangers, not to a phone, workplace or to a house.
- Who to go home with – when at a setting, both the child and childcarers should know who the child is allowed to leave with.
- They should never answer the door unless an adult is with them (in the case of younger children).
- The child should learn their personal details: full name, address and telephone number.

- Stranger Danger – who strangers are, what to do if approached.
  If an unknown person talks to them, they need not be rude – they can pretend they haven't heard and walk away quickly, telling an adult if they feel worried. But if a stranger asks or invites the child to go with them, they should run away and tell a safe adult immediately. They must learn to 'Say no and never go!' If children are touched, grabbed or feel otherwise frightened or worried they might be in danger, it's alright to break the usual behaviour rules. They should attract attention by shouting and screaming, and punch, kick, etc. if they feel they need to. Police officers often visit settings to talk to children about being lost and stranger danger, which helps to establish them as a safe person in the minds of children.

Identifying and expressing feelings:

- They can express their feelings, including worry and fear, knowing they will be taken seriously, and not dismissed or ridiculed.
  Children learn this through experience of being respected.

General activities that encourage naming, thinking about and expressing feelings are good for all children.

- They don't have to keep secrets unless they want to, even if it's an adult's secret.
  Using the word 'surprise' is often better than using the word 'secret' with young children. Surprises are usually thought of as pleasant things that are only secret for a little while before everyone finds out about them – birthday presents and treats are good examples of this. Older children can learn that they should not keep secrets that worry them. A touch, kiss, etc. should never be a secret.

If they are bullied:

- They should know who to tell and to tell them immediately. Most settings and all schools have anti-bullying policies.
- At the time, they should resist, saying firmly or shouting 'NO!' Friends should stick together as there is safety in numbers.

The charity Kidscape have devised the 'Keepsafe Code' suitable for children over five. It's especially helpful for children who have experienced bullying and may be afraid of it happening again. You can find further details online at www.kidscape.org.uk. Kidscape's telephone number is 020 7730 3300.

Vulnerability

Abuse occurs in all cultures and socio-economic groups. It happens to boys, girls and babies from families of different kinds within different communities. Abusers can be men or woman. Children are most likely to know their abuser, and they are likely to be in a position of trust – they may be a family member or a family friend. Some children are made a scapegoat; they are abused within a family, whilst other children are not. This child may be chosen because of their personality – they may be naturally reserved for instance. Children can also be vulnerable because of the following factors:

- Disability.
- Being a loner.
- Being the result of an unwanted pregnancy.
- Being the opposite gender to the one a parent wanted.
- Being the eldest child.
- Being a step-child.
- Being a child who doesn't feed well or doesn't like eating (particularly as a baby).

Statistics have shown that a child who has been abused is more likely to be abused again, even at the hands of a different person.

Children are also more likely to be abused if they don't meet a parent's expectations – this can be for a range of reasons.

Social factors

Social factors can also lead to abuse. If parents or carers are abusing substances, the focus of their life may shift. Someone who is addicted to alcohol or drugs may not notice the needs of their child, or be aware that they are being abusive. People dealing with addiction may find that it takes over their lives, leaving them unable to deal with other things.

People who are addicted may go to places that are inappropriate for young children. They may take a child

with them, or leave them at home alone while they buy alcohol or drugs. They may use substances at home. It can be very frightening for a child to see their parent or carer under the influence of these substances. If drugs or alcohol are kept in the home, young children may ingest them accidentally or as a result of copying a parent.

Whistle blowing

Whistle blowing is the term used to describe when a practitioner alerts superiors or outside professionals to their concerns relating to their own setting. All those within the sector have a duty to safeguard children, and they must take action to blow the whistle if necessary, even though it may be uncomfortable.

You must report concerns about colleagues to superiors if you suspect them of abuse. If you have reported to superiors any concerns about abuse but you feel they haven't taken your concerns seriously or taken the appropriate action, you should report this to Social Services. (This relates to suspicions you may have about children being abused outside of the setting as well as concerns you have about colleagues.)

FOCUS ON...
your learning

In this section you've learnt about child protection and safe working practices. We've looked at the indicators of child abuse and explored what you must do if you suspect a child is being abused. You've learnt techniques to support children in protecting themselves.

Questions

1 Give examples of physical and behavioural indicators of:
   a) physical abuse
   b) sexual abuse
   c) emotional abuse
   d) neglect.
2 What would you do if you suspected a child in your care was being neglected?

Learning Outcome 3

FOCUS ON...

the role of adults in working with children to manage conflict

In this section you'll learn about some of the causes and effects of positive and negative behaviour in children. You'll also learn how adults can work in ways that help children to manage their behaviour and situations that may be difficult for them.

This links with Assessment Criteria **3.1, 3.2**

Behaviour

Encouraging children to behave appropriately is a key aspect of your role. If children don't learn to behave appropriately, they won't be accepted in society as they grow up. This would have a negative affect on their welfare. It's in the interests of individual children, and society as a whole, for children to learn how to behave acceptably.

There are many ways of encouraging positive behaviour. But it's generally accepted that children need to be given boundaries to keep to and goals to reach to help them learn how to behave in acceptable ways. It's your job to encourage children to behave acceptably, whilst managing inappropriate behaviour (that oversteps the boundaries) when it occurs.

Children want to be accepted ▼

Valuing and encouraging positive relationships

Children need to discover how to develop positive relationships with each other, and with adults. Through experience children begin to understand other people's feelings and learn about acceptable ways of behaving. Children will need the support and encouragement of caring adults as they develop their social skills.

Most children display a very strong need to be liked by other people. Children want to be accepted, and they pay attention to messages that tell them what is and is

Learn the lingo

Primary socialisation = when children learn how to behave within the family/home from parents or primary carers.

Secondary socialisation = when children learn how to behave in society from people outside of the family or home

not acceptable to other people. This process is known as 'socialisation'. It takes two distinct forms. **Primary socialisation** occurs first, as children learn, from their parents or primary carers, how to behave within their family and home. **Secondary socialisation** occurs as children learn, from people outside of their family or home, how to behave in society. In the case of settings this may be from other children, childcarers and other adults, including other children's parents and carers, visitors and outside professionals.

You can help promote children's secondary socialisation by encouraging and supporting positive relationships between children and adults. This encourages children to form friendships, to develop rapports and to behave in socially acceptable ways. You can do this by:

- Making all adults aware of the importance of promoting positive relationships between themselves and the children.
- Inviting appropriate visitors into the setting to interact with children (under the supervision of staff).
- Introducing stories that promote friendship, citizenship and community spirit, featuring characters who celebrate individuality.
- Talking with children about how to help people and how to be a friend.
- Giving children the opportunity to undertake a range of activities in pairs, small groups and large groups as appropriate to their age and stage of development.
- Introducing older children to teamwork activities and activities that value individuality.
- Giving children opportunities to help.
- Praising children when they behave in socially acceptable ways.
- Encouraging children to participate in activities that help them to get to know each other better.
- Demonstrating that you respect other people's individuality yourself.

Promoting positive behaviour

You can promote (encourage) positive behaviour by rewarding children when they behave in acceptable ways. Children enjoy being rewarded, so they are encouraged

to behave in the same way again. When children repeat behaviours, over time they become an ingrained, natural part of what the child does. The more a child is given positive attention for behaving appropriately, the less inappropriate behaviour they are likely to display.

Practical example

Deepak sits at the table

Three-year old Deepak doesn't like to sit at the table to eat at snack time. He often gets up and runs around with his food. Staff have to correct him and return him to his seat.

Today, Deepak has stayed at the table without a fuss. Pre-school assistant Chris says, 'Well done Deepak. You're sitting up very nicely today.' Later, Chris tells Deepak's dad how well Deepak sat up at snack time. He makes sure Deepak hears.

1. *Why is Deepak more likely to sit up without a fuss now Chris has praised him?*

Rewards

The rewards that can be given to children fall into two categories: tangible and intangible. Tangible rewards are real items that physically exist and can be seen. Intangible rewards are not physical items, but something that children can experience. Some examples are shown in the table below. Settings use mainly intangible rewards. They are extremely valuable. They show children that they're earning approval from adults. They also demonstrate how to interact positively with other people – how to thank them, for example. Intangible rewards can be used to encourage children throughout an activity or task, showing them that they're behaving correctly and giving them the confidence to continue. You can give children warm praise, thanks and smiles frequently throughout every day. It would be impractical to do the same with tangible rewards.

Tangible items are often used to reward individual children who are working towards specified behaviour goals that have been identified for them (see page 163).

They're also good for rewarding and celebrating occasional achievements that are out of the ordinary, as they can be kept as a reminder of that time. Some tangible rewards, such as money, may be given by parents and carers, but in most settings it would be considered inappropriate to use them.

Certificate of Achievement

Awarded to: .... On: ....

For: Helping a friend

Signed.. Well done!

A certificate rewarding achievement ▲

Rewards ▼

Tangible rewards	Intangible rewards
Prizes	Praise
Stickers	Smiles
Certificates	Cuddles
Stars/ink stamps	Round of applause/cheers
Trophies/awards	A thank you
Toys	Public acknowledgement (praise given in front of other people to draw their attention to an achievement)
Money	Pats on the back
Allowed to choose something tangible from a shop	Opportunities to pick a game or story for the group
Work displayed/published (in a newsletter for instance)	Special trips or the provision of favourite activities (e.g. going to the park or baking cakes)

Children should be rewarded in a way that values them as an individual. For instance, some children feel uncomfortable with public acknowledgement or being physically touched – they may not appreciate a pat on the back. While it's natural for childcarers to cuddle a young child, this is not considered to be appropriate in all environments (such as the classroom) or with all children, particularly as they get older. You must keep to the accepted policies and procedures of your setting. It's important to consider how children feel about the rewards being given to others. Tangible rewards in particular may lead to jealousy or a feeling of being treated unfairly if they are not handled carefully.

GOOD PRACTICE

Consistency is very important in terms of managing behaviour. Without it, children become confused and insecure. It can be very worrying for them not to know what response their behaviour will receive from one moment to the next, or from one childcarer to the next. In addition, it can lead to an increase in inappropriate behaviour. See the case study below for an example.

Behaviour policies and boundaries

All registered settings are required to have a behaviour policy in place. This identifies the types of behaviour that the setting considers to be both appropriate and inappropriate. There should be a statement addressing how the setting encourages appropriate behaviour, and how staff deal with inappropriate behaviour when it occurs. The policy must be based on the values of fairness and anti-discriminatory practice. The policy not only tells individual staff how to deal with behaviour in the appropriate way, it also helps to ensure that all staff respond to behaviour in the same way. This promotes fairness and consistency. Policies also make the setting's approach to behaviour clear to children's families.

Have a go!

Read your setting's behaviour policy carefully. If there's anything that you don't fully understand, ask your supervisor to explain things to you. This is important as you will deal with behaviour constantly. The whole team must have a consistent approach, or children will become confused about what's expected of them.

There will be many, many rules at any setting. Lots of them will be connected with keeping children safe. There may be rules about how many children can play on the climbing frame at once for example, or about removing shoes when visiting the baby room. Over time, children will pick up the cues for how they should behave during different activities.

Practical example

Shopping with Millie

Four-year old Millie is 'playing up at the supermarket because she wants some sweets. Her Mum has told her 'no', but Millie continues to whine and cry. Mum tells her 'no' again. Millie throws herself on the floor, crying loudly. Other shoppers have noticed. Feeling embarrassed, Mum says, 'Alright, have the sweets! Just stop making such a fuss!' Millie chooses her sweets and puts them in the trolley.

1. *What has Millie learnt she should do to get what she wants when her Mum says 'no'?*
2. *How would you respond to Millie in the same situation?*

It's usual for settings to draw up a short list of the main rules that underpin the values of the setting, and guide general behaviour. Some settings refer to their list as a 'code of conduct', and others use the term 'boundaries'. This list may be displayed as a visual reminder of the rules that should apply to everyone within the setting, including all adults. It's essential to discuss the boundaries with children, as appropriate to their age and stage of development. Children can be actively involved in devising the boundaries. This helps them to think carefully about acceptable and unacceptable behaviour. Involving older children in devising the boundaries helps to give them a sense of ownership of their setting, and it shows respect for their opinions. Older children may also be more willing to follow boundaries they have helped to design.

Remember that:

- Children understand boundaries best when they are expressed simply, and there aren't too many.
- Your aim should be to help children not just to know and follow each boundary, but to understand why it exists.

Playground rules ▼

GOOD PRACTICE

Phrase boundaries in a positive way whenever possible. A list of things not to do doesn't tell children what they should do. For instance, if you were to say, 'Don't hurt other people', you would be focusing on the inappropriate behaviour that children should avoid. It would be better to say, 'Please be kind and respect other people'. You then focus on the appropriate way to behave. You can talk about why children should be kind and respectful and ways in which they can achieve that.

Challenging behaviour

All adults have felt frustration when it comes to relationships, the behaviour of other people and keeping to rules and regulations. Children are no different and they have even less experience of life to draw on than adults. While you should have high expectations of children, make sure they are realistic. All children occasionally display challenging behaviour. Young children learn through repetition and it's natural for children to test their boundaries as they grow up and enter new stages of development. Some children frequently display challenging behaviour over a long or short period. So why does this behaviour occur, and how should we manage it?

Challenging behaviour is often a response to a child's immediate feelings and emotions, or an event in their life. Finding the reason helps you to approach the behaviour in the best way. Sometimes causes are easy to spot. Examples include:

- Tiredness.
- Heightened excitement.
- Boredom.
- Illness.
- Hunger or thirst.
- Changes at home (living circumstances within the home or moving home).
- Changes in routine (different timings or layout of environment, for instance).
- New children or adults at setting.
- Temperature (feeling too hot or cold, or changes in the weather).
- Lack of opportunity for physical play.

- Frustration/anger (at not being able to have what they want or not being able to achieve something. New tasks and activities may be particularly frustrating, or daunting).
- Jealousy (of another child's possession, ability or the affection they're being given).

See Unit 2 pages 99 – 108 for information on helping children deal with transitions in their lives.

More serious and ongoing factors may lead to prolonged periods of challenging behaviour:

- Bereavement.
- The child becoming disabled or seriously/chronically ill.
- A close family member becoming disabled or seriously/ chronically ill.
- Parents' relationship breaking down/parents becoming separated/divorced.
- Parent/s beginning new serious relationships.
- Becoming part of a step family.
- Having new carers.

This links with the information about the behavioural indicators of abuse in Learning Outcome 2 of this Unit.

Sometimes reasons for inappropriate behaviour are hidden, unconscious or in the past. This is complicated further by the fact that different children may respond to the same events or the same feelings by behaving in very different ways. For instance, one child who has been abused may become very quiet and withdrawn as a result, whilst another may become aggressive or violent. In these cases, challenging behaviour may be presented over a longer period of time.

You can track development in these areas in the development charts on pages 38–51, by following the sections colour-coded in yellow and pink.

To have realistic expectations for children's behaviour, it's important that you have good knowledge and understanding of children's development patterns for the following areas:

- Social and emotional development.
- Behavioural development.

Communication difficulties, learning difficulties and attention deficits are also likely to impact on children's behaviour. You'll learn more about this later in this section.

FAST FACT

Frequently praising children for positive behaviour is the best strategy of all for dealing with inappropriate behaviour – avoidance. The more you reinforce appropriate behaviour, the less challenging behaviour you will have to deal with.

Strategies for managing behaviour

It's essential that you understand what strategies are acceptable and unacceptable when dealing with behaviour. You must become confident in your ability to handle challenging behaviour appropriately. This takes time and practical experience. As we've learnt, settings must have

agreed strategies in place to challenge and deal with inappropriate behaviour. **CHILDREN MUST NEVER BE PHYSICALLY PUNISHED, FRIGHTENED OR HUMILIATED.** Watch the experienced staff at your setting to see how they put the strategies into practice.

Have a go!

Make a point of paying close attention to how the staff at your setting deal with inappropriate behaviour. What strategies work well? Have you tried these approaches yourself? What have you learnt?

You must follow your own setting's policy on behaviour management. But brief general guidelines to appropriate strategies for different types of behaviour are outlined below.

Attention seeking

Children may throw tantrums, cry frequently or refuse to settle at activities for long unless an adult is beside them. Children may be hostile or jealous towards another person receiving attention. Children displaying this type of behaviour may be feeling insecure and in need of adult reassurance. Or they may simply be used to lots of adult attention.

Strategy: Go out of your way to praise positive behaviour, and try to ignore inappropriate behaviour when possible. Otherwise, you reward the inappropriate behaviour with the attention the child is seeking

Children may hurt others ▼

Aggressive/destructive behaviour

Children may hurt others, by hitting or kicking, etc. They may throw or kick over equipment or furniture. Children may be experiencing frustration, and may have been feeling unhappy for some time. This behaviour has often 'built up' with older children, but may be more spontaneous in younger children.

Strategy: Be firm and in control, to stop the child becoming out of control. Calm the child quickly, in a quiet place if possible. Children who have lost control may be quite scared, and eventually tearful. When the child is ready, find out the source of the upset and resolve the issue. Talk with children about the consequences of their behaviour.

Offensive comments

Children swear or use offensive words or comments that they've heard. They may not understand what they're saying.

Strategy: Tell children why their words are unacceptable within the setting, making it clear that they cause hurt and upset. This also applies to name calling, which should also be viewed as completely unacceptable and should be taken seriously.

Learn the lingo

Making restitution
= saying sorry; making things up to someone who has been hurt.

In all cases it's important to encourage children to acknowledge the feelings of other people they may have hurt, and for them to apologise. They can also do what they can to make-up for it if appropriate (known as **making restitution**).

Rewarding compliance

When a child who has been behaving inappropriately complies by altering their behaviour, you should respond immediately by demonstrating your approval – a smile, nod or a thank you will do the trick. It's important to acknowledge compliance so that a child can see that they are valued as an individual – it was only their behaviour that was disapproved of and now they have altered it they can feel acceptance once again. This protects children's self-esteem, and helps to prevent them feeling labelled as a 'naughty' or 'bad' child. Children will also be more likely to comply again in the future. Never call a child a 'naughty boy/girl.'

If an adult doesn't notice or reward positive behaviour, but does take notice of inappropriate behaviour, children may begin to behave inappropriately to seek attention. They may feel that even negative attention is better than no attention at all.

Dealing with conflict

All children will have problems with other children sometimes. Learning to get along and co-operate with other people is an important life skill for everyone. You can help children to learn how to handle disagreements and disputes positively. The extent to which children are able to this will depend on their age, needs and abilities.

When conflict arises between children, encourage children to think about the situation carefully. With encouragement, older children will often be able to sort out their own conflicts. They will be familiar with finding fair compromises, and can sometimes be quite creative in their approach to finding a resolution. This is important as there won't always be adults on hand to step in as children grow and become more independent. Resist the temptation to intervene in children's problems right away, giving them the opportunity to resolve things for themselves, as long as their behaviour is not dangerous or so inappropriate that it should be stopped immediately (in the case of bullying for example).

Younger children will need much more support and you may well need to start them off. Encourage children to identify the problem as they see it, and then help them to hear the other side of the argument. This helps them to understand the feelings of other people. Ask children, 'What do you think we can do about it now?' If they can't think of a solution, you could suggest one or two and help them to consider their options.

It's important to teach children what to do when they can't handle conflict for themselves, or when they feel themselves becoming angry or frustrated. The following three basic strategies are helpful to children:

- Tell an adult as soon as possible.
- Walk away from the person or the immediate situation as long it's safe to do so.
- Count to ten and take a few deep breaths.

Friends are good ▶

Children who are upset need sensitive comforting – they often begin to feel better if they receive an apology – but they should only get one if it's due to them of course! Friends are often very good at comforting one another. Most children (even toddlers) will show concern if someone else is upset.

A firm and respectful approach

You must always maintain a respectful approach when you're interacting with children, even if they're in trouble. Never try to control a child by intimidating them. You must always intervene sensitively. Remember that you're a role-model for children. You don't want children to lose their temper with people or to shout at them, so you mustn't behave like that yourself. You must stay calm and controlled.

When you're setting boundaries and dealing with instances of inappropriate behaviour, you should be firm and clear about the behaviour you want, whist staying respectful. Pay close attention to how experienced staff respond to inappropriate behaviour. It will help you to adopt the right tone yourself.

Individual behaviour programmes

Sometimes it's necessary to plan a behaviour programme for an individual child. This is in line with, but in addition to, the behaviour policy that applies to all. (The policy should cover individual behaviour programmes as one of the strategies used for managing children's behaviour.) This means that particular behaviour goals are identified to suit an individual child, and strategies are planned to help them achieve the goals.

An example of this is the use of a sticker chart. A child may receive a sticker for reaching behaviour goals throughout the day – for sitting at the table at mealtimes for instance. When a child has earned a set number of stickers, this may lead to a further reward – a small toy or a trip to the park perhaps.

There may also be planned strategies for dealing with inappropriate behaviour from that child, again tailored to suit them. Individual behaviour programmes may be necessary if:

Sticker chart ▶

Days of the week	Morning	Lunch-time	Afternoon
Monday			
Tuesday			
Wednesday			
Thursday			
Friday			

- A child frequently/persistently displays challenging behaviour.
- A child's behaviour is inconsistent with their age.
- A child's behaviour has changed recently.
- A child has been identified as in need of specialist help and the setting is working on this with outside professionals and the family. This could be due to impairment such as a learning difficulty, communication difficulty or attention deficit.

(see page 173).

Your setting will have procedures in place for developing individual behaviour plans. This will include how:

- Evidence of the child's behaviour will be collected.
- Behaviour goals will be identified.
- Parents and carers will be involved.
- Outside professionals will be involved if necessary.
- The child will be involved.

- The child will be supported.
- Appropriate behaviour will be rewarded.
- Inappropriate behaviour will be handled.
- The programme will be monitored and reviewed.

Communication difficulties, learning difficulties and attention deficits

Communication difficulties, learning difficulties and attention deficits are likely to impact on children's behaviour. All children are different though, and much will depend on the degree of the difficulty or deficit.

Children with communication difficulties, learning difficulties and attention deficits may have an Individual Education Plan (IEP) that has been drawn up as part of their special needs assessment. In this case, behaviour programmes must complement and fit in with the IEP. There's more about this in Unit 9. Communication difficulties may impact on behaviour because:

- Children may have difficulty understanding language and therefore understanding boundaries and instructions.
- Children may have difficulty expressing themselves, leading to frustration when other people don't understand their feelings.

In addition, children with learning difficulties may have difficulty understanding and learning to comply with behaviour boundaries and goals.

Children with attention deficits may have a range of traits that make it difficult for them to behave as their peers do (see the diagram below). The majority of the traits are either rooted in difficulties with inattention or difficulties with impulsivity (being impulsive). Some children may display only one or two traits, others may have many. The degree of the traits may also vary. Some children take medication that helps them – some children's behaviour can start to change as their medication wears off. There may be a time gap before the next dose is due to be taken.

Some traits of children with deficit disorders ▼

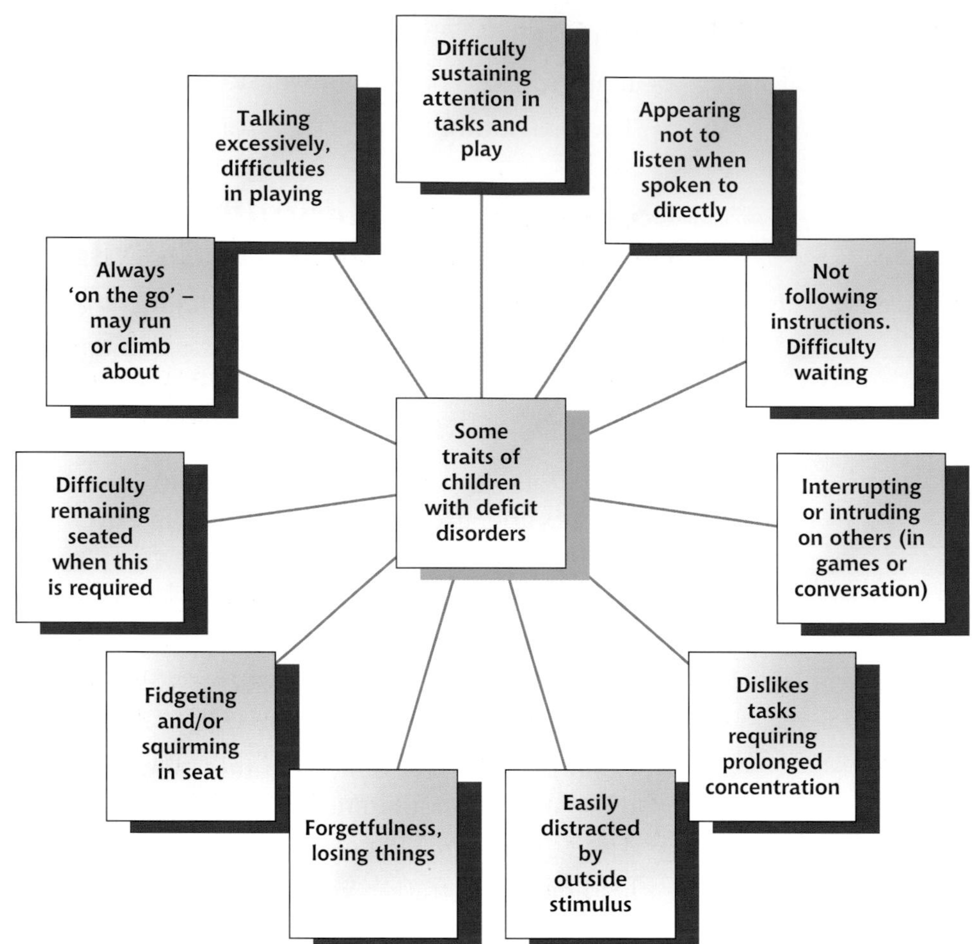

FOCUS ON...
your learning

In this section you've learnt about some of the causes and effects of positive and negative behaviour in children. You've learnt strategies for dealing with inappropriate behaviour and techniques that promote positive behaviour. You've also learnt ways to help children to manage their behaviour.

Questions

1 Name three possible causes for long-term inappropriate behaviour.

2 Explain why promoting positive behaviour is the best way to avoid instances of inappropriate behaviour.

RAPID RECAP

Learning Outcome 1

By law, settings have to comply with health and safety regulations and requirements. Settings draw up their own policies and procedures explaining how they will do this in practice. You need to know about and understand all of the policies and procedures at your setting and you must always work in line with them. It's expected that you will undertake first-aid and food hygiene training and qualifications as part of your role.

Learning Outcome 2

Everyone who works with children has a duty to protect them from harm. You should learn how to recognise the indicators of child abuse and report any concerns you have to a senior practitioner as soon as possible. You must only give confidential information to those who 'need to know'. If a child discloses abuse, you must believe them, listen carefully remembering what they say. Do not ask any leading questions. You should always follow your settings' guidelines for safe working practice.

Learning Outcome 3

All children behave inappropriately sometimes. It's important for you to stay calm and follow your setting's behaviour policy when handling challenging behaviour. There can be many reasons for inappropriate behaviour. Understanding the root cause of the behaviour helps you to respond to it effectively. Promoting positive behaviour is the best way to avoid instances of inappropriate behaviour. With support, children increasingly learn to manage conflict with other children.

FAQ

Q **How will I be assessed on this Unit?**

A *You'll complete an assignment entitled 'Safe, healthy and nurturing environments for children.'*

What will I have to do?

A *Your tutor or Centre will help you to understand the task. It involves you writing about how you would explain the main requirements that relate to a setting to a new family who are having a look around. See Unit 1 Learning Outcome 5 for more information on study skills.*

Weblinks

You may like to visit te followng websites:

- www.kidscape.org.uk
  For advice on tackling bullying
- www.nspcc.org.uk
  The home of the Campaign to Stop Child Abuse
- www.childline.org.uk
  For details of the Defeat Bullying Campaign
- www.donthideit.com
  Help and advice for children about tackling abuse
- www.thinkroadsafety.gov.uk
  For details of road safety campaigns

Children and play

Learning Outcomes

In this unit you'll learn about:

1. The importance of play and activities and how these link with development.

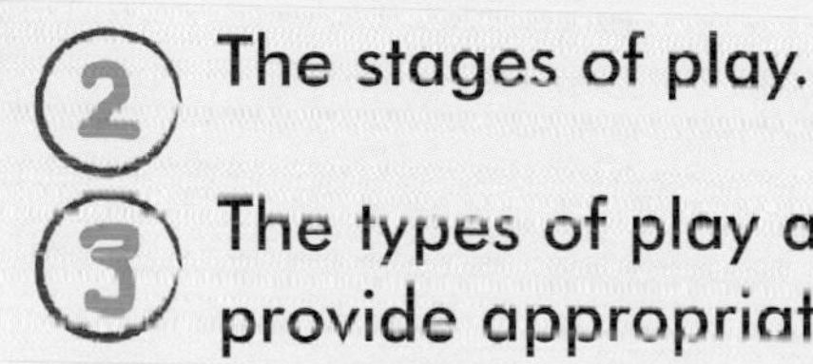

2. The stages of play.
3. The types of play and how to provide appropriate activities for learning.

Learning Outcome 1

FOCUS ON...

the importance of play and activities and how these link with development

In this section you'll learn why play is important for learning and development. You'll also learn about key theories of play.

This links with Assessment Criteria **1.1, 1.2**

Learn the lingo

Play
= Physical or mental activity that has no objective other than for enjoyment or amusement.

Creativity
= a mental process involving the generation of new ideas and concepts or new associations between existing ideas and concepts.

Why is play important?

Playing is great fun for children and it's also the main way in which young children learn. **Play** has both long-term and short-term benefits for children.

Play provides children with the opportunity to interact with both adults and children, at whatever level is appropriate for them. This helps children gain the social skills they need to get on with others and become part of a group. Children learn and practise a wide range of skills when they're playing – how to ride a tricycle for example. They also make discoveries and learn concepts – at the water tray they may learn that pebbles sink, for instance. The activity, game or experience will finish when children stop playing, but the learning will eventually be remembered. These are all long-term benefits of play, which develop over time. Other long-term benefits gained through play include increasing:

- Independence.
- Self-esteem.
- Knowledge and understanding.
- Well-being, health and development.
- **Creativity**.
- Capacity to learn.

The short-term benefits of play occur at the time a child is playing. They include the opportunity to:

- Enjoy freedom.
- Have fun.
- Test boundaries.

- Explore risk.
- Exercise choice and control.

FAST FACT

The benefits of play were outlined in 'Best Play: What play provision should do for children', published by the National Playing Field Association in 2000. You can read this document online – see the website section for details.

Social skills and relationships

Play acts as a bridge to social skills and relationships. Young children need to gain skills such as:

- Sharing.
- Taking turns.
- Co-operating.
- Making and maintaining friendships.
- Responding to people in an appropriate way.

Listed below are some play activities and experiences that help children to develop these skills. By grouping children thoughtfully and being a good social role-model, adults can enhance children's learning about how to behave sociably when they play

Learn the lingo

Socialising
= practicing social skills such as making conversation, sharing ideas, active listening and reading body language.

Socialising opportunities include:

- Circle games.
- Rhymes and songs.
- Packing away time, with all children encouraged to participate.
- Snack/meal times, with children helping to set up, serve and clear away.
- Pretend play in pairs or groups.
- Any activity where there are limited resources that the children need to share, for example, painting at easels or playing at water and sand trays.
- Board games and table-top activities.

Playing in the sand ▶

Learn the lingo

Play theory
= someone's idea about why and/or how children play

Theorist
= name used for people who come up with theories

FAST FACT

Psychologists do not always agree with one another! There are many opposing theories as you'll read below...

Theories about play

Psychologists and other **theorists** have studied play for hundreds of years and developed different theories about how children learn and develop through play.

Some of the most well-known theories are outlined below, but there are many books dedicated to the subject of learning, development and **play theories**. You may find it interesting to learn about additional theories and the research and experiments that underpin them.

Piaget

Jean Piaget was born in 1896. He developed theories that have been influential, although they have been challenged over the years. Piaget was the first to say that when children play they can make discoveries for themselves without being taught. He observed that children generally learn in the same sequence. He noted that children of the same age often made the same mistakes. This led him to believe that children's cognitive development (their ability to think, reason and understand) was developed through a series of stages of development that occur in sequence. He believed that children should not be hurried through these stages – he said they should be allowed to pass through them naturally in their own time.

Piaget only focused on children's cognitive development. He didn't consider other areas, such as children's social and emotional development. He referred to children as 'lone scientists' believing that adults should try to provide environments where children could make their own discoveries. The idea that adults should only intervene sensitively in children's play stemmed from Piaget. This is widely accepted today.

Piaget referred to children at play as 'active participants in their own learning'. He believed that children use their first-hand and previous experiences to learn. He thought children made assumptions based on experiences. He called these assumptions 'schemas'. Piaget called the process of applying one schema to another circumstance 'assimilation'. For example, imagine a child had only ever poured water through a funnel. One day at the sand tray they discover that dry sand will also pass through the funnel. They have assimilated a new concept into their existing schema – sand and water can both pass through funnels.

Piaget believed that when children cannot fit a new experience into an existing schema, they create a new schema that will fit. He called this process 'accommodation'. For example, a child may assume she likes all biscuits even though she's only ever eaten custard creams (which she enjoyed). When she tries another type she finds out this is not the case – she hates coconut creams! She accommodates a new schema – different biscuits have different tastes and she doesn't like them all.

Piaget's stages of cognitive development ▼

Stage One: Sensory-motor. Child's Age: 0–2 yrs
Key Aspects: Babies use their sense to learn. They can only see things from their own point of view – they are 'egocentric'. They do not know that something they cannot see still exists, e.g. if a ball rolls out of view, they will not look for it. At about 18 months this changes. They have then achieved 'object permanence'
Stage Two: Pre-operational. Child's Age: 2–7 yrs
Key Aspects: Children are still 'egocentric'. They believe animals and inanimate objects have the same feelings as people – they are 'animalistic'. They use language to express their thoughts, and use symbols in their play, e.g. they pretend a length of string is a snake
Stage Three: Concrete Operations. Child's Age: 7–11yrs
Key Aspects: Now children 'decentre' – they can see other points of view and understand that inanimate objects do not have feelings. They are establishing complex reasoning skills, and they can use writing and other symbols, e.g. mathematical symbols – this is called 'conservation'
Stage Four: Formal Operations. Child's Age: 11– adulthood
Key Aspects: Children can use logic and work methodically. They can think 'in abstract' – doing mental arithmetic and thinking things through internally. They can problem solve thoughtfully

Piaget believed that children pass through four stages of cognitive development. He did not believe that everyone would attain every stage, particularly stage four. Piaget's theory is called the 'constructivist theory'.

Vygotsky

Lev Vygotsky, born in 1896, was one of the first to disagree with Piaget. He died while in his 30s, so his career was short, but he has had a major impact on current thinking. He believed that children learn through social interaction and relationships, through the social tool of language.

Vygotsky believed that all play contains an imaginative element and that this is freeing for children. He agreed

with Piaget that children at play are 'active participants in their own learning'. But he felt that the emotional aspect of play was as important as the learning aspect. He believed that play was a good way to learn, but he did not think it was the only way.

Vygotsky's most well-known theory is called 'The zone of proximal development'. Vygotsky said that children should always be challenged by some activities that are just beyond their current stage of development. He said this would motivate them and move their learning forward. (He called a child's current stage of development the 'zone of actual development'.) The process of offering activities that will slightly stretch children in this way is referred to as 'scaffolding learning'. Vygotsky called the stage of development that children could move onto with scaffolding learning the 'zone of proximal development'.

In summary, through scaffolding learning with some challenging activities just beyond what a child can do, children can move from the actual zone of development to the proximal zone of development. This disagrees with Piaget's view that children should be allowed to pass through the stages of development naturally with little intervention.

Adults should provide opportunities for children to learn ▼

Bruner

Jerome Bruner was born in 1915. He extended Vygotsky's theories and called his new theory the 'spiral curriculum'. Bruner believed that children learn through discovery with the direct assistance of adults. The adults should provide opportunities for children to return to the same activities (in terms of materials and ideas) again and again. He believed that by doing this children would extend and deepen their learning of the concepts and ideas that adults introduce to them.

He observed how children like to return to activities over a period of some years. He said children do this because they are motivated to learn through the spiral curriculum. You may have observed children returning to activities yourself. Have you noticed children who enjoy building the same model time and again, or drawing the same pictures? Resources like interlocking bricks can be a favourite of children for some years.

Hughes

Modern play expert Bob Hughes studied children and young people's play extensively. He identified different types of play. He gave each type of play a name and defined the characteristics of each, explaining the role he believed each type of play had in children's development. He called his research findings the 'taxonomy of play types'. This is referred to in the publication 'Best Play'.

Learn the lingo

Playwork = name given to the sector that works with children of school age in their leisure time, within play settings.

Playworker = people who work within playwork settings.

Playwork is the name given to the sector that works with children of school age in their leisure time, within play settings. Leisure time for school-aged children is anytime they're not required to be in school. Playwork is carried out in settings such as out-of-school clubs and adventure playgrounds. You may work in a playwork setting during your career.

It's now widely accepted within the playwork field that playworkers should support children's development within each type of play identified by Hughes. Many **playworkers** aim to provide good opportunities for children and young people to experience them all.

The table on below gives further details. The information is adapted from Hughes' Taxonomy of Play Types and Best Play (1996, PLAYLINK, London).

Play types ▼

Play type	Characteristics of play type	Examples of how this play type can be provided for by practitioners
Communication play	This is play that uses words, gestures or nuances, including conversation, debate, jokes, singing, poetry, play acting	Through musical activities, group circle time/debate time, consultation activities, drama games and performances
Creative play	This occurs when children play in a way that allows them to transfer information, respond in new ways and develop an awareness of new connections with an element of surprise. An example of this would be to create a sculpture from clay or to paint a picture, for the sake of creation	Through art and craft activities such as drawing, painting, collage, chalking, sculpture with malleable materials and tools. Access to a broad range of materials both natural and man-made including wool, fabrics, cellophane, tissue paper

Play type	Characteristics of play type	Examples of how this play type can be provided for by practitioners
Deep play	This play occurs when children participate in experiences that are risky, perhaps even potentially life threatening. It allows children to conquer fear and to develop survival skills. Examples of this play include balancing on a high beam and skateboarding along a wall	Through exhilarating play within adventure setting – using zip wires, climbing trees, caving, mountain biking. Participating in sports/physical activities such as skateboarding, rollerblading or sledging. (As always, practitioners must carry out a risk assessment before these activities)
Dramatic play	This occurs when children dramatise events that they do not participate in directly. This includes playing TV shows or games based on cartoons or super-heroes, or the enactment of a religious/festive event, perhaps even a funeral	Through time and space for children to develop their own such games and activities. Practitioners can support this play by not interrupting unless play becomes dangerous, and allowing children to use resources and materials freely to develop 'sets' and so on
Exploratory play	This occurs when children gain factual information through manipulation or movement. This can include handling objects in a range of ways, such as throwing, banging or mouthing – this allows children to assess the properties of the object and to assess its possibilities. An example of this is the way in which children manipulate recycled objects to make a model	Provide interesting resources for children, and regularly introduce new objects, both man-made and natural. This could include autumn leaves for example. Allow children to find their own way of using tools and objects as long as this is safe – do not insist on showing them the 'right' or 'proper' way unless children ask for help
Fantasy play	This takes place when children rearrange the world in a way that is unlikely to occur, but that appeals to them. For instance, they may play at owning a zoo, or an expensive car, or play at being a pop star or a pilot	Through allowing children the time and space to develop fantasy play and worlds themselves. Practitioners can support this play by not interrupting unless play becomes dangerous, or they are invited to participate. In this case practitioners should follow the child's lead, and not impose their own ideas on the child's fantasy world

Play type	Characteristics of play type	Examples of how this play type can be provided for by practitioners
Imaginative play	This occurs when the conventional rules that govern our real physical world have no meaning or do not apply to the world of children's play. For example, children may pretend to be a plant, scarecrow or an aeroplane. Or they may act out pumping petrol from an invisible pump	Through allowing children the time and space to develop their imaginary play. Practitioners can support this play by not interrupting unless play becomes dangerous, or they are invited to participate. In this case practitioners should follow the child's lead, and not impose their own ideas or rules on the child's play. Practitioners should accept without question the rules children have devised
Locomotor play	This occurs when children move around in any and every direction for the sake of doing so. Examples of this include playing playground games such as tag and climbing apparatus and trees	Through allowing plenty of free-play time in large areas, so that children can develop their own games and travel around the play space spontaneously. Practitioners can also organise and join in with playground games such as Sticky Glue (also known as Stuck-in-the-Mud)
Mastery play	This occurs when children's play controls the physical and affective ingredients of the environment. Examples include making fires, building dams, digging holes and creating shelters	Through activities that involve the elements, such as building a camp fire and cooking on it or making and flying windsocks or kites. If necessary (depending on the nature of the play space) practitioners can arrange visits/trips so that children can experience making shelters in the woods or digging trenches in the sand
Object play	This occurs when children handle an object using an interesting sequence of manipulations and movements. This includes examining properties of objects closely, or using items in a new or novel way – using a ruler as a twirling baton for instance	Through providing interesting resources for children and regularly introducing new objects likely to stimulate curiosity and imagination (both man-made and natural). Allowing children to find their own way of using objects as long as this is safe

Play type	Characteristics of play type	Examples of how this play type can be provided for by practitioners
Rough and tumble	This occurs when all children involved are obviously unhurt and enjoying themselves while they play chasing, wrestling or playful 'fighting' games. This 'close encounter play' is about discovering physical flexibility, gauging relative strength and the exhilaration of display. It involves safe touching	By not stepping in too soon if children are enjoying rough-and-tumble play – monitoring the play enables practitioners to step in if rough and tumble escalates to play that is outside safe or acceptable limits. Resources such as soft play equipment and soft play zones are helpful for facilitating this type of play in otherwise 'formal' areas – within a classroom used for an after-school club for instance
Social play	This occurs when children play together. Rules and criteria for social engagement and interaction between the children can be revealed, explored and amended (changed during play). Examples are activities where children involved are expected to stick to rules or protocols such as in games or conversations	Through allowing children plenty of time and space to develop rules and protocols for themselves. Practitioners should support children when the rules of play and interaction are explored or changed, as long as behaviour does not become unsafe. Team activities and opportunities for children to design their own board games can facilitate this type of play
Socio-dramatic play	This occurs when children act out experiences of an intense personal, social, domestic or interpersonal nature. The experiences acted out may have really happened to children, or they could potentially occur. Examples of this play include playing homes/families, playing shopping and even arguing	Through providing play areas such as home corners and the provision of prop resources such as play money, play telephones and so on. Older child may enjoy role-play or moral dilemma games where they act out or describe how they would behave in certain situations – if they missed the last bus home for example
Symbolic play	This occurs when children use an object to symbolise something else, e.g. a piece of wood may become a snake, or a piece of string may be used as a wedding ring. Symbolic play allows control, gradual exploration and increased understanding, without children risking being out of their depth	Through providing interesting resources for children, and regularly introducing new objects likely to stimulate curiosity and imagination (both man-made and natural). Allowing children free access to resources, so they can get out items they want to play with

Imaginary play ▼

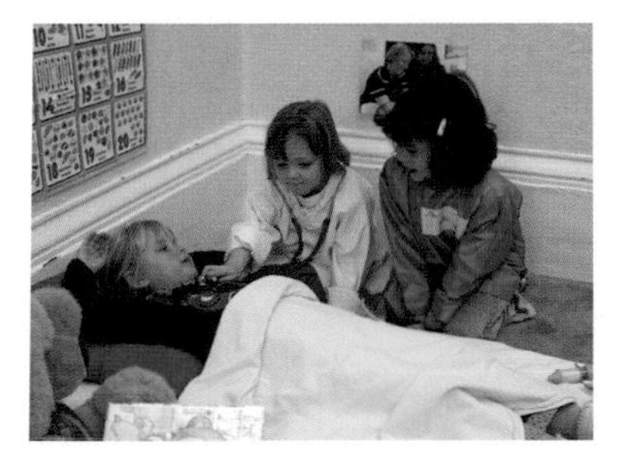

Neuro-scientists

New theories about the way in which human beings think, remember and learn are being developed in light of new technology that has emerged in recent years. Using advanced imaging techniques, neuro-scientists (brain scientists) can now look right inside living, functioning brains. They can actually watch what happens when people are playing, thinking, remembering and learning. Interesting new research is being carried out around the world. Childcarers are advised to keep themselves up to date with developments. Professional journals (magazines) are a good source of new information as it is released.

Practical example

What children can learn through play

Four-year old Josh came to playgroup with his broken arm in plaster. The children were fascinated to hear about the accident and what happened afterwards. The playleader decided to read them a book about hospitals. Because the children had been so interested, she set up a hospital role-play area the next day, complete with beds, bandages and a doctor's set. She read the book to the group again, this time pointing out the pictures of equipment and how it is used. The children then played in the imaginary hospital area.

1. *How did this play promote the children's learning and development?*

Play settings

A range of settings where children play is given on page 3 and page 315.

FOCUS ON...
your learning

You've learnt about the short-term and long-term benefits of play and how play promotes learning and development. You've also learnt about some of the key theories of play.

Questions

1 Name three long-term benefits of play.

2 Name three short-term benefits of play.

Learning Outcome 2

FOCUS ON...

the stages of play

In this section you'll learn about the stages of play and how children play at different ages and stages of their lives.

This links with Assessment Criteria **2.1, 2.2**

Parten's five stages of play

In 1932, researcher Mildred Parten was studying the play of children aged between two and five years of age. She focused on the children's social interactions during their play. She identified five stages of play that children pass through:

1. Solitary play.
2. Spectator (or 'onlooker') play.
3. Parallel play.
4. Associative play.
5. Co-operative play.

FAST FACT

Despite her research being carried out almost 80 years ago, Mildred Parten's findings are still valid today and are generally accepted.

Further details about each of the play stages are given below. The diagram shows the approximate age at which children reach each stage.

Solitary play

Solitary play occurs when a child plays alone, completely independent of others. Babies and very young children play on their own.

Spectator play

The word 'spectator' means someone who is watching. Spectator play occurs when a child watches another child or children at play but does not join in. The spectator either will not be playing themselves, or will be doing a different activity to the one they are watching. This is sometimes called 'onlooker play'. Toddlers can often be observed watching others from a distance.

Practical example

Felix wants to watch

Shobna is a new learner on placement. She's at the water tray with a group of children. She notices two-year old Felix watching nearby. She invites Felix to come and play. He doesn't. Shobna doesn't want to just leave him there. She thinks he must want to join in but is too shy. She tries hard to persuade him again but he wanders off.

1. *Shobna inviting Felix to play was fine. But what should she have done when he didn't want to join in? Give the reason for your answer.*

Parallel play

At this stage the child plays alongside others and may share resources, but they remain engrossed in their own activity. The child has companionship, but even in the middle of a group, the child remains independent in their play. They do not look at other children.

Associative play

Learn the lingo

Play agenda
= what a child wants to achieve in their play.

During the associative play stage, children share resources and talk to each other. But they each have their own **play agenda** (their own idea of what they want to do). The children don't co-ordinate their play objectives or interests. This means there will be trouble! Conflicts arise when children have separate ideas that others do not share. Children especially have trouble when trying to play imaginatively together.

Co-operative play

The co-operative play stage occurs when children fully interact and can participate together in play with specific goals in mind. They can play their own imaginary games, organising themselves into roles, etc., e.g. 'You be the doctor and I'll be the patient...' The older children in Parten's study were capable of co-operative play.

The stages of play ▼

Solitary play

Spectator play

Parallel play

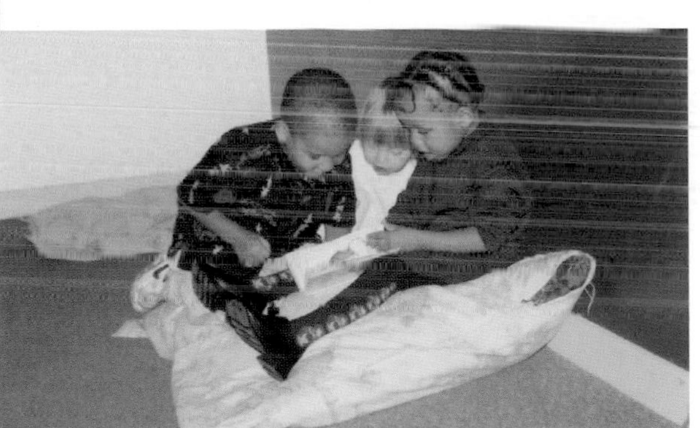

Associative play

Co-operative play

The pattern of play development is shown in the pictures on pages 191.

Although Parten's work was with children aged two to five years, you will find you can observe older children playing in the ways she describes. Once children achieve the next stage of play, they will still at times play in the ways they have before. For instance, all children like to have the personal space to play alone sometimes. Most children will also stand back and watch others without joining in at times, especially in new circumstances. Older children will be seen playing alongside each other with little interaction when engrossed in an art or craft activity, such as drawing or making jewellery. Because of this, some people like to think of the stages of play more as 'phases' of play, because children phase in and out of them.

To progress effectively through the stages of play development, children need the opportunity to play with other children and the support of skilful adults.

FOCUS ON...
your learning

In this section you've learnt about Parten's stages of play and how children progress through them.

Questions

1 Name each of the five stages of play identified by Parten.

2 A child is playing alongside others, but she is engrossed it her own activity and does not interact. Which phase of play is she currently in?

Learning Outcome 3

FOCUS ON...

the types of play and how to provide appropriate activities for learning

In this section you'll learn about the types of play and how to provide appropriate activities for learning.

This links with Assessment Criteria **3.1, 3.2**

Types of play

Further details about opportunities and resources specifically for the older age range are included on the Play Types table on page 186.

Children play in lots of different ways. Different types of play have names such as 'imaginary play' and 'physical play'. It helps us to divide play up into categories when we're discussing it and when we're planning, resourcing and monitoring children's play. But it's important to know that for children play is seamless. It doesn't happen in categories.

Children can slip from one type of play into another easily. They can also play in many different ways with one resource. For instance, if a child gallops a hobby horse around the playground she will be engaging in both physical and imaginary play at the same time. If she does this with a friend, she'll also be engaging in social/emotional play. Different types of play are outlined below. (Different settings sometimes use different terms to describe types of play. Don't worry – just ask your workplace supervisor or tutor to explain any new terms you come across during your training.)

FAST FACT

It's important that a range of play activities are provided for children. This ensures that there are plenty of opportunities for children to learn and develop in all areas of their play.

Learn the lingo

Consolidate learning – term used to describe the process of learning becoming strengthened and fixed in children's minds over time.

We often describe a good range of activities as 'broad and balanced'. This means that activities that promote each area of play are provided regularly. There must be enough repetition of activities to enable children to practice skills and **consolidate** their **learning** over time. But children need new challenges as well as they develop. Children need a variety of opportunities and resources that support each type of play to ensure a range of skills are developed.

Physical play (gross motor) and exercise

Also, see Unit 8 for further information and practical activity suggestions for children aged between three and 16 years.

Children need opportunities to develop, practise and refine their gross motor body movement. This includes:

- Whole-body and limb movements.
- Co-ordination.
- Balance.

Developing control of bodily movement allows children to develop skills such as running, climbing, kicking, skipping, hopping, throwing, catching, swimming and riding a bike.

Playing freely outside and playing with large equipment (both indoors and outdoors) provides good opportunities for developing these skills. Children need lots of time and space to explore and to experience equipment such as slides and climbing frames. Older children will need and enjoy new physical challenges as they grow up – building a den big enough for three children for instance, or weaving through posts on a bike. Children will continue to practice and develop skills and exercise their bodies into adulthood through activities such as dancing and sport.

Tunnels can be used to support physical play ▲

Opportunities/resources that support physical play (gross motor) and exercise include:

- Tunnels.
- Balancing beam.
- Ride-on toys and bikes.
- Wheeled toys to push and pull.
- Climbing frame.
- Slide.
- Large bricks and other large construction equipment.
- Den making and building equipment.
- Hoops and ropes.
- Large and small balls.
- Bats and rackets.
- Participating in sport (older children).

Children need plenty of exercise in order to be healthy and strong. Physical play provides children with exercise. Physical play can take place indoors as well as outdoors.

Fine motor/manipulative play

Manipulative play enables children to practise and refine their fine motor skills. Children need a lot of practice. It's important to provide a range of activities and experiences to meet the needs of children at all levels of fine motor development. Levels can vary widely. Within a group, there may be children who cannot yet build a tower of bricks, while others may be making complex buildings. There should be opportunities for children to use an increasing range of tools and equipment as their skills develop.

Opportunities/resources that support fine motor/manipulative play include:

- Threading.
- Jigsaws and puzzles.
- Large and small construction.
- Free drawing with a variety of crayons and pencils.
- Free painting.
- Play with malleable materials and tools, e.g. dough and cutters.
- Dressing and undressing dolls and themselves.
- Craft activities, e.g. making a collage with sequins or seeds.
- Sewing (older children).
- Building models from kits (older children).
- Making jewellery (older children)

Imaginative play

Imaginative play involves activities and experiences that enable children to use their imagination and develop their own imaginative ideas. Children need the time, space, resources and, when appropriate, sensitive adult support, to express their thoughts and ideas.

Opportunities/resources that support imaginative play include:

- Domestic play, for example in a home corner.
- Role-play; for example, Goldilocks in the three bears' house.
- Play with dolls.
- Dressing up.

- Play with puppets.
- Small world play, for example a model farm or hospital.
- Outdoor pretend play, e.g. pretending a climbing frame is a boat and the playground is a sea full of sharks, or pretending to fill up a ride-on car with petrol.
- Play with large and small construction equipment.
- Art and craft activities where the children are free to think of and develop their own ideas – also see creative play.
- Drama (older children).

Play with puppets supports imaginative development ▶

Creative play

A creative activity involves expression of children's imaginative ideas. 'Creative process' is the name we give to all the things a child does when they're playing creatively (such as the way they use paint and paintbrushes) in order to end up with 'product' (a painting). Whether children are painting, creating sculptures or making their own music, it's important to value the *process* of creative activity, rather than just the *product*. Or in other words, the experience a child has creating their end result should be valued – what the end product looks or sounds like is not the priority.

For an activity or experience to be creative it should have a number of the following features:

- Involve the imagination.
- Begin with an open-ended outcome (children aren't told what they should create).

- Be a personal expression of ideas.
- Be unique in terms of process (children create in their own way).
- Have the process as equally important as the product.

Opportunities/resources that support creative play include:

- Art and craft activities, e.g. collage, painting, drawing.
- Exploration of sound.
- Musical instruments.
- Singing.
- Making up stories.
- Dance.
- Play with natural materials such as sand, water, wood, clay.
- Creative writing (older children).
- Creative thinking (older children, e.g. solving brainteasers, thought-storming ideas in a group).

Very young children will need to explore the resources to become familiar with them and to develop and use their emerging skills. They need the time, space, materials and encouragement to develop their ideas, skills and knowledge. Older children, who are familiar with the materials, will enjoy setting themselves challenges such as creating a moon buggy from cardboard boxes. Also, see imaginary play.

Making music supports creative play ▶

Intellectual play

Intellectual play (sometimes called 'discovery play') occurs when children use their thinking and understanding skills. It can be difficult to define intellectual play activities and experiences, as children are thinking, learning and understanding whenever they're engaged in play.

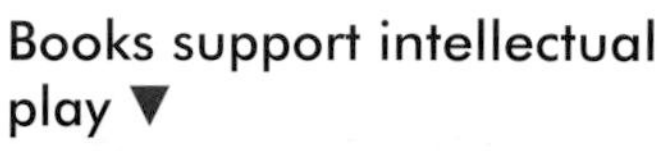
Books support intellectual play ▼

Opportunities/resources that support intellectual play include:

- Books
  Firstly for learning about how books work, turning pages, looking at pictures, seeing words. Later on for learning to read, and for discovery/study.
- Board games
  For developing strategy and concentration.
- Sand, water and sand/water toys
  For learning about capacity, volume, similarities, differences and change.
- Interest tables
  For making discoveries about particular topics or themes, e.g. autumn, or shopping.
- Quizzes
  For testing and increasing knowledge.
- Internet
  For research.

Social and emotional play

Social and emotional play occurs when a child plays with one or more other people. During this type of play, children learn and practice how to interact with others, how to form relationships and how to be part of a social group. As children progress through the stages of play, they need opportunities to play with other children in pairs, small groups and large groups. Activities that help children to learn about and express feelings also come under the heading of social and emotional play. (Expressing feelings also links with creative and imaginary play.)

Opportunities/resources that support social/emotional play include:

- Story time
  For sharing the experience of sitting and listening together, as well as empathising with story characters.

- Board games and playground games
  For playing together, taking turns, following rules, experiencing winning and losing.
- Music, singing, drama/imaginary play
  For the experience of creating something unique with others.
- Team games and activities (older children)
  For working together for a common purpose, learning to give and take and supporting one another.

Free play and planned activities

We've already learnt that it's important for children to have plenty of opportunities for free play. We can support this by providing a range of resources that promote different types of free play (creative play, imaginative play, etc.).

Most settings also provide additional planned activities alongside free play. Planned activities generally have a learning focus or aim. This means that they are intended to teach children a particular skill, or to develop their knowledge and understanding of something specific.

For instance, when we provide a home corner for children to play in, we know that children's social and emotional development and imaginary development is likely to be promoted in their free play. We provide the resources with this general promotion of their development in mind. We probably won't specify exactly what children might learn, and we accept that different children will play in the area in very different ways, and so the benefits will vary greatly. But planned activities with a learning focus/aim are different.

For instance, you might plan to plant cress seeds with children because you want them to learn that plants need light and water to grow. You might also want them to observe the seeds growing as they learn to take care of them over the next few days. Children wouldn't learn this for themselves through free play with the seeds and other resources. So the planned activity enables you to introduce children to the concept of growing in a way free play could not have done.

Broad and varied play opportunities

It's important for settings to provide broad and varied play opportunities for children. This takes some planning. Settings generally plan out a timetable of activities.

Most settings have a basic routine – set times that children arrive, depart, have snacks and meals. Some other activities are also included during every session, such as story time and free-play time. These regular features give the overall plan a basic structure. Around them, childcarers allocate time to planned activities and special events, such as a visitor coming to talk to the group, or an outing. They also plan what resources will be made available during free play, as this will influence which areas of children's development are likely to be stimulated. What will happen in the regular activities will also be recorded – which books will be read at story time for instance.

Settings need to schedule time carefully to ensure that children are given plenty of opportunities for physical activities as well as enough time for rest, access to indoors and outdoors and a balance of busy and quieter pursuits. The only way to keep track of all this is to write it all down or enter it on a computer. Settings generally display their plans so that staff as well as families can see what will be going on when.

You can learn about this in Unit 10. If your setting works to a learning framework, you should read Unit 10 alongside this Unit.

In settings where learning frameworks apply, staff will plan activities and experiences that promote the outcomes or goals of the framework. The plans will be referenced to the framework to show how the outcomes or goals will be promoted.

Short-, medium- and long-term plans

There are various ways to make plans. Settings have different methods of deciding what they will offer to children and their own way of recording plans in writing. But staff generally share the task of planning. Many settings like to have changing themes or topics that link activities together. Topics such as seasons, shopping and the farm are popular. Where themes are used, staff tend to get together and make long-term plans for the whole year, allocating themes to each week. The time given to each theme will vary accordingly – some may last for one week, others for longer.

Next, groups often make medium-term plans, perhaps focusing on onc term. Staff will suggest activity ideas linked to the theme and the ones selected will be

scheduled on the plan. After this stage, individual staff may have activities allocated to them. It will be their responsibility to plan the activity in detail, which is part of short-term planning. This may only be done a week or two ahead of the activity taking place. You'll find out more about planning individual activities below.

Have a go!

You'll probably have seen your setting's short-term plans, which tell you what's happening each day. If you haven't been involved in the planning at your workplace, ask your supervisor to explain the planning process to you. Does the setting make long-, medium- and short-term plans? Do staff share the task of planning? Are there pre-printed planning sheets to fill in?

The planning cycle

Planning takes place in a cycle. Many settings call this the 'plan, do, review cycle', as this is easy to remember.

We've learnt that settings make and record plans in their own way, and you must follow the methods of working at your own setting. Your supervisor (or tutor) will probably give you an activity planning form to complete. But generally, at the 'plan' stage of the cycle, childcarers plan activities in detail, considering the following:

- What exactly will children do?
  What is the process (method)? How will children play?
- How will children benefit from the activity? (Or in other words, what's the aim/purpose?)
  What do you intend children learn? What areas of play and development will be promoted?
- Does the activity meet the needs of the group?
  Is it appropriate for the children's ages and stages of development? Does it suit children's abilities?
- What resources are needed?
  How will they will be organised and who will organise them? Do you need to arrange to buy or borrow resources (if so, make sure your supervisor gives permission).
- Health and safety.
  A risk assessment must be carried out

see Unit 3, page 117

There's more about this in Unit 9

- What level of support/supervision will be needed?
  Will the activity require close supervision? How many adults will be needed? How should adults support the children? Will children with individual needs require additional support, equipment or space to participate? Does the activity need to be adapted in any way to meet individual needs?
- How children will be grouped.
  Will they take part alone, in pairs, small groups or large groups?
- When the activity will take place.
  Date and time.
- Where the activity will take place.
  Indoors/outdoors, which part of the room or outside play space.
- Preparation on the day.
  How will the area will be set up, and who will do it? Who will do any other tasks (such as making up paint, etc.)?

At the 'do' stage of the planning cycle, children take part in the activity and adults fulfil their roles in supporting them.

The 'review' stage of the cycle takes place after the activity, when childcarers reflect on and evaluate the activity as a whole. It's a time to consider whether the activity fulfilled its aims, how individual children responded and how the activity should be followed up.

For instance, you may notice that a child is having difficulties learning a particular skill and/or understanding a certain concept. Extra support or learning opportunities may be planned to help them. See the case study below for an example of this.

Where children are progressing well, childcarers can plan for continued progress. This can be done by considering what children should learn next. What opportunities should be provided for them? What support might they need to continue their progress? The answers to these questions start childcarers off planning once again and so the plan, do, review cycle continues.

Plan, do, review cycle ►

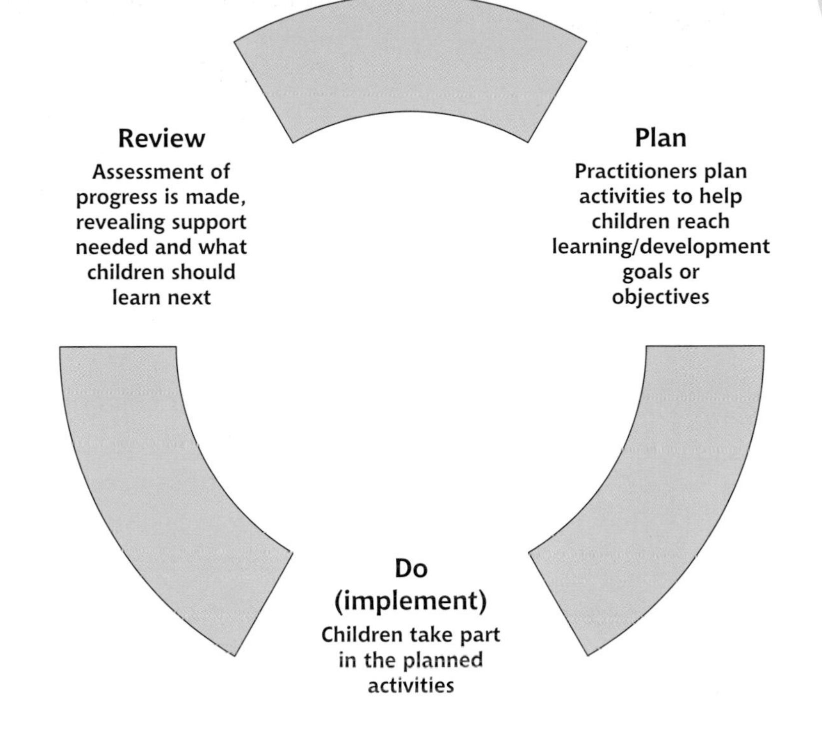

In Unit 3 you learnt that you must risk assess play activities and experiences to ensure they're suitable for children. You learnt a level of risk is acceptable in children's play because we would stifle children's development if we didn't let them take reasonable risks.

Risk and challenge in play

As a general rule, where there's a risk, there's a challenge. As you've learnt, children need all sorts of challenges to develop and progress. Physical risk and challenge often add excitement to activities, which is why children are attracted to them. Adventurous play such as swinging from a zip wire in an adventure playground can be a thrilling experience. Taking part in activities like this can be good for children's confidence and self-esteem. The important thing is to balance risk and challenge with safety and common sense when planning activities. For instance, the zip wire in the adventure playground may be fine for older children, but you wouldn't send pre-school children hurtling along on it!

Encouraging exploration and investigation through play

You now know that children naturally learn through play. But you can encourage further exploration and investigation with sensitive support. The most effective way to encourage exploration and investigation is to provide an environment that is:

GOOD PRACTICE

While activities shouldn't become stale and boring, remember that children learn from and like repetition. Settings can ring the changes by presenting old favourites in fresh ways sometimes. Combining resources in unusual ways can be effective. Children will delight in finding the dolls in the water tray to be 'bathed' for instance and it's great fun to take percussion instruments outside for a marching jamboree parade. Even small differences such as putting the sand tray on the floor instead of on its stand can change the way children engage with the activity.

Practical example

Lyle and India make a scrapbook

Childcarer Kazia carries out a planned activity at her nursery, which involves making a scrapbook. During the activity, Kazia notices that four-year old Lyle is having difficulty mastering the skill of cutting with scissors. Three-year old India is new to the nursery, so Kazia makes a point of observing her carefully. She notices that India has little idea of how to handle a book, and doesn't seem used to turning pages.

Kazia makes a note of her observations when she evaluates her activity. Later she plans further opportunities for Lyle to use scissors and sets aside some time for India to share books on a one-to-one basis with an adult.

1. *Can you suggest another activity or experience that would help India to become familiar with books?*

Children need an element of risk and challenge ▼

- Purposeful
  Play and activities should benefit children in terms of learning and experience. (Remember that having fun is an experience!)
- Supportive
  Activities and play are planned with regard to the support that individual children may need. They are also planned with children's sense of confidence, self-esteem and general well-being in mind.
- Challenging
  Opportunities that challenge children are offered as well as those that consolidate learning. This encourages motivation and progression in terms of learning.
- Varied
  There should be both planned adult-led activities as well as free-play and child-led activities. Play and learning should take place both indoors and outside. A range of physically active pursuits should be offered as well as those that require quiet concentration.

- Balanced
  Opportunities should be provided to stimulate children's learning in all areas of their development and learning.
- Vibrant and exciting
  Interesting, exciting activities motivate children, helping to foster a love of learning and discovery, which will hopefully last a lifetime.

Promoting exploration and investigation with objects of interest

Children take in information through all of their senses. Just like us, they are often attracted to interesting objects. An object may interest a child because it is unusual, or perhaps because of its texture, appearance or the sound it makes. Coming across interesting objects encourages children to explore and investigate further – just as you might do when something catches your interest.

Have a go!

Spend a minute or so thinking about objects that interest and attract you. Do you love to look at and touch sparkling jewellery? Or do you find yourself feeling lots of fabrics when you're shopping for clothes? Perhaps you like trying the fragrances in department stores. Could you spend hours looking at old photos, stamps or postcards? Are you interested in how things work, such as watches or technology?

Children feel the same attraction and motivations to touch, explore and investigate when you provide interesting objects for them to handle.

Introducing objects of interest to babies and toddlers

Learn the lingo

Heuristic play
= play with a range of diverse objects, often provided in a treasure basket for babies and toddlers.

Play with objects is known as **heuristic play**. This type of play is sometimes provided for babies and toddlers via treasure baskets containing a selection of interesting objects for the child to handle and explore. These would not be familiar toys but everyday items that the child could experiment with. Obviously safety must be considered when selecting these items, remembering that babies and toddlers explore with their mouths, as well as with their hands and their eyes. Babies should always be supervised during heuristic play, although adults shouldn't intervene in

the play unless it's necessary. A good selection will offer the chance to explore interesting and contrasting textures and items that stimulate hearing and smell. A treasure basket may contain items such as a hairbrush, kitchen whisk, shiny paper, jars, ribbon, sturdy cardboard tubes and natural objects such as seashells, fir cones and pebbles.

Introducing objects of interest to children

One of the ways in which settings introduce children to objects of interest is by providing an interest table or area. Here, selections of interesting objects are attractively displayed. The aim is to entice children over to look, touch and generally explore and investigate further. Settings often link their interest table to their current theme. So if the theme was autumn for instance, the interest table may feature conkers, acorns, leaves in a variety of colours, shapes and textures, etc.

Interest tables should stimulate children's curiosity ▼

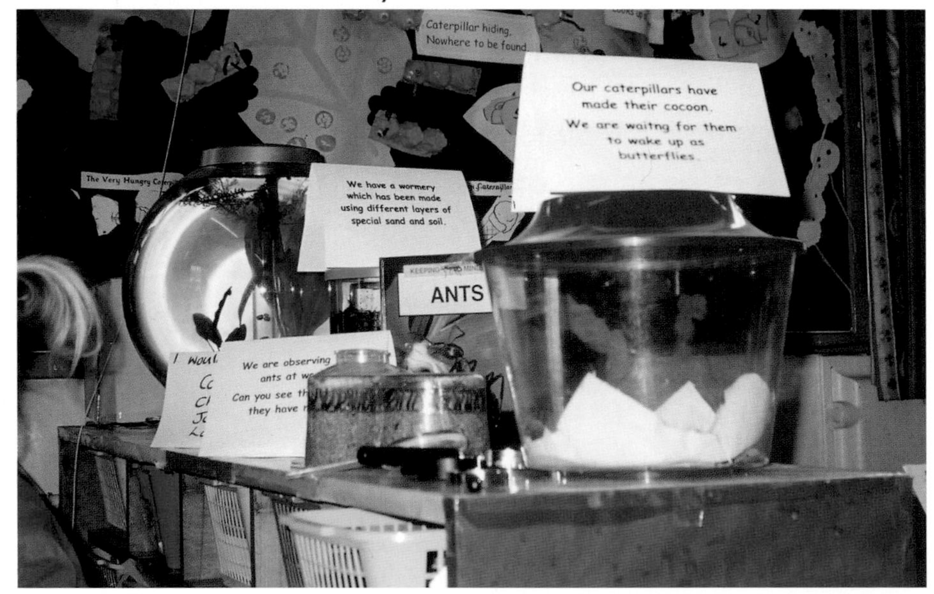

Introducing children to objects of interest promotes other aspects of their learning and development. For instance:

- Holding and handling objects will promote children's physical development.
  A range of differently sized and shaped objects should be provided. Fine manipulative skills and hand-eye co-ordination will be practised when picking up and holding.

- Introducing children to unfamiliar objects will promote language skills.
  Naming the objects and describing their features will introduce new vocabulary in a meaningful way.
- Interesting objects stimulate children intellectually.
  By promoting children's natural curiosity and widening their horizons. Older children will be able to think about where the object comes from, who owns it and what it might be for.
- Exploring and investigating objects together as a group promotes social skills.
  Children will take turns. They can begin to learn about other people and cultures through examining and exploring objects. For example, handling a collection of divas (special lamps) would be a good starting point for children to find out about the Hindu and Sikh celebration of Diwali.
- Handling beautiful and unusual objects will promote emotional development.
  Children may experience and show a range of feelings such as wonder, joy and fascination. When children bring in items from home for others to examine and explore, this is likely to have a positive effect on their self-esteem.

Handling objects

Young children will need to be shown how to handle objects that are fragile and delicate. Demonstrate how to handle objects with respect, showing children how to hold and touch. If you have borrowed objects, it's likely that these are special to someone and children need to know this. If children are examining living things, plants or small animals (such as minibeasts in bug boxes) it's particularly important to ensure gentle handling.

All children should be provided with opportunities to explore and examine objects. When planning an activity and selecting items, ensure that all children can participate fully. If there are any children with a visual impairment, objects that can be explored through the senses of touch, sound and smell, as well as sight, should be selected. Children who have a hearing loss won't appreciate the 'noisy' aspects of objects but can explore with their other senses. Some children may have difficulty picking up and holding on to objects, so items that are easy to grasp should be included, perhaps on trays close to the child.

Care and thought needs to be given to choosing objects to ensure children enjoy and learn from exploring them, whilst staying safe.

Providing a range of objects

Over time, it's good practice to provide a range of objects for exploration, such as:

- Natural materials with interesting features, e.g. pine cones, cork, bark, sponges, pumice, rocks and pebbles, fossils, etc.
- Items associated with animals, e.g. feathers, nests and eggs (abandoned), a chrysalis, shells, wool from sheep, etc.
- Manufactured items, particularly unfamiliar and unusual items, e.g. a sundial, chiming clocks, timers, etc.
- Objects that reflect people and their culture, e.g. cooking utensils, music (recordings and instruments), fabrics, clothes, games and 'special' items such as candlesticks, prayer mats, statues. (*It's important to note that we're talking about real artefacts here. Everyday play opportunities should reflect diversity in terms of people and cultures*).
- Things from the past, e.g. photographs, toys, household equipment, clothes and, for older children, printed material such as ration books, certificates, newspapers.

see page 298 for further details.

Where to find them

- Ask parents, friends and families, but remember that items might be precious and you would need to be sure that you could look after them. It's best not to borrow anything that is irreplaceable.
- Make your own collection from your cupboards, your travels, charity shops and car boot sales.
- Make contact with local community groups. They may have items to lend or can suggest where to borrow them.
- Many local museums have collections that can be borrowed for use with children.

Conservation

Remember to emphasise conservation. Children should be encouraged to care for and protect the natural environment. Wildlife must not be disturbed to provide objects for interest tables!

Safety

To make sure objects are safe for children to handle, consider the following:

- Babies and toddlers will explore by sucking and chewing. Check that objects are made of non-toxic materials, are clean and with no loose, small pieces.
- Older children can be warned about sharp edges or any other concerns. Make sure you look for possible hazards beforehand.
- Many plants have poisonous berries. They are not suitable to be used.
- If any of the children in the group are allergic to certain substances (such as feathers) do not use them.

Have a go!

Imagine that your supervisor has asked you to set up an interest table for three- to five-year olds. It must link up with the current theme of 'The Seaside'. List what you would provide and where you would get each item.

Handling objects of interest ▶

Exploring and investigating the natural environment

Children can learn a great deal from exploring investigating the outside environment. Activities include:

- Planting/growing seeds and bulbs helps children learn about nature and growth.
- Caring for a pet can help children to understand about life cycles and develop a sense of caring and responsibility.
- Observing wildlife in its natural habitat helps children understand the natural world. Bird tables can be set up where children can see them easily. Minibeasts can be found and examined in a garden area, perhaps using magnifying glasses and bug boxes.
- Studying the weather can fascinate children. They can watch puddles form and evaporate, measure rainfall and find out the direction of the wind. Children love to feel snow, to experience its texture as they build with it and watch it melting away. Icy puddles and icicles provide interesting experiences too.
- On a walk in the neighbourhood, you can draw children's attention to street furniture such as signposts, letter boxes, lamp posts and shop and road signs. They can look for architectural features such as doorways, roofs and chimney pots too.

There's further information on how to provide activities to encourage learning and development in Unit 10. You may find it helpful to read that unit now.

FOCUS ON...
your learning

In this section you've learnt about different types of play. You've learnt how to plan and provide play activities, and how to encourage exploration and investigation through play.

Questions

1 Why is it important to provide activities and experiences that promote each of the play types?

2 Why does providing objects of interest encourage exploration and investigation through play?

RAPID RECAP

Learning Outcome 1

There are several different play types. It's important to provide a wide range of activities that promote each type of play so that children can make progress in every area of the development. This takes planning. Settings plan what resources and activities will be available for free play, as well as planning activities with a specific learning focus or aim. Exploration and investigation through play should also be promoted.

Learning Outcome 2

There are five stages of play identified by Parten. These are solitary play (child plays alone), spectator play (child watches others play but doesn't join in), parallel play (plays alongside others but does not interact), associative play (interacts with others but has own play agenda) and co-operative play (fully interacts, capable of sharing ideas and co-operates to play imaginary games effectively with others). Children generally progress through these stages by the time they are five years old. But they will still revisit them in phases of their play.

Learning Outcome 3

We use categories to divide up different types of play when we're talking about them, e.g. 'physical play' and 'creative play'. But for children play doesn't have categories. When they play, children may experience several types of play at once. Childcarers should plan play opportunities that meet children's needs and promote all areas of development. Play opportunities should be broad and balanced.

FAQ

Q How will I be assessed on this unit?

A *You'll complete an assignment entitled 'Children and play'.*

Q What will I have to do?

A *Your tutor or Centre will help you to understand the task. It involves you writing about play activities that might take place in three different settings. See Unit 1 Learning Outcome 5 for more information on study skills.*

Weblinks

You may like to visit the following websites:

- www.playlink.org.uk/publications/
  To view the publication "Best Play: What play provision should do for children," which is about how children benefit from play and how the benefits can be provided.
- www.mirandawalker.co.uk
  For play activity ideas.

Communication and professional skills within child care and education

Learning Outcomes

In this unit you'll learn about:

How to develop effective communication skills to work with children and adults in a variety of settings.

How to use your developing knowledge and skills to improve your practice and develop professionally.

How to investigate employment opportunities and routes of progression.

Learning Outcome 1

FOCUS ON...

how to develop effective communication skills to work with children and adults in a variety of settings

This links with Assessment Criteria **1.1, 1.2, 1.3**

Communicating well with children

The way in which you talk with children communicates much more than just the words that you say. By communicating well, you can demonstrate good use of language. You can also show children that you value what they say and feel. It's important to communicate well with both children and adults, as we build relationships through communication and interaction. Children also learn from their conversations with adults.

Communication methods

Language is generally thought of as the main way in which we:

- Communicate with one another.
- Express ourselves.

Learning how to use language is essential for the social development of babies and young children. We use language in our social interactions in many ways, including to:

- Share information.
  Children learn through listening and talking. They can also demonstrate what they know and put forward their own ideas.
- Share our feelings and experiences
  Children develop emotionally when they can use language to express themselves. For example, rather than crying they can explain to a carer what's wrong. They can share their interests and news and receive feedback.
- Ask questions.
  Children become more independent when they can ask questions and ask for what they want (such as a drink).

- Negotiate.
  Children's social relationships develop when they can negotiate with language – they can agree to share toys and take turns.
- Organise and plan.
  Children's independence, confidence and self-esteem grows when they can plan and organise for themselves – 'I'll meet you on the bench in the playground at lunchtime.'
- Get to know each other.
  Conversations are the starting point for most friendships.

Language is also a tool for thinking. Most of us think in words when we mentally direct ourselves. For example, you may think, 'I need to buy a birthday card on my way home'. People sometimes say their thoughts aloud to themselves without even realising they're doing it. It happens because thinking in words comes so naturally. Words can also help us to bring to mind information we have stored in our brains. If someone mentions the word 'beach', a visual image of the seaside may come to you, or perhaps you will think back to your last holiday.

But communication isn't just about language. There are a range of communication methods you can use with babies, children and adults. They are not all verbal. For example, think how easy it is to let someone know whether you approve or disapprove of something they're doing, just by the expression on your face. A range of communication methods is shown on the diagram below.

Communication methods chart ▶

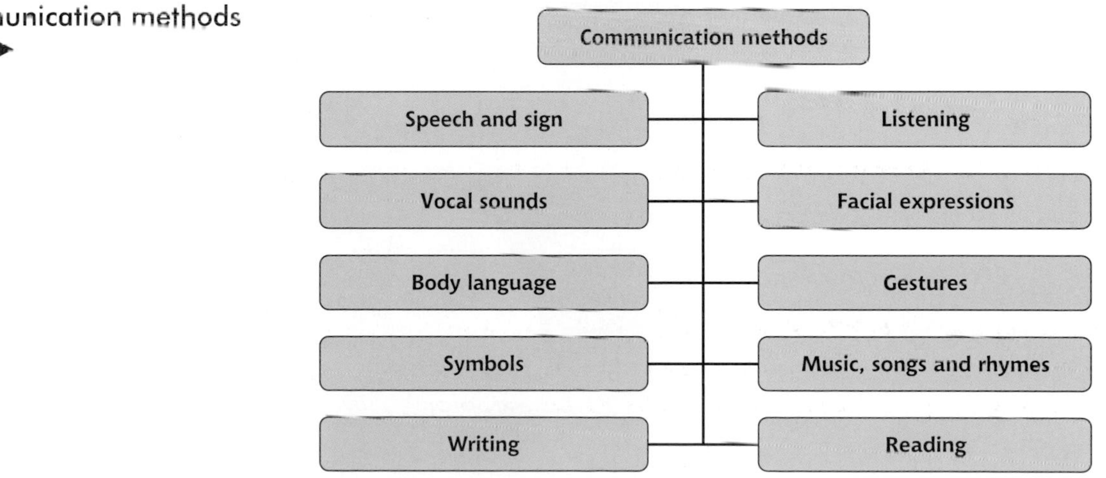

You need to select methods of communication that are appropriate to the children and adults you're working with and the situation or activity at hand. To do this, you need to have good knowledge and understanding of:

- How babies and children learn to communicate.
- How to communicate effectively with babies, children and adults.
- Individual children's developmental stages.
- Individual children's communication needs.

Patterns of communication

Age birth to three months

Babies express their feelings (such as tiredness, hunger and emotional distress) by crying. They learn to recognise the sound of their parents' and carers' voices through listening. They can be soothed with gentle tones from a well-known adult. They will smile. They are interested in faces – they watch them and respond to them.

Methods to engage and interest:

Spend plenty of time talking to babies in a lively tone when they're content, and soothe them reassuringly with gentle tones when they're distressed. Ensure babies can see your face and make eye contact. An ideal time to communicate is when attending to babies' care needs. The baby and carer can look into each other's eyes during nappy changing and bottle feeding, for example.

Making eye contact is very important ▶

Age three to six months

Babies start to make a range of playful, short sounds – they babble and coo. They experiment with sounds, rhymes and volume. They enjoy vocal exchanges with adults. They laugh and squeal to express delight and cry to express distress.

Methods to engage and interest babies:

Join in with babies' playful babbles, repeating sounds back to them. Talk to babies often and engage them in 'conversation' – talk to them, then pause to allow the baby to 'reply', then 'answer' them once again. Respond with delight with your facial expressions, body language and your speech when babies communicate their delight to you. Show sympathy in your facial expressions, body language and your speech when babies communicate their distress to you. Remember to talk WITH babies, not TO them.

Age six to 12 months

Babies learn to use sound deliberately to imitate and to get attention. They may make sounds whilst gesturing to show adults what they want. Babbling begins to sound tuneful. Babies play around with sounds, joining them together. Most of the sounds needed for language can now be made. By 12 months most babies understand the meaning of around 15–20 words.

Methods to engage and interest:

Continue talking with babies. Look out for signs that they are using sounds for deliberate communication. Respond to this to encourage babies to repeat their efforts. Babies enjoy getting to know simple songs and rhymes. They like to anticipate the fun endings to old favourites such as 'Round and Round the Garden'.

Age 12–18 months

Babies begin to say single words at around 12 months. The **vocabulary** expands to about 15 words within the next three months. Babies become more aware of other people's body language. They may follow someone else's gaze.

Methods to engage and interest:

Make sure that you respond encouragingly to babies' first words, so that they will be motivated to keep talking to you. Babies enjoy sharing first picture books with adults.

abc **Learn the lingo**

Vocabulary
= the term given to refer to all the words someone knows.

They enjoy learning the names of objects they see in the pictures. They also enjoy learning the sounds that familiar animals make. As they become aware of body language, children enjoy simple songs with actions they can copy.

Age 18–24 months

Children start to use two words together first as they begin to say simple phrases. Most children can communicate their meaning to parents/carers by two years or shortly after. They have a vocabulary of about 200 words. They say up to 20 new words each month.

Methods to engage and interest:

Show lots of interest in what children have to say. Ensure that you reply to children whenever they talk to you. Take what they say seriously, even if words are missing, or you're not sure what is meant. It's important that children feel their efforts at communicating are worthwhile. Opportunities to interact with their peers and slightly older children are helpful. Read children short, simple stories, and sing familiar songs slowly so they can join in with words or phrases they know.

Age two to three years

Children speak in simple sentences. They begin to ask simple questions (what/where). They pick up new words easily, and their vocabulary continues to expand. They make mistakes such as saying, 'I goed' rather than 'I went', or 'I sleeped' rather than 'I slept'. Children now use plurals and negatives, e.g. 'dolls' and 'No drink left'. Children may need time to stop and think during speech, which can be mistaken for stammering.

Methods to engage and interest:

Make sure children are in an environment rich with exciting language, including conversation, songs, rhymes and stories. Children's questions should be answered, even if they are repetitive. Introduce children to expressive words for feelings and describing, e.g. happy, sad, excited, angry, wet, dry, soft, hard. Demonstrate language for thinking by using it aloud yourself, 'I wonder what will happen if I pour this water into the sand... oh look, it's all wet now!'

Language will now continue to develop, with most children talking fluently by the age of five.

Reading

It's never too early to read to babies and young children. The youngest infants will enjoy hearing the rise and fall of an expressive voice reading aloud, even if the words aren't yet understood. Children enjoy stories long before they can read words. An early love of stories will motivate children to want to learn to read later on.

Just as children learn that spoken words carry meaning, they will learn that the words on the page are meaningful too. Children often learn this before the age of three. Think how often a two-year old will bring you a book to read to them. Most children will learn to recognise letters and odd words that are familiar to them by the time they leave nursery education, but most will not read until they start school.

It's never too early for children to enjoy books ▶

Writing

Mark-making is the term we use to describe any activity in which children can deliberately make a mark. The obvious activities are art based – children make marks when they draw, crayon, paint, print, stamp, etc. But children can draw with a twig in the sand, or trace patterns on the ground with water and so on.

Whenever children deliberately make marks they're practising the skills they'll need to write. They're learning the techniques for pencil control and how to make their marks stop, start, flow and join. They're discovering how to move their arms and hands to make big shapes, small

ones, thick ones and thin ones. They feel the satisfaction of leaving their mark.

At between three and four years most children start to make small symbols in a row, which are their first attempts to write. We call this **emergent writing**. It's often mingled with real letters children have learnt from their own name. This emergent writing, which eventually progresses into actual writing, stems from early mark-making opportunities.

abc Learn the lingo

Emergent writing
= marks made by a child when they first attempt to write. Symbols drawn in a line are often mingled with real letters.

Sign language

Sign language is generally used with children and adults who have a hearing impairment. Makaton, a basic form of sign language, is often used with children who have learning difficulties that affect their ability to communicate through speech. There's recently been some interest in using signs with hearing babies. Some experts believe that teaching babies simple signs can help them to communicate before they have the ability to express themselves with words. They believe that this reduces frustration in babies and that it does not delay verbal communication.

Adult and child signing ▼

Conversation

To show that you value and respect children, it's important that you pay attention to them when they tell you that they want to communicate with you. Young babies may do this by cooing or babbling whilst looking at you, particularly

GOOD PRACTICE

You should always be open to what children have to say. If a child feels that you may judge them or that you're not interested in them, they may become reluctant to interact with you. Try to be objective and listen carefully. Don't assume you know what children are going to say.

when you're attending to a care need (such as changing a nappy). An older child may tap you on the arm and then gesture towards something that they want.

Sometimes several children want to talk to you at once. In this situation, let the children know you have noticed them and will listen to them all in turn. Once a child knows their turn will come, they're generally happy to wait. You might say something like, 'Were you starting to tell me something, Jack? I'll just finish listening to Sadie, and then I'll listen to you.' Make sure you always remember to listen to the child as you promised. When children are keen to share their thoughts they may interrupt one another Allowing interruptions sends the message that one child's thoughts are more important than another's. When a child interrupts, try acknowledging them, but encouraging them to wait. You might say, 'Hold on to that idea Maria. Let's finish listening to Declan, and then we'll hear from you.'

Practical example

Waiting to talk

Pre-school assistant Cheryl is playing animal lotto with a small group of three- and four-year olds. She asks if anyone has a pet. Tom, Lottie and Carlos are keen to talk about their pets, and all try to talk at once. Cheryl says, 'Let's all listen to Tom first. Then Lottie can tell us about her dog, and after that we'll all listen to Carlos.' The children listen to Tom. Then Carlos tries to talk about his pet again. Cheryl says, 'Just a minute, Carlos. We're listening to Lottie next, and then we'll all listen to you.'

1. *Why was Cheryl's approach good in terms of valuing what each of the children had to say?*

Tone and expression

Aim to show the warmth and affection that you have for children in your tone of voice when you're communicating with them. This makes communication more enjoyable for

children, and it's likely to motivate them to communicate with you. Expression is also important. The way in which your voice rises and falls engages babies and young children. Your tone and expression also lets them know that you're being friendly or playful – even before they can understand the actual words that you're saying to them. Babies and children learn to trust people who interact with them sensitively. This is at the heart of building a good relationship with babies and children.

Remember that your face and your body 'speak' for you even when you don't intend them to! Make sure that your facial expressions and body language are appropriate to each situation. Speak with children at a level they can understand and a pace that suits them. Your knowledge of child development and individual children will help you.

GOOD PRACTICE

You must always use appropriate language when talking with or in front of children. Language that labels children or makes them feel bad about themselves should never be used. For instance, a child may need to be told that an aspect of his behaviour is inappropriate, but he should never be told that he is a 'naughty boy' or a 'troublemaker'. A child may need to be reminded to be quiet and to listen at story time, but she should never be told to 'shut up'. Using language in this way is hostile, unnecessary and unprofessional.

Encouraging communication through play

Role play ▼

Many activities can be used to encourage communication through play. Some encourage talking, others listening and some encourage non-verbal communication. Touch, mark-making and pretend play are all valuable ways to encourage children to communicate through different media. Here are some more ideas:

- Role-play with dressing-up clothes, a home corner and other props.
- Play opportunities with dolls, puppets and soft toys.
- Small world play with resources such as a farmyard and animals.
- Playground games such as 'Ring-a-ring-o-roses'.
- Use of toy telephones.
- Playing side-by-side at the water tray, sharing resources.

- Interesting objects to explore, such as items that scrunch, squelch, rattle or jingle.
- Ball games between two or more players.

Joining in alongside babies and children and talking with them about their activities helps to develop relationships as well as communication skills. With experience it will become a very natural, intuitive part of your role.

Active listening

Listening ▼

Listening well is important. It shows that you value what children say and feel. This helps to give children confidence and self-esteem. Here are some active listening strategies:

- Let children see you're interested in what they're saying.
  Establish eye contact, getting down to the children's level whenever necessary. Smile and nod encouragingly if appropriate.
- Give children time.
  Children need time to think as they speak. Listen for long enough to let them finish what they have to say.
- Ask children questions about their topic.
  This encourages children to talk further (and to think). It also shows you're interested.
- Clarify and confirm.
  Ask questions to check you're following what a child is telling you.
- React to what children say.
  Show empathy for children's feelings when they are expressed. Be aware of your facial expressions – look happy for children, or concerned, or whatever is appropriate.
- Respond.
  Make sure that you answer children when they talk to you. Even if they haven't asked you a direct question, make a comment, e.g. 'That's interesting' or, 'That sounds like fun'. These small acknowledgements are important.

The following types of behaviour could indicate to children that you do not value their ideas and feelings:

- Not really listening.
- Not making eye contact.
- Looking bored.

- Not contributing to the conversation.
- Not responding.
- Not acknowledging or answering.
- Interrupting.
- Rushing children to get to the point.
- Not acting upon children's ideas.
- Not thanking or praising children for their contributions.

Have a go!

Ask a friend to do this communication exercise with you. Sit facing each other. Talk to your friend for one minute (you will need to time yourself). Your friend can answer you as usual, but they should not make eye contact with you at all. At the end of the minute, tell your friend how you felt during the exercise. This task will help you to understand just how important eye contact is to active listening.

Asking questions and offering ideas

Encouraging children to ask questions promotes curiosity and a thirst for learning. Asking questions is a key way for children to check their understanding and expand their knowledge. It also gets children involved in two-way conversation, encouraging them to practise active listening themselves.

Children can also be encouraged to suggest ideas and then test them. This promotes the skills of investigation. (Perhaps children have suggested ways of sinking a toy boat in the water tray – they can then try out their ideas and find out what actually sinks the boat.) You can encourage children to ask questions and to share their ideas and suggestions by:

- Inviting them to.
  'Has anyone got a question they'd like to ask?' or, 'What games could we play outside later?'
- Role-modelling.
  Let children hear you put forward your own ideas and questions.
- Planning questions with children.
  For instance, if a visitor is coming to the setting, you can plan questions to ask them beforehand. What do children want to find out?
- Having a suggestion box.
  This is popular with older children.

FAST FACT

Many settings are introducing 'consultation and participation' policies. These set out intentions to consult with children by seeking their opinions, ideas and suggestions. Groups may consult children about their setting's rules, activities and resources. This is most common in settings for older children.

- Responding positively when children ask questions or make suggestions.
  Answer questions fully. Praise children's efforts, and thank children for their contributions, 'I'm glad you asked me that' or, 'What a good idea!'
- Giving opportunities for children to listen to one another.
  Circle time or news time are popular ways of doing this.

Communication differences and difficulties

You'll read more about this in Unit 9.

Some children will experience communication difficulties, which may be long or short term.

Some children learn more than one language. When this is the case, there may be noticeable differences in the way in which children's patterns of communication develop.

Communicating with adults

Everyone working at a setting needs to establish positive relationships with the other adults. Good communication is the key to positive relationships. You'll need to communicate well with colleagues, other professionals, and parents/carers.

Listen actively to other adults in the workplace ▼

Positive working relationships lead to a pleasant, comfortable atmosphere in the working environment. This is good for staff and children because your working environment is the child's play and learning space. When positive relationships are formed it's easier for colleagues to give and receive trust, support, help, advice, information and encouragement. It's more likely that any problems arising between colleagues will be positively approached and resolved. It's also more likely that skills and knowledge will be shared. Good teamwork depends on good communication.

Communicating with respect

You should always communicate politely. This means that you need to address people appropriately. People's names are part of their identity, so find out how people would like to be addressed. Don't assume that it's acceptable for you to use a parent's first name. Not all parents share the same

last name as their child and not all mothers go by the title 'Mrs'. Don't shorten anyone's name (including children) unless you're invited to.

GOOD PRACTICE

By being polite yourself you will encourage children to use good manners too.

Good manners show respect for other people. I'm sure you can think of a time when you have been offended by someone else's lack of manners. Perhaps someone asked you to do something without saying please, talked over you when you were speaking, or brushed past you without saying excuse me.

Communicating appropriately

Aim to communicate clearly, in a way that's appropriate for individual adults. To do this, you should consider:

- The methods of communication available to you – see the diagram below.
- What you need to say.
- Whether it is urgent.
- Whether it is confidential.
- The policies and procedures at your setting – e.g. your setting may prefer to write to parents rather than to email.

Methods of communicating with adults ▶

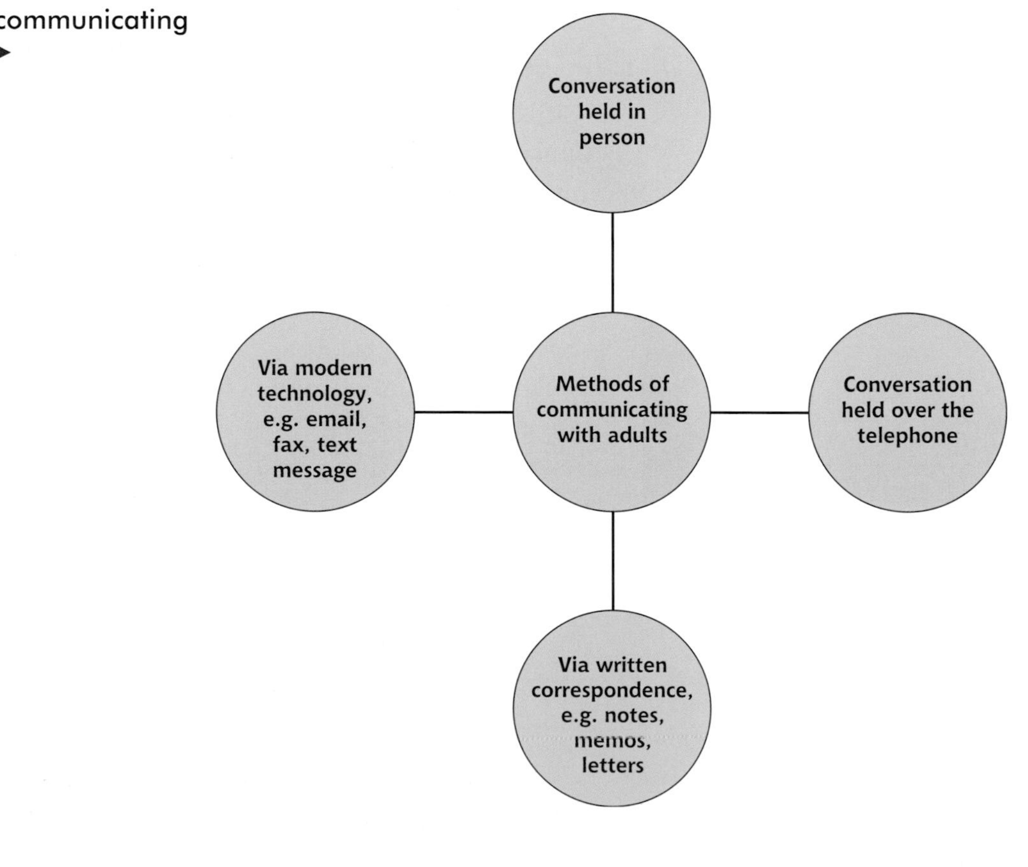

Most communication between colleagues takes place in conversation. But when staff are with the children, it's their duty to focus their attention on the children's care, learning and development. Remember this when you need to talk with colleagues. Unless there's a reason for urgency, avoid interrupting colleagues when they're working closely with children, or when they need to concentrate fully on the task in hand. If you're unsure about this, you can always ask a colleague if it's a good time to talk. Detailed discussions are best scheduled for non-contact time, when you and colleagues aren't responsible for children's care.

Always behave professionally within the setting – only have appropriate discussions within earshot of children. Friendly chats about subjects unrelated to the setting should be kept for free time, spent away from the children. Children should never be aware of any conflict between staff.

There may be guidelines at your setting about how you should communicate formally. For instance, there could be procedures for passing information to staff working on a different shift.

Communication needs

Adults and children can experience the same communication difficulties. You may need to adapt your communication techniques to meet the needs of others. It's important that you're as sensitive to the communication difficulties of adults as you would be to those of children.

You can adapt your communications in a number of ways to suit individual needs. Strategies may include:

- Learning some signs (sign language).
- Talking clearly and facing anyone who is lip reading.
- Arranging for an interpreter (for adults for whom English/Welsh is an additional language).
- Translating signs, letters and other written communications into the languages required (this can be done via computer and/or with assistance from bi-lingual parents).
- Arranging to talk in a quiet area free from background noise.
- Taking the time to give key information verbally as well as in writing (for adults who have difficulty reading).

You should practise the principles of active listening with adults, just as you would when talking with children. See page 223.

Communicating clearly

It's essential to communicate clearly to ensure that your message is received. Once you've chosen the appropriate communication method, you're on the right track. But there's a key question to ask yourself – what exactly are you trying to say? You need to be clear about the point of your message before you try to communicate it to someone else. These strategies can help:

- Thinking through/writing down key points in advance.
  So that you don't forget anything, and you feel focused.
- Practising or seeking advice.
  If you're unsure about how to phrase something, practise a few different ways aloud, or in writing, or seek advice from a colleague.
- Considering whether you need an answer.
  Do you need to wait for a reply, or some information in response?

GOOD PRACTICE

It's important that you're clear about the communications that you receive. To avoid making mistakes ALWAYS CHECK WHENEVER YOU'RE UNSURE ABOUT INFORMATION GIVEN TO YOU, OR WHAT'S BEING ASKED OF YOU. Nobody will mind you checking. It's far better to ask than to get something wrong.

Responding to requests for information

Part of your role is to supply other adults with information. For instance, colleagues often share information about children. A parent may ask for further information about the setting, or you might be asked to give information to an outside professional working with a child, such as a speech therapist or social worker. Whatever the request, you should be clear about what is being asked for and when the information is needed by. You should aim to give accurate information on time. But you must consider confidentiality before passing information on – see below for further details.

Confidentiality

During your career you will be aware of many personal details about the families that you work with. You may be given confidential information verbally, and you may have access to confidential records, depending on your position. Respecting confidentiality is extremely important.

Passing on information when you should not do so can have serious consequences. It can upset people. Trust may be lost, causing damage to working relationships. Your professional reputation can be affected and disciplinary action may be taken by employers. Make sure that you

read and understand your setting's confidentiality policy. You should treat any personal information about the people at your setting as confidential – that includes information relating to children, parents, carers and colleagues. Types of confidential information include:

- Personal details such as those recorded on the registration form, including addresses, telephone numbers and medical information.
- Information about children's development and individual needs. This includes information held in development reports and on special educational needs registers.
- Details about family circumstances, including things you may know about the current or past relationships within families, or details about people's jobs or events in their lives.
- Financial information, including details about how children's places are funded.
- Information relating to past incidents or experiences of a sensitive nature. For instance, a family may have suffered a traumatic event. Or perhaps you know that social workers, therapists or other professionals are working within a family.

Sensitive information should be made available to practitioners on a 'need-to-know basis'. That means that different practitioners in the same setting will not necessarily have access to the same information. Therefore, you should not discuss confidential matters with colleagues unless you are sure that it's appropriate to do so and it can be done privately. If you're not sure about any issue of a confidential nature, check with your supervisor before disclosing information to anyone else.

Sometimes, confidential information needs to be discussed with a parent or carer. In this case, childcarers should arrange to talk privately, ideally in another room. Childcarers should also consider whether it is appropriate for the parent's child to hear the discussion.

Confidential information contained within the records of a setting must be handled with care and stored securely. Don't leave sensitive paperwork or files where people who do not need to know will have access to them.

Practical example

Carly's invitations

Three-year old Carly goes to nursery. She's having a birthday party. Her dad asks her keyworker, Jodie, to supply him with the addresses of Carly's friends, so that he can send out invitations in the post. Jodie explains that this would break confidentiality. She offers to take the invitations and give them out by hand at the nursery instead.

1. *Why did Carly do this?*

Parents and carers should be aware of information held about them and their children. If a setting stores records on computer, they must be registered on the Data Protection Register. There are rules about what information can be recorded and how information should be kept.

Disclosing information

You must respect confidential information about children, as long as doing so will not affect their welfare. For instance, if you suspected that a child was being abused, you would have a duty to disclose this information, but only to the relevant person or authority.

See Unit 3 for further details.

FOCUS ON...
your learning

In this section you've learnt about the communication patterns of babies and young children. You've also learnt how to communicate effectively with both children and adults.

Questions:

1. How can you show that you're actively listening to someone?
2. Why should you ask children questions?

Learning Outcome 2

FOCUS ON...

how to use your developing knowledge and skills to improve your practice and develop professionally

This links with Assessment Criteria **2.1, 2.2**

Personal and professional development

You should continue to develop your skills and professional knowledge throughout your career. This will help you to:

- Improve your practice.
- Expand your knowledge and understanding.
- Keep up to date.
- Stay motivated and interested in your role.

An important aspect of professional development is learning from past experiences. This involves thinking about your practice, noticing areas for development and planning how to improve your knowledge, understanding and skills.

Reflective practice

Reflecting on how you do things, what you do and what you achieve helps you to see how well you're working in practice. Reflective workers regularly:

- Think about their practice.
- Analyse their actions.
- Record their reflections, e.g. in a diary.
- Discuss their reflections with others.
- Ask for feedback from others to help them improve.
- Identify their strengths.
  By asking themselves: 'What do I do well or to a high standard?'

- Identify their weaknesses.
  'What don't I do all that well? What don't I feel confident doing?'
- Notice their achievements.
  'Where have I made progress? What targets have I reached?'
- Identify their development needs.
  'What new information and/or skills should I learn? How can I address my weaknesses?'
- Solve problems.
  'What problems do I currently have, and how can I tackle them?'
- Improve practice.
  'What can I do to improve my practical work with the children/ parents/carers/my colleagues?'

Reflection also helps you to see which of your practical work strategies and techniques are successful, and where a fresh approach is needed. This increases your professional knowledge, understanding and skills.

Throughout your career, you'll need to devote regular time to thinking about your professional development. Do this during non-contact time, when you're not responsible for children. Quiet time to think things through properly can give you a deeper understanding of how you're working and how you can develop.

Plan some quiet time to reflect your practice ▶

Reflection techniques

Several techniques can be used to reflect on and analyse your practice:

- Questioning what, why and how.
  For instance, imagine you've previously had difficulty keeping children seated at story time. Today, one child got up and took another's cushion, causing them to cry. You might question, 'What actually happened, and why did the event occur? How did I respond and why?'
- Seeking alternatives.
  'How else could I have handled things?'
- Keeping an open mind.
  'There could be a better way to handle or prevent such situations'.
- Viewing from different perspectives.
  'How might colleagues have responded? How were the children involved feeling at the time?'
- Asking 'what if?'
  'What if I'd given children more time to settle in their seats?'
- Thinking about consequences.
  'A colleague came to deal with the situation while I tried to carry on with the story. But what would have happened if I'd stopped reading the story to the rest of the group until the situation was resolved?'
- Testing ideas through comparing and contrasting.
  'What similar events have I experienced, and were they handled effectively? Could techniques used then work in this situation?'
- Bringing ideas together.
  'I've thought about the issue myself, and discussed it with a colleague. I remember reading that it's good to take time to settle children at story time. It can help them to concentrate and feel engaged.'
- Seeking, identifying and resolving problems.
  'On reflection, I think the problem was that the children hadn't settled before I started reading. Next time I'll try giving them more time. I'll ask if they're comfortable and if everyone can see the book.'

Good reflective workers learn to use all of these techniques, applying one or more of them to each situation or issue they reflect on. They keep a record in their diary.

Feedback

Throughout your career the feedback you receive from others will be valuable to you. It helps to have someone objective to comment on your skills and understanding. It can give you a new insight into your own practice. Feedback can come from:

- Tutors.
  This may be given in tutorials on a one-to-one basis, in comments made in class, or in written reports.
- Workplace supervisors.
  In reports made to your tutor, on a one-to-one basis in a ***staff appraisal*** *(a regular meeting to discuss your work performance), casually given during a session ('Well done, your story-telling skills are really coming along now.')*
- Colleagues.
  Colleagues may work more closely with you than your supervisor, and so they're well placed to give you feedback on your practical work. In a group setting other staff will always be on hand to let you know how well you've dealt with a situation, or to give you help and advice when you need it.
- Parents and carers.
  What families have to say is valuable feedback. Parents and carers may raise concerns or praise the provision when they drop off and collect their children. Settings sometimes ask families to complete a regular questionnaire to let them know how they feel about the provision.
- Children.
  They'll soon let you know if they enjoy or dislike an activity. How well children respond to you in different situations can give you a good idea of your strengths and weaknesses.

Learn the lingo

Staff appraisal
= a regular meeting with supervisors to discuss your work performance.

FAST FACT

Staff appraisals usually take place every six to 12 months, depending on the setting. At the end of the meeting, targets will be set for developing skills, knowledge and understanding. At the next appraisal, progress towards the targets will be monitored.

GOOD PRACTICE

To get the most out of meetings with supervisors/tutors to discuss your progress and development, spend some time thinking about it yourself first. Have a look back over your diary. Where are you making progress? Where can you improve further? What support from your tutor/supervisor would help you? What would you like to achieve next, and by when?

Planning professional development

You've learnt that professional development should be continuous, and that you should plan regular non-contact time for reflection. This ensures reflection isn't forgotten and that you have the time to think. Records kept in your diary will build into a helpful account of your development. You might plan reflection time in response to:

FAST FACT

Tutors and supervisors are there to support and guide you through your ongoing professional development.

- A naturally occurring event.
  When you've come across a new situation, or when you feel something has gone particularly well or badly.
- Feedback received.
  From tutors, colleagues, supervisors, parents, carers or children.
- Regulations.
  As new discoveries are made and new theories are developed, what we consider to be best practice changes. You may be able to see how this has happened in your life time.

An appraisal meeting ▶

GOOD PRACTICE

If you ever feel you are struggling with your professional development or if any aspect of your performance is worrying you, approach your tutor and/or supervisor and arrange a time to talk to them.

Have a go!

Think back to how you learnt and played in various settings when you were a child and compare this with how children are encouraged to learn and play now. Regulations are often changed to reflect what is newly considered to be best practice. You must adapt and develop your own practice in accordance with regulations throughout your career. This may mean that you'll need to learn new information or skills.

- Appraisals.
- Policy/procedure reviews.
  Most settings review their policies and procedures each year. Staff members consider how effective the policies are. They also evaluate how well their practice promotes the policies. It may be decided to develop a

policy in the interests of improvement. If regulations alter, it may be essential to change policies and practice to stay in line with them.

- Organisational evaluations.
  Settings may regularly review a number of aspects of their provision, such as the success of activities, or the partnership with parents and carers. Staff, children, parents, carers and outside agencies may all be involved in the evaluation process.

Setting targets

Once you've identified an aspect of your practice that would benefit from professional development, the next step is to set yourself a target.

Targets should always be written down. It's important to make them SMART. This stands for specific, measurable, achievable, realistic and time-bound. The table below explains how to do this.

SMART ▼

Specific	State exactly: ● what you are planning to achieve ● how you will achieve it. This will help you focus clearly on your target.
Measurable	Decide: ● how you'll know when you're on the way to achieving your target ● how you'll know when you've achieved your target
Achievable	Make sure your target is achievable. A large target is sometimes best broken down into several smaller targets. The task seems more manageable then, and you see that you're making progress.
Realistic	Worthwhile targets can be challenging. But be realistic about how and when you can achieve things or you may become disheartened or discouraged.
Time-bound	Timescales help motivate you to get on with working towards your targets. Set dates for when each target should be met, and monitor your progress. Set dates for monitoring, and enter them in your diary so you don't forget them.

Review, update and amend targets

When you monitor your progress towards a target:

- Review what you've done so far. Have you achieved what you wanted to within the timescale you set?

GOOD PRACTICE

When you're planning your development, it's a good idea to set a range of targets that can be achieved in the short term (perhaps in the next few days or weeks), in the medium term (perhaps in the next few weeks or months) and in the long term (perhaps in the next year). Short-term targets can help you to improve your practice continually in small but regular steps. Medium-term targets help you to take on professional development tasks that are a bit more challenging. Long-term targets help you to think about the bigger picture. For instance, you may undertake a new professional qualification that will take a year or more of study.

- If you're working on a large target that you've broken down into smaller targets, what will you do next? Plan the next step in more detail, and set a new timescale. Remember to set dates for monitoring, and enter them in your diary.
- If a timescale has turned out not to be realistic, you can adjust it. If you're having difficulty meeting a target, try to work out why. Is there a different way to approach the target? Do you need to ask a tutor, supervisor or colleague for guidance? Set the target again, stating any new method of achieving it.
- If you've finished working on the target, reflect on your progress. What have you learnt? How have you developed? Has there been improvement in your skills and/or understanding? Make notes in your diary. Is there any follow-up work to do now? If so, set a new target to help you achieve it.
- If the target has been completely achieved, well done! Make a point of rewarding yourself with a treat. It doesn't have to cost anything (how about a long soak in a bubble bath or putting your feet up with a DVD?) If you've achieved a big target you could have a small celebration with colleagues – a plate of homemade biscuits or cakes in the staff room usually go down well! Once you've enjoyed your reward, it's time to tackle the next target for your continual professional development.

There'll be times when you'll need to access further learning opportunities as part of your continuing professional development. See Learning Outcome 3 for further information about this.

A training session ▶

Practical example

Sophia gets SMART

After reflecting on her practice, Sophia feels that she could improve her communication with adults. She sets the following SMART target:

'My target is to improve my communication with adults because I often feel nervous when I'm interacting with them. I will attend a communication skills training course, and read about the subject. I will use the techniques I learn to help me feel more confident, particularly when I'm interacting with parents and carers. I'll know I'm on my way to achieving the target when I've done some reading and found a course. I will be closer to achieving it when I've completed the course and learnt some communication techniques. I'll have achieved my goal when I feel more confident when I'm communicating with adults.

Timescale:
Find an appropriate course and book a place – by 1st March
Use the library and internet to research communication skills – by 14th March
Attend course and use communication techniques – date to be set by 1st March as it depends on the date and length of the course.'

1. *Why is it important that Sophia's objectives are specific, measurable, achievable, realistic and with timescales?*

FAST FACT

Your tutor will mark your Practice Evidence Diary. Your work placement supervisor will be asked to verify that it gives an accurate account of your practice.

Practice evidence diary

As part of your evidence to achieve PERS you're expected to complete a Practice Evidence Diary. The diary consists of tasks that you need to complete during your work placements. You'll need to demonstrate that you can evaluate and reflect on your practice. You'll also have the opportunity to show your understanding of the practical skills you've learnt in placement. Your tutor will explain to you how to keep your diary.

Personal experiences

Something to bear in mind when reflecting on your practice is how your own background, life history and experiences can affect your practice. For instance, if as a child you hated having to play outside in cold weather, you may be tempted only to take children outside in fine weather. If a childminder was bitten by a dog as a child, she might pass her fear on to children in her care by becoming anxious whenever a dog crosses their path. Many people were brought up to know only their own family's religion or beliefs. By being aware of how your experiences can influence your practice, you can take deliberate steps to avoid any pitfalls – by finding out about a range of religions and beliefs for instance.

FOCUS ON...
your learning

In this section you've learnt how to reflect on your practice and use feedback as part of your continuing professional development. You've also learnt how to set short-term, medium-term and long-term professional targets.

Questions:

1 What are the benefits of reflecting on your practice?

2 Who can you ask to give you feedback on your practice?

Learning Outcome 3

FOCUS ON...

how to investigate employment opportunities and routes of progession

In this section you'll learn how to find out about the employment opportunities available to you, and how you can progress in your career.

This links with Assessment Criteria **3.1**

Professional development

You learnt about the importance of continual professional development in Learning Outcome 2. There'll be times in your career when you'll need to access further learning opportunities as part of your continuing professional development.

There's a range of ways for you to learn including:

- Training for higher-level qualifications. This could be via a college or centre, or you could do a distance learning course via mail or email.
- Undertaking short courses to gain specific skills/ qualifications, e.g. first aid, food hygiene, child protection.
- Training to understand new developments such as The Early Years Foundation Stage.
- Training and seminars to develop general skills and knowledge, e.g. managing challenging behaviour, heuristic play, baby massage.
- Undertaking your own learning and research using books, magazines and the internet. It's important to keep yourself up to date with developments in childcare and education. Subscribing to an industry magazine is a good way to do this. (Many settings leave magazines in the staff room for staff to borrow.)

To find out about learning options you can:

- Enquire about in-house learning opportunities at your workplace, and let your workplace know the type of development opportunities you are looking for. It's good practice to negotiate a learning plan with your employer.

The internet is a good source of information ▶

- Contact the local Early Years Development and Childcare Partnership (EYDCP) or Sure Start. They may also have details of funding for learning.
- Request details of learning opportunities from colleges and other training organisations. Enquiries can also be made to Learn Direct – advisers will help you to find the learning opportunity you're looking for in your area. The telephone number to call is 0800 101 901.
- Read about and research up-to-date developments, making use of resources such as the internet, the public library and your workplace reference information. When undertaking web-based research, the sites of national organisations are a good starting point. Ofsted, National Day Nurseries Association, Pre-School Learning Alliance, National Childminding Association and 4Children all have websites, and useful links are provided to further informative sites. See the Follow up section at the end of the unit.

Also, see the Follow up section at the end of the unit.

Employment opportunities

We identified a range of voluntary, statutory and private/independent sector settings for children on page 2. All of these settings will provide employment for childcarer practitioners.

Childcarers now work in a wider range of settings than ever before. There are increasing opportunities within the private and voluntary sectors in settings such as private day nurseries for example, and in play facilities such as out-of-school clubs. Many tour operators employ childcarers abroad in holiday resorts, and there are also employment opportunities in UK holiday venues.

Disabled children are now more widely included in a full range of settings. Happily, this means you should have the opportunity to work with disabled children and non-disabled children side-by-side in the same setting. In the past, childcarers had to work in settings such as residential homes and special schools if they wanted to work with disabled children.

The number of nannies working in the homes of private families continues to increase. Nannies may be residential (live-in) or daily (live-out). There's nanny work available both in the UK and abroad. There are nanny agencies who recruit childcarers and find them work with families, although many families will advertise a nanny position themselves in newspapers and/or magazines. Other families who would like their child to be cared for in a home environment choose a registered childminder. Parents will take the child to be cared for at the home of the childminder each day. Nannies and childminders work with children of all ages and may drop off/collect children from school.

In recent years government strategies have encouraged more multidisciplinary childcare services. This means there are increasing opportunities for professionals whose roles are quite different to work side-by-side in a multidisciplinary team. For instance, someone with a childcare qualification may work with a health visitor or a play worker.

Finding available jobs

Employment opportunities may be advertised in:

- Magazines/journals.
- Local and national newspapers.
- Local authority job bulletins.
- The Job Centre.
- Employment agencies.
- Online.

It makes sense to use all channels open to you to find out about possible employment opportunities. Your family and friends, and the staff and students where you have undertaken training, are all useful contacts. You may like to let the settings you've been to on work placement know when you are looking for a job. They may be interested in

taking you on when they have a vacancy if you impressed them as a student.

Your local Job Centre advertises jobs. They'll also be able tell you which websites, newspapers and so on advertise childcare jobs locally. You'll find your local Job Centre listed in the telephone book. You may also like to look up Connextions, an organisation that helps young people to find work and training. See the Follow up section for further details.

Visit your local Job Centre to find information on current vacancies ▶

Learn the lingo

Job description = list of general tasks or functions and responsibilities of a job.
Terms of employment – contract between the employer and the employee that usually includes details for holiday pay, sickness benefit, pension provision and details of any probation or notice period.
Person specification = profile of the type of person needed to do a job – their qualifications, required experience and personality type. This is usually produced alongside a job description.

Requirements of employers

When you find a job you're interested in, you'll need to contact the person advertising the job. The advertisement will tell you who to contact and whether to call or write in. If you're interested in a job with a statutory, private or voluntary organisation, it's likely that you'll be sent a **job description** and/or **terms of employment.** The job description will outline the role and responsibilities involved in the job. The terms of employment will include details about the hours, holiday entitlement and the pay. A **person specification** may also have been drawn. This will list the qualifications, experience, skills, knowledge and attitude required in any applicant. (This is less likely to be the case when seeking employment as a nanny with a private family.) When you receive employment details from an employer, it's important to go through the details carefully to decide whether to apply for the post.

There's more about this below.

Applying for employment

The Job Centre and Connextions offer job seekers help with applying for jobs, compiling a CV and even interview techniques. (CV stands for curriculum vitae, a document that lists the personal information a potential employer will need to know about you.) You may also have a careers advisor at your centre whose role it is to support you. It makes sense to take advantage of the help available to you. Mock interviews are especially helpful, so do ask your careers adviser about arranging one for you. You can practise answering common questions such as 'Why did you apply for this position?' and get used to telling someone about yourself.

Career progression

In time, it's likely that you'll want to progress in your career. For instance, you may want to become qualified to Level 3, become a team leader or even make a sideways move into another connected field such as playwork.

The Job Centre and Connexions can help you to find out about career progression at any point in your career. They'll advise you about the opportunities available to you, and tell you about any training and qualifications you might need.

Have a go!

Have a go at compiling your own CV following the guidelines below. Ask your supervisor to have a look at it and give you feedback. Is it up to the standard she'd expect from job applicants? Amend your CV if necessary. Remember to update it when you gain new qualifications, complete work experience or attend training.

See Follow up section.

The following guidance is adapted from the book *A Practical Guide to Child-Care Employment* (Hobart and Frankel)

- The CV should be typed or word processed and presented tidily on white A4 paper.
- Stick to a plain font and black print as it looks professional.
- Spelling and grammar must be correct.
- Keep it brief. It should be no more than two pages long.

- Avoid solid blocks of script.
- Use space to emphasise points and make sections stand out.
- Get a tutor or supervisor to check your CV. It may be clear to you but confusing for someone else to read.
- Update your CV regularly.

Your basic CV should include:

- Personal details – full name, address, date of birth, telephone number, email address if relevant.
- Education and qualifications – the schools and college you've been to and the qualifications you've gained, with dates.
- Training – the training you've done that hasn't led to a qualification, e.g. short courses and seminars, with dates.
- Work experience and history – where you've been on placement, where you've worked and your role. This should include all jobs (including part-time/Saturday jobs). Include the date, e.g. 'Nursery Assistant, Apple Day Nursery September 2006 – March 2008.'
- Personal Interest and Hobbies – e.g. do you go to the gym? Do you like to read? Are you an artist? Do you play an instrument?
- Other relevant information – e.g. do you belong to any organisations? Do you do any volunteer work?

Some employers may ask you to complete an application form instead of sending a CV. Read any information sent with it carefully. Complete the form neatly and clearly. All questions should be answered honestly. Use your CV as a guide.

FOCUS ON...
your learning

In this section you've learnt about the organisations that provide employment. You've also learnt how to find out about career progression, and the professional development opportunities that are available to you.

Questions:

1 Name three places to look for a job.

2 How can you find out about career progression?

RAPID RECAP

Learning Outcome 1

You must develop good relationships with the children and adults you work with. Good communication is the heart of forming good relationships. You should communicate sensitively and respectfully in a way that meets the needs of other adults and children. You should practise active listening, and value the communications made to you. You should also be aware of the non-verbal communication of others and yourself.

Learning Outcome 2

Throughout your career it's good practice to reflect regularly on your practice and record your reflections in a diary. Feedback from tutors, supervisors, colleagues, parents/carers and children will aid your reflection. When you've identified areas for professional development, you should set short-, medium- and long-term targets and monitor your progress towards them.

Learning Outcome 3

You can find out about employment opportunities and career progression from the Job Centre, Connextions and your centre's career advisor. There are many other ways to find out about jobs too, including magazines and newspapers. You can access help with job applications and preparing for interviews. You should undertake professional development throughout your career. A range of opportunities is open to you, from higher qualifications to one-off seminars.

FAQ

Q How will I be assessed on this Unit?

A *Your portfolio provides the assessment for this unit.*

Q What will I have to do?

A *Your tutor or Centre will help you to understand the task. It involves providing evidence of your ability 1) to work as a competent practitioner and 2) to be an effective communicator with children and adults.*

See Unit 1 Learning Outcome 5 for more information on study skills.

Weblinks

You may like to visit the following websites:

- www.learndirect.co.uk
  For information about professional development opportunities.

The following sites give up-to-date information about developments in childcare and education:

- www.ofsted.gov.uk
  The site of Ofsted.
- www.ndna.org.uk
  The site of the National Day Nurseries Association
- www.pre-school.org.uk
  The site of the Pre-School Learning Alliance
- www.ncma.org.uk
  The site of the National Childminding Association
- www.4children.org.uk
  The site of 4Children

The following sites are relevant to finding employment and career progression:

- www.connexions-direct.com
  Provides information and advice for young people.
- www.jobcentreplus.gov.uk
  The site for the job centre

The childcare practitioner in the workplace

Learning Outcomes

In this unit you'll learn about:

The professional standards of the practitioner

How to observe development

How to carry out planned play/activities

4 How to use effective communication skills and contribute to positive relationships

This unit has a strong practical focus. You will be assessed via your Placement Summary, Practice Evidence Records and Professional Development Profiles. Because this unit asks you to pull together all your learning and apply it in your practical work with children, there are many links to other units in this book.

Learning Outcome 1

FOCUS ON...
the professional standards of the practitioner

This links with Assessment Criteria **1.1, 1.2, 1.3**

Professionalism

Your aim should be to achieve **professionalism** in your role. You need to take all of the things you learn during your course about what you should do and how you should behave and apply them to your practical work in the setting. You must meet the minimum standards that are required of professional childcarers. But why aim at minimum standards? It's far better to aim high and do the very best work you can for children, families, your setting and for yourself.

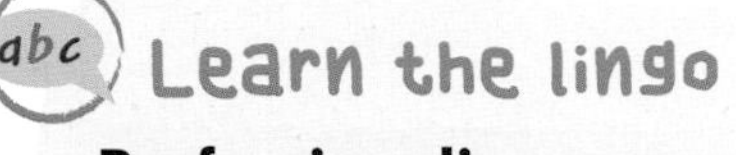

Learn the lingo

Professionalism
= a professional approach to work

Team work and initiative

In all group settings you will need to work as a member of a team of professionals. This may be a **multidisciplinary team**. This means it may include workers from a number of other professional groups, for example teachers and social workers. You need to know who leads/manages the team and their expectations of you as part of the team. You also need to understand the line management of the team, that is, who's in charge of what and whom.

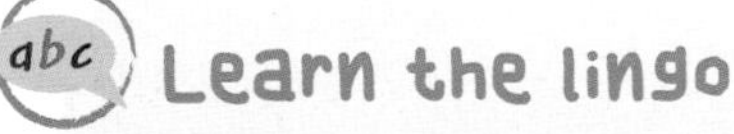

Learn the lingo

Multidisciplinary team
= team including workers from a number of professional groups, e.g. childcarers, teachers, social workers, etc.

You must always act in line with the policies and procedures of the setting, and you mustn't overstep the limits of your role as a learner (as explained in Unit 1). You must also follow the instructions you are given. But once you've settled into a setting and got used to when and how things are done, you'll find that you can start to use your initiative. This means you will start to become of aware of what needs doing and you'll do it without being asked.

Developing the confidence to use your initiative in a range of situations and circumstances in the setting is part of your professional development. You have used your initiative to some degree from your first day in placement. For instance, if a child sitting at the table had dropped a

toy by your feet, you would have picked it up and given it back to them wouldn't you? You wouldn't have waited for a member of staff to ask you. You wouldn't have asked a member of staff if you should pick it up. You would have gotten on and done it because it was obvious to you that it was the right thing to do. As you gain experience and knowledge on your course it will become increasingly clear to you what you should do in a range of circumstances. You'll be able to use your initiative and get on with things.

Most settings have a routine. Make a point of noticing things that get done at a similar time each day. They present a good opportunity to use your initiative. For instance, when the children are asked to tidy up the toys after morning free-play, an adult may go to push the tables together and put the chairs around ready for snack-time. This is something you could do. At first it's a good idea to offer by saying to a member of staff, 'Shall I get the tables ready for snack?', just to be sure they don't mind you taking the initiative. But after that you may feel confident enough to just go and do it. The same applies to lots of other tasks, such as getting the outside toys out of the shed. You'll also develop the confidence to take the initiative necessary to handle issues that arise when you're working directly with children, such as dealing with inappropriate behaviour or comforting a child who is upset.

You can take the initiative by getting outside toys ready ▶

Meetings

Within the work setting there will be many groups meeting formally and informally: staff team meetings, groups of parents/carers, children and other professionals. Groups can be very effective at stimulating new ideas, managing projects, making decisions, monitoring and reviewing progress and supporting group members. Attend meetings if you're given the opportunity as a learner. You may be asked to just listen, depending of the type of meeting. But you

may have the opportunity to contribute ideas, particularly at activity or theme planning meetings. If staff need to discuss something confidential you may be asked to leave the room. Don't be offended as this will be a necessary part of complying with confidentiality procedures.

Carrying out instructions

It goes without saying that you should do as you're asked on placement. But you should also do so willingly! There are some jobs in childcare that few people enjoy – washing up paint pots, cleaning the toys and so on, but they do need to be done and they are part of the job. Approach them with a positive attitude. Your supervisor will be taking notice of how you respond to instructions.

You may need to jot down instructions to make sure that you're able to follow them accurately. You should then try your best to carry out the tasks to the standard required and in the time allocated, making sure that you are aware of the policies and procedures of your workplace.

You will need to ask questions if you don't understand what to do. You may need to say that you can't do some tasks until you've been shown how to do them by someone in a supervisory role, or until you've received appropriate training. It's perfectly fine to say this. Your setting may have several learners coming in and out and staff may not remember what you have yet to learn. You should never overstep your limits as a learner.

Recording information

Your role is likely to involve recording information for a range of purposes. The list below gives an idea of the types of information:

What?

- attendance
- health
- progress
- accidents/incidents
- child protection
- planning
- child observations.

Who for?

- yourself
- line manager
- parents/carers
- team members
- other professionals.

Always make a sure you present written information in the format required by your setting. Work in line with policies and procedures at all times.

Have a go!

Document an imaginary accident/incident in a nursery setting, as you would if completing the accident/incident record book within the nursery.

Unit 1 contains relevant information on professional practice, including details of:

- Confidentiality.
- Timekeeping.
- Dress.
- Personal hygiene.
- Being a good role-model for children.

Details of how you can develop professionally are included in Unit 5.

Personal time management

You will need to manage your time effectively in the work setting. You may also find it helpful to:

- Make lists and add dates/times by which the task needs to be accomplished.
- Prioritise the tasks on the list, i.e. put them in order, which is most important, which must be achieved first, etc.
- Observe and learn from experienced staff how they manage to achieve their tasks within the allocated time.

Commitment

You need to have commitment to both your work in the setting and to your course. The diagram below highlights some ways of bringing commitment to your role.

Commitment ▼

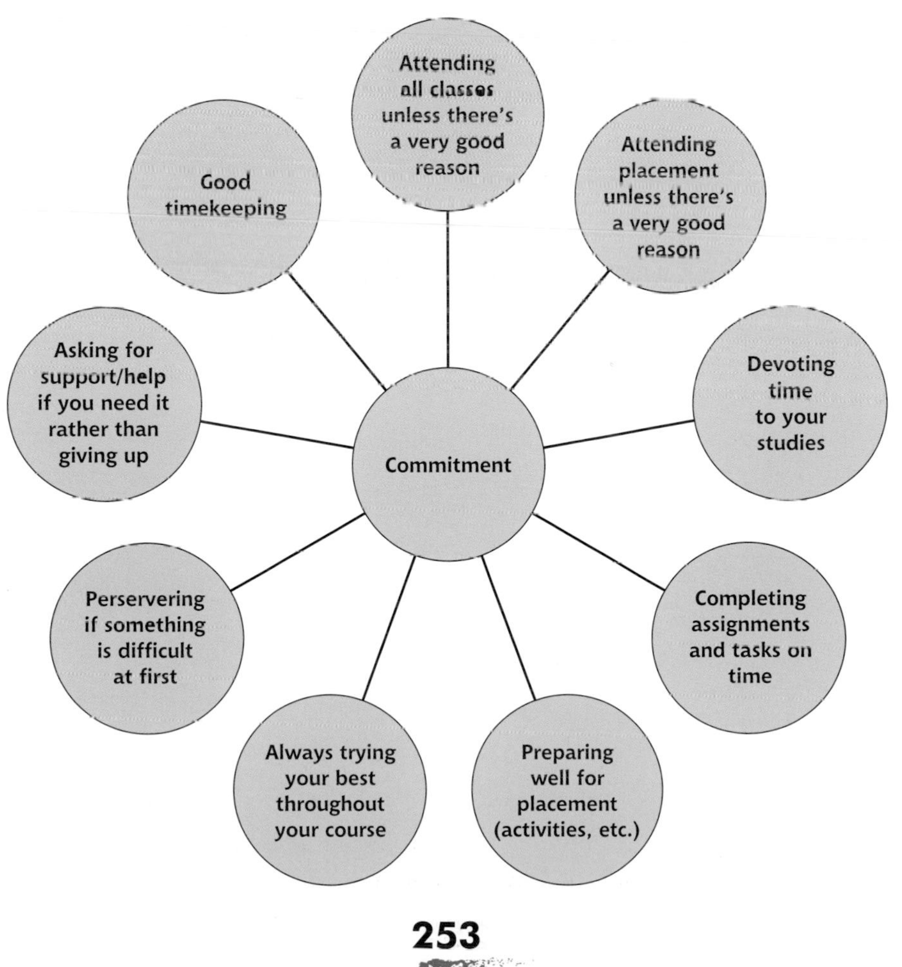

FOCUS ON...
your learning

In this section you've learnt about meeting the professional standards for a childcare practitioner. You've learnt that you need to take all of the things you learn during your course, about what you should do and how you should behave, and apply them to your practical work in the setting.

Questions:

1 What does 'professionalism' mean?

2 What should you do if a colleague asks you to do something you haven't been shown how to do?

Learning Outcome 2

FOCUS ON...
how to observe development

In this section you'll learn about observing children's development and using observations to plan play and activities.

This links with Assessment Criteria **2.1, 2.2**

Observing children aged from birth to 16 years

In Unit 2 you learnt how to carry out observations using a range of methods. It's important to select an appropriate observation method to suit the age of the child you're planning to observe. For instance, some methods, such as checklists, are better suited to observations of babies or young children, especially when you're focusing on the development of skills.

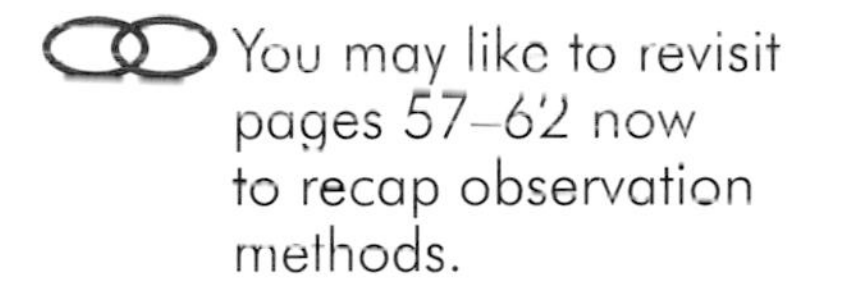

You may like to revisit pages 57–62 now to recap observation methods.

A childcarer observing ▼

Using observations to plan play and activities

It's important that childcarers provide play and activities that meet the needs of all children at the setting. This will help them to reach their full potential. As you learnt in Unit 2, observations help us:

- To assess a child's current stage of development.
- To monitor ongoing development and progress towards national targets that apply to the setting.
- To identify any particular difficulties a child may have.
- To know and understand an individual child better.
- To record any behaviour that causes concern.

Completed observations are useful tools that you should use to inform your planning of play and activities for children. After all, there's little point in carrying out observations if the information isn't put to good use.

Children's development

Childcarers collect information about a new child's current stage of development by carrying out baseline observation. This is very important. Once you know where a child is in terms of their development in different areas, you will have a good idea of the types of play and activities they need and enjoy at this stage. You can now plan effective play and activities for them. You will need a good knowledge of children's patterns of development, as explained in Unit 2.

Children's development progresses over time of course, so the play and activities that a child should experience changes too. Childcarers carry out regular observations to monitor children's ongoing progress. These observations should continue to inform your play and activity plans. When planning, consider what children are likely to learn next and think about activities you can provide to support this development.

When difficulties are identified

During the observation process, you may identify difficulties that an individual child is experiencing. These difficulties could be with particular tasks, such as dressing themselves or counting. Using this information to inform your planning, you can provide play and activities that will help them, such as dressing up or number rhymes. You may plan extra help as well, as shown in the case study below. This enables you to meet children's needs.

You can read more about this in Unit 9, which also gives information about adapting play and activities to meet children's individual needs.

Sometimes you may identify a difficulty not just with a skill or concept, but with a broader aspect of development, such as communication. Or a child may continue to have difficulties for longer than you would expect. When this happens, childcarers need to plan how to support the child.

Think about what children might learn next ▶

Practical example

Sunita dresses up

Children Centre assistant Rachel has learnt from her observations that Sunita is having difficulty putting on and removing her clothing. Today, the dressing-up clothes are available to everyone during free-play time. Rachel has made a note on today's plans to make a point of supporting Sunita when she plays in the dressing up area. She's going to focus on encouraging Sunita to use different fastenings, including zips and buttons.

1 Why did Rachel make the note on the plans?

Knowing and understanding a child better

Observations can help you to get to know individual children better. This knowledge can be very useful when it comes to planning play and activities. Knowing about children's interests and preferences can help you to plan opportunities to appeal to them and engage them. This is helpful generally, but it can be particularly useful when you're working with a child who's struggling with a task, or who's reluctant to join in.

Dressing up gives opportunities to practice using fastenings ▶

For instance, imagine that a child shows little interest in books and tends to stay away from them if possible. You know that he loves to play with the toy farm, particularly the tractors. By borrowing some books from the library containing pictures of tractors and animals and getting hold of one or two stories about farms, it's more likely that you'll be able to motivate the child to look at books and engage with a story. This will create a positive connection to books, which you can build on.

Behaviour

You may have observed behaviour that is cause for concern in a child. In this case, you can plan activities that will help them to overcome the problem. You can also plan how you can support the child during play and activities that might trigger the behaviour.

For instance, imagine an older child becomes aggressive and argumentative when he's out during playground games such as Dodge ball. You may plan to keep a close eye on the game. This will enable you to resolve any disputes about whether the child was out fairly. You'll also be prepared to step in quickly should he become aggressive with his peers. You may also plan plenty of opportunities for him to experience winning and losing in other, less excitable circumstances over the coming weeks. Play activities could include board games, quizzes and competitions for instance.

FOCUS ON...
your learning

In this section you've learnt about how you can use observations to plan play and activities for children. This builds on your learning from Unit 2 about how to carry out observations.

Questions:

1. How can you use your knowledge and understanding of individual children effectively in your planning?
2. How should baseline information about a child's current stage of development inform your planning?

Learning Outcome 3

FOCUS ON...
how to carry out planned play/activities

This links with Assessment Criteria **3.1, 3.2**

Information about planning play activities for children is included in Unit 4 and Unit 10. Details of how to provide a safe and hygienic play environment are included in Unit 3.

Carrying out planned play activities

Encouraging children to participate in activities

You should aim to encourage children to participate in the play activities available to them so they will gain the benefits of each opportunity. But it's important to respect children's freedom of choice too. As you learnt in Unit 4, there are stages in the development of children's play when they can be expected to watch activities from a distance, or to play socially but with little interaction with others. Children need to be supported sensitively through the phases of play. If a young child feels they're being pressurised to do certain tasks they may feel even more like avoiding them in the future. The best way to encourage children to participate is to make activities interesting, attractive and inviting, so children will want to come and take part in them.

Joining in alongside children often gives them the motivation and confidence to try an activity. If a friendly adult sits at a play activity, extra children will usually come along. You have probably had experience of this yourself. To encourage children to stay for a period and engage, try talking to them about what they're doing. You can also ask questions that help them to focus. For instance, you may say, 'Mia's building a house. What are you going to build with bricks, Joe?'

This links with information on exploration and investigation on page 203.

When you notice that a child is engaged and immersed in their play, don't intervene unless it's unavoidable (if they're about to do something unsafe, for instance). Children's concentration is fleeting especially when they're young, so don't distract them needlessly from the important business of focused play.

Have a go!

The next time you want to attract a group of children over to an activity, try out this technique. Let children see you notice the activity and make your way over. Get busy! Become engaged in doing the activity, whatever it is. Be intent. Concentrate. Being interested is interesting! You will probably find that children are soon coming over. They'll be curious about the activity. They'll want to see what you're doing, and hopefully they'll be motivated to try it for themselves.

Don't disturb children immersed in their play needlessly ▼

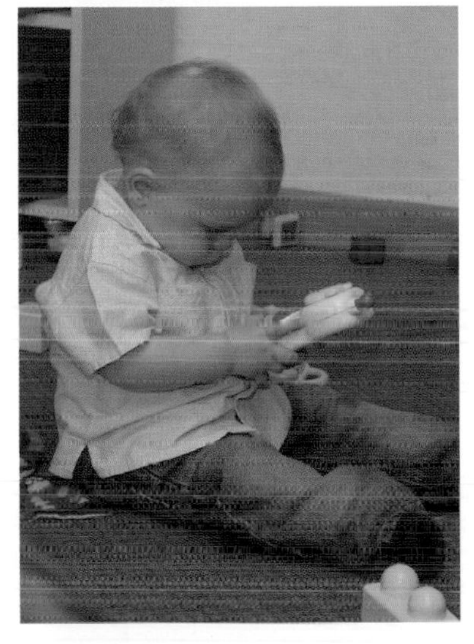

Set activities out attractively ▼

Setting out activities

When setting out activities there are several things to consider:

- Choose an appropriate space – make sure there's enough room, don't block exits or walkways, keep busy activities away from quiet areas such as book corners.
- Keep messy activities in the appropriate place – cover the floor, table, etc., if necessary, make protective clothing available for children.
- Use any safety equipment needed and take any other precautions necessary for health and safety reasons – safety mats, etc.
- Check the condition of resources as you put them out. If any are broken, remove them and let your supervisor know.
- Set out the activity in an attractive, inviting way – take note of how experienced staff do this. For instance, if setting out a home corner you might set the table, put some pans on the cooker and sit a couple of teddies up ready for their dinner. Children are likely to come over to 'feed' them.
- Check you've remembered to put out everything needed.

Clearing away activities

Things to remember when clearing away activities are shown on the diagram on page 262:

GOOD PRACTICE

Helping with tidying up promotes social skills and encourages children to respect their environment. Realistic expectations of what children are likely to achieve are important. It's reasonable to expect younger children to 'show willing' by trying to help, while older children will be able to take more responsibility.

FOCUS ON...
your learning

In this section you've learnt about encouraging children to participate in planned play activities and how to support children in becoming immersed. You've also learnt how you should set out and clear away activities.

Questions:

1 Why shouldn't you disturb a child engaged in play needlessly?

2 Give two examples of how you can encourage children to participate in activities.

Learning Outcome 4

FOCUS ON...

how to use effective communication skills and contribute to positive relationships.

This links with Assessment Criterion **4.1**

Information about how to communicate effectively with children and adults both verbally and non-verbally is given in Unit 5.

Communication skills

Learning how to communicate well is a key part of your role.

Positive relationships

In Unit 5 you learnt that effective communication is important because it's at the heart of maintaining positive relationships with:

- Children
- Staff
- Other professionals
- Parents and carers.

Contributing to positive relationships

Positive relationships have a huge part to play in the quality of provision offered by a setting. The building might be fantastic. The resources might be impressive. But if there aren't positive, professional relationships between children and staff, amongst colleagues and between staff and families, the provision will not rate very highly.

You have a role to play in contributing to positive relationships. Good communication skills and a positive attitude go a long way towards achieving this. You read about displaying a positive attitude in Unit 1, Learning Outcome One. You may like to recap now. You'll also find further information about relationships in the same section.

FAST FACT

There are rare occasions when a professional needs to takes time off for 'compassionate reasons' such as the death of a family member.

Professional relationships between staff and parents are important ▲

Conflict

There are very few relationships that don't experience conflict at some time. In all settings there are times when conflict arises between adults. You're bound to experience conflict in the workplace at some point in your career. But there are strategies that will help you to resolve conflict positively, while maintaining a good relationship. Typical situations that cause conflict include:

- Workers feeling that others are not sharing responsibilities or tasks. They may express this by saying that a colleague is not pulling their weight.
- People have different ways of doing things, and adults may feel that their way is the right way, or the best way. So they may be unwilling to compromise.
- Change is challenging for many people. Adults may find changes of plan and staff changes unsettling, and they may be reluctant to accept new circumstances.
- People making comments that are insensitive, or inappropriate, to or about another person. This can lead to hurt feelings and resentment.

Resolving conflict

It's important to act professionally. Conflict should normally be worked through in a discussion between the people involved. This should be done at an appropriate

GOOD PRACTICE

When you work with children it's important that your temperament is steady and consistent, whatever is happening in your own personal life. You may have heard it said that you shouldn't 'bring your problems to work'. This means that you must put your personal problems, issues and feelings aside when you come into a setting. It's unfair to the children and staff not to. You must always be a professional with a positive attitude.

time, away from the children. Children should not be aware of conflict between adults.

If disagreements arise when adults are with the children, they can be raised and resolved later on. Knowing this should help you to feel prepared to overcome any negative feelings you may have at the time, and to get on with working professionally. But you should make sure that you don't leave matters longer than necessary. It's better to catch conflict early and deal with it before resentment builds up. If you have an issue, always raise it with an appropriate person at a suitable time, rather than grumbling or gossiping behind someone's back. This leads to bad feeling and it is unprofessional.

There may be exceptional circumstances when you have to speak up right away on a matter of conflict because not to do so might harm a child's safety or welfare. If a colleague was about to do something you considered unsafe, for instance.

Techniques for resolving conflict

There are various techniques for resolving conflict. Some settings have guidelines and procedures to help staff and you should work in line with these. It can be helpful to read through the procedures again at times of conflict.

Resolution techniques centre on discussion, and will vary according to the situation. They include the following steps, which can be helpful in most circumstances:

- Approaching the resolution process positively.
  There may be an issue, but you are going to sort it out calmly – think positively.
- Understanding an issue fully.
  Knowing what exactly an issue is. If you have an issue, you should think it through carefully before you raise it with someone else. If someone raises an issue with you, make sure you fully understand their source of conflict – repeat it back to them. Check you have understood correctly.
- Noticing and identifying feelings.
  Take time to notice how you, and other people, are feeling about an issue. Does everyone feel the same? Sometimes understanding each other's feelings is enough to resolve conflict.

- Looking for solutions.
  There may be an outright solution that will work for everyone, or a good compromise. However, compromises may not be possible, not only because they can be difficult to reach, but because it may breach regulations to compromise on certain issues, for instance safety or confidentiality.
- Referring to senior staff if you need support.
  You may want the advice of senior staff before dealing with conflict. Or, you may want to refer to a superior if a solution cannot be agreed. Sometimes a superior may act as a mediator for adults (someone on neither person's side who helps to resolve the conflict).
- Reviewing.
  Set a time to review the situation. Has the solution worked, or do you need to think again?

GOOD PRACTICE

If you experience conflict while on placement, it's a good idea to talk to your workplace supervisor and/or your tutor for advice before taking action.

Information about an inclusive approach can be found in Units 1, 4 and 11.

An inclusive approach

Treating everyone fairly is essential to maintaining positive relationships.

FOCUS ON...
your learning

In this section you've learnt about the importance of using effective communication skills and a positive attitude to contribute to positive relationships. You've also learnt how to resolve conflict professionally while maintaining positive relationships. There are links with information contained in Units 1, 4, 5 and 11.

Questions:

1 Name two factors that contribute to positive relationships within the setting.

2 Who can you ask for advice if you experience conflict on placement?

RAPID RECAP

Learning Outcome 1

You must meet the professional standards for a childcare practitioner. You need to take all of the things you learn during your course about what you should do and how you should behave and apply them to your practical work in the setting. You must be a good role-model for children at all times, and aim to work effectively as part of a professional team. You should bring professionalism and commitment to your role.

Learning Outcome 2

Observing helps you to know and understand children better. You'll gather information about their development, any difficulties they may have, and notice behaviour that causes concern. You should use this information to help you plan play and activities that promote development and meet children's needs. You can also plan to support children during their free play.

Learning Outcome 3

You should aim to encourage children to participate in the play activities available to them so they will gain the benefits of each opportunity. But it's important to respect children's freedom of choice too. To appeal to children, plan interesting activities and set them out attractively in an appropriate place. Support children sensitively to help them to concentrate and engage. Don't disturb a child focused on their play needlessly. Clear away thoroughly after your activities. There are links with information contained in Units 3, 4 and 10.

Learning Outcome 4

Effective communication skills are important. They are at the heart of developing and maintaining positive relationships with others. In order to contribute to good relationships you must communicate well and display a positive attitude. If you experience conflict you should resolve it professionally through calm discussion. There are links with information contained in Units 1, 4, 5 and 11.

FAQ

Q How will I be assessed on this Unit?

A *You will be required to complete your Placement Summary, Practice Evidence Record and Professional Development Profiles.*

Q What about my placement diary?

A *It will be marked by your tutor and verified by your placement supervisor as part of the evidence you need to provide for you Practice Evidence Records.*

Weblinks

You may like to visit the followng websites:

The following sites give information and advice on providing high-quality childcare and education

- www.ofsted.gov.uk
  The site of Ofsted.
- www.ndna.org.uk
  The site of the National Day Nurseries Association
- www.pre-school.org.uk
  The site of the Pre-School Learning Alliance
- www.ncma.org.uk
  The site of the National Childminding Association
- www.4children.org.uk
  The site of 4Children

Also see the activity related sites listed at the end of Unit 4.

Working with children from birth to age 5 years

Learning Outcomes

In this unit you will learn about:

1. How to plan and support environments for children.

2. How to contribute to working with parents as part of a team.

3. How to recognise the importance of working with other professionals.

4. How to meet the diverse needs of babies and young children.

This Unit contains several links to other Units within this book.

Learning Outcome 1

FOCUS ON...

how to plan and support environments for children

In this section you'll learn how to plan and support environments for children from birth to 5 years.

This links with Assessment Criteria **1.1, 1.2**

The importance of children's welfare

Further information about this is included later in this section and also within Units 2 and 3.

Children's welfare **should always be your first concern** as a childcarer. YOUR MAIN RESPONSIBILITIES ARE TO MEET CHILDREN'S NEEDS AND TO PROTECT THEM FROM HARM.

Layout and organisation of the environment

An important part of the childcarer's role is to provide a healthy, hygienic and safe environment for young children.

Group provision is provided in different kinds of premises. This includes purpose-built accommodation, village halls and family homes. A well-planned layout can make a setting a welcoming, safe, secure and reassuring environment for children. The diagram on page 271 shows the factors room layout can affect.

Most settings will vary the use of their premises throughout sessions, changing the position of tables and so on to suit the activities currently taking place. Other pieces of furniture such as storage units may be rarely moved. The selection and position of furniture and equipment contributes greatly to the overall effect of the environment. Safety must be a priority.

Safety within settings is covered within Unit 3.

Key issues to consider when selecting furniture and equipment include:

- Is the furniture/equipment appropriate for the children's age and stage of development?
  If not, it could be unsafe. Look for the manufacturer's guidance and the safety marks. Chairs and tables should be of the correct height for the children. Weight

Factors room layout can affect ►

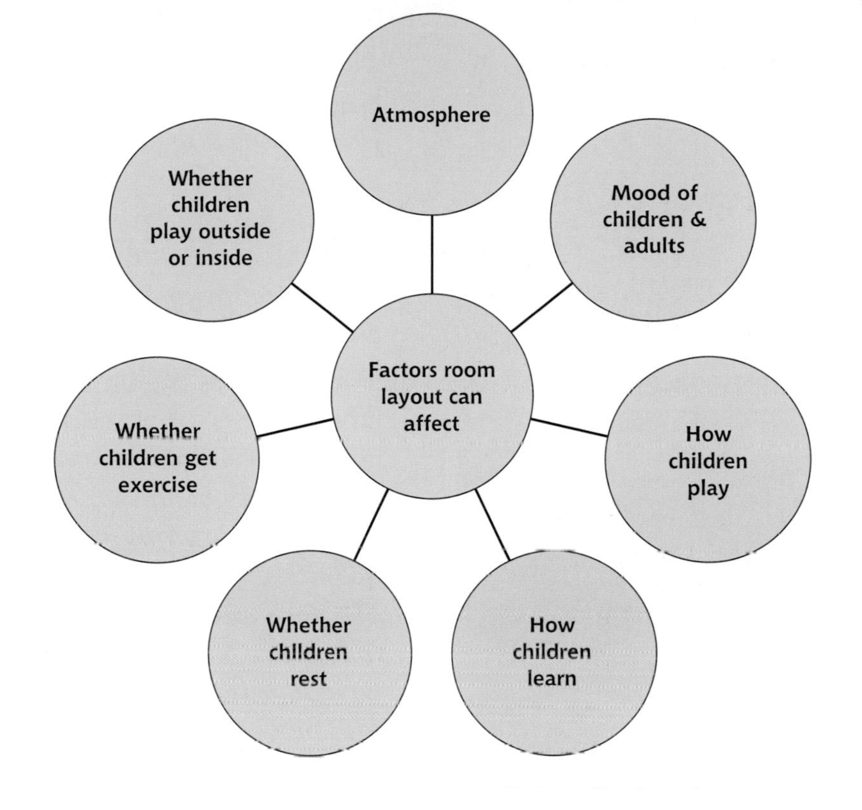

restrictions may be given for furniture such as high chairs or babies' floor seats. Sometimes, settings may need to consult specialists, parents and carers if a piece of equipment/furniture must meet the needs of a child with additional needs.

- What size is the furniture/equipment?
  It's always best to measure new items to be sure they are the right size for the setting.
- How will the furniture/equipment be used?
  Because both space and money is limited, many settings try to purchase furniture/equipment that can be used in different ways or for a number of different activities. For instance, a storage unit may have a work surface. A bookcase may have a cork board attached.
- Where will equipment/furniture be stored?
  If it won't be in use all the time, settings need somewhere suitable for storage.
- Is the furniture/equipment durable and easy to clean?
  Choosing equipment that won't withstand group use and frequent cleaning isn't good value for money in the long run.

The temperature of the setting should be kept between 16–24°C (60–75°F) and ventilation should allow fresh air to circulate.

When deciding on the layout of the environment, it's important to:

- Provide comfortable, quiet areas for rest.
  This may be done through the provision of large floor cushions/children's beanbags/upholstered children's furniture such as sofas. The area should be away from noisy, busy activities. Screens may be used to give the area a feeling of separateness. In the case of settings caring for young children, this area will be in addition to the sleeping area, where cots/beds will be provided.
- Provide areas for physical activity and exercise.
  Physical exercise is essential to children's health and their development. Settings should ensure children have regular opportunities and enough space for physical activities. While the ideal is to have an outdoor area of a good size, outdoors shouldn't be thought if as the only space for physical activities. Large equipment can be used inside if necessary. Activities such as music and movement and dance often take place inside. The outdoor play space should be safe and secure. It should ideally provide a variety of surfaces, covered areas for wet weather, shady areas for sunny days and space to run around and use the wheeled toys safely. Trees and plants and an area to be used for growing add to the children's learning experiences.

Physical activity is essential to children's health ▼

- Promote hygiene and cleanliness.
  Set up messy activities in areas that have furniture and flooring that can be cleaned easily. Make sure there's easy access to sinks for hand-washing. You don't want children trailing paint over carpeted areas on their way to the bathroom.
- Choose the location of each activity carefully.
  Position quiet activities away from noisy or busy ones. This helps children not to disturb each other and they won't have to be told to keep the noise down needlessly. Give activities the space they need. Overcrowded areas or equipment can be dangerous and difficult to supervise. Restrict the number of children permitted in an area/at equipment at one time if necessary, e.g. only four on the climbing frame at once. Follow safety procedures such as putting the slide on even ground and using safety matting. Ensure that resources don't obstruct fire exits at any time.

- Meet everyone's needs.
  Considering the needs of all the children, leave sufficient room for children to move around the play space between the activities, furniture and equipment. Also ensure that activities, furniture and equipment are accessible.

See Unit 9 for further details.

- Ensure a balanced layout.
  Children need opportunities to engage in different types of play and the layout of the environment (and the activities offered) should enable this. For example, children need opportunities for imaginative play as well as physical play. They need opportunities for rest as well as for exercise.

  Childcarers must make sure the environment supports planning for children's play and learning, and supports the curriculum if one applies to the setting.

There's more about this in Units 4 and 8.

There are further details about this in Unit 10.

Details are given on page 380.

- Use appropriate safety equipment.
  There are various pieces of safety equipment available. Using such equipment can effectively minimise the risk of accident or injury to children.

Full details are included within Unit 9.

- Adapt the environment.
  It's important that the environment meets the needs of all children, whatever their age, gender, individual needs and abilities. You must identify and address barriers within the environment that prevent children from participating.

There's further information on page 125.

- Ensure security.
  Young children should not be able to leave the setting themselves, and visitors should not be able to enter without the knowledge of staff. Follow the security arrangements in your setting strictly, e.g. shut doors and gates behind you, make sure the outside gate is shut before letting children into the outside area.

Details of the health and safety requirements that apply to premises and working with young children are included with Unit 3

Have a go!

Imagine you're going to provide a morning crèche in your room for children aged two and a half to five years. Decide what areas you would divide the room into, e.g. a quiet place for rest, messy areas, somewhere to eat and drink etc. When you have a list, mark on your outline where you would position each area. Draw on key pieces of furniture or resources, e.g. the messy play table.

Also see page 138.

- Ensure pets are kept safely.
  Pets must be kept well away from any food preparation areas. Pets and their homes must be kept clean and healthy.

Large equipment can be used inside ▶

Have a go!

Part one

Choose an indoor space you know well that isn't currently used for childcare purposes, such as a classroom at your Centre. Sketch the outline of the room on a large piece of paper, showing where features like doors, windows and radiators are. Make a second copy of the plan to use in the second part of this task, which appears later in this section.

Planning environments for babies and toddlers

Babies and toddlers need to have plenty of clear floor space. Very young babies will need room to lie out comfortably on baby mats placed on the floor. There should be enough space for them to roll around freely. They'll also spend some time in baby chairs. As babies start to crawl they need plenty of room to manoeuvre and explore. When babies first start to walk they fall over often. Moving around in an open area means there's less chance of babies injuring themselves on furniture.

FAST FACT

Lighting should be adequate for the activities provided. Diffused lighting may be used in rest and sleep areas. Children with visual impairments may need additional task lighting to be provided at activity points.

As they grow into busy toddlers, children enjoy moving around a room quite quickly, making the most of the space they have to play in. They have not yet developed the concentration span needed to spend very long in one place doing one activity.

There's more about this on page 270.

GOOD PRACTICE

Floor space must also be allocated to the equipment that's needed by this age group – high chairs and cots take up quite a lot of space in group settings. The stability of the furniture chosen is important as babies will use it to pull themselves to a standing position. They will also hold onto it for support when they first start to walk. Because childcarers need to ensure that the layout leaves plenty of clear floor space, it makes sense to keep furniture to a minimum. Settings generally ask adults and children to remove their outdoor shoes before entering baby rooms. This helps to keep carpets and soft furnishings clean and hygienic.

Feeling secure and reassured

Welcoming children into an attractive and thoughtfully arranged environment will help to reassure them and help them settle in. Settings should be geared to the needs of the children with child sized equipment, attractive displays and a pleasant, calm atmosphere. Using attractive curtains, soft furnishing and wall coverings will add to the general attractiveness and comfort of the setting. Cloakrooms, washbasins and toilets should be easily accessible and ideally child-sized to promote security and growing independence.

Providing a routine will help children to feel secure. They will become familiar with the structure of the day and will become more confident as they recognise familiar times and begin to know where they fit in.

A sense of belonging

Children need to develop a sense of belonging. They will feel more at home in a setting that contains things that are personal and familiar to them and that reflect their own experiences and culture.

- Each child should have a coat hook, ideally labelled with their name and a picture that they'll learn to recognise.
- Other equipment such as bags and lunch boxes should be named.

There's more about this on page 298.

- The activities, displays and resources in the setting should reflect the diversity of society. Children should be able to personally identify with their surroundings.
- The displays should contain the children's work and reflect their interests.

Children need plenty of space to play, but smaller areas should be provided for some types of activities, such as messy play and imaginative play areas. This will help children to concentrate more easily and work with a partner or in smaller groups. But it also helps children not to feel overwhelmed or insecure in a huge space. This is particularly important for settings such as pre-schools who may meet in a large community hall. A carpeted area is good for bringing the children together for stories and circle time.

FAST FACT

Working in partnership with parents and carers and involving families in the setting helps young children to feel reassured and secure. You'll read more about this in Learning Outcome 2.

Access to activities and play materials

Most settings will put out some activities and play materials before the children arrive. This is good because it makes the environment welcoming and stimulating. It allows children to come in and settle down to play right away. But if staff only allow children to play with the items they've chosen for the group, they're not truly promoting free play because the children are not exercising free choice. When encouraging children to select and access materials independently, consider:

- Labelling containers of resources with words and/or pictures for easy selection.
- Using low, child-sized furniture for storage.
- Making art and craft resources freely available as well as toys and equipment.
- Encouraging children to put away the resources as they finish with them. This avoids the setting becoming cluttered. Sometimes you may need to ask children to wait until some resources are finished with before any more are set out.
- Ensuring resources that are too heavy/awkward/big for children to manage are still accessed by adults – let children know they can ask for these things. Adults should also be responsible for assembling equipment that must be put together carefully for safety reasons.

GOOD PRACTICE

It's good practice to allow children plenty of choice in the resources they use. Ideally play materials should be stored safely, somewhere that children can easily access them. This allows children to be independent in selecting and fetching resources. Children can also be independent in tidying away resources after use. Children should be encouraged to value and care for their environment.

- Ensuring resources that require close supervision (such as tools) are not freely accessible.
- Ensuring children only have free access to materials suitable for their age, needs and abilities.

Have a go!

Part two

Using the second outline you made of a room in part one, repeat the task, this time planning an environment suitable for children aged birth to two years.

Involving children in decisions about their environment

Children generally enjoy being involved in decisions about their environment. This helps them to have a feeling of ownership of their setting, and gives them a sense of belonging. Young children may be involved in making small decisions at first. For instance, you might ask whether the group would like to have story time inside or outside today. As children grow up they'll be able to make more and bigger decisions.

Consistency and stability

Children tend to feel more settled and secure when they have consistency and stability in their lives. Settled and secure children are more likely to be happy and to learn and play well. The following diagram shows factors that can contribute to consistency and stability.

Children tend to need less structure as they grow up, but things like a consistent home life and good relationships with childcarers remain important for all children. Many settings use a keyworker system because of this.

See page 69 for information about the role of the keyworker, and pages 396–408 for details about supporting children and families who are new to the setting.

Changes to environments

Sometimes unforeseeable changes occur within children's environments. Some emergency maintenance work may be needed to a room of a setting's premises, for instance. When this happens, childcarers should explain changes clearly to children and families, as they can be unsettling.

Consistency and stability ▶

You should also be sensitive to the fact that young children especially may require reassurance and comfort when unforeseeable changes occur. If changes to a room for young children are planned, it's best to introduce them gradually if possible.

Positive, enabling environments

Childcarers want to help children to develop and progress. You've learnt how providing the right resources, activities and experiences helps children's development. But there's more that can be done. You can support children further by providing an environment that's both positive and enabling.

You can help create a positive and enabling environment by:

- Showing respect for every child you work with.
  Helping children to develop a sense of self-worth and self-respect.
- Removing barriers to participation.
  Helping children to learn and experience that everyone can join in together, and that individuality is valued
- Encouraging children to try new things.
  Helping children to develop confidence and self-esteem.

See Unit 9.

- Encouraging children to be independent when appropriate.
  Helping children to develop self-reliance and confidence.
- Ensuring that resources are accessible.
  Helping children to be independent and resourceful.
- Acknowledging individual children's contributions.
  Helping children to develop confidence and self-esteem, and teaching them to value other people's contributions.
- Acknowledging individual children's achievements.
  Helping children to develop confidence and self-esteem and fostering a love of learning.

Displays encourage children to look and think ▼

Displaying children's work

Displays and interest tables are an effective way of creating a stimulating and attractive environment for children.

Display has many values. It can:

- Show children that their work is appreciated.
- Encourage children to have a sense of pride in their work.
- Be used as a tool for learning.
- Encourage children to look, think, reflect, explore, investigate and discuss.
- Provide a sensory and imaginative experience.
- Encourage parental involvement in their children's learning (parents/carers will see displays when they enter the setting).
- Be used to promote positive images and to reflect our diverse society.
- Make the environment attractive, adding colour, vibrancy and texture.

See page 300 for further details.

FAST FACT

The entrance area gives the first impression of the setting to children, parents and visitors. A welcoming entrance with displays of children's work will contribute to giving a positive impression.

Where to put displays

Displays should be placed where they can be seen easily and touched if appropriate. It's worth getting down to children's level to view surroundings. This will give you the best idea of where to put displays. The obvious place is on a wall, where many settings have large framed corkboards dedicated to displays. But the ceiling can also make an effective display space, especially for hanging artwork.

Doors and the ends of furniture such as bookcases can be used. Displays can also be placed in windows. Work that contains materials that catch the light (such as shiny paper) or that light will pass through (such as cellophane or tissue paper) look particularly effective here.

What to include in displays

Variety makes displays interesting. Displays can include:

- Children's paintings and other individual work.
- Children's co-operative efforts.
- Natural materials and plants.
- Objects of interest, such as photographs, pictures, collage and real objects.
- Use of different colours, textures and labelling.

On page 196 you learnt to value the process children experience when creating artwork, as well as their end product.

FAST FACT

Using labels and captions on displays helps to introduce young children to the concept that print carries meaning. Written questions such as, 'How many bears can you see?' encourage adults and children to interact with a display together.

It's important to remember this when selecting work for display. What the work means to children is much more important than how it looks to an adult. All children should be able to contribute to the displays in their environment. When looking around their room, every child should have at least one piece of their work displayed or have taken part in a group display. This will help children to feel they're part of the setting and that their work is valued. Children should be involved in the choice of work that will be displayed and, where possible, in the mounting of work and the creation of the display.

Labels and captions must be:

- Clear.
- An appropriate size.
- In lower case letters, except at the beginning of sentences and proper nouns.
- Correctly spelt.

Settings should also include the home languages of the children amongst their display (parents are often willing to help with this). If labels and captions are hand-written they should be carefully printed. It's important to practise printing using guidelines to help you until you're confident enough to print free-hand. Many settings use

pre-cut letters or computer printouts. The style of printing used varies from setting to setting. Always check your own setting's requirements before starting work on a display.

You've learnt that displays should reflect our diverse society. Children should also be given the opportunity to represent themselves accurately in their artwork. Crayons, pencils, felt-tips and paints are available in a range of skin tones.

Have a go!

Taking your notepad with you, stand in front of a display you like at your workplace. What is it that appeals to you exactly? Make notes about the display's striking features. Is there a good use of colour? What about texture? Does the backing and/or border complement the display? Is it for touching as well as looking at? How have the labels/captions been printed? Think about how you could incorporate similar features in your own displays.

Planning displays

It's important to plan displays, thinking everything through first. Once you've decided what to include and where to put the display, think about colours, backing and borders. Good presentation is essential, including good mounting and well-produced lettering. Staples, sticky tape or sticky tack should be used discreetly so they don't detract the viewers' eyes from the work.

There are no rules when it comes to colour. Bright colours can be effective, while contrasting colours like black and white make for a bold look that catches the eye. Use of pastels can draw viewers to a display, but are best used in areas where children will be able to get right up close to the work. Mounting pastel-coloured work on a darker background will help to make it stand out.

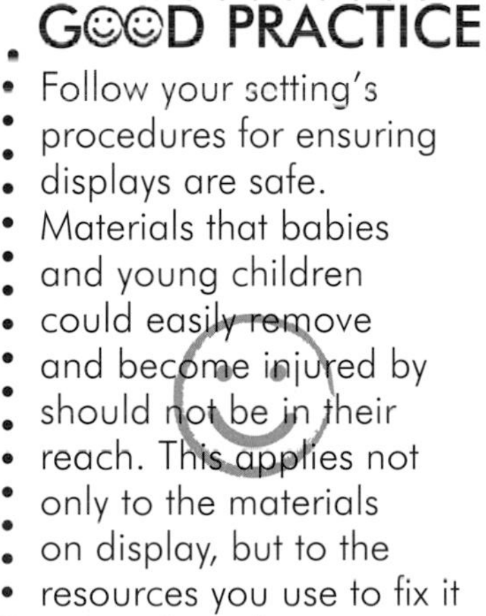

Think about safety while putting up your display too. Don't leave potentially dangerous objects such adult's scissors or staplers within children's reach. It's good practice to involve children in mounting a display when appropriate to their age and abilities. But it may be necessary to put up the backing paper yourself first when children are not around. This is because it's a fiddly job that involves using adult tools and it's difficult to supervise children safely at the same time. After working on a display, check carefully that you haven't dropped any resources such as pins or staples.

Interest tables

Interest tables can be used to follow a theme or topic. They can also be used to display work, or collections from a recent outing. The display should be at children's height and positioned in a quieter area of the setting. The table should be covered and any objects that are not intended to be touched should be placed in a protective container, such as a sealed plastic tank.

Helping children to learn about the natural world is important and seeing how things grow and develop is part of learning about the world. Children can collect and display natural objects such as leaves and plants (be aware of the dangers of poisonous plants). Adding non-fiction books to the table gives children and adults words and pictures to refer to and can extend learning and understanding.

See page 205 for details.

Interest tables are not generally suitable for babies and very young children. But you can introduce objects of interest through heuristic play with this age group.

Adding interest to displays

Interest can be added to displays by good use of:

- *colour* – backing, mountings and borders can be used to display the children's work to its best advantage.
- *texture* – include things that are interesting to touch and contrast with each other, for example smooth silver foil and rough, flat sandpaper.
- *movement* – including hanging displays and objects that move (such as windmills).
- *sound* – including objects that crunch, rustle, crackle. Interest tables may feature shakers and musical instruments made by the children for instance, or a collection of bells.
- *characters that are familiar to the children* – from books read at story time, people they have met on a trip or people who have visited the setting. Photos can be used as well as drawings.

FAST FACT

The length of time a display remains should be considered and planned. Any display that has become old or faded should be replaced.

Physical and health needs

It's important to have responsive, reflective and knowledgeable adults caring for babies and young children. 'Responsive care' is the term used to describe

how childcarers identify and respond to the care needs of children. You must be able to provide responsive care for babies and very young children as they don't generally have the language to explain to adults what they need. You must learn to interpret this for yourself. This will depend on your knowledge and understanding of:

- The development pattern of babies and children.
- The individual baby or child.

Look out for signs of tiredness ▼

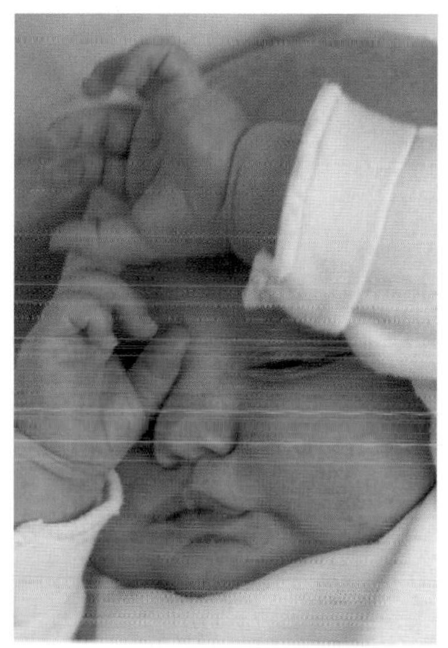

For instance, a baby may cry for a number of reasons. You need to find out what's wrong so you can attend to the child. You'll need to look for signs accompanying the crying in order to work out what the baby needs. You'll need to consider what you know about babies in general, as well as what you know about the individual child. This will help you to find out if the baby is:

- Tired
  Are they rubbing their eyes or yawning? Are they blinking heavily and slowly? When did they last sleep? Do they often sleep around this time?
- Hungry
  When did they last have a feed? Did they take all of their feed? Are they ready to start weaning – perhaps they're the right age and seem to be hungry again a short time after feeding?
- Lonely
  Are they alone? Do they need a cuddle or someone to play with? In the case of a baby who cannot crawl yet, do they need to be repositioned nearer other children for company?
- Bored
  Have they been in the same position or playing with the same toy for some time? Have they got access to resources or activities likely to stimulate them at their stage of development?
- Unwell
  Is the child displaying any signs or symptoms of illness? Is the child the right age to be teething, and are they showing any signs of this (dribbling, red cheek, inflamed gums)?
- In need of a nappy change
  A quick check will reveal if the child is wet or dirty.

This links with Unit 3.

- Frightened
  Has the baby been startled by a sudden or loud noise? Have they seen a stranger? Do older, mobile children scare certain younger babies when their play becomes boisterous or too close to them?
- Frustrated
  Is the child experiencing difficulty with a task? Are they frustrated because they can't reach a toy they've dropped? Or are they hungry but struggling to feed themselves – has most of the food ended up on the floor?

FAST FACT

With experience, responsive care becomes a very natural, intuitive part of a childcarer's role.

Good childcarers are constantly using their **responsive care** skills. These skills are informed by experience – the more time you spend with babies and young children, the more 'tuned in' you'll become to recognising their care needs.

Learn the lingo

Responsive care = the term used to describe how childcarers identify and respond to the care needs of children.

One of the most effective ways to learn from experience is to be a reflective practitioner. Reflective practitioners think about their practice, notice areas for development and plan how to improve their knowledge, understanding and skills. Reflection is a key part of developing the skills of responsive caring. It's important to have reflective and knowledgeable childcarers working with this age group, because responsive caring is at the heart of providing high-quality care for babies and young children.

See Unit 5 for further details.

Have a go!

Further information about meeting the needs of babies and young children are included within Unit 2. You're advised to re-read Unit 2 as part of your study towards Unit 7. There's more information about policies and procedures on page 164.

Staffing levels and supervision

There's information about levels of supervision and the required ratios of adults to children on pages 112 and 118.

Babies and very young children need constant and close supervision. They must not be left unsupervised at any time. In addition, much adult time is spent attending to their physical care needs. Childcarers will be making up feeds, feeding, changing nappies and so on. Babies and very young children also need to have the time and attention of adults to meet their emotional needs.

FOCUS ON...
your learning

In this section you've learnt about how to plan and promote a healthy, hygienic and safe environment for children. You've learnt how the environment can offer reassurance and security, and how to make good use of displays. You've also learnt how to meet basic health and physical needs through responsive care. Links to other Units give information on health and safety, meeting physical and health needs, adapting environments and promoting positive images.

Questions:

1 Why is responsive care important?

2 What are your main responsibilities as a childcarer?

Learning Outcome 2

FOCUS ON...

how to contribute to working with parents as part of a team

This links with Assessment Criteria **2.1, 2.2**

Relationships with families

You must always respect and value the important role family members play in their children's lives. Parents are usually the primary carers of children. They usually know their children best and have a closer bond with them than anyone. It's your role as a childcarer to form partnerships with families based on this fact. Children generally feel a deep sense of love and connection with their parents and carers. They are usually the most consistent people throughout a child's life to provide them with love, affection and care. Children share experiences with family members that they will remember for the rest of their lives.

Benefits of good relations between families and childcarers ►

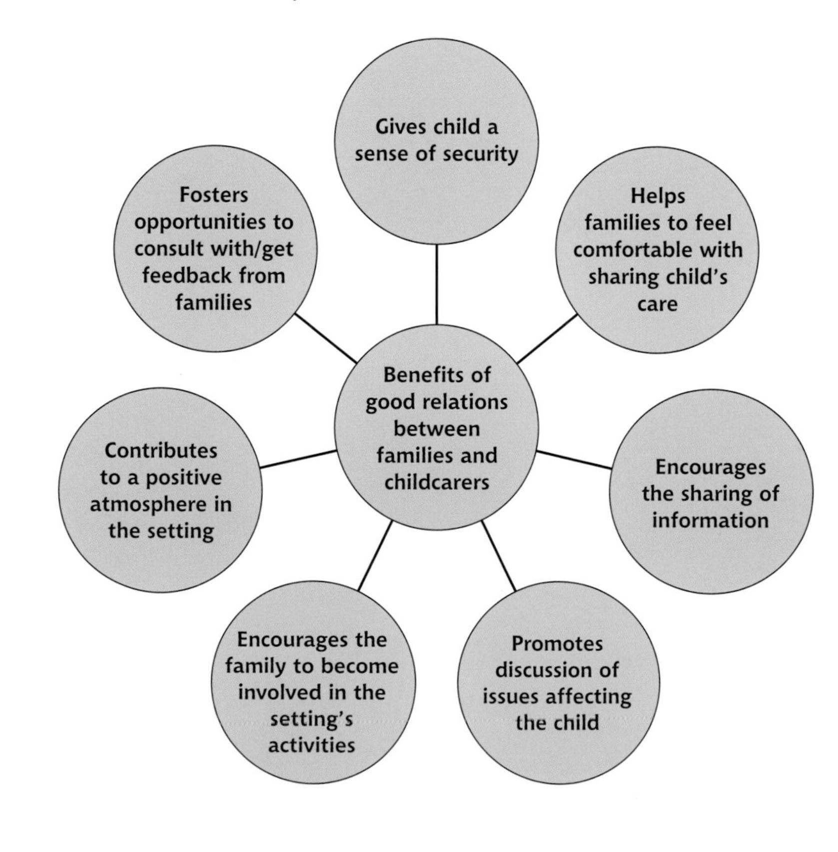

The diagram above shows the benefits of good relationships between families and childcarers. The benefits explain why good relationships are so important.

Shared care

We know that children are generally regarded as very precious by their parents and other family members. It's normal for parents to feel anxious at first about sharing the care, learning and development of their child with childcarers. But as a positive relationship is established between parents and childcarers over time, trust is built. Parents generally begin to gain confidence in both the individual staff members and the setting as a whole. Good relationships and sharing information are key to effective shared care.

GOOD PRACTICE

Good childcarers work in partnership with parents and carers. But this can only be achieved when a positive relationship has been established. The relationship between a child's keyworker and their parents is particularly important, as the keyworker will normally be the parent's main point of contact with the setting.

The role of the keyworker

You'll find further details about the role of the keyworker on page 69.

Keyworkers are particularly important for babies and young children. This is because sharing information about care matters (such as how/when children have slept and taken feeds) is crucial. The younger the child the more necessary close bonds with consistent adults are to promote feelings of security and reassurance.

FAST FACT

Families are much more likely to share important information and concerns with childcarers when a positive relationship exists.

Effective communication

Good general communication skills are necessary when working with families.

Details of these are included within Unit 5.

Following the procedures of your setting, choose the most appropriate method of communication for your message. For instance, details of when a baby slept and their feeds throughout the day may be provided in a written report handed to a parent when they collect their child. The findings of observations and development checks may be shared in a one-to-one meeting between families and their keyworker.

Always respect confidentiality when dealing with information. See page 228.

Family backgrounds will reflect different cultures, religions and beliefs ▼

Childcarers must also follow their setting's procedures for recording information given to them by families, and for passing it on the colleagues and managers when appropriate. As mentioned in Unit 1, when you're a learner on work placement you mustn't overstep the limits of your role. If a parent or carer asks for or tries to give you information about their child, you should tell them you're a learner and so you must fetch a member of staff for them.

Valuing diverse family backgrounds

A wide range of types of families love and care successfully for children. Family backgrounds will reflect different cultures, religions, beliefs and relationships between adults. Some children will live with family members other than their parents. Some children will live with carers they are not related to biologically (by blood). Some children may live within social care facilities rather than a family home. Some children may divide their time between more than one home. You should value and accept the diverse family backgrounds of all children and the homes in which they live.

Encouraging participation within the setting

When you encourage families to participate within a setting, you show them that they're valued and respected by childcarers. You can also strengthen the partnership between the setting and families, which is good for everyone concerned. There are many ways to encourage families to participate, including:

- Invitations to social activities, such as fundraising events or coffee mornings.
- Invitations to join the setting's committee.
- Invitations to annual general meetings (AGMs), perhaps with a crèche facility to enable attendance.
- Running family sessions, where adults can attend with their child and the child's siblings.
- Having training or information evenings on topics of interest, such as first aid, or baby massage.
- Organising family trips.
- Organising family festival celebrations, a Christmas party for instance.

- Inviting family members to volunteer during sessions, or to help by using their skills, e.g. making dressing-up clothes or story sacks, or playing a musical instrument to the group.
- Holding exhibitions of children's art and craft work.
- Holding open days.
- Organising children's concerts or plays.
- Holding a toy library or book exchange.

Some settings may also offer a parents group, which may organise their own events, including some of those mentioned above. A parent's room may also be provided within the setting. Newsletters and notice boards help families to feel involved and up to date with activities within the setting.

Have a go!

Imagine your setting has put you in charge of organising an event to encourage families to participate within the setting. Choose an event that appeals to you from the list above, or think of one of your own.

Now write the invitation you would send to families. Explain what the event is and what will happen. Include the reasons why you'd like them to come. You can design a poster instead if you prefer.

Meeting the needs of parents

Information about identifying and meeting the needs of individual families can be found within Learning Outcome 4.

FOCUS ON... your learning

In this section you've learnt about developing good ongoing relationships with families, and the importance of valuing diverse family backgrounds. You've also learnt about the role of families in children's lives and the importance of effective shared care between the home and the setting.

Questions

1. Who is usually the primary carer of children?
2. Suggest three ways settings can encourage the participation of parents and carers?

Learning Outcome 3

FOCUS ON...

how to recognise the importance of working with other professionals

This links with Assessment Criteria **3.1, 3.2**

Multi-professional teams

All children have a range of needs, including needs for health, education and care. Traditionally services for young children have been organised separately to meet these needs through:

- Health services.
- Education services.
- Social care services.

Workers from health, education and social care services will liaise and work together with children and families when necessary. This enables them to meet families' needs in a co-ordinated way. Childcarers will liaise with workers from each of these services when appropriate. Health service workers include:

- Health visitors.
- Doctors.
- Nurses.
- Physiotherapists.
- Speech therapists.

Education workers include:

- Teachers.
- Specialist teachers.
- Classroom assistants.
- Learning support workers.
- Psychologists.
- Educational welfare officers.

Social care workers include:

- Social workers.
- Residential care workers.

Teachers are part of a multi-professional team ▼

- Outreach workers.
- Youth workers.
- Probation officers.

It's becoming more common for professionals from these separate services to work to together on a day-to-day basis, perhaps alongside professionals from the voluntary and private sector. We call this a **multi-agency or multi-professional** team.

The purpose of the team is to work closely together for the benefit of children and families. Team members will share their knowledge, skills, understanding and perceptions (opinions). This is good for families because it means professionals can provide them with a fully co-ordinated service that meets their needs holistically (meaning wholly, or altogether). The professionals within the team will be aware of each other's work with the family at every stage.

When professionals work together from the same premises, it's much more convenient for families to access services on a practical level. For example, multi-professional teams can be based within:

- Sure Starts
  Where workers organising projects for families and young children might include: early years workers, social workers, health visitors and outreach workers.
- Children's Trusts
  New organisations for families, children and young people. Trusts bring together health, education and social care services locally. Some Trusts have responsibility for all children's services, while others do not at present. Workers might include: early years workers, social workers with different specialities, health visitors, speech therapists, educational psychologists, youth workers, playworkers and teachers.

Child protection
The multi-agency approach in relation to child protection is explained in Unit 2.

Legal frameworks

The legal frameworks that support working with children and children's welfare are outlined in Units 3, 9 and in Learning Outcomes 4.

Practical example

Multi-professional support

Ten-year old Claire has additional needs. She and her family receive services from a team of professionals who work together to meet their needs. The team comprises of a doctor, a physiotherapist, a specialist teacher, a social worker and play worker.

1. *What are the benefits of this multi-professional approach to meeting the needs of Claire and her family?*

FOCUS ON...
your learning

You've learnt about the roles of different professionals that may work with children. You've also learnt how a multi-agency approach supports and benefits children and their families. Links to other Units give information about relevant legal frameworks, and the multi-professional teams that work within child protection services.

Questions

1. What does the term "multi-agency team" mean?
2. Which service do youth workers traditionally work within – education, health or social care?

Learning Outcome 4

FOCUS ON...

how to meet the diverse needs of babies and young children

This links with Assessment Criteria **4.1, 4.2**

Equality

In Unit 1 you were introduced to the issues of prejudice, discrimination, anti-bias practice, equal opportunities and meeting everyone's needs. We will be building on this learning throughout this section.

Have a go!

It's a good idea to refresh your memory by re-reading the information on pages 17–19 now, before moving on with this unit.

The rights of children and families

There is legislation in place covering children and adult's rights, equality and inclusion. An outline is given below. Your setting will have its own Equal Opportunities policy in place, which must be in line with the relevant requirements of your home country. All childcarers should know and understand these and work in line with them at all times.

UN Convention on the Rights of the Child

The UK Government made this convention law in 1991. It contains Articles that refer to the rights and needs of children. The acknowledgements include:

- Children have the right to non-discrimination – all the rights within the Convention apply equally to all children regardless of their race, sex, religion, disability or family background.
- Children have the right to rest, play and leisure, and opportunities to join in with activities including those that are cultural and artistic.

There's more about this on page 334.

Childcarers should ensure that disabled children have full opportunities to join in with play, since they may experience inequality in this area. A range of different cultural activities should be provided for all children, whatever their own culture.

- Children have the right to freedom from exploitation.
  Childcarers must prevent children from being abused, bullied or used.

There's more about this on page 298.

- Children have the right to a cultural identity.
  Settings should recognise, respect and value the cultural identity of individual families, and celebrate diversity throughout the group.
- Disabled children have the right to live as independently as possible and to take a full and active part in everyday life.
  Childcarers should consult with families to support disabled children's independence in the most effective way.
- Parents and guardians have the right to support in carrying out their parental responsibilities.
  Settings must work in partnership with all families.
- Children have the right to have their views heard.
  Childcarers should consult with children, particularly about decisions affecting them, and take notice of what they say. Childcarers should seek out and respect the views and preferences of children. This may be done through discussion, 'All About Me' theme work, or even through artwork. Practice should be adapted to suit the child's age, needs and abilities.
- Children need a strong self-image and self-esteem.
  Children should feel valued and accepted for who they are within the setting. This is achieved through showing children respect.
- Children also have a right to be aware of their rights.
  Childcarers should let children know that they have equal rights within the setting. Children should know they will be accepted for who they are, and respected when they are there. Children also have the responsibility to respect other children and adults within the environment. Young children will learn this from your actions and attitudes towards them. But childcarers can be more direct with older children and talk to them about these issues.

Children should feel valued and accepted for who they are ▼

Care Standards Act 2000

Settings registered with Ofsted must meet the requirement of this Act. The guidance from Ofsted tells us that:

- There must be an equal opportunities policy consistent with current legislation.
- Equal opportunities must be given to children and adults (including staff), and anti-discriminatory practice must be observed.
- Children's records must contain all information that is required to enable appropriate care to be given.

This links with Unit 9.

- There must be regard to the Special Educational Needs Code of Practice and Assessment of Special Educational Needs.
- Settings must have a written statement giving guidance about special needs and disabilities. It must be available to parents. It must be in line with current legislation.
- Staffing arrangements should meet the individual needs of children with additional needs.
- The physical environment must be 'as far as is reasonable' suitable for children with disabilities.
- Children with additional needs should have access alongside their peers to facilities, activities and play opportunities.
- Parents and carers should be consulted about the need for special services or equipment for their child.
- Privacy must be ensured for children with special needs when intimate care is being provided.

The Human Rights Act 1998

This Act was brought into force in 2000. It allows people in the UK to enforce rights given under previous laws in the British courts. Before the Act it was necessary to take cases to the European Court in Strasburg. A key previous law is the European Convention on Human Rights, which was ratified by the UK in 1951. It guarantees rights and freedoms for all as identified in the United Nations Declaration on Human Rights.

Race Relations Act 1976

This Act states that racial discriminatory practice is unaccepted, and defines in law what that means. The

Act was introduced to make discriminatory practice illegal in the UK. This was due to 'substantial ingrained discrimination' being present within our society.

All children should have equal opportunities ▼

Children Act 1989 and 2004

This Act requires all settings to have an equal opportunities policy that takes account of children's:

- Religion.
- Racial origin.
- Cultural background.
- Linguistic background (language background).

For details of additional regulations relating to inclusion, see Unit 9.

Discrimination

Discrimination occurs when people are treated unfairly because of stereotypical views held about a group they belong to or are perceived to belong to. There are all kinds of stereotypes and people treat others unfairly based on a broad range of them. However, discrimination is commonly based on:

- Disability.
- Ethnicity.
- Culture.
- Race.
- Religion.
- Gender.
  (Evidence shows women are still discriminated against)
- Age.
- Sexuality.
- **Low socio-economic group** (families with low income).

Inequalities are embedded in our society, throughout the UK. There isn't a certain area of the country or certain group of people that are more or less likely to be prejudiced. But on a positive note, we have more equal opportunities legislation and awareness now than ever before. Children are growing up in settings that are required to promote equal opportunities. Your setting's equal opportunity policy is a public commitment to equality. It promises families that they will be treated fairly.

abc Learn the lingo

Low socio-economic group
= families with low income

Types of discrimination

There are four types of discrimination:

1. Direct discrimination.
   This occurs when obvious action is carried out to the detriment (disadvantage or damage) of a person, because of their age, sex, race, religion, ethnicity or disability. For instance, if a setting were to refuse a child admission because they are Asian.
2. Indirect discrimination.
   This occurs when a condition is applied that will favour one group over another unfairly. For instance, a multi-lingual setting (where some families speak languages other than English) might offer extra places to parents on completion of forms, but only supply the forms in English.
3. Segregation.
   This is when people are unfairly separated when there's no reason for this. For instance, a setting with a separate area set aside for disabled children to eat in.
4. Victimisation.
   This occurs when people are purposely treated unfairly after complaining about previous discrimination. For instance, a parent complains that they were not given a chance to book an extra place because they couldn't understand the form. As a result the setting manager says there's been a double booking, and their child won't be able to come at all.

If a group of workers are jointly discriminating, the term **institutionalised discrimination** may be used.

FAST FACT

The effects of discrimination are serious and far reaching. Once experienced, children may suffer the impact of discrimination throughout their lives

GOOD PRACTICE

It's good practice for a setting to make it clear how places are given to families. This shows that it's done fairly. Many private/independent settings have admissions policies stating that places are allocated on a first-come-first-served basis.

Learn the lingo

Institutionalised discrimination – occurs when a group of workers jointly discriminate.

Effects of discrimination and inequality

Within families that experience it, discrimination can lead to:

- Missed opportunities that may affect a child's experiences. This can have a negative impact on development.
- Low self-esteem.
- Low confidence.
- Little sense of self-worth or self-value.
- Confused identity.
- Fear of rejection.

Inequality has a negative effect on all children, even if they haven't been the target of discrimination. If one child is stopped from participating within a group, then the rights

of all the children to participate equally, alongside one another, are affected. Children shouldn't be exposed to inequality, regardless of whether they are the target of it. If children are introduced to discrimination they are being introduced to criminal behaviour.

Practical example

Tara discriminates

Supervisor Tara thinks it will be too much trouble to have disabled children in the setting. Whenever a parent or carer of a disabled child enquires about a place, she lies and says the setting is full.

Tara is directly discriminating against disabled children and their families. But this inequality affects the children who do attend too. Tara is not allowing them to play and make friends with disabled children. She is keeping them segregated from disabled children. This is unacceptable.

(1) What affects may Tara's discrimination have?

Meeting the needs of families

Strategies to meet the needs of families
See Unit 9 for details of the barriers to participation that disabled adults and children may experience, and how to overcome them.

It's up to childcarers in the setting to put the Equal Opportunities policy into practice by promoting and meeting the needs of families. The first step is to find out what the needs of families are. This is done by getting to know them, as explained in Learning Outcome 2. The key-worker has a very important part to play.

There are likely to be families with diverse needs within any setting. Once needs have been identified, childcarers need to find develop strategies (ways) of meeting the needs. Keyworkers can do this in consultation with families and colleagues, remembering to respect confidentiality. Example of needs that may be identified and how they might be met are given in a series of case studies below.

Supporting a diverse environment

Settings should be diverse environments, or in other words, places where the diversity of our multi-cultural society is reflected. Childcarers can foster a diverse

Practical example

Breaking down a language barrier

A Polish couple have booked a place for their new baby. They have just started to learn English as an additional language. There is a language barrier between the staff and the parents.

Using the computer, the setting manager translates into Polish the setting's 'Welcome Pack'. This contains the information given to all new parents. She arranges for a Polish-speaking interpreter to come to a meeting with the family and the keyworker. They talk about ongoing strategies to meet the family's needs. At the meeting, the childcarers find out that the baby's uncle will soon be living locally. He speaks English, and will be staying with the family. It's agreed that the uncle will act as an interpreter in the future if required. The manager will carry on translating written material for as long as necessary.

1. *If no action was taken to meet the family's language needs, what negative affect might it have?*

Information on meeting the care needs of babies and young children is provided in Unit 2.

environment in several ways, including providing opportunities for children to find out about a range of cultures and beliefs. Celebrating a range of festivals and cultural events is a key way of introducing children to cultures other than their own. Many settings take festivals such as Diwali, Eid and Christmas as topics and plan a range of linked activities. This might include making Rangoli patterns for instance (a form of Indian art). A range of cultural artefacts such as a collection of divas (special lamps) may also be introduced on the interest table.

These activities are valuable. But it's important that diversity is embedded in the setting too. It should be a part of every day. It shouldn't be seen as something that's 'done' now and again in connection with a topic. Promoting positive images of people goes a long way towards achieving a diverse environment (more about this below).

Settings can show that they value all of the languages spoken within the group by making print available in as

Practical example

Literacy support

A dad meets his daughter's keyworker on her first visit to a holiday club. He tells the keyworker he has difficulties with literacy. He struggles to read and write without support. He's worried this will be a problem because there's information to read and registration forms to fill out.

The keyworker tells him there's no need to worry, she can talk him through the written information. She suggests she takes responsibility for verbally telling him about new information contained in newsletters and so on. They agree she should also give a copy to the child to take home as usual. When forms need to be completed, the keyworker invites the dad into the office. She asks him questions verbally and records the answers on the form.

1. *Why is it important that the keyworker still sends newsletters home with the child as usual?*

Some stockists of multi-cultural resources are listed in the web links on page 305.

many language as appropriate. Families can be involved in helping to write signs in various languages. Many settings like to have a multi-lingual 'Welcome' sign by their entrance. Story books written in various languages are available at the library.

Positive images

Childcarers should promote positive images of all people within the setting, reflecting the wider society. In other words, they should show, through the way they portray people, that all different kinds of people are valued in the setting.

This can be done by making sure that the pictures children see in books, displays, on puzzles, etc., show males and females, people of all sizes, ethnicities and cultures, and people who have a range of impairments. Positive images should also be reflected in the toys that you choose and the activities you plan, whenever these represent people.

Practical example

Staying in touch

The mum of Liam, a child at nursery, has become seriously ill. She doesn't leave her home very often, but she still wants to feel involved in her son's life at nursery. His Gran will be bringing him in and collecting him from now on.

The setting makes really good use of a home-to-nursery diary, recording details of Liam's experiences. They take digital photos of nursery activities and displays, and email them to Liam's mum often. If she isn't well enough to visit the setting to discuss Liam's development from time to time, Liam's mum knows the setting will arrange for their keyworker to visit her at home or talk to her on the phone. She also knows she can call the keyworker at any time.

1. *Can you think of any other measures that would help to support Liam's family?*

For instance, when setting out a collection of baby dolls you may include dolls of different ethnicities. When you plan an activity featuring people puppets, you may have different ages represented in the puppets provided. Your doll's house may feature a ramp and a doll using a wheelchair, or perhaps crutches, or a hearing aid. The aim is to represent the diversity of society overall. (It would be unrealistic to attempt to cover every eventuality in each collection of resources.) You should find that you end up with images that each child within the setting can personally identify with.

Include images each child can identify with ▼

You should also make sure that you show people in a positive light. Strong images of those people who may be discriminated against are particularly important. Some examples of strong image resources on the market are:

- A set of jigsaw puzzles that each show a family of a different culture eating a meal together.
- A poster on the theme of celebrations, which shows six families of different religions celebrating.

- A set of picture postcards showing athletes competing in the Paralympics.
- A set of doll's house dolls, featuring four elderly couples of different ethnicities.
- A set of puppets with the theme of 'People who help us' – including a female police officer and an Asian doctor.
- A set of jigsaw puzzles showing children helping, which includes a child with learning difficulties washing a car.
- Stories that are not about a child's disability, but the lead character just happens to be disabled.
- Doll accessory set that includes glasses.

Avoid images that aren't positive. For instance, in a story or picture disabled people are sometimes shown as being dependent on non-disabled people for instance, perhaps by being cared for or pushed in a wheelchair. Also, females may be shown as the underdogs to male characters.

To weave the thread of diversity throughout their setting, childcarers should extend this further wherever they have the opportunity. For instance, childcarers can make sure that different styles of clothing are represented in the dressing-up clothes and that cooking utensils and food in the home corner represent the wider world (these might include woks and balti pans). Crayons can be bought in a

Practical example

Nina's choice

Nina is planning to buy some toys to promote positive images. She comes across a doll's house doll that she likes the look of at first. It's a doll version of a woman sitting in a wheelchair. It's made of one piece of plastic.

It occurs to Nina that this may be a problem. The woman can't be taken out of her wheelchair. The wheels of the chair don't go around. Nina wonders if this toy promotes positive images and if it would give good play value.

1. *What do you think? Should Nina buy the toy with the money earmarked for promoting positive images? Why?*

range of flesh tones for art activities. There are so many possibilities. Find out more about them for yourself by completing the Have a go! task below. Also, the next time you visit a children's library, have a look for books that show positive images of people.

Have a go!

Positive images

Educational supplies sell resources and equipment suitable for group use in a range of settings. You may have access to educational catalogues at your workplace. Most also have a website. Referring to either supplier's catalogues or websites:

- Find three different resources that could be used in a home corner to reflect diversity.
- Find three resources that show a positive image of disabled people.
- Find a toy that will help children to identify with elderly people.
- Find three examples of dressing up clothes or doll's outfits that represent different cultures/ethnicities.

The website addresses of three educational suppliers are given in the weblinks section.

Supporting an inclusive environment

Full details on providing an inclusive environment and identifying and meeting children's individual needs are included in Unit 9.

FOCUS ON...
your learning

You've learnt about the rights of children and their families to be treated fairly. You've also learnt about the causes and effects of discrimination. You've learnt strategies to promote and meet the needs of individual children and their families. Links to other Units give information on protecting children, meeting children's care needs, identifying and supporting children with additional needs and providing an inclusive environment.

Questions

1 What are the four types of discrimination?

2 How can settings promote positive images of people?

RAPID RECAP

Learning Outcome 1

Childcarers must provide a healthy, hygienic and safe environment for children. The environment can affect many aspects of the provision, including atmosphere, how children learn and play and whether children get exercise and rest. With careful planning the environment can offer young children reassurance and security. Attractive, well-thought out displays of children's work can enhance learning and give children a sense of pride and belonging. You should meet the physical and health needs of babies and young children through responsive care.

There are links to information about meeting physical and health needs, health and safety and adapting environments within Units 2, 3, 4 and 9.

Learning Outcome 2

Parents and carers are usually the primary carers of children. They generally have the closest ongoing bond with children and know them best. You must form and maintain good relationships with children's families. This is the foundation for providing shared care for children. All types of families successfully love and care for children. You must value and show respect for diverse family backgrounds. You must communicate effectively with parents and carers, sharing, recording and reporting information according to your setting's procedures.

There are links to information about communication within Unit 5.

Learning Outcome 3

A multi-agency approach allows a team of professionals to work closely together to provide families with co-ordinated services to meet their needs. Professionals may come from the services of health, education and social care. Childcarers may be part of a multi-agency approach. Multi-agency teams may include doctors, health visitors, teachers, specialist teachers, social workers, psychologists, etc.

There are links to information about relevant legal frameworks, and the multi-professional teams that work within child protection services, within Units 3 and 9.

Learning Outcome 4

Children and families have the right to be treated fairly. You must work in line with your setting's equal opportunity policy. Prejudice leads to discrimination. The effects are serious and far reaching, and can include missed opportunities affecting experiences and development. Childcarers must identify the needs of families, then develop strategies to meet them. Settings should be places where the diversity of our multi-cultural society is reflected. Childcarers can foster this in several ways, including providing opportunities for children to find out about a range of cultures and beliefs, and promoting positive images.

There are links to Units 1, 2, 3 and 9.

FAQ

Q How will I be assessed on this Unit?

A *You'll complete an assignment task. CACHE publishes a task for each optional unit every year.*

Q What will I have to do?

A *Your tutor or Centre will help you to understand the task.*

See Unit 1 Learning Outcome 5 for more information on study skills.

Weblinks

You may like to visit the following websites:

- http://www.parentscentre.gov.uk/
  The Government site for parents offering advice and support. Includes a guide to using childcare.
- http://www.parrotfish.co.uk/calendar.htm
  To download a free festival calendar and view multi-cultural resources.

Educational suppliers' websites. You can use these for the Learning Outcome 4 Have a Go! task:

- www.nesarnold.co.uk/
- http://www.theconsortium.co.uk (select 'Early Years' from the menu)
- http://www.kidslikeme.co.uk

Also see the web links provided in Unit 9.

Unit 8

Play activity for children from birth to age 16 years

Learning Outcomes

In this unit you'll learn about:

How to meet the diverse play needs of children.

How to support a range of play opportunities for children.

The role of the adult in providing play activity for children.

Learning Outcome 1

FOCUS ON...

how to meet the diverse play needs of children

In this section you'll learn how the main stages of play relate to the diverse needs of children, and how you can further children's interests, views and play.

This links with Assessment Criteria **1.1, 1.2**

This unit is about play activity for children up to the age of 16 years. Relevant information about play activities and environments for babies and toddlers is given in Unit 7.

Play with older children

As explained on page 183, learners undertaking this qualification may work in a playwork setting with older children during their careers. If you're working with a broad age range of children (which is likely if you've chosen this optional unit), you need to learn how to adjust the way in which you work to suit the needs of older children and young people.

The Playwork Principles explain the values playwork is based on. You should always promote them in your work with older children in play settings. The Principles themselves appear below. They are rather wordy. You should know that the information given in this Unit reflects and promotes the principles, so you will be learning and understanding more about them as you work your way through this part of the book.

Playwork principles

These Principles establish the professional and ethical framework for playwork and as such must be regarded as a whole. They describe what is unique about play and playwork, and provide the playwork perspective for working with children and young people. They are based on the recognition that children and young people's capacity for positive development will be enhanced if given access to the broadest range of environments and play opportunities.

1. All children and young people need to play. The impulse to play is innate (built in). Play is a biological, psychological and social necessity, and is fundamental to the healthy development and well-being of individuals and communities.

2. Play is a process that is freely chosen, personally directed and intrinsically motivated. That is, children and young people determine and control the content and intent of their play, by following their own instincts, ideas and interests, in their own way for their own reasons.
3. The prime focus and essence of playwork is to support and facilitate the play process and this should inform the development of play policy, strategy, training and education.
4. For playworkers, the play process takes precedence and playworkers act as advocates for play when engaging with adult-led agendas.
5. The role of the playworker is to support all children and young people in the creation of a space in which they can play.
6. The playworker's response to children and young people playing is based on a sound up to date knowledge of the play process and reflective practice.
7. Playworkers recognise their own impact on the play space and also the impact of children and young people's play on the playworker.
8. Playworkers choose an intervention style that enables children and young people to extend their play. All playworker intervention must balance risk with the developmental benefit and well-being of children.

You may work in a playwork setting with older children ▼

Self-directed play

Self-directed free play is a natural and spontaneous activity with many benefits for children. It's essential for children's growth and development. It's not just enjoyable but vital to children and young people's well-being. Good play opportunities and environments can make a real difference to a child's quality of life.

Throughout this Unit the term 'play' refers to self-directed play that is freely chosen by children (free play).

Stages of play and development

The stages of child development influence children and young people's play needs and behaviour. All children develop at different rates and so their play needs and behaviours will also vary. Children tend to have different

Information about child development is included within Unit 2. Details of the stages of play can be found within Unit 4.

interests and be drawn to different types of play as they grow up and develop. The amount of independence that children are comfortable with increases over time. A good knowledge and understanding of children's development is essential to the provision of good, appropriate play opportunities.

Play needs and preferences

You need to know about the play needs and preferences of the children that you work with. This enables you to provide play opportunities that will meet the needs of children and young people and promote their development. It also enables you to provide experiences that children will enjoy and will find engaging and interesting. You can find out about children's play needs and preferences by observing children at play.

Observing children at play

You'll find that you naturally observe things about individual children's play needs and preferences as you:

- Interact and play with children.
- Stand back and supervise children.

See pages 53–64 for further details about formal observations.

These naturally occurring observations are informative. Some workers find jotting them down in a notebook a helpful way to gather information. Planned observations of children are also valuable.

Have a go!

Think about a child you work with regularly in your setting. Just going on what you've picked up about them naturally, make a rough list of their play needs and preferences. What do they like to do? What are they interested in? What support do they need when they're playing? You may be surprised at how much you've picked up about children's play needs and preferences in the course of your work.

Consulting with children

Childcarers working in play settings should consult with (or in other words ask) children and young people about their play needs and preferences. This becomes more important as children grow up. Through consultation you

can interact with children, finding out what they want and need from their play. You can then provide appropriate play that children will enjoy participating in. But consultation has other advantages too. It can help children and young people to feel:

- Listened to:
  When workers actively seek out everyone's opinion, they have the opportunity to encourage everyone to have their say, including those children unlikely to put forward their opinion without it being asked for and those children who don't tend to approach adults or gain their attention easily.
- Valued and worthwhile:
  We know as adults how good we feel when others ask for our opinions and ideas. It's good to feel that your thoughts are worthwhile and so your opinion is sought out and valued. The same is true for children.
- Included:
  Consultation promotes participation. The more children are involved in devising play opportunities or play spaces, the keener they are to participate.

Children and young people can also learn and practise skills during consultation. They will have opportunities to:

- Form and explain ideas and opinions.
- Listen to and respect each other.
- Discuss and debate.
- Adapt and negotiate.
- Plan.
- Take responsibility.
- Evaluate.
- Give feedback.
- Record information.

FAST FACT

Consulting children can lead to increased self-esteem and confidence and help to encourage feelings of empowerment.

Consultation can take place during casual conversation as workers interact with children and young people. But planned consultation activities can also take place during:

- Meetings.
- Circle time.
- Planning sessions.
- Evaluations and reviews.

Workers should always choose a method of consultation that suits the ages and abilities of the children in the group. Consultation methods include:

- Discussion:
  You can talk with children individually or in groups about their play needs, preferences and play spaces, asking for their opinions and ideas.
- Questionnaires:
  These can be written or pictorial (made up of pictures), depending on the ages and abilities of the children.
- Interviews:
  As an alternative to questionnaires, an 'interviewer' can verbally ask children questions and record their answers. They could use audio recording equipment (such as a digital recorder) or a video camera.
- Suggestion boxes:
  Children can write and draw their ideas, thoughts and feelings and put them into a box anonymously (without giving their name). Suggestion video tapes/audio tapes can also work well.
- Voting:
  A good, quick way of consulting. Children can vote on the layout of the play space at the start of the session for instance, or vote on what playground game to play together. This can be as simple as a show of hands or can involve a ballot (an anonymous paper vote).
- Evaluation:
  Involving children in the evaluation of play sessions reveals what they've enjoyed. This can inform future planning. There are several visual ways of recording evaluations. It's common to ask children to rank, in order of preference, the activities they've participated in. For example, you could:
  1. *Draw out a large bulls-eye target and ask each child to place a cross on it to show how they felt about a particular experience. The nearer to the bulls-eye the cross is, the better they enjoyed the experience. See the diagram opposite.*
  2. *Draw up a list of play experiences. Give children a gold, silver and bronze sticker each. Ask them to place the stickers next to the experiences on the list awarding them first, second or third in terms of their favourites.*

The evaluation target ▼

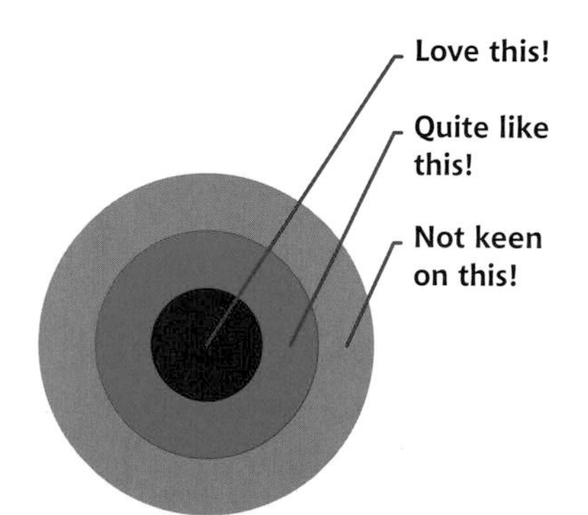

3. *Tell children the four corners of the play space represent 'really liked it', 'liked it', 'didn't like it', and 'really didn't like it'. Call out play experiences and have children run to the relevant corner depending how they felt about the experience.*

- Thought-storming:
  This is a method of collecting ideas from a group of contributors, in our case, children. Your tutor probably uses thought-storming as a way of collecting ideas from you and other learners in your class. The case study that follows gives an example of thought-storming with children.

Children can record their ideas using audio equipment ▶

To encourage children and young people to participate in consultation:

- Make the process fun.
- Tell children the purpose of the consultation – let them know that what they have to say will influence future play experiences.
- Ensure everyone gets their say.
- Choose methods to suit the children.
- Acknowledge and accept everyone's contribution.
- Ensure all contributions are respected by other children.

Planning inclusive play

Details about this are included in Unit 9. Further information about planning activities can be found in Unit 4.

Some children and young people with additional needs may experience barriers that affect their access to play. Settings must take action to identify and remove barriers to ensure that all children are given equal opportunities to play. Play opportunities and environments should meet the individual needs of all children.

Have a go!

Arrange a visit to a play setting different from your own workplace, such as an adventure playground. It's a really good way of broadening your experience of play. Look at the activities and resources. Notice the way children play. Talk to children about what they like to do at the setting, and ask them what they're interested in.

It's also helpful to visit settings that cater for children of a different age range to your current workplace.

See page 4 for details of how to find out about settings in your local area.

FOCUS ON...
your learning

In this section you've learnt about how to recognise the play needs, interests and preferences of individual children, and the importance of consulting with children. You've been introduced to the Principles of Playwork. There are links to other Units that give information on the stages of play, planning for play and inclusion.

Questions:

1 Why is it important to consult with children and young people?

2 Why do you need to know about children's play needs and preferences?

Learning Outcome 2

FOCUS ON...
how to support a range of play opportunities for children

This links with Assessment Criteria **2.1, 2.2**

Play environments

A range of different types of play environments (or play spaces) can meet the play needs of children and young people. These can be both indoor and outdoor including:

- Out-of-school clubs, often run on school premises in a classroom or hall, with the use of the school playground. These may open before school, after school and/or in the school holidays.
- Adventure playgrounds, featuring outdoor space for adventurous/exhilarating play such as climbing trees or using zip lines (cables fixed between two high points that children can hang off and slide down). Some may also have indoor facilities for play. These are generally open after school and during the holidays.
- Holiday clubs run in sports centres, providing a range of play opportunities and usually featuring a broad range of physical activities and sports.
- Play buses or other mobile facilities that visit places that would not otherwise have much in the way of play facilities (for example, in remote locations). The buses are specially converted inside so that children can get on the bus and play. They generally visit during the holidays and at weekends for older children and on weekdays during term time for pre-school children.
- Residential centres where children stay overnight, for a weekend or perhaps a week during the holidays. A range of activities may be offered off-site and on-site, including opportunities for adventurous activities such as canoeing, caving and team games.
- Public parks and fields, where children may go to play without supervision. Some public sites may be staffed by a play ranger or a park keeper offering 'low-level' supervision. There may or may not be play equipment installed.

Additional places where children play are listed on page 3.

Planning and creating play spaces

Settings must plan play spaces that will meet the play needs and preferences of the children and young people with they work with. Planning will be informed by:

- Observations made of children's play needs and preferences.
- Consultation with children.
- Evaluations of the play experiences and environments.

The design and layout of a play space will depend on the type of space available. What can be offered within a school hall is clearly different from what can be offered within an adventure playground. There are many ways of planning play spaces, but you must always take your setting's own unique play space into consideration. One method of planning is shown in the diagram below.

Also, staff will want to provide play opportunities that promote all of the play types. Guidelines for this are given on pages 193–200. You'll find information about play environments and activities for babies and toddlers within Unit 7.

Planning ▼

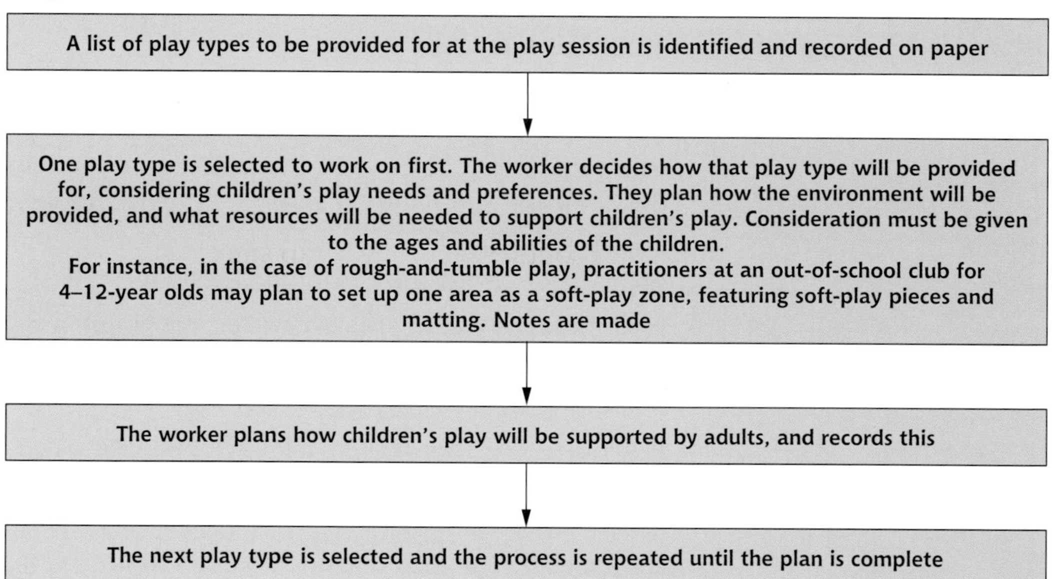

Aim to create spaces that children can adapt during play according to their age, needs and abilities. This gives them freedom and control within their play and the opportunity to explore and develop their own play ideas, activities and experiences. Many experts agree that ideally the following types of resources should be included in the design of a play space:

- 'Loose parts' that can be moved around the setting to create new and interesting structures and/or play experiences. Parts may include logs and other pieces of wood, plants, containers, screens, toys, etc. (This

Physical resources should be included in the design of a play space ▼

idea came from 'The theory of loose parts' developed by Simon Nicholson in 1971.) Loose parts can be used in an endless combination of ways. The parts used can change over time.

- Permanent fixed resources that stay in one place, such as large apparatus or trees.
- Physical resources (within a space suitable for physical play) such as climbing frames, ladders, stilts, balls, skateboards, bicycles.

Resources that stimulate play

In addition to toys and equipment, staff need to collect a wide range of resources to effectively support children self-directed play, such as those described in the 'loose parts' section above.

Many resources can be obtained cheaply or can be adapted with some creativity. For instance, many areas have a scrap stores. Settings can join these, then help themselves to supplies of many scrap resources for a small fee. Items to be found in scrap stores include wooden planks, tall cardboard tubes from carpet rolls, large sheets of card, paper and cellophane. Your local council should be able to tell you about your nearest scrap store.

Involving children

We looked at the importance of consulting with children in Learning Outcome 1. You can also involve children in the design and creation of play spaces. Children can be involved in:

- Helping to draw up plans by suggesting and discussing ideas.
- The gathering of resources.
- Setting out the play space and resources, making use of 'loose parts'.

Access for all

Play spaces and resources for play must be accessible to all the children. But children will be encouraged to develop their own play, using and changing resources and play spaces as play develops. So staff must monitor the changing nature of activities, experiences and play spaces, and be ready to make adaptations if they're needed.

Encouraging children to explore and investigate

It's important for children to have opportunities to choose and explore play spaces for themselves, according to their age, needs and abilities. This gives children freedom and control within their play and the opportunity to explore and develop their own play ideas. You can encourage children to explore and investigate in their play by:

You'll learn more about this in Learning Outcome 3.

There's further information about exploration and investigation on page 203.

- Providing activities that interest them, engage them and meet their play needs (as outlined in Learning Outcome 1).
- Providing a stimulating environment.
- Providing stimulating resources.
- Supporting self-directed play

Have a go!

Throughout your course you'll be required to provide activities for children. You must choose activities suitable for the age, needs and abilities of the children you're working with. You may like to try some of the following play activities with younger children, older children and young people...

Games

Traditional playground games are a favourite at play settings. Younger children enjoy:

Traffic Lights

What to do:

Explain to children that you'll call out the traffic light colours. When they hear 'Amber' they should 'get ready' by walking around the play space. When they hear 'Green' they should 'go' and run around. When they hear 'Red' they should stop and stand still. You can adapt this game by making pictures of traffic lights that are amber, green and red and holding up the cards in turn. This would support children with hearing impairments and would help children learning to recognise colours.

Captain's Coming

Older children enjoy this game played on an imaginary boat.

What to do:

1. Choose a volunteer to stand in front of the group. Their job is to call out instructions to the rest of the children. Each instruction has a corresponding action. Players must do the right action until the next instruction is called.
2. The last child to comply with each instruction is out.
3. The last child remaining is the winner.
4. The instructions and corresponding actions to teach the children are:
   - Captain's coming = salute
   - Bow = run to the front of the play space
   - Stern = run to the back
   - Starboard = run to the right
   - Port = run to the left
   - Scrub the decks = on hands and knees, mime scrubbing the floor
   - Climb the rigging = mime climbing upwards
   - Sharks = lie down and snap arms together in the manner of jaws
   - Submarines = lie down on back with one leg in the air as a periscope
   - Man overboard = mime throwing a lifeline

Children can also suggest their own additional instructions and actions.

Kangaroo Conga

Dancing the conga ▼

Older children and young people enjoy this activity. What to do.

1. Have the group line up one behind the other. Players should hold the waist or shoulders of the person in front of them (except for the person at the head of the line, who will be the leader).
2. The leader shouts out '1, 2, 3!' On 3, everyone should jump forward together, attempting to keep the line intact. They'll be some laughter as the first couple of attempts go wrong! When players have got the hang of it, move on to step 3.
3. The leader calls '1, 2, 3, left!' or '1, 2, 3, right!' Practice until the players can move sideways keeping the line intact.

4. Now practice moving backwards.
5. The leader should now be able to shout out instructions at random for the group to respond to, e.g. 'Left! Back! Right! Forwards!'
6. Young people can add their own moves into the mix, turning around so the line is reversed, or adding a Mexican wave for example. They can even try a conga to music.

Drama and imaginative play

To encourage imaginative play amongst young children you can provide:

- Small world toys such as farms and animals, doll's houses and dolls, vehicles and road play-mats.
- Imaginary areas such as home corners for role-play. These can be changed to represent other familiar places for a period of time, such as a doctor's surgery or a shop.
- Dressing up resources.

Children of primary school age often enjoy opportunities to:

- Put on their own puppet shows.
- Act in their own improvised 'stage' shows.
- Play their own complex fantasy games.

Young people may enjoy drama activities and opportunities to act out written and improvised scenes and plays. You can also try the following game.

Improvise!

What to do:

1. Players stand in a circle. Place a number of props in the centre.
2. The first player chooses a prop and does a mime with it. The group must guess what the player is pretending the prop is. (The trick is to provide inanimate props that can be used several different ways, e.g. a long cardboard tube can become a golf club, a flute, etc.)
3. Once the mime is guessed, the prop is passed to the next player. When inspiration for the use of the prop runs out, a new prop can be chosen from the middle of the circle.

Percussion free play ▼

Music, movement and rhythm

To promote music, movement and rhythm play amongst children and young people you can provide:

- Musical instruments.
- Recordings of music (make sure your setting has the right to play these).
- Opportunities and space for dancing.

A marching jamboree

Younger children enjoy this.

What to do:

1. Allow children to choose a percussion instrument from a selection on offer.
2. Have the group line up one behind the other.
3. Lead the group on a marching jamboree!

You can extend this activity by playing a simple rhythm and having children play it back to you. Give them all the chance to lead the band.

A disco karaoke

For older children.

What to do:

1. Clear an area for dancing.
2. Dim the lights and use disco lights if available (avoid strobe lighting with children).
3. Fix up a microphone.
4. Put on the music. Children can sing and dance along.

Young people enjoy.

- DJ-ing with real decks.
- Music quizzes in teams – try playing just the introductions of pop songs and challenge teams to name the song and artist.
- Writing their own songs, or writing new lyrics to songs they know.
- Learning or choreographing (making up) dance routines.

Physical play

You should support children during their physical play. Many of the activities described above involve physical

See page 194 for further details. A list of resources to support self-directed physical play is given on page 194.

play, including the games and movement activities.
It's important to provide children with an element of challenge and risk in their physical play You may like to try the following physical activities:

Making dens

For older children. What to do:

1. There are several ways to make dens. Children can simply push tables together and throw a couple of blankets over them. Or three tall cardboard tubes or wooden poles can be tied at the top with cord to make a tepee frame, over which a sheet is draped.
2. Dens create a cosy, darkened atmosphere, perfect for play with torches, or for storytelling.

Get knotted game ▼

Get Knotted!

For young people.

1. You need an even number of players for this game. No more than 12 players can make-up each 'knot', but you can have more than one knot in play at the same time.
2. Have players stand in a circle facing inwards.
3. Players close their eyes and reach their right hands across the circle. When they feel the hand of another player, they should grasp it as if shaking hands. Players open their eyes.
4. Sill holding right hands, players should reach out their left hands and grasp the free hand of another player. (Everyone should now be holding hands with two different players.)
5. Without letting go hands, the group must now work as a team to untangle themselves by stepping over arms, etc. This should eventually end up either in one big circle or two entwined circles with no 'knots'.

Expressing creativity

Many of the activities mentioned above involve expressing creativity, including those relating to imaginary play and music and movement. You can also encourage children to express themselves through art and craft activities using resources such as:

- Mark-making materials (pens, pencils, crayons, paint, charcoal, air-brushes, etc.).

- Malleable materials (dough, Plasticine, clay, etc.).
- Decorative/collage materials (paper, glue, sequins, glitter, beads, etc.).

Craft activities may include:

- Making greetings cards.
- Making jewellery.
- Making sculptures (from wood, papier-mâché, sand, marshmallows, etc.).

You can also try the following:

Water painting

For young children.What to do:

1. Go outside on a dry day. Give children pots of water to use with paintbrushes and trays of water to use with paint rollers and sponges.
2. Encourage children to 'paint' freely with their water. They can make marks and pictures on the floor, or 'paint' the walls and fences.
3. Remind children that painting freely in this way can only be done with water, not real paint!

Face painting encourages creativity ▼

Face painting

For older children. Equip children with a mirror and face-paints, and encourage them to get creative! Some children may like to paint each other's faces in pairs.

You must:

- Check children don't have allergies to face-paint.
- Get parental permission for children to participate (your setting may have a permission slip for families to sign).
- Follow the instructions on the face-paint (children may need to apply a base of face cream, and there will be directions for removing the face-paint later).

Special effects photography

For young people.

1. Young people can work alone or in pairs. Using a digital camera, demonstrate how to achieve the following special effects when taking photos (always hold the camera firmly with one hand):
   - For a motion/speed effect = turn the flash on. Spin the camera downwards as you take the photo. This

Young people can create photos using special effects ▼

gives a blurred edge, but the middle of the picture is clear. Also try panning the camera across as you take the photo.

- To create silhouettes = take photos against a bright sky (but don't shoot into the sun). Turn off the flash for a bold image.
- To create a soft effect = experiment with breathing on the lens before taking a photo. You can also place a piece of stocking over the lens and shoot through that.

When children express creativity, they may be taking an emotional risk. Read on to find out how you can support emotional risk taking.

Many of the activities suggested here have been adapted from "A Practical Guide to Activities for Older Children," Miranda Walker (2007) Nelson Thornes. See the Follow up section for further details.

Emotional risk

Emotional risk taking is a life skill. Children and young people (and adults) take emotional risks whenever they pluck up the courage to do something that stretches them emotionally or that risks personal failure or rejection. Examples of emotional risk taking include:

- Speaking in front of a group of peers or adults.
- Performing in public (singing, acting, dancing, playing musical instruments).
- Auditioning.
- Trying to make a new friend.
- Saying no to friends or refusing to give in to peer pressure.
- Showing others your own creative work (art or creative writing, for instance).
- Entering a competition.
- Suggesting your own ideas to peers/adults.
- Telling a joke.
- Applying for a college course or a job.
- Doing something independently for the first time (e.g. using public transport, living alone).

Activities that feel like a risk to one person may come easily to another. Children are individuals who are comfortable doing different things. The things that children are comfortable with are sometimes referred to as being within their 'comfort zone'. But if children are to

continually move on and progress in their development, they need to step out of their comfort zone every so often and take an emotional risk.

Children with good levels of self-esteem and confidence are generally more willing to take emotional risks. You can help children to feel equipped for emotional risk taking by providing activities that foster high levels of confidence and self-esteem, including:

- Team activities.
- Trust games.
- Games that give all children the opportunity to be the leader.
- Consultation.
- Displays of art/craft work.

Ensure you offer children plenty of praise generally, and specifically, for having a go or trying hard. This helps to communicate that there's value in being prepared to step out of the comfort zone, whatever the result of taking the risk.

FOCUS ON...
your learning

In this section you've learnt about creating play environments that stimulate play opportunities and how to encourage children to explore and investigate through play. You've also learnt how to support and provide opportunities for the following: drama and imaginary play, creativity, music, movement, rhythm, games, physical play.

Questions

1. Suggest three activities you could provide for children aged 3–5 years to promote creativity.
2. Suggest three activities you could provide for children aged 8–12 years to promote physical play.

Learning Outcome 3

FOCUS ON...
the role of adults in providing play activity for children

This links with Assessment Criteria **3.1, 3.2**

Health and safety

Health and safety information (including how to risk assess play activities) is given in Unit 3.

Although risk assessments will be carried out before activities take place, the level of risk can change during play. This is due to the way in which children and young people decide to play and use the resources. Staff must continually monitor the changing levels of risk. There's no need to intervene in children's play unless the level of risk becomes unacceptable. If this happens, staff must intervene and bring the level of risk back to an acceptable level.

There's further information about this on page 125.

An effective technique to keep intervention at a minimum is to encourage children to develop an awareness of hazards and how to manage risk themselves. This is also an important life skill.

Policies and procedures

Throughout Units 1–6 you learnt about the policies and procedures that settings put in place to ensure staff work in line with legislation, requirements and the setting's own values. You must continue to work in line with these in relation to children's play. Your setting may have written guidelines about the way in which staff should support children's play.

Children's right to play

This links with page 293.

Under the UN Convention on the Rights of the Child, children have the right to play. Children should be allowed to make their own choices and their own decisions about their play. But there are still things you can do to support children's self-directed play.

Supporting self-directed play

The support that children need in their self-directed play depends on their age, abilities and personalities. But even older children and young people may need adult support in choosing and exploring play spaces.

Also see page 196 for information about valuing process as well as product.

For example, when children first arrive at a play setting they may show signs of feeling overwhelmed or self-conscious. This can apply whether or not it's the child's first day. You can help children by:

- Helping them to find friends who have already arrived.
- Providing suggestions of play, e.g., 'Would you like to get the paint out?'.
- Pointing out a feature of the play space, 'Have you seen that the ball-pool is set up inside today?'.

Drawing on your knowledge of children and their play needs and preferences will help you to offer appropriate support.

Learn the lingo

Content of play = what children want to do in their play and how they want to do it.
Intent of play = the purpose or reason for play.

Supporting the content and intent of play

You must respect that children and young people's play belongs to them. It should be up to children to decide what they want to do in their play and how they want to do it – this is the **content** of the play. The **intent** of the play is its purpose or reason. Sometimes there may be an end product such as a painting or sculpture. But in many cases there is not. Play may be driven by many things, including curiosity or exploration.

As you learnt on page 260, it's important for workers to allow children and young people to play uninterrupted whenever possible.

Allowing uninterrupted play

Interruptions can disturb or destroy the play 'world' that children have created and are playing within. A child may not be able to recapture this. Ideas or trains of thought can be lost in an instant when interruptions occur.

GOOD PRACTICE

When children are playing, resist the temptation to show them 'better' or 'proper' ways of doing things unless:

- They ask to be shown.
- Behaviours are potentially dangerous (the dangerous misuse of a tool for instance).

Play is not about the right or wrong way of doing things. It's about exploration, discovery and individual creativity.

Ending a play session

Sometimes workers have to interrupt play due to timing. It may be time for a child to go home before they've finished their play, or it may be time to have a meal that's ready.

Don't disturb children needlessly when they're absorbed in their play ▶

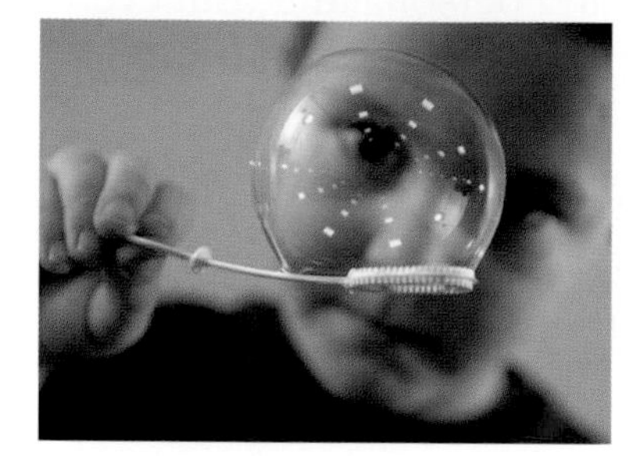

When this is likely to happen, prepare children by giving them a warning. You might say, 'There's only 15 minutes left before we need to go and have our lunch.' This advance notice gives children the opportunity to wind up their play accordingly. It can also help to leave resources and play spaces as they are, if possible, instead of packing away, so that children can return to their play later if they want to.

Responding to play cues

You should avoid interrupting children when they're engaged in play. But you should look out for signs that children want you to play with them, so you can respond. Sometimes children or young people will ask you to play with them. But sometimes they give a more subtle **play cue**.

Learn the lingo

Play cue = a signal that a child gives to show that they want to play.
Play return = a signal someone gives to show that they're willing to play. This is given in response to a play cue.

A play cue is a signal that a child gives to show that they want to play. They are hoping their cue will get a favourable response. For instance, if a child kicks a ball towards you they are indicating that they want to play – they are hoping you will give them a 'play return'. This is a signal that you're willing to play. In our example, you would kick the ball back as a 'play return'. Play returns encourage children's play.

If you observe a play cue you can respond in a number of ways. It may be appropriate to join in with children's play or to make a suggestion, provide resources or offer support and/or encouragement.

Imagine you've responded to a play cue and joined in a child's play. You will not play with them forever! So after being careful to intervene in play sensitively, how should you end your intervention sensitively?

There may be a natural end to the play – perhaps a board game has finished or a model has been made. Children tend to get what they want from their play activities and experiences and then they are over. This is sometimes confusing for adults as children may throw away a picture they've spent time and effort working on, or knock down a construction they've built. Whenever possible you should follow children's lead in terms of the end of play.

There's more about supporting children as appropriate to their age, needs and abilities in Units 2, 9 and 10.

Working with colleagues

There's more information about this on pages 250–253.

When working in group settings, you'll be required to work effectively with colleagues in a team. In play settings,

resources and play opportunities may require a lot of organising. You must always do what you've agreed to do on time, or the children may have to miss out on planned activities. This would be a shame and a waste of the time spent on planning and organisation. It could also leave an awkward gap in the setting's schedule and cause conflict within the staff team.

Practical example

Responding to a play cue

Seven-year old Amy has been playing alone with a balloon. She has been hitting it around the room with her hand. As playworker Lana passes by, Amy hits the balloon towards her. Lana hits it back and then stands still to see how Amy responds. Amy hits the balloon back to Lana again. Lana recognises the play cue and continues to play the game with Amy. After a few turns Amy begins to hit the balloon in the air. She claps her hands before she catches it. The game is over and Lana moves away as Amy carries on alone with her new game.

(1) Why did Lana respond in this way?

FOCUS ON...

your learning

You've learnt about the importance of children's right to play freely, and how to encourage self-directed play. You've also learn how to support children's play according to their age, needs and abilities, and how to end play sessions effectively. There are links to other Units that give information on health and safety, policies and procedures and working with colleagues to promote play.

Questions

1 Which Convention gives children the right to play?

2 What strategies can you use to end play sessions effectively?

RAPID RECAP

Learning Outcome 1

The Principles of Playwork underpin the work carried out by staff working with older children and young people in play settings. In order to provide appropriate play opportunities that children enjoy and engage with, you need to find out about their play needs, interests and preferences. You can then plan play opportunities that appeal to the children and meet their needs.

There are links to information about development, planning and inclusion within Units 2, 4 and 9.

Learning Outcome 2

Both indoor and outdoor play environments should stimulate a range of play. Play spaces should include loose parts, permanent fixed resources and physical resources. Encouraging children to explore and investigate gives them freedom and control within their play and the opportunity to explore and develop their own play ideas. You should support and provide opportunities for the following: drama and imaginary play, creativity, music, movement, rhythm, games, physical play.

Learning Outcome 3

Children have the right to play freely. You should encourage and support children's self-directed play according to their age, needs and abilities. You should not intervene needlessly when children are engaged in play. But you should look out for and respond to play cues that show children want to play with you. You should end play sessions sensitively. You must work in line with your setting's policies and procedures relating to play. You must effectively work in a team with colleagues to promote play.

There are links to information about health and safety, policies and procedures and teamwork within Units 3, 4, 5 and 9.

FAQ

Q How will I be assessed on this Unit?

A You'll complete an assignment task. CACHE publishes a task for each optional unit every year.

Q What will I have to do?

A Your tutor or Centre will help you to understand the task. See Unit 1 Learning Outcome 5 for more information on study skills.

Weblinks

You may like to visit the followng websites:

- www.playlink.org.uk/publications/
  To view the publication "Best Play: What play provision should do for children," which is about how the benefits of play can be provided by play settings
- www.skillsactive.com/playwork
  The home Skills Active, for information about playwork
- www.mirandawalker.co.uk
  For play activity ideas
- www.nurseryworld.co.uk
  The home of Nursery World magazine, with archived activity ideas.
- www.gameskidsplay.net/games
  For playground game ideas

Supporting children with additional needs

Learning Outcomes

In this unit you will learn about:

How to support children with additional needs and their families.

How to support children with additional needs within the setting.

The role of the adult in enabling children with additional needs to participate in activities and experiences.

Learning Outcome 1

FOCUS ON...

how to support children with additional needs and their families

In this section you'll learn about the legal requirements and other sources that support children with additional needs, and the main reasons for working in partnership with their families.

This links with Assessment Criteria **1.1, 1.2**

Inclusion is a right that all children have ▼

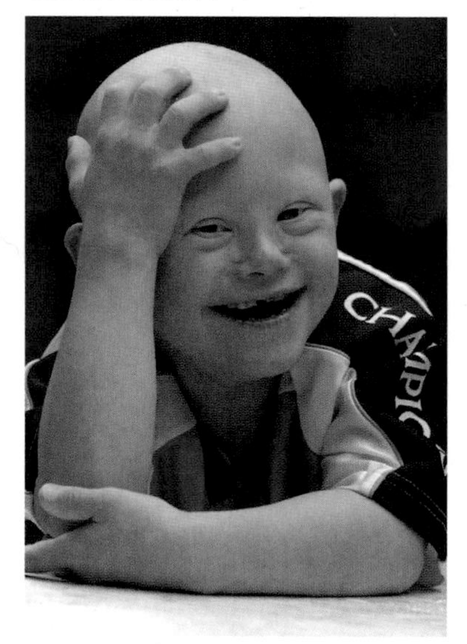

The principles of participation and inclusion

The Disability Discrimination Act 1995 (DDA 1995) was introduced to give legal rights to disabled adults and children, who have a right to be included in society and to participate within it. We call this the right to 'inclusion'.

But things haven't always been that way. Although disabled people have always been part of society, they haven't always been treated equally. Historically, disabled people have been regarded as 'abnormal' or even 'evil'. Some cultures believed that disabled people had mystic powers, while others thought that children were born disabled to punish their parents for a past wrongdoing. There were times when disabled children were drowned at birth or when they spent their lives locked away in institutions, shunned by society and living in fear. The way disabled people lived was dictated by non-disabled people and their attitudes towards disability.

In the more recent past there has been the assumption that disabled people (children and adults) have a problem. Their impairments have been regarded as personal tragedies. It's been seen as the responsibility of non-disabled people to either cure or care for the disabled person, taking steps to fit them into society. Treating disabled people as sick patients in this way is not empowering. This way of thinking is known as the 'Medical Model of Disability'.

There's a worldwide organisation called the Disabled People's Movement. The British Council of Disabled

People (BCODP) is a branch of this, formed in 1981. The BCODP believe that disability is not an inevitable consequence of a person's impairment (or in other words, that disability is not bound to happen because a person has an impairment).

The BCODP believe that disability arises from the negative way in which disabled people are treated by society. They believe that disabled people are dis-abled by society's structure, its attitudes and its lack of access, which exclude disabled people from activities that non-disabled people take for granted. It's believed that society should change to meet the needs of disabled people. This gives disabled people rights and choices. This is known as the 'Social Model of Disability'.

The DDA 1995 supports the Social Model of Disability by giving disabled people rights regarding the way they receive services, goods and facilities. Read on to find out more.

It's the Government's long-term vision that by 2025, disabled people in Britain should have full opportunities and choices to improve their quality of life and will be respected and included as equal members of society.

Learn the lingo

There are several specialist terms connected to disability. Some disabled people, families and professionals use different terms to mean the same thing. This is a bit confusing at first, but you will pick up the language. Some definitions are given below. But the best advice is to pay attention to the terms used within your setting and by your tutors. Some old-fashioned terms are considered inappropriate and in some cases offensive and are no longer used. For instance, we would say 'disabled' rather than 'handicapped'. We would say 'learning difficulties' rather than 'mentally handicapped.'

Children with additional needs = all children have needs that must be met. But this term refers to children who have extra needs due an impairment. Some people use the term 'special needs', but there's some disagreement about this. Some people don't like this term because they feel all children are special. Some disabled people think it's inappropriate as there's nothing 'special' about being disabled. Others think that 'special' is just another way of labelling disabled children as different from their peers. But families of young disabled children often feel more accepting of the term 'special'. Generally, if this term is used by a family, then practitioners will use it when working with them. The term 'disabled' may also be used to mean the same thing.

Impairment = term used to identify an individual's child's disability, e.g. a visual impairment, hearing impairment, speech impairment, physical impairment, etc. A child may have more than one impairment, e.g. a learning difficulty and a visual impairment. The word 'disability' or 'difficulty' may be used to mean the same thing.

Individual needs/specific needs = terms used describe how an impairment impacts on the needs of an individual child. This will be specific to them. For example, Emily, a wheelchair user, needs assistance with toileting and dressing. Nina, also a wheelchair user, does not.

Special educational needs (SEN) = Children with SEN learn differently from most children of the same age and may need extra or different help to learn. Not all disabled children need extra or different help to learn. It depends on their individual needs. The term SEN is used by national and local education departments.

Accessible = a facility that a disabled person is able to access, e.g. an accessible toilet, parking space, building.

Special setting = a setting just for children with additional needs/SEN, e.g. special school, special youth club.

Mainstream setting = a setting that is not just for children with additional needs/SEN, e.g. most schools, nurseries, etc.

Inclusion = occurs when a child with additional needs is included within a setting/activity.

Inclusive = an inclusive setting includes children with additional needs. Mainstream settings are required to be inclusive.

Rules and regulations

To support children with additional needs and their families, settings and childcarers must work in line with the current legislation, regulations and codes of practice that apply in their home country. The examples given here apply in England. The assessment and intervention framework outlined in this Unit apply to early years settings.

All children have the right to participate in society and to be given equal opportunities, regardless of whether they have additional needs. It's very important for settings and individual staff to practice inclusive ways of working. (Or in other words, to work in ways that promote inclusion within the setting). The main laws that safeguard these rights are:

The Disability Discrimination Act 1995

The Disability Discrimination Act 1995 (DDA 1995) was devised to support the rights of disabled people to take a full and active part in society. It gives them equality of access, or in other words, the same opportunities to participate in society as non-disabled people. This important piece of legislation gives disabled people (adults and children) rights regarding the way in which

they receive services, facilities or goods. This includes education, care and play services.

The DDA 1995 was introduced in three stages:

- In 1996 it became illegal for service providers to discriminate against disabled people by treating them less favourably than non-disabled people.
- In 1999 service providers became required by law to make reasonable adjustments for disabled people, such as providing extra assistance.
- In 2004 service providers became required by law to make reasonable adjustments to their premises. This means that it mustn't be unreasonably difficult for disabled people to access the provision because of physical barriers, such as narrow doorways or steps. If a premise's physical features cause a barrier for a disabled person, that feature may be removed or altered. Or a service may provide a reasonable way of avoiding the feature or may make their service available in a different way, e.g. a pre-school may replace steps into the front of their building with a ramp. Or they may open a fire door around the side to let a wheelchair user in.

A disabled person is defined in the DDA 1995 as someone who has a physical or mental impairment that adversely affects their ability to carry out normal day-to-day activities. This will be long term – it will have lasted for 12 months or be likely to last for more than 12 months. This includes some chronic illnesses, such as ME, which affect some people's ability to carry out normal day-to-day activities.

Service providers must make reasonable adjustments to premises to give disabled people equal opportunities ▼

The UN Convention on the Rights of the Child

The UN Convention on the Rights of the Child was ratified by the UK Government in 1991. All of the 41 Articles of the Act apply to all children, both disabled and non-disabled. Article 23 'Disabled Children' states that disabled children must be helped to be as independent as possible. They must be helped to take a full and active part in everyday life.

The Care Standards Act 2000

The Care Standards Act 2000 sets out 14 quality outcomes that all daycare settings registered with Ofsted must comply with. These are known as the 14 'standards'. The standards apply to practitioners' work with all children. They include:

Also see Unit 1.

- Standard 9 Equal opportunities.
  This tells us that staff must actively promote equality of opportunity and anti-discriminatory practice for all children.
- Standard 10 Special needs.
  This tells us that the setting must be aware that some children may have special educational needs. The setting must make sure that appropriate action can be taken when a child with special needs is identified or admitted to the provision. Steps must be taken to promote the welfare and development of the child within the setting, in partnership with families and outside agencies.

Special Educational Needs and Disability Act 2001

This Act was introduced to extend the rights of children. It strengthens the right for disabled children to be educated in mainstream schools, although special schools are acknowledged as having a vital role to play. LEAs must provide information and advice to families. Ways of resolving disputes over the provision of education must be in place.

Every Child Matters

Also see page 368.

Every Child Matters: Change for Children aims to improve outcomes for all children and young people, including disabled children. As many disabled children's needs are

complex and cross traditional service boundaries, they are one of the groups who stand to gain the most from this programme of change.

Every Child Matters is supported by a number of policies and strategies that should work together to improve outcomes for disabled children, young people and their families. You can find further information on this on Government websites – see the Follow up section for details.

The Special Educational Needs Code of Practice

The Special Educational Needs Code of Practice (SEN Code) was introduced in 1994 and revised in 2002. It applies to schools and early-education settings offering the Early Years Foundation Stage.

Children with special educational needs are identified as:

- Children who learn differently from most children of the same age.
- Children who may need extra or different help to learn.

The SEN Code sets out procedures to be followed in order to meet the needs of children with special educational needs.

Under the SEN Code, early years settings must:

- Adopt the recommendations of the SEN Code.
- Train staff to identify and manage children with special educational needs.
- Devise and implement a Special Educational Needs policy in line with the SEN Code. This must explain how the setting promotes inclusion, which means how it includes children with disabilities and/or special educational needs within the setting.
- Appoint a Special Educational Needs Co-ordinator (SENCO), who will have responsibility for overseeing how the setting meets the needs of children and follows the SEN Code.

Settings must do these things even if there are currently no children with SEN in attendance.

Assessment and intervention frameworks

Under the SEN Code, settings are required to intervene and take action to support children with SEN. There are two stages:

1. Early Years Action
   This is the first stage in which a child's special educational needs are identified. To meet the child's needs the setting should then devise interventions (strategies) that are additional to or different from those provided under the setting's usual curriculum.
2. Early Years Action Plus
   This is the second stage in which practitioners feel it's appropriate to involve outside specialists/professionals. These people can offer more specialist assessment of the child and advise the setting on strategies to support them.

Parents, carers and families are at the heart of provision as they know most about their child. Some parents are 'experts' with wide-ranging and in-depth knowledge of their child and their disability and/or special educational need.

Early Years Action

Staff working in the early years are often the first to notice that a child may be experiencing difficulties with their learning and/or development, although sometimes it's a parent or carer who first expresses a concern about their child. When it's suspected that a child is having problems, staff need to make focused observations of the child to see if they can identify specific difficulties. These observations should be recorded. As you learnt in Unit 2, childcarers often first notice that a child is experiencing a difficulty when they make observations to monitor children's learning and development. They will then plan activities and support to help the child progress.

See Unit 2.

The SEN Code explains that practitioners will have cause for concern when, despite receiving appropriate early education experiences, one or a combination of the following criteria applies to a child:

- Makes little or no progress, even when staff have used approaches targeted to improve the child's identified area of weakness.

- Continues working at levels significantly below those expected for children of a similar age in certain areas.
- Presents persistent emotional and/or behavioural difficulties that are not managed by the setting's general behaviour management strategies.
- Has sensory or physical problems and continues to make little or no progress despite the provision of personal aids and equipment.
- Has communication and/or interaction difficulties, and requires specific individual interventions (one-to-one attention) to learn.

Once it's been established that a child meets one or more of the above criteria, childcarers should:

- Arrange a time to meet with parents or carers to discuss the concerns and to involve them as partners in supporting the child's learning. A childcarer (usually the child's keyworker) should explain the role of the setting's SENCO, and discuss the involvement of the SENCO with the parents or carers. Staff should ask the parents and carers for their own observations of their child's learning and, if appropriate, for information about health or physical problems, or the previous involvement of any outside professionals such as speech therapists. Parents are the first and best source of information in many cases.
- Meet with the SENCO. Staff should make available as much helpful information as possible, e.g. observations, assessments, health details.
- The childcarer and SENCO should work together with the parents and carers to decide on the action needed to help the child progress. The SEN Code states that action should 'enable the very young child with special educational needs to learn and progress to the maximum possible'. The diagram below gives examples of strategies (actions) that may be used.
- An Individual Education Plan (IEP) should be devised for the child. This should record three or four short-term targets set for them and detail the strategies that will be put in place to help them work towards the targets. The IEP should only record that which is additional to or different from the general curriculum plan of the setting (see Unit 10 for details of curriculums). The IEP should be discussed with the family and the child concerned.

- IEPs should be working documents, which means they will be amended over time. Regular reviews should take place in consultation with families to check on how effective the strategies implemented are and the progress made towards targets. The SEN Code states that reviews need not be 'unduly formal', but a record of them must be kept in the IEP. New targets and strategies decided on at review must also be recorded. There should be a review at least every three months.

Your setting will have adopted a set of record keeping documents to complete throughout the stages of Early Years Action and Early Years Action Plus. The blank documents may have been bought or the SENCO may have devised them.

Strategies ▶

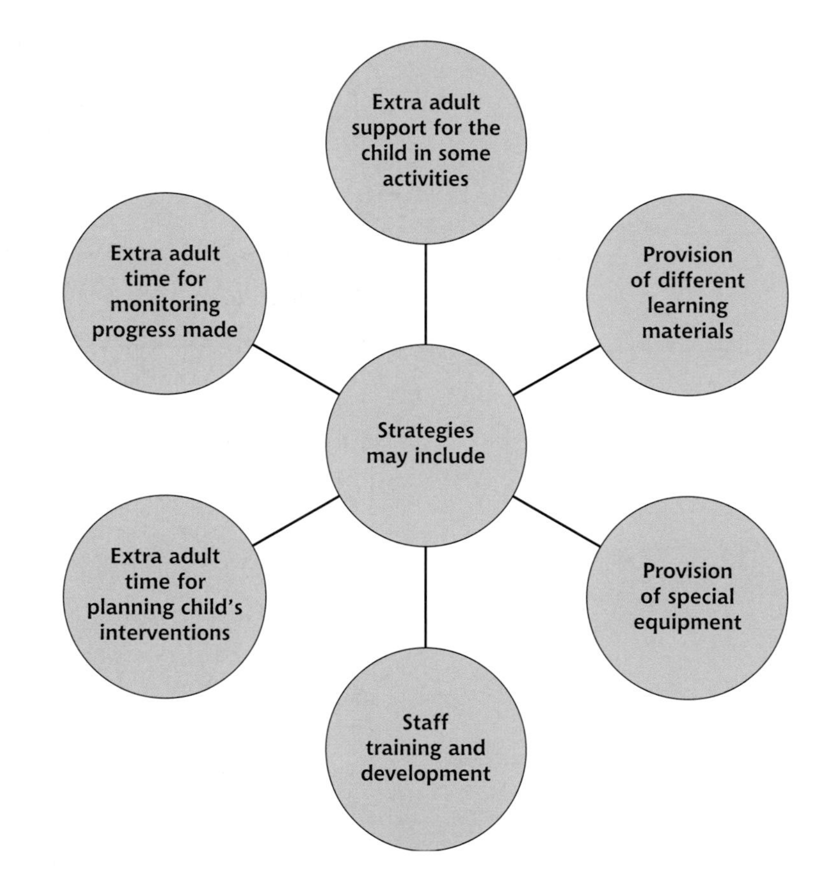

Early Years Action Plus

The decision to implement Early Years Action Plus (that is to involve outside support services and professionals) is generally taken in consultation with a family at a meeting to review a child's IEP. The SEN Code identifies that the implementation of Early Years Action Plus is likely to be triggered when, despite receiving support tailored to their needs, a child:

- Continues to make little or no progress in specific areas over a long period.
- Continues working at a level substantially below that expected of children of a similar age.
- Has emotional difficulties that substantially interfere with the child's own learning or that of the group, despite an individual behaviour management programme
- Has sensory or physical needs and requires additional equipment or regular specialist support.
- Has ongoing communication or interaction difficulties that are a barrier to learning and social relationships.

See page 171.

The type of support services and professionals available to settings at this stage varies according to local policy. But there will be support available.

To find out about the provision made in your local area by your Local Education Authority (LEA) you can:

- Contact your LEA. You may find relevant information on their website.
- Ask the SENCO at your setting.
- Ask your tutor.

Your LEA's support services or local health or medical services may be able to provide support and help with:

- Assessment.
- Advice on IEPs.
- Strategies.
- Activities.
- Equipment.
- Specialist support for children during some activities.

At the Early Years Action Plus stage, outside specialists should be consulted as part of the review process while they are involved with the child.

Although the procedures of 'Early Years Action' and 'Early Years Action Plus' apply to schools and settings offering the Early Years Foundation Stage, they can effectively be used by childcarers working with younger children.

Statutory assessment

In some cases, children don't make the expected progress despite the intervention of Early Years Action Plus. At this stage the family, childcarer, SENCO and outside

professionals meet to discuss if a referral should be made to the LEA requesting a statutory assessment of the child. If agreed, an application for assessment is made.

The LEA asks for all relevant records including observations, IEPs and assessments. These are considered and the LEA decides (within 26 weeks) if the child should be made the subject of a Statement of Special Educational Needs. The statement is legally binding. It sets out a child's needs and outlines what special educational provision must be made to meet them. The LEA must then provide this for the child by law. This applies to all LEAs in England. The nature of the provision made by the LEA will depend on the child's need. Examples of provision include:

- A transfer to a specialist setting.
- A place at a mainstream setting with additional one-to-one support.
- A place at a mainstream setting with additional resources and equipment.
- Support of an educational or clinical psychologist.
- A home-based programme, such as Portage (a programme of activities tailored to suit individual children. Parents and carers carry out the activities with the child at home. A Portage worker will support the family).

Statements for children under the age of five must be reviewed by the LEA every six months. Because of the time it takes to go through the stages of intervention, most children are not referred for statutory assessment until they are over the age of five, by which time they will have started school.

Working in partnership with families

It's important to respect and value the role of family members. Parents are usually the primary carers of children and they know their children best. You should always form partnerships with families based on this fact.

Childcarers working with children with additional needs should be informed by families' knowledge and experience of their child. Remember that having good knowledge about a specific impairment or special educational need is helpful, but it doesn't tell you much about an individual child.

For example, a childcarer may be very well informed about Down's syndrome. But although there will be some general commonalities (things in common) between children with Down's syndrome, each child is an individual, just like all other children. So children with Down's syndrome will develop at different rates and have differing abilities. Some may have additional impairments or special educational needs. They will have different likes and dislikes, different personalities and different learning styles. They will respond differently to activities and experiences. Parents and carers know all of these personal details about their child. When a good partnership is built, this information can be shared and the quality of the childcarers' work with that child will be better as a result.

Ongoing, two-way communication is at the heart of a good partnership between a family and the setting. You've learnt that it's valuable to communicate:

- When a child's additional needs are first identified.

  or
- When a child who has already been identified as having additional needs starts the setting.
- Throughout the Early Years Action/Early Years Action Plus processes, including at reviews.

It's also valuable to communicate:

- When the child is dropped off/collected. To share information about how the child has been, what they've done and so on. A home-to-setting diary may be used to share information, which will build into a record. If a child has limited communication abilities, this contact is especially important as it will be up to adults to make meaningful links between the setting and home. For instance, if a parent tells you their child got a pet rabbit at the weekend, you can talk about this with the child and share the news with their peers at circle time.

Communication with families is important ▶

- Feedback on strategies or breakthroughs in learning as they occur.
- Any difficulties that have arisen, and how they've been approached or resolved.

The impact on families

It's important that a child's difficulties are recognised early on. This leads to early intervention, designed to identify and meet a child's current needs whilst preventing further difficulties from developing.

It's important to understand how a child with a disability can impact on parents ▼

You've learnt that early years workers are often the first to identify problems with children's learning or development. This means they're often the first to raise these issues with parents and carers. In other cases, families may already be aware of a disability or special educational need, but if the child is young they may still be adjusting to this news. It's important for you to understand how having a child with a disability can impact on parents, carers, siblings and members of the wider family such as grandparents, aunts and uncles.

It's often a shock for family members to be told that a child has a disability and/or special educational need, and so the matter must be handled with honesty and sensitivity. A traumatic time may follow, and family members may go through a range of emotions similar to those that are experienced by the bereaved (i.e. people who are grieving for a loved one who has died). These emotions may include:

- Disbelief.
  For example, a parent may think that the childcarer, doctor or specialist is mistaken.
- Denial.
  A grandparent may be convinced the child will grow out of it or catch up.
- Grief.
  A father may grieve for the child he has 'lost' – the one he imagined would be perfect, whose future he had thought about.
- Self-blame.
  A mother may think it was her fault – she must have done something wrong during pregnancy. Was she too active? Did she eat the wrong things?

- Aggression.
  A parent may feel angry, cheated out of the child they imagined. A sibling may feel angry about the extra attention their brother or sister needs.

Childcarers need to be supportive and understanding, even if families find it hard to accept what they are saying at first. The setting must be a non-judgemental environment where family members can feel safe to express their feelings, whatever they are, and find support.

Families of children with disabilities can also feel isolated and ill-informed. Childcarers should liaise closely with SENCOs, who will know about local and national sources of support and information for parents and carers, including organisations, professionals, books and leaflets. These details should be passed on when appropriate.

But some parents who were already aware of their child's disability may feel quite differently. In the case of Down's syndrome for instance, the condition will have been identified at birth (or perhaps during pregnancy) and the family will have had some time to adjust to this. Parents and carers may already be well informed about the syndrome and may have received support from professionals and organisations. They may even be 'expert parents', with wide-ranging knowledge of their child and the disability or special educational need. If so, they may be well placed to offer support to other parents who find themselves in a similar situation.

Learn the lingo

Respite care = temporary care that is provided for a short period to give families a brief break, or to support them in a difficult period (e.g. if a main carer has to go into hospital). This is usually provided outside of the family home.

The material and personal resources available to families of children with disabilities and/or special educational needs will also vary and so the experience of the families is likely to differ. Free services for children without a statement of special educational needs depend on local policy. Some families may be able to pay for additional specialist support, **respite care** or equipment for their child, while others will not. Some parents or carers may have a good support network of extended family, while others may be isolated.

In summary, families have differing needs. It's the job of childcarers to be aware of the needs of families and to tailor the support they offer to them accordingly, so that needs are effectively met. You should always follow the procedures of your setting that relate to working in partnership with parents and carers.

Participating in activities

It helps all children, including those with additional needs, when their families and their setting share a joint approach and a pleasant relationship.

There are various ways of involving families in activities including:

- Inviting parents and carers into the setting to take part in activities alongside their child.
  This helps the family members and the childcarers to establish a consistent approach as they become familiar with each other's ways of working with the child. It's also helpful if families are feeling isolated.
- Suggesting activities that family members can do with their children at home to follow up those done within the setting.
  This helps to consolidate and reinforce the work done in the setting, allowing further opportunities for learning and progress. This can be particularly important for children who need extra time to master particular skills or concepts.
- Ensuring families know about opportunities to socialise with other children and their families, e.g. the setting's fundraising events, summer trips or festival celebrations.
  This encourages wider participation and inclusion and helps to avoid the isolation of families.

Advantages and disadvantages of inclusion

The advantages of inclusion include:

- All children are given equal opportunities within the same setting.
- Disabled children get to know, interact and routinely participate alongside non-disabled peers.
- Non-disabled children get to know, interact and routinely participate with disabled children.
- Children can attend a setting close to home.
- Disabled children play and make friends with local children they may also see outside of the setting.

The disadvantages of inclusion include:

- Children/families may feel different and/or isolated within a setting.
- Children may not have opportunities to make friends with other disabled children.
- Families may not have opportunities to get to know other families of disabled children (who can be part of an extended network of support).
- There may still be some barriers to participation (see below), e.g. specialist aids and equipment may not be readily available, staff may not have appropriate training and experience.

With sensitive support, many of the disadvantages of inclusion can be tackled within an inclusive setting.

Settings should be inclusive ▶

FOCUS ON...
your learning

In this section you've learnt about the legal requirements and code of practice that relate to supporting children with additional needs. You've learnt about inclusion, and the importance of working in partnership with families, providing necessary support.

Questions

1 There's a range of terms and words associated with disability. What's the best way to pick up the appropriate language to use within settings?

2 Suggest ways in which you could communicate with families.

Learning Outcome 2

FOCUS ON...

how to support children with additional needs within the setting

This links with Assessment Criteria **2.1, 2.2**

Observing and identifying children's needs

The process of observing and identifying children's needs is covered in Learning Outcome 1 of this unit, and also in Unit 2.

Families should be encouraged to participate in the observation of their child and the identification of their needs. Parents and carers can assist childcarers with the observations carried out in the setting and the analysis of these, which leads to the identification of needs. But they can also be encouraged to share the observations that they make outside the setting. As the child's primary carers they will be familiar with the child's experiences at home and in other environments. This helps to give a well-rounded picture of the child. The parents and carers should remain involved as an IEP is drawn up and then reviewed over time (as explained in Learning Outcome 1).

Details of the individual children in your care

Childcarers should develop a good knowledge of individual needs as they affect the children in their care. You learnt in Learning Outcome 1 that the same impairment can be experienced by different children in very different ways. You need to understand how the children you're working with are affected so that you can meet their needs appropriately.

You should also be aware of the expected pattern of development of the children with additional needs that you're responsible for. Children generally (but not always) master skills or achieve learning in a similar sequence, even though they may not do so at the same rate as peers of the same age. But some children may not be expected to achieve certain milestones 'in order', or to achieve them at all. For instance, some children will not be expected to

carry out large motor skills such as walking, jumping or running. But it may be appropriate to work with such a child on other ways of travelling, such as rolling across the floor or floating in water. These issues would be discussed at an intervention meeting when devising or reviewing an IEP in consultation with the SENCO, family members, the child and perhaps outside professionals.

Understanding the needs of the individual children is important ▼

Understanding the needs of the individual children in your care will enable you to feel confident within your roles and responsibilities. It will help you to have realistic expectations of children's development, and help you to work effectively with children with additional needs and their families.

Special educational needs may be due to:

- Physical impairments.
- Visual impairments.
- Hearing impairments.
- Communication/speech difficulties.
- Emotional/behavioural difficulties.
- General learning difficulties or developmental delay.
- Specific learning difficulties (such as dyslexia).
- Medical conditions.

Planning to meet children's needs

In addition to making IEPs to support children with additional needs, it's important for childcarers to make sure that all the activities and experiences offered within the setting are fully inclusive. Everyone should have equal opportunities to participate.

So when short-term session plans are drawn up, staff should consider the individual requirements of the children who will be in attendance. Careful attention should be given to the activities planned and the free-play resources to be offered.

Inclusive planning checklist

When you're planning an activity, always ask yourself the questions on this checklist:

- Does the activity suit all the children's needs?
- Are adaptations or alternatives necessary to ensure participation? (see below)

- Are specialist aids or equipment required?
- How should children be grouped? (Will some children benefit from being in a smaller group?)
- What level of supervision is needed? (Will some children need closer supervision than others?)
- What support will be needed? (Will some children benefit from one-to-one support from an adult?)
- Might there be a good opportunity to implement a strategy identified within a child's IEP? (Such as encouraging them to sit within a social group for example).

This links with Learning Outcome 3

Ensure all children can participate in activities ▶

GOOD PRACTICE

After children have taken part in activities and experiences, take some time to review how well they went. Were the children's needs met effectively? If not, what can you learn from this? What can you do differently next time? Remember to consult with children if appropriate. They're the best people to tell you if they felt fully able to participate, and to make suggestions about improving inclusive practice.

Communication difficulties

The SEN Code tells us that 'most children with special educational needs have strengths and difficulties in one, some or all of the areas of speech, language and communication. Their communication needs may be both diverse and complex'.

'Communication' means the process of interacting with others. Children who have difficulties communicating may have difficulties forming relationships as communication is the cornerstone of our relationships with other people. Children may feel isolated, left out or frustrated and may not feel motivated to communicate. Behaviour and social development may be affected. Children use language to think as well as to speak and so there may also be an affect on intellectual development.

The range of communication difficulties will include children with:

- Speech and language delay, impairments and disorders.
- Specific learning difficulties such as dyspraxia and dyslexia.
- Hearing impairments.
- Visual impairments.
- Mental/emotional health issues.

Communication difficulties also occur in:

- Children who demonstrate features within the autistic spectrum.
- Some children with learning difficulties.

The difficulties listed above are known as 'barriers to communication'.

Alternative and Augmentive Communication

Alternative and Augmentive Communication (AAC) describes any system or special method of communication that's used to overcome communication barriers. Using AAC can help children with communication difficulties to make the most of their available senses and experiences. Methods of AAC include:

- Symbols.
  A child may carry a deck of symbol cards, using them to signify meaning. These can be personalised. For instance, a child may have cards showing pictures of different resources. He may show staff the relevant card to indicate what he'd like to play with.
- Communication boards.
  These generally contain a number of symbols or words. Children express themselves by pointing to them. Some boards are designed to fit onto wheelchairs.
- Voice output communication aids.
  These may be connected to an electronic speaking communication board, or a laptop computer, that enables a child to 'talk'.

- Sign language.
  Including Makaton – a basic version of British Sign Language that may be taught to younger children or those with learning difficulties. Gestures may also be used.
- Facial expressions.
  Useful for expressing emotion.

It's important to identify methods of breaking down communication barriers for individual children. Sometimes very simple steps can make a real difference. For instance:

FAST FACT

Specialist help and advice from outside professionals (such as speech therapists) is often needed. Young children with speech or language delay are most likely to overcome their problems when they receive intervention early on.

- Hearing aids.
- If a child lip reads, adults and peers can be encouraged to face the child when speaking directly to them or to the group they are playing or working within.
- If a child has partial hearing, it may help to eliminate all unnecessary background noise when communicating with them. Slowing the pace of conversation and speaking clearly may also help.
- Children with learning difficulties may find it easier to understand sentences that are short and simple.

Some children may communicate via AAC methods ▶

Attention deficits

Attention deficit disorders are thought to be caused by a chemical imbalance in the brain that affects the parts of the brain that control attention, concentration and impulsivity (being impulsive). This means that a range of behaviours may be displayed by children with attention deficits. There are three core symptoms of attention deficits:

Hyperactivity

Signs:

Children may squirm and fidget when seated, or have difficulty remaining seated when this is required of them. They may tend to run about excessively or when it's inappropriate to do so. They may be 'always on the go'. They may talk excessively and have difficulty playing or listening quietly.

Effect on learning, social relationships and self-esteem:

Children may miss out on learning and the development of skills because they aren't listening, concentrating or participating – they may be busy fidgeting or moving around the room. They may unintentionally distract the rest of the group, or ruin their games or activities. They may play too roughly for their peers. They may often be in trouble and this may have a negative effect on their self-esteem. They may believe they are unable to behave.

Impulsivity

Signs:

Children may have difficulty taking turns. They may interrupt other people and intrude in conversations and games. They may not wait for the end of a question before attempting to answer it. They may blurt things out without thinking about them first, making them socially inept (or in other words, socially unskilled). They may have volatile and unpredictable moods. They may lash out when frustrated and have a short temper.

Effect on learning, social relationships and self-esteem:

Being socially inept in these ways can make children unpopular with their peers, which affects their self-esteem and confidence. Some children may be afraid of the impulsive child as unpredictable outbursts can be frightening and they may have been hurt by the child in the past. Some children may enjoy the reaction from a child with a short temper, enjoying winding them up or getting them into trouble.

Inattention

Signs:

Children may have difficulty concentrating and may dislike and/or avoid activities that require sustained concentration. They may be easily distracted, finding it difficult to finish tasks. Children may not seem to listen when they are talked to directly and they may not follow instructions given to them. The child may frequently lose things and be forgetful.

Effect on learning, social relationships and self-esteem:

Children may have difficulties joining in group games and activities as they may forget the rules, lose concentration and not finish what they start. This can deter other children from playing with them, affecting self-esteem. Children may not concentrate in learning situations, and children of school age may avoid study or forget what they should do. This added to poor memory may lead to poor performance in tests and exams. Changing rooms or teachers often can confuse older children. Children may believe they are stupid or unable to learn.

Attention deficits and associated problems may be treated with a combination of approaches that can include:

- A behavioural management programme.
- Behavioural therapy.
- Medication.
- Psychotherapy.

It's essential that childcarers liaise carefully with children, families, SENCOs and outside specialists when working with children with attention deficits. Generally, childcarers will be guided by outside specialists about how to best support the individual child they're working with, depending on the child's difficulties and individual circumstances.

Stereotyping must also be avoided. Be careful not to make broad assumptions about children and their capabilities for instance, or about families and their feelings. Get to know individual children and families, and the issues that affect them personally.

GOOD PRACTICE

It's good practice to avoid labelling children. There are many terms and words associated with disability, but you must not let these stop you from seeing the individual child. For instance, it's better to think of Maisy as a child who has Down's syndrome, rather than a 'Down's child'. Elliot is a child who has epilepsy, rather than 'an epiletic'.

FOCUS ON...
your learning

You've learnt that it's important to have a good understanding of how impairments affect individual children and to have realistic expectations of children's development. This will help you to plan activities and learning opportunities to meet children's needs. You've also learnt about specific communication methods and the importance of avoiding labelling and stereotyping.

Questions:

1 It is good practice to review activities. What factors should you consider in your reviews?

2 What are the three core symptoms of attention deficits?

Learning Outcome 3

FOCUS ON...

the role of the adult in enabling children with additional needs to participate in activities and experiences

In this section you'll learn about the barriers to participation, and how they can be overcome to enable children to participate in activities.

This links with Assessment Criteria **3.1, 3.2**

Barriers to participation

It is important that all children can participate in activities and experiences ▼

It's important that childcarers promote inclusive ways of working. Or in other words, ways that are suitable for all children and families, so that everyone can be included in the group, jointly participating in the activities and experiences offered within the setting.

In order to promote inclusion, childcarers must be aware of features that may cause a barrier to participation. A barrier can be anything that prevents children from participating fully. Barriers fall into three categories:

1. Attitudinal.
   The belief held by some people that disabled children are incapable, or to be pitied or feared. These barriers may be overcome with training.
2. Environmental.
   Including physical barriers, e.g. premises that are inaccessible due to steps or poor lighting, or other difficulties that occur within the environment such as the use of complex language. The barriers may apply to the provision as a whole or to particular activities or experiences. These barriers may be overcome with changes to the layout of premises or the organisation of activities/experiences – more information follows.
3. Institutional.
   A lack of anti-discriminatory policies or procedures.

These barriers may be overcome with training and the introduction of policies and procedures.

Settings must:

- Examine their provision, identifying existing barriers to participation. Childcarers must be proactive, anticipating features of the setting that are likely to be barriers, regardless of whether those features present a barrier to the children currently attending.
- Take action to remove barriers, whenever possible and reasonable, or
- Whenever possible and reasonable, alter the barrier so that it no longer has the same effect, or
- Whenever possible and reasonable, find an alternative way to offer the activity or experience.
- Monitor the effects of the action taken, introducing new action if necessary.

Adapting the physical environment

It's likely that your setting will have already identified and overcome some of the barriers to participation that occur within your physical environment.

But you may find new potential barriers when:

- A new child with additional needs starts attending the setting.
- The needs of children already in attendance change over time.

By considering the layout of a room carefully you can effectively overcome physical barriers. For instance:

- Furniture of different heights may be used to ensure that wheelchair users can participate in tabletop activities.
- Furniture may be positioned and activities set out to allow easy passage for children using wheelchairs, crutches or other aids.
- Furniture and equipment may be kept in the same position to assist children with visual impairments to locate and navigate.
- Equipment and resources may be stored at a height that makes it accessible to all children.
- Scent clues or bright colours may be used to mark out certain areas (e.g. lavender in the book corner, mint in the play dough).
- Task lighting may be used to brighten activity areas.

- Comfortable soft areas may be provided for children who need to rest during play sessions.

You may need to change the layout of furniture to make activities accessible ▼

Adapting activities and experiences

As you learnt in section 2, it's also important that you consider the needs of children in relation to the activities and experiences that you offer. This can be done at the short-term planning stage. Once barriers to participation have been identified (there's a checklist to help you in Learning Outcome 2), you can consider ways of overcoming them.

Specialised aids or pieces of equipment may be available to assist children – there's more information about this below. But simple strategies can often be used effectively too. It may be appropriate to:

- Devise your own adaptations.
- Change the way an activity is organised.
- Offer an alternative.

The following table gives examples of simple strategies that could be used to overcome barriers.

Specialist aids and equipment

You should be aware of the relevant specialist aids and pieces of equipment that are available for the children you work with. You must be confident that you know how to use these safely. Your SENCO and outside professionals will be able to offer advice.

Barriers and strategies to overcome them ▼

Activity	Barrier	Strategy
Painting with rollers	Child with a physical impairment cannot grip the roller effectively	Practitioners mould thick Plasticine around the handle. The child grips it, altering the shape of Plasticine to suit her grip. The roller has been easily adapted to suit her individual grasp
Game of catch to be played in pairs	Child with a visual impairment has difficulty seeing the ball approaching, and therefore difficulty preparing to catch it accurately	Practitioners attach a tail of bright ribbon to some of the balls, and tie bells (from a textiles shop) securely to the ends. The balls are now more easily located, and they can also be caught by the tail
Game of musical bumps	One child with a hearing impairment cannot hear the music, while a wheelchair user cannot sit on the floor and get up again easily	Practitioners play musical statues instead, and devise two hand signals, one that is used to indicate when children should dance, and another for when they should freeze like statues
Singing songs	A child with communication difficulties has difficulties joining in	Practitioners encourage the group to come up with actions they can do as they sing. They also slow the pace of the singing. They allow time to play along with musical instruments too

FAST FACT

Barriers to participation within the setting don't just affect disabled children and their families. A non-disabled child may have a disabled family member who is affected. Disabled staff members may also experience barriers.

GOOD PRACTICE

It's good practice to consult children about the way in which barriers are tackled if this is appropriate to their age and ability. Also see Learning Outcome 2 for details of how to review inclusive activities and experiences.

Some children will already be using aids and equipment at home, in which case parents and carers will be the setting's first source of information. Educational catalogues and care catalogues are useful. Most settings receive new editions regularly and they're a good way to keep up to date with new innovations and designs.

There are many specialist aids and pieces of equipment available for children. What individual children use will of course depend on their needs, but you may come across:

- Specially angled cutlery designed for children with physical impairments who have difficulty feeding themselves.

Practical example

Adapting for Jade

Playworker Will works at a holiday club. Ten-year old Jade, a wheelchair user, has recently started attending the club. The staff have planned some parachute games and Will needs to ensure that Jade can participate. He thinks that she could join in effectively if the other children played kneeling down instead of standing up. He asks Jade what she thinks of this idea. Jade says her teacher plays parachute games in the same way at school and that this adaptation works for her.

1. *Why did Will include Jade when deciding how to adapt the activity?*

- Non-slip matting that has flexible use – it can be placed under plates or bowls at mealtimes to stop them sliding away, or perhaps under pots of paint at the craft table.
- Light boxes that can be used to back-light objects making them easier for children with visual impairments to see.
- Hearing loops that can be installed for those with hearing impairments.
- Communication boards that can be used by those with communication difficulties.

Have a go!

Have a look at an educational or care catalogue or website. Make a list of specialist aids, equipment and play resources that may help children aged three to five years with the following impairments:

(see the weblinks on page 365).

- A physical impairment of the hands, leading to difficulty with fine movements including feeding and fine motor play.
- A visual impairment, leading to difficulty locating and tracking moving objects such as balls.

FOCUS ON...
your learning

You've learnt about the barriers to participation for children and families and how to overcome them. You've also learnt about specialist aids and equipment and how to review activities to ensure an inclusive approach.

Questions:

1. What are the three categories of barriers to participation?
2. Who can give you advice about specialist aids and equipment?

RAPID RECAP

Learning Outcome 1

Childcarers and settings must work in line with the legal requirements and codes of practice that relate to supporting children with additional needs within their home country. Disabled children and adults have the right to participation, so inclusion within settings is important. Each setting must appoint a SENCO and have a SEN policy. Staff should work in partnership with families in order to support both the family and the child with additional needs effectively. There's a range of local and national support available for families.

Learning Outcome 2

You must have a good understanding of how impairments affect individual children and have realistic expectations of children's development. This will help you to plan activities and learning opportunities to meet children's needs. You should check that all activities and experiences offered are inclusive and take steps to make them inclusive where necessary. Specific communication methods are helpful for some children. You must avoiding labelling and stereotyping children and families.

Learning Outcome 3

Barriers to participation stop children and families from being included within settings, activities or experiences. Barriers can be physical, attitudinal or institutional. Childcarers must identify and overcome barriers, promoting inclusion. This may be done in a number of ways, including the use of specialist aids and equipment, adapting activities and changing the physical premises or layout of activities.

FAQ

Q **How will I be assessed on this Unit?**

A *You'll complete an assignment task. CACHE publishes a task for each optional unit every year.*

Q **What will I have to do?**

A *Your tutor or Centre will help you to understand the task.*

See Unit 1 Learning Outcome 5 for more information on study skills.

Weblinks

You may like to visit the following websites:

- www.essentialaids.com
- http://www.independentliving.co.uk/kids
- http://www.dlf.org.uk/public/suppliers/play.html
  To see a range of specialist aids, equipment and resources.
- http://www.cafamily.org.uk/
  Home of Contact a Family, which provides information and support to the parents of all disabled children.
- http://www.direct.gov.uk/en/CaringForSomeone/CaringForADisabledChild/index.htm
  For information about laws and policies relating to disabled children, and available support for families and carers.
- http://www.ncb.org.uk/Page.asp?sve=785
  Home of the Council for Disabled Children.
- http://www.ndcs.org.uk
  Home of the National Deaf Children's Society.
- http://www.nbcs.org.uk/
  Home of the National Blind Children's Society.
- http://www.mencap.org.uk/
  Home of Mencap, which works with people with learning disabilities and their families and carers.

Introduction to children's learning

Learning Outcomes

In this unit you'll learn about:

1. The different frameworks for learning for children from birth to age 16 years.
2. The principles of how children learn.

3. The role of the adult in supporting children's learning from birth to age 16 years.

Learning Outcome 1

FOCUS ON...

the different frameworks for learning for children from birth to age 16 years

In this section you'll learn about the frameworks for learning for children from birth to age 16 years, which apply in England.

This links with Assessment Criteria **1.1, 1.2**

The Early Years Foundation Stage

From September 2008 *The Early Years Foundation Stage* will be mandatory for:

- All schools.
- All early years providers in Ofsted registered settings.

It will apply to children from birth to the end of the academic year in which the child has their fifth birthday.

In the *Statutory Framework for the Early Years Foundation Stage* the Department for Education and Skills tells us that:

Statutory framework for the Early Years Foundation Stage ▼

"Every child deserves the best possible start in life and support to fulfil their potential. A child's experience in the early years has a major impact on their future life chances. A secure, safe and happy childhood is important in its own right, and it provides the foundation for children to make the most of their abilities and talents as they grow up. When parents choose to use early years services they want to know that provision will keep their children safe and help them to thrive. The Early Years Foundation Stage (EYFS) is the framework that provides that assurance. The overarching aim of the EYFS is to help young children achieve the five *Every Child Matters* outcomes..."

Every Child Matters is the government agenda that focuses on bringing together services to support children and families. It sets out five major outcomes for children:

- Being healthy.
- Staying safe.
- Enjoying and achieving.

- Making a positive contribution.
- Economic well-being.

The EYFS aims to meet the *Every Child Matters* outcomes by:

- **Setting standards** for the learning, development and care young children should experience when they attend a setting outside their family home. Every child should make progress, with no children left behind.
- **Providing equality of opportunity and anti-discriminatory practice**. Ensuring that every child is included and not disadvantaged because of ethnicity, culture, religion, home language, family background, learning difficulties or disabilities, gender or ability.
- **Creating a framework for partnership working between parents and professionals**, and between all the settings that the child attends.
- **Improving quality and consistency in the early years through standards that apply to all settings**. This provides the basis for the inspection and regulation regime carried out by Ofsted.
- **Laying a secure foundation for future learning** through learning and development that is planned around the individual needs and interests of the child. This is informed by the use of ongoing observational assessment.

FAST FACT

From September 2008 the EYFS will replace *The Curriculum Guidance for the Foundation Stage, the Birth to Three Matters Framework* and *The National Standards for Under 8s Daycare and Childminding.*

Themes, Principles and Commitments

The EYFS is based around four **Themes.** Each theme is linked to a **Principle**. Each Principle is supported by four **Commitments**. The Commitments describe how their Principle can be put into action. The Themes, Principles and Commitments are shown in the table that follows.

Additional statements are provided within the EYFS to explain each Commitment in more detail. You can see these on the Department for Education and Skills' 'Principles into Practice' poster, an extract of which is reproduced below.

Themes, principles and commitments ▼

Theme	Principle	Commitments
1. A Unique Child	Every child is a competent learner from birth who can be resilient, capable, confident and self-assured.	1.1 Child development 1.2 Inclusive practice 1.3 Keeping safe 1.4 Health and well-being
2. Positive Relationships	Children learn to be strong and independent from a base of loving and secure relationships with parents and/or a key person.	2.1 Respecting each other 2.2 Parents as partners 2.3 Supporting learning 2.4 Key person
3. Enabling Environments	The environment plays a key role in supporting and extending children's development and learning.	3.1 Observation, assessment and planning 3.2 Supporting every child 3.3 The learning environment 3.4 The wider context
4. Learning and Development	Children develop and learn in different ways and at different rates. All areas of learning and development are equally important and interconnected.	4.1 Play and exploration 4.2 Active learning 4.3 Creativity and critical thinking 4.4 Areas of learning and development

Principles into Practice ▼

The Early Years Foundation Stage: Themes and Commitments

A Unique Child	Positive Relationships	Enabling Environments	Learning and Development
1.1 Child Development Babies and children develop in individual ways and at varying rates. Every area of development – physical, cognitive, linguistic, spiritual, social and emotional – is equally important.	**2.1 Respecting Each Other** Every interaction is based on caring professional relationships and respectful acknowledgement of the feelings of children and their families.	**3.1 Observation, Assessment and Planning** Babies and young children are individuals first, each with a unique profile of abilities. Schedules and routines should flow with the child's needs. All planning starts with observing children in order to understand and consider their current interests, development and learning.	**4.1 Play and Exploration** Children's play reflects their wide ranging and varied interests and preoccupations. In their play children learn at their highest level. Play with peers is important for children's development.
1.2 Inclusive Practice The diversity of individuals and communities is valued and respected. No child or family is discriminated against.	**2.2 Parents as Partners** Parents are children's first and most enduring educators. When parents and practitioners work together in early years settings, the results have a positive impact on children's development and learning.	**3.2 Supporting Every Child** The environment supports every child's learning through planned experiences and activities that are challenging but achievable.	**4.2 Active Learning** Children learn best through physical and mental challenges. Active learning involves other people, objects, ideas and events that engage and involve children for sustained periods.
1.3 Keeping Safe Young children are vulnerable. They develop resilience when their physical and psychological well-being is protected by adults.	**2.3 Supporting Learning** Warm, trusting relationships with knowledgeable adults support children's learning more effectively than any amount of resources.	**3.3 The Learning Environment** A rich and varied environment supports children's learning and development. It gives them the confidence to explore and learn in secure and safe, yet challenging, indoor and outdoor spaces.	**4.3 Creativity and Critical Thinking** When children have opportunities to play with ideas in different situations and with a variety of resources, they discover connections and come to new and better understandings and ways of doing things. Adult support in this process enhances their ability to think critically and ask questions.
1.4 Health and Well-being Children's health is an integral part of their emotional, mental, social, environmental and spiritual well-being and is supported by attention to these aspects.	**2.4 Key Person** A key person has special responsibilities for working with a small number of children, giving them the reassurance to feel safe and cared for and building relationships with their parents.	**3.4 The Wider Context** Working in partnership with other settings, other professionals and with individuals and groups in the community supports children's development and progress towards the outcomes of *Every Child Matters*: being healthy, staying safe, enjoying and achieving, making a positive contribution and economic well-being.	**4.4 Areas of Learning and Development** The Early Years Foundation Stage (EYFS) is made up of six areas of Learning and Development. All areas of Learning and Development are connected to one another and are equally important. All areas of Learning and Development are underpinned by the Principles of the EYFS.

ST IVES DIRECT 02-2007

department for education and skills   ISBN 978-1-84478-886-6   00012-2007DOM-EN © Crown copyright 2007   recycle When you have finished with these cards please recycle them   80% recycled These cards are printed on 80% recycled paper

Areas of Learning and Development

Theme 4, Learning and Development, also contains six Areas of Learning and Development. These are shown on the diagram below:

Areas of learning and development ▶

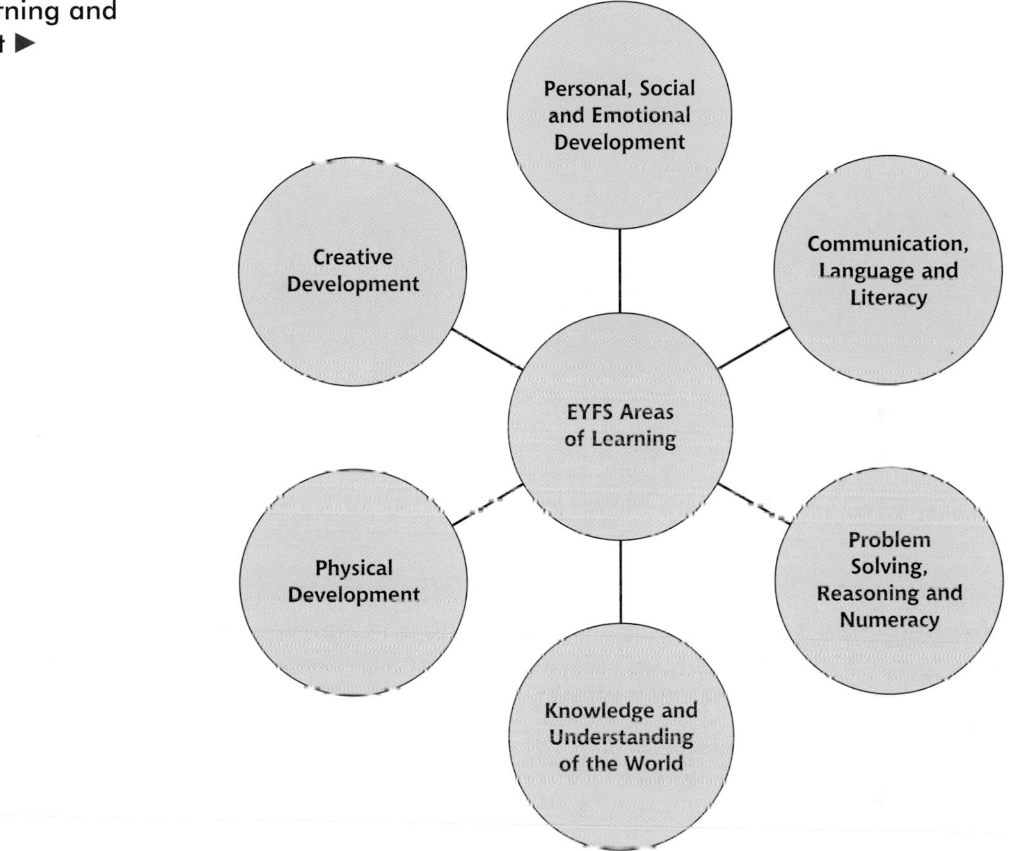

FAST FACT

All areas of Learning and Development are connected to one another and are equally important. They are underpinned by the principles of the EYFS.

Each Area of Learning and Development is divided up into **Aspects**. You can see these on the Department for Education and Skill's Learning and Development card, reproduced on page 372. Together, the six areas of Learning and Development make-up the skills, knowledge and experiences appropriate for babies and children as they grow, learn and develop. Although these are presented as separate areas, it's important to remember that for children everything links and nothing is compartmentalised.

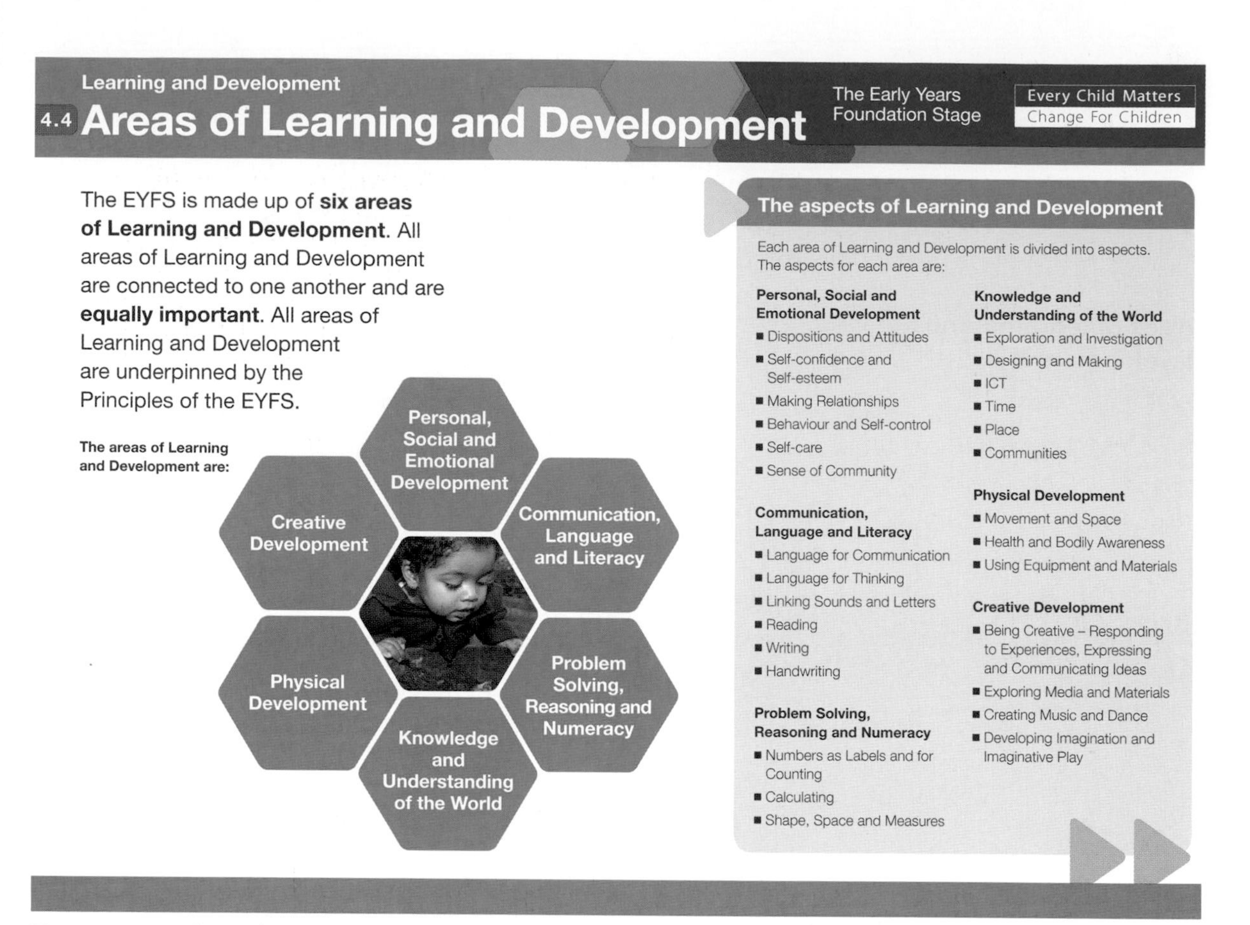

Department for Education and Skill's Learning and Development card extract ▲

So what does all this mean?

Childcarers working in settings following the EYFS need to meet the standards for learning, development and care. Their responsibilities include:

- Planning a range of play and learning experiences that promote all of the Aspects within all of the Areas of Learning.
- Assessing and monitoring individual children's progress through observational assessments.
- Using the findings of observational assessments to inform the planning of play and learning experiences.
- Ensuring that children's individual interests and abilities are promoted within the play and learning experiences.

In their 'Key Elements of Effective Practice' (KEEP) The Department for Education and Skills tells us that:

Effective practice in the early years requires committed, enthusiastic and reflective practitioners with a breadth and depth of knowledge, skills and understanding. Effective practitioners use their own learning to improve their work with young children and their families in ways that are sensitive, positive and non-judgemental.

Therefore through initial and ongoing training and development practitioners need to develop, demonstrate and continuously improve their:

- relationships with both children and adults;
- understanding of the individual and diverse ways that children learn and develop;
- knowledge and understanding in order to actively support and extend children's learning in and across all areas and aspects of Learning and Development;
- practice in meeting all children's needs, learning styles and interests;
- work with parents, carers and the wider community;
- work with other professionals within and beyond the setting.

Key elements of effective practice ▲

EYFS resources for childcarers

The EYFS pack of resources for providers includes:

The Statutory Framework for the Early Years Foundation Stage

This booklet sets out:

You can find out more about the welfare requirements on page 110.

- The welfare requirements.
- The learning and development requirements.
  These set out providers' duties under each of the six areas of Learning and Development.

Practice Guidance for the Early Years Foundation Stage

This booklet provides further guidance on:

- Legal requirements.
- The areas of Learning and Development.
- The EYFS principles.
- Assessment.

24 cards

These give the Principles and Commitments at a glance, with guidance on putting the principles into practice. They include an overview of child development.

See the web link section at the end of the Unit.

CD-ROM

This contains all the information from the booklets and cards. It includes information on effective practice, research and resources. This can also be accessed via a website.

Have a go!

Using the web link at the end of the Unit, visit the EYFS website. Now:

- Take the overview tour to familiarise yourself with the site.
- Follow the links to the Areas of Learning and read more about the Aspects.
- Follow the links to the 'Principles in practice' for examples of how practitioners following the EYFS work with children within their settings.

The National Curriculum

The English National Curriculum (National Curriculum) sets out the minimum curriculum requirements for all maintained schools, including:

- The subjects taught.
- The knowledge, skills and understanding required in each subject.
- Attainment targets in each subject.
- How children's progress is assessed and reported.

Within the framework of the National Curriculum, schools are free to plan and organise teaching and learning themselves. Many schools choose to use Schemes of Works from the Qualifications and Curriculum Authority. These help to translate the National Curriculum's objectives into teaching and learning activities for children.

Key stages

The National Curriculum is divided into four **key stages** that children pass through as they move up through the school system. These stages are in addition to the Early Years Foundation Stage described earlier:

- Year 1 and Year 2 of primary school are known as Key Stage 1.
- Years 3 to 6 of primary school are known as Key Stage 2.

- Years 7 to 9 of secondary school are known as Key Stage 3.
- Years 10 to 11 of secondary school are known as Key Stage 4.

Subjects at Key Stage 1 and 2

The compulsory National Curriculum subjects for Key Stages 1 and 2 are:

- English.
- Maths.
- Science.
- Design and technology.
- Information and Communication Technology (ICT).
- History.
- Geography.
- Art and design.
- Music.
- Physical education.

Schools also have to teach:

- Religious education.
  Parents have the right to withdraw children from the religious education curriculum if they choose.

Schools are advised to teach:

- Personal, social and health education (PSHE).
- Citizenship.
- One or more modern foreign language.

It's acceptable for schools to use different names for the subjects, as long as they're covering the National Curriculum.

There are **attainment targets** and a **programme of study** for each subject. Programmes of study describe the subject knowledge, skills and understanding pupils are expected to develop during each key stage.

Levels and formal teacher assessments

Attainment targets are split into **levels.**

Teachers carry out regular checks on children's progress in each subject. There will also be **formal teacher assessment** at the end of Key Stages 1–3 (pupils will usually take GCSE/equivalent exams at the end of Key

Stage 4). This indicates which National Curriculum level best describes individual children's performance in each subject. Schools send parents a report telling them what National Curriculum levels their child has reached in formal assessments.

Art and design is a compulsory subject at Key Stage 3 ▼

Subjects at Key Stage 3 and 4

Key Stage 3 compulsory National Curriculum subjects are:

- English.
- Maths.
- Science.
- Design and technology.
- Information and Communication Technology (ICT).
- History.
- Geography.
- Modern foreign languages.
- Art and design.
- Music.
- Citizenship.
- Physical education.

Schools also have to provide:

- Careers education and guidance (during Year 9).
- Sex and Relationship Education (SRE).
- Religious education.
  Parents can choose to withdraw their child from religious education curriculum.

In Year 9, children do national tests and choose what to study at Key Stage 4, when they will study both compulsory and optional subjects. Most pupils work towards national qualifications. Pupils are advised to choose a balance of options to give them more choice when deciding on courses and jobs later on. Pupils may also choose from a growing range of vocational qualifications. The compulsory Key Stage 4 subjects are:

- English.
- Maths.
- Science.
- Information and Communication Technology (ICT).

- Physical education.
- Citizenship.

Schools must also provide:

- Careers education.
- Work-related learning.
- Religious education.
- Sex and Relationship Education (SRE).
- One subject from each of the four 'entitlement' areas.

The entitlement areas are:

- Arts subjects.
- Design and technology.
- Humanities.
- Modern foreign languages.
  Parents can choose to withdraw their child from religious education curriculum.

Review of the curriculum

A new secondary curriculum was published in September 2007. Its aims include cutting back on compulsory subject content and developing pupil's personal attributes and practical life skills. The Department for Education and skills tells us that:

The review of the curriculum ▼

The new Key Stage 3 curriculum will be brought in over a three-year period. It becomes compulsory for Year 7 pupils in September 2008. From September 2009, it will apply to all Year 7 and Year 8 pupils, and from September 2010 it will apply across Years 7, 8 and 9. Changes to the Key Stage 4 curriculum will be brought in from September 2009.

As part of changes to the curriculum for 14 to 19 year olds, from September 2008 a new Diploma qualification will be introduced alongside GCSEs and A levels in selected schools and colleges.

Have a go!

For more information about the new secondary curriculum, visit the Qualifications and Curriculum Authority website. The address is given in the web links section at the end of the Unit.

FOCUS ON...
your learning

In this section you've learnt about frameworks for learning that apply in England. You've learnt about their structure and content. You've also learnt about the principles and approaches related to the frameworks.

Questions:

1. What is the purpose of observational assessment in the Early Years Foundation Stage?
2. Which Key Stages of the National Curriculum will children follow in primary school?

Learning Outcome 2

FOCUS ON...
the principles of how children learn

This links with Assessment Criteria **2.1, 2.2**

Supporting different approaches to learning

Throughout your course you've been learning about different approaches to learning. You will know by now that there are many of them! There's more information about learning approaches here. It's important that you take the time to understand the approaches to learning that are used within your own setting. You will then be able to support children's learning effectively, in partnership with families and your colleagues.

Environments that encourage learning

Some studies have shown that good-quality care and learning experiences are more important than the environments in which children learn. A range of settings that can successfully encourage learning are shown on the diagram below. This includes leisure settings, as children will learn through play, as you know.

Factors that can affect children's ability to learn

There are some factors that may negatively affect children's learning:

- Low self-esteem.
  If a child has low self-esteem, they may feel that they are incapable of doing all sorts of things well. They may expect to fail, or expect adults and their peers to disapprove of them. When a child feels that way, they may stop trying to achieve, or only attempt tasks half-heartedly. They may withdraw from activities and/or the group. This is a self-fulfilling prophecy (or in other words, the child gets what they expect). The less a child

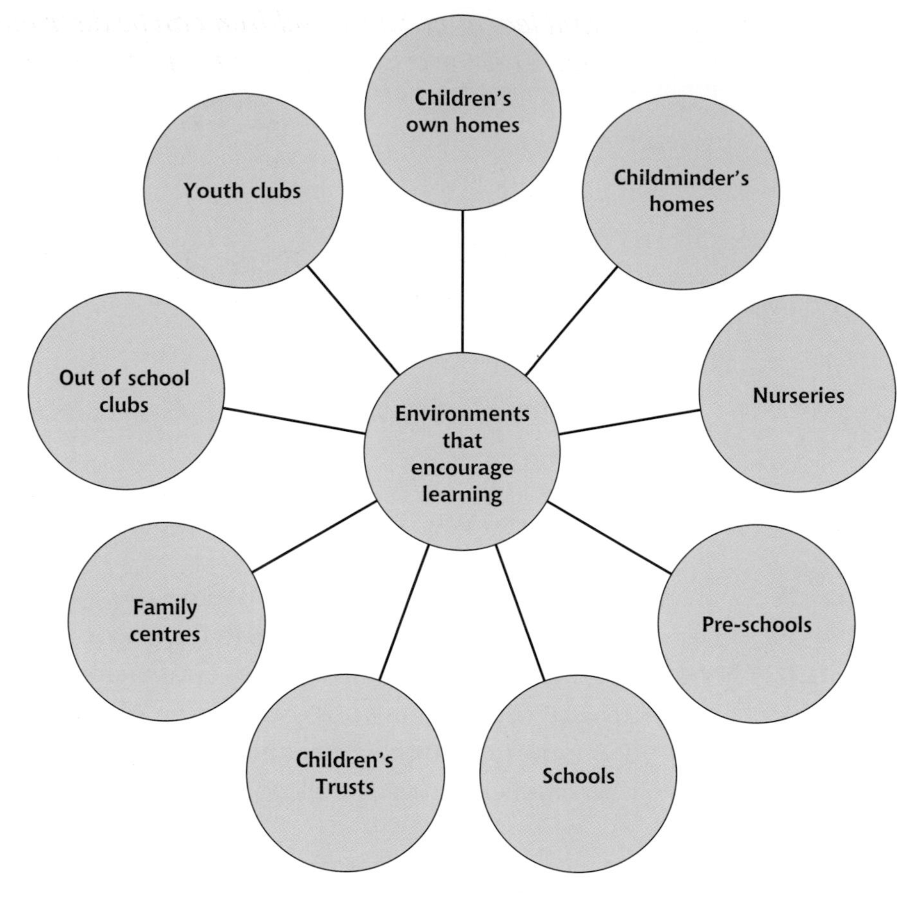

Environments that encourage learning ▲

tries, the more likely they are to fail. This reinforces their belief that they will fail and they may try even less as a result.

- A lack of confidence.
  All children lack confidence sometimes, particularly when they find themselves in a new situation. But some children experience an intense lack of confidence, which may persist for long periods or occur in many different situations. This can stop children from participating in activities, or they may only partially join in, limiting their experience and their learning. Children can't become fully absorbed and engaged in an activity if they feel unable to relax. Children who feel tense and unsure are less likely to learn as much as their peers.
- Being the subject of discrimination.
  If a child is the subject of discrimination, they may have low self-esteem and/or a lack of confidence as a result. Children who are discriminated against are not given equal opportunities, which can affect their experiences

There's more about this on page 296.

and learning. Sadly, children can be discriminated against in many ways, for a range of reasons.

See below.

- Poor concentration.

Children who have low self-esteem and/or a lack of confidence:

- Are often reluctant to try activities or experiences.
- Often show little enthusiasm.
- Are often reluctant to join in.
- Often seem tense or worried.
- Often say phrases like, 'I can't' or 'I won't be able to'.

Children with low self-esteem and/or confidence need:

- To have their problem identified.
- To have activities and experiences planned sensitively to help them develop their self-esteem and confidence – you may participate alongside them for instance.
- Gentle encouragement, but they should not be pushed into things.
- Lots of praise when they do try or participate.

Encouraging concentration

Learn the lingo

Concentration span = the period of time someone is able to focus completely on one activity or task.

One of the key factors that affects children's learning is the development of their **concentration span**. That is the period of time that they are able to focus completely on one activity or task. Children's concentration span typically lengthens as they get older and develop.

Three-year-olds can generally concentrate for a short period. By the time they are five this period has generally lengthened considerably. But concentration spans vary widely from child to child and even from activity to activity. Children with attention deficits may have considerable difficulties concentrating.

See page 354 for details.

Older children can also have problems concentrating. This can be tougher to deal with. The tactic of providing interesting and engaging activities is more difficult to apply when children have to study a subject they're not interested in and complete homework that doesn't appeal. Studying in 'bite-size' stints can help, with plenty of breaks and small rewards built in. Promoting learning methods that suit children's preferred styles of learning is also helpful, especially when revising for tests and exams. Some

See page 21 for further details.

older children work best in peace and quiet, while others may like to have background music or the radio on.

GOOD PRACTICE

It's important to provide interesting, engaging activities for children, which will capture their attention and encourage them to concentrate. It also helps to minimise distractions. For instance, by ensuring adults can't be heard talking at story time when you want children to listen, or by keeping noisy and quiet activities separate as far as possible. But it's still important to have realistic expectations of children's concentration spans.

Cognitive development

Information about the stages and sequence of cognitive development is included on pages 34–37, and within the development tables on page 38–51.

You need to have a good understanding of the stage of development of the individual children you're working with, as well as a good general understanding of the patterns of development. Understanding children's stage of cognitive (intellectual) development is important. This enables you to have realistic expectations of children's learning, and to plan activities and experiences that are suitable for them at critical periods for their learning (see below).

Critical periods for learning

FAST FACT

Evidence for a critical period for learning language is particularly strong.

Some experts believe that humans are born with an innate (built in) 'hard wiring'. This makes us predisposed (inclined) to notice and pay attention to certain aspects of our environment at certain times of life.

There's more about the development of communication from birth to 16 years on pages 34–37 and within the development tables on page 35–51.

Some experts believe that a young child's family and carers can shape children's predisposition in this period of critical learning, e.g. if children don't receive good opportunities to learn language during the critical period, it will be harder for them to learn later on. Some experts think that while children may learn language later, they are unlikely to have an affinity (flair) with language later in their lives.

The importance of play

Play is an effective vehicle for children's learning because:

- Children enjoy playing.
- Children are intrinsically motivated to play (they are driven from within).
- Children can make their own discoveries through play.

Information about learning through play is provided in Learning Outcome 3, and within Units 4 and 8.

- Children can initiate their own activities and explore their own thoughts and ideas through play.
- Children can actively learn through play – the learning is a real, vivid experience.

Active learning

The EYFS identifies active learning as effective practice. The term 'active learning' refers to the way in which, 'babies and young children learn to make sense of their world by actively investigating what it contains and through social activity with significant people.'

Active learning ▼

Guidance goes on to explain how babies and young children construct ideas about the things they encounter (come across) in their lives. As they encounter more objects, situations, people and ideas, they need to adjust their knowledge to make sense of these new things. In other words, they apply, revise and reapply what they know, creating their own meaning. The EYFS tells us children are also, 'creating a framework for thinking and learning that will help them to develop as learners.'

To engage children in active learning you need to understand and build on what each child is familiar with, knows and can do. You need to:

- Value and understand children as individuals.
- Get to know children and their families well.
- Understand family circumstances, e.g. children who live in a bedsit with no garden may have less opportunities for large physical play than those with a garden.
- Understand that different children will learn the same thing in different ways.
- Provide a range of activities and experiences, making sure there will be things to engage and interest every child.
- Personalise learning, building on things individual children know and can latch on to, so they have a base from which to explore something new.
- Encourage children to make decisions about what they're going to do and how.
- Plan activities based on children's real-life experiences, such as going to the dentist.
- Make full use of the outside space to extend learning, as many practical experiences benefit from freedom to move.

Although this theory centres on babies and young children, the principles of active learning can also be applied to older children and even to adult learners.

Have a go!

Part one

An outline of active learning and how you can promote it is given above. Visit the EYFS site, using this link:

www.standards.dcsf.gov.uk/eyfs/resources/downloads/4_2_ep.pdf

It will take you to the Active Learning information. You can further your understanding of how to support active learning by reading the 'Key Messages'.

Part two

Re-read the information about Piaget's theories of learning on page 180.

You'll notice the similarities between Piaget's ideas and the active learning theory.

FOCUS ON...
your learning

In this section you've learnt about your role in supporting approaches to learning and the environments that can encourage learning. You've learnt about the importance of play, active learning, critical periods of learning and factors that can affect learning. You've also learnt about the stages of cognitive development and how to encourage concentration.

Questions

1 Name three factors that negatively affect children's learning.

2 How can you encourage concentration?

Learning Outcome 3

FOCUS ON...

the role of the adult in supporting children's learning from birth to age 16 years

This links with Assessment Criteria **3.1, 3.2, 3.3**

Supporting children's learning

When planning your work with children, you should always consider the starting point of each individual child – what do they already know and understand? What do they have experience of? This allows you to pitch your activity to the right level for the children. The starting points will differ within any group of children, even those of the same age, so this will require knowledge of the children and some careful thinking. (This links with the information in Learning Outcome 2 on active learning).

Consider the best way to group children for activities, and what the role of adults will be in terms of supporting children's learning. For instance, through effective deployment of adults and thoughtful grouping of children, it's possible to plan activities that operate on more than one level. This meets the needs of different children working on the same activity. The case study below gives an example.

Encouraging participation

Children need to engage with activities and experiences in order to learn effectively. Practitioners sometimes make the mistake of thinking that children have experienced or learnt all of the things that the setting offered that day, or that week or month. But children may have benefited little or not at all if they have not actually participated actively themselves. You can promote participation by:

- Providing activities that meet the needs of the children.
- Providing a balance of activities across the areas of development and any curriculum framework that applies to your setting.

Free play ▼

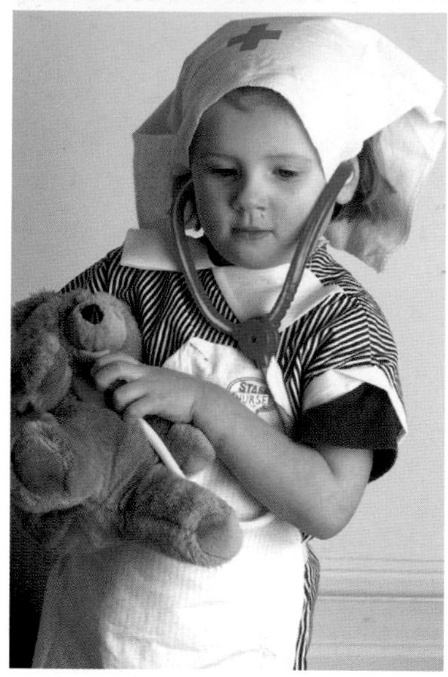

- Providing activities that are fun and playful, and present them to children in a playful or engaging manner.
- Providing a balance of structured activities and free play.
- Providing a balance of adult-directed and child-initiated activities.
- Providing a balance of activities for all styles of learning.
- Providing a balance of indoor and outdoor activities.
- Grouping children appropriately.
- Providing appropriate adult support.
- Initiating an activity by participating yourself (try going into the dressing-up corner alone and trying on hats – you are likely to have company very soon).
- Participating alongside children.

Practical example

Lisa's games

Nursery worker Lisa is planning some tabletop games for her group. She decides to split the group into three sub-groups for the activity. One group of mainly four-year olds will play a game of sound lotto. An adult will be on hand, but they will be encouraged to manage the game themselves and to operate the tape recorder. A group of mainly three-year olds are going to play a sequencing lotto game. An adult will work with them, encouraging them to talk about what is happening in the pictures, and the order the pictures should go in. A third group of mainly two-and-a-half-year olds will play a game of picture lotto with two adults. They will focus on sharing out the cards, taking turns, naming the pictures and matching.

1. *Why has Lisa decided to split the group?*
2. *Why is she planning three groups in total?*
3. *Why is the focus of the game different, despite the fact all groups are playing lotto games?*

Consolidating, extending and challenging

It's generally accepted that children need a variety of activities and experiences appropriate to their age and abilities that will allow them to:

- Consolidate.
  Consolidation is when children have opportunities to repeat activities and experiences, confirming their previous learning, practising skills and perhaps developing a deeper understanding. Children are naturally drawn to consolidating in their play, e.g. a child may frequently build the same house or aeroplane from small interlocking bricks.
- Extend.
  Extension occurs when children's existing learning is moved forward in a new way, perhaps by applying consolidated learning and skills to a new situation. For example, a child who has learnt to use a sewing machine may learn to hem a garment. We can link activities to encourage this (see the Practical Example below). Extension activities are particularly helpful when you're working with groups of children with different levels of development. For instance, you can plan a core activity for all of the children and follow this up with an extension activity for the children who are ready for it.
- Challenge.
  Children are challenged when they are introduced to new activities and experiences that are just beyond their current competence, e.g. a child who has learnt to jump is introduced to the skill of hopping on one leg.

These strategies promote learning and development.

Look out for naturally occurring opportunities to support and extend children's learning. It may be appropriate to offer your support if children:

- Could be encouraged to think or discuss further if they were asked a question.
- Need a suggestion to initiate an activity or experience.
- Show signs that their play/learning is flagging and new input is needed.
- Are becoming frustrated or struggling.
- Seem nervous, reluctant or unsure.

- Need a demonstration of a skill, e.g. how to hold scissors or how to add fractions.
- Are not understanding something.
- Are beginning to behave inappropriately or have given up.

Practical example

Antonio extends learning

Key stage one teacher Antonio has planned to read a story about a bird that drops pebbles into a bottle of water to make the water level rise. The bird can then take a drink from the bottle. Afterwards, the children retell the story themselves using props – a bird puppet, pebbles, water and a bottle. They measure the water level and record how much it rises when they drop in the pebbles.

1. *How did the extension activity extend the children's learning?*

Supporting development of skills

You should have high expectations of children and commitment to supporting the development of their skills. Some studies within schools have found that the attitudes of teachers can influence how well children actually achieve. In one study, teachers were told completely at random that certain children were high achievers. With their teachers believing in them, many of the children actually performed better than they had before.

You should base your expectations on a realistic appraisal of what children's current capabilities are, and what they might achieve next. But always aim to let children know that you believe they are good at learning, and remember to praise them for both achieving and trying their best. Key skills that help children to become effective learners are shown on the diagram that follows:

Skills that promote effective learning ▶

You can encourage these skills in a range of ways, including:

- Determination and motivation.
  Encourage children to persevere when they can't get something right at first. Motivation and determination are linked, because a child who is motivated to achieve a goal grows in determination. You can motivate children by celebrating their achievements and praising them for trying. A small reward to look forward to often helps to motivate older children, even if it's as simple as saying to them, 'When you've finished your assignment, why don't we hire that film you wanted to see?' But the best motivation of all is the desire to learn. That's why it's so important to foster a love of learning and an interest and curiosity about the world when children are young.
- Confidence.
  Children who feel nurtured (cared for) and respected for who they are as an individual are likely to develop confidence. Children also develop confidence when they take emotional risks successfully. Experiencing physical risk and taking on challenges in a supporting environment also helps. Teamwork can give confidence a boost too.

See pages 324 and 380. Some team activities for older children are suggested on page 318–323.

- Independence.
  Confidence breeds independence. Children experience a desire to do things for themselves and in their own way from an early age. Most of us will have experienced a frustrated two-year old who can't quite manage a task such as putting on shoes themselves, but definitely doesn't want our help! It's important to encourage independence as appropriate to children's age and abilities from early on. This helps children to become increasingly independent as they grow up. Adults won't always be with children in the older age range, so independence is a very important life skill.

Also see pages 81–96.

- Self-reliance.
  Independence breeds self-reliance. Self-reliant learners trust themselves to pick up the knowledge and skills they need. This helps children to feel relaxed, which makes it easier for them to concentrate and participate in activities and experiences. In turn, this helps them to learn. It can help to remind children of their past learning successes.

Promote children's understanding of healthy food ▼

Everyday routines

Everyday routines are essential to the care of children, and they also provide them with a sense of security and structure to their day. But they should not be overlooked as learning experiences. Settings can plan to enhance learning through everyday routines. For instance, in a pre-school you could:

- Promote children's understanding of healthy foods through discussion at snack times and mealtimes.
- Promote good manners at the table.
- Make sets when setting the table (e.g. putting in order the things that belong together) and talking about position, e.g., 'The fork goes opposite the knife.'
- Count out how many cups and plates are needed.
- Encourage children to pour their own drinks.
- Encourage children to put on and fasten their own outdoor clothes.
- Talk about hygiene with children when washing hands and toileting.
- Discuss respect for the environment when tidying up.

- Use name-recognition opportunities when marking the register.
- Allow children to see you writing when you make notes.

Have a go!

Make a list of five everyday routines that exist within your setting. Now have a think about each routine in turn. Is it currently used as a learning activity? If so, how? Think of a least one other way to use each routine as a learning opportunity with the children in your group.

You may like to share your list with colleagues, and discuss ways of putting your ideas into practice.

In December 2007, the Government published the 'Children's Plan' which sets out ambitious new goals for 2020. For more information, see the web links section at the end of the Unit.

Different types of activity

Activities may be:

- Adult directed.
  When an adults tells children what to do.
- Child initiated.
  When an activity is a child's idea.
- Structured.
  When an activity is planned with a learning focus or objective.
- Spontaneous.
  When children spontaneously start an activity (free play).

See Unit 8.

Children learn best from a range of activity types. The table that follows gives examples of the different types of activities that children may experience.

You learnt about the principles of effective communication with children in Unit 5. You can use your communication skills to extend children's learning, as explained on pages 214–224.

Effective communication

It's important to apply the principles of effective communication when supporting children's learning. You need to communicate clearly and appropriately for each child you work with. You can't support learning effectively if children don't understand the way you communicate with them.

Principles into practice ▼

Age	Adult-directed activity	Child-initiated activity	Structured activity	Spontaneous activity
3–5	Setting the table	Sinking boats in the water tray	Clapping out the rhythm of a nursery rhyme	Jumping from one paving stone to the next
5–8	Preparing food for snack time	Imaginary games	Putting objects into sets (e.g. all the red buttons together, all the hexagons together)	Telling a joke
8–12	Rehearsing a play	Making a birthday card for a friend	Visiting a museum	Singing along to background music
12–16	Writing about a personal experience	Setting out a skating area with ramps, jumps, etc.	Doing science experiments	Dancing with a friend

The information on responsive care on page 282 will help you. So will the information about responding to play cues on page 328.

There's further information about consulting with older children on pages 310–313. A Practical example introduces methods.

Consultation

It's important to consult children when supporting their learning, as appropriate to their abilities. This promotes the theory of 'active learning' you leant about in Learning Outcome 2. It also helps you to plan activities that meet children's needs and to work with children in the ways that suit them best. Babies and very young children won't be able to tell you what they want verbally. But by being a responsive carer, you can notice what they want and how they want to do things. Think of it as a kind of 'silent consultation'.

FOCUS ON...
your learning

You've learnt about how to support children in becoming effective learners and how to provide an environment that supports and encourages learning. You've learnt about using everyday routines as learning experiences and the different types of activities that meet the diverse needs of children aged from birth to 16 years. You've also learnt about using effective communication skills and consultation to support learning.

Questions

1 How do effective communication skills help you to support children's learning?

2 What skills can encourage effective learning?

RAPID RECAP

Learning Outcome 1

From September 2008 *The Early Years Foundation Stage* will be mandatory for all schools and all early years providers in Ofsted registered settings, applying to children from birth to 5 years. The aim of the EYFS is to help young children achieve the five *Every Child Matters* outcomes. The EYFS is based around four **Themes**. Each theme is linked to a **Principle**. Each Principle is supported by four **Commitments**. Theme 4, Learning and Development, also contains six **Areas of Learning and Development**, which are divided into **Aspects**. Practitioners make **observational assessments** to monitor progress and plan for the next stage of children's learning.

The National Curriculum sets out the minimum curriculum requirements for all maintained schools, applying to children aged five to 16 years. It's divided into four **Key Stages**. There are compulsory **subjects**. There are **attainment targets** and a **programme of study** for each subject. Teachers carry out regular checks on children's progress in each subject. There will be **formal teacher assessment** at the end of Key Stages 1–3, used to assess pupils' **level**. Pupils usually take GCSE/equivalent **exams** at the end of Key Stage 4.

Learning Outcome 2

It's part of your role to support your setting's approach to learning, whatever framework may be followed. A range of settings that provide good quality care and activities can be effective environments for learning, from children's own homes to secondary schools. Play is an effective vehicle for learning. You need good knowledge of the patterns of cognitive development and individual children's current abilities in order to offer appropriate learning experiences. Some experts believe there are 'critical periods of learning.' You can encourage concentration by providing engaging activities, minimising distractions, breaking study into manageable chunks and promoting ways of working that suit children's preferred learning styles.

There are links to information within Units 7, 8 and 9.

Learning Outcome 3

You can support children in becoming effective learners by developing their skills for learning that include confidence, motivation and determination. Children should experience a range of activities that are **adult directed, child initiated**, **structured** and **spontaneous**. You must communicate effectively in ways appropriate for the children you're working with. You should consult with children when supporting their learning.

There are links to information within Units 5, 6 and 8.

FAQ

Q **How will I be assessed on this Unit?**

A *You'll complete an assignment task. CACHE publishes a task for each optional unit every year.*

Q **What will I have to do?**

A *Your tutor or Centre will help you to understand the task. See Unit 1 Learning Outcome 5 for more information on study skills.*

Weblinks

You may like to visit the following websites:

- www.everychildmatters.gov.uk
  For further information about Every Child Matters
- www.standards.dcsf.gov.uk/eyfs/
  The EYFS site. This link will help you with the Have a go! tasks in Learning Outcome 1.
- www.direct.gov.uk
  Follow the links for information about the National Curriculum
- www.qca.org.uk/qca_13575.aspx
  For information about the new secondary curriculum
- www.desf.gov.uk/publications/childrensplan/
  For details of the Children's Plan

Also see the links provided in Unit 8

Unit 11

Supporting children and families

Learning Outcomes

In this unit you'll learn about:

The range of support available for children and families.

How to build positive relationships with children and their families.

The role of the adult when supporting children and their families in a social care setting.

This Unit contains several links to other Units within this book.

Learning Outcome 1

FOCUS ON...
the range of support available for children and families

This links with Assessment Criteria **1.1, 1.2**

Children's social services

In each local authority, a Director of Social Services oversees the statutory services of Education and Social Services for Children (Social Services). Social Services work with children and families facing a range of challenges when:

- Children have been identified as being 'in need'.
- Children are 'looked after' by their local authority. *This includes children living in residential care homes and within the homes of foster carers.*
- Children are placed for adoption.
- Children may have experienced or may be experiencing 'significant harm'. *This includes children who have experienced or may be experiencing child abuse.*

Children are recognised as being 'in need' if:

- They are unlikely to achieve or maintain, or to have the opportunity of achieving or maintaining, a reasonable standard of health or development without the provision of services.
- Their health or development is likely to be significantly impaired, or further impaired, without the provision of services.
- They are disabled.

See pages 290–291 for further information about multi-professional teams and the role that childcarers and childcare settings play within them.

Support will generally be provided for vulnerable children and families through a multi-agency approach.

A range of social care settings are available for children and families. The diagram that follows gives further examples of settings where social care may be provided.

You'll find more information about a range of statutory, private and voluntary settings on page 2.

Social Care Settings diagram ▶

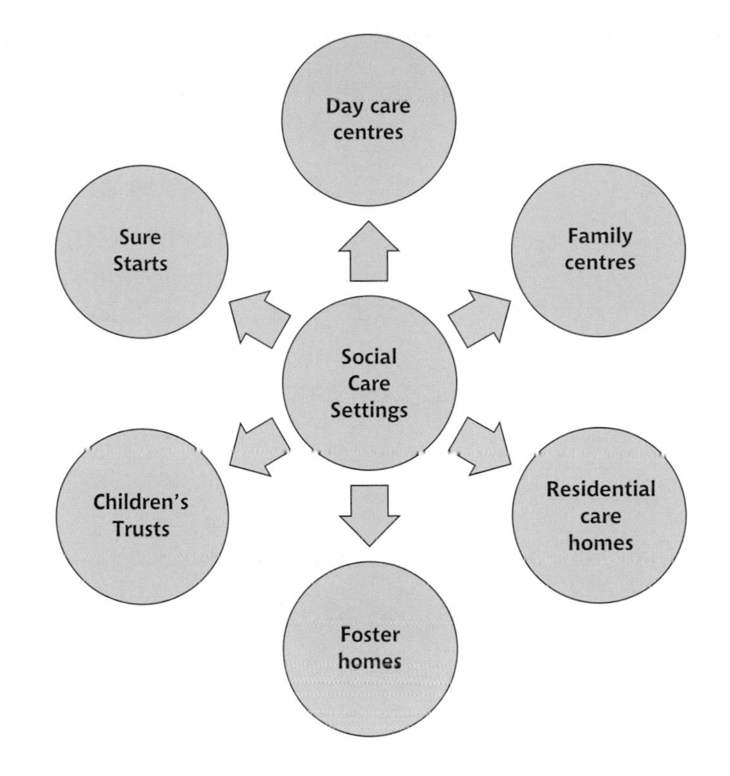

The Practical Example that follows gives an example of the range of services that may be provided within a social care setting.

Social Services supports families and tries to keep them together when appropriate by:

- Offering them support in the community and through settings.
- Providing counseling and short periods of relief care.
- Giving practical support in the home.
- Giving advice on welfare rights.

Contacting Social Services

Information about your local Social Services can be obtained from its offices (listed in the telephone directory) or your local library. Social Services have a range of leaflets to inform the public about their services.

Information about the multi-agency approach to child protection is included within Unit 3.

Child protection

Social Services have a duty to investigate the circumstances of any child believed to be at risk of harm, and to take action on their behalf.

Practical example

Support for Gemma and Ajay

Gemma is 18. She's a young mum to two-year old Ajay. Gemma and Ajay go to their local family centre at least three times a week. They attend family drop-in sessions, where Ajay plays alongside his mum. This gives Gemma the chance to socialise with other parents. She also picks up tips from the staff on caring for and playing with Ajay. Once a week, Ajay attends a crèche at the centre, while Gemma takes part in an adult literacy course. Gemma wants to improve her basic skills as she's planning to find a job when Ajay starts pre-school next year.

Gemma doesn't have contact with Ajay's dad. But every Saturday she drops Ajay at the centre at 9am. The staff care for him until his dad collects him at 9.30am. Dad spends the day with Ajay, returning him to the staff at 5pm. Gemma collects Ajay from the centre at 5.30pm.

1. *What impact do you think the Family Centre has on Gemma's life?*

Organisations that support children and families

There are a range of statutory, private and voluntary organisations, both locally and nationally, which provide support for children and families. A sample of national voluntary agencies is outlined in the table that follows.

National Voluntary Agencies ▼

Name of organisation	Support offered	Website address
Barnados	Works with children and their families to help relieve the effects of disadvantage and disability. It runs community projects and day centres, and provides residential accommodation for children with additional needs.	www.barnardos.org.uk
ChildLine	Provides a national telephone helpline for children in trouble or danger. The helpline number for children to call is 0800 11 11.	www.childline.org.uk
The Children's Society	Offers childcare services to children and families in need. It aims to help children to grow up in their own families and communities.	www.childrenssociety.org.uk
Citizens' Advice Bureau	Provides free, impartial advice and help to anyone. They have over a thousand local offices providing information, advice and legal guidance on many subjects.	www.citizensadvice.org.uk
Contact a Family	Helps families caring for disabled children to meet and support each other. It organises community-based projects that assist parents' self-help groups. Runs a national helpline (0808 808 3555)	www.cafamily.org.uk
The Family Welfare Association	Offers services for families, children and people with disabilities. Provides financial help for families in exceptional need, gives social work support and runs drop-in centres.	www.fwa.org.uk
Gingerbread	Provides emotional support, practical help and social activities for lone parents and their children.	www.gingerbread.org.uk
Jewish Care	Provides help and support for people of the Jewish faith and their families. Among other things, it runs day centres and provides social work teams and domiciliary (home) assistance.	www.jewishcare.org/

Name of organisation	Support offered	Website address
Mencap	Aims to increase public awareness of the problems faced by people with learning difficulties and their families. Supports day centres and other facilities.	www.mencap.org.uk
MIND	Concerned with promoting mental health and mental health services for families.	www.mind.org.uk
NCH (National Children's Homes)	Provides services for children who are disadvantaged. It runs many schemes including family centres, foster care and aid and support schemes for families.	www.nch.org.uk
NCT (National Childbirth Trust)	Works through a network of branches to provide and support local services, training and evidence-based information for parents, families and health professionals.	www.nct.org.uk
The National Deaf Children's Society	Gives information, advice and support directly to families with deaf children.	www.ndcs.org.uk
The National Society for the Prevention of Cruelty to Children (NSPCC)	Has a network of child protection teams throughout Britain. Runs a 24-hour referral and counselling telephone line, and offers support via family care centres.	www.nspcc.org.uk
Parentline	Offers a telephone support helpline for parents who are having any kind of problem with their children. (0808 800 2222)	www.parentlineplus.org.uk
National Toy Libraries Association	Promotes awareness of the importance of play for the developing child. Libraries are organised locally, loaning toys to families with young children.	www.natll.org.uk
RELATE (National Marriage Guidance Council)	Trains and provides counsellors to work with people who are experiencing difficulty in their relationships.	www.relate.org.uk

Name of organisation	Support offered	Website address
The Samaritans	Offers befriending service to anyone in despair, via telephone (08457 90 90 90), email (jo@samaritans.org), letter and face-to-face in local centres.	www.samaritans.org/
Women's Refuges	Provides 'halfway houses' for women and children who are the victims of violent male partners until they can be re-accommodated. Offers a free domestic violence helpline (0808 2000 247)	www.refuge.org.uk/

Local voluntary/community organisations

In most areas there are a wide range of local voluntary/community organisations that have grown up to meet the needs of the local people. Some are self-help groups; others meet the needs of people from particular minority ethnic groups. They may provide specific information services, advice and support. They are often listed and co-ordinated by a local Council for Voluntary Services and can be found under 'voluntary organisations' in Yellow Pages.

- African-Caribbean, Indian and Pakistani community centres exist in areas where there are significant numbers of people of Caribbean and Asian origin. They offer a range of advice and support services for local people. There are also a wide range of local organisations that aim to meet the needs of other minority communities.
- Parent and toddler groups – here parents and carers can bring very young children, but are required to remain with them while they play.

Private sector services and facilities

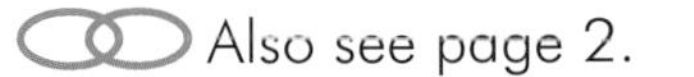
Also see page 2.

Some services are provided by individuals and organisations that make a profit. They have identified a demand and people are willing to pay for these services. Personal support services include personal and family therapy, different forms of counselling, domestic (home) and care assistance and respite care. These services tend to be expensive and beyond the means of many.

FOCUS ON...
your learning

In this section you've learnt about the range of settings that are available for vulnerable children and families. You've also learnt about the national and local support available to children and families via statutory, private and voluntary organisations. Links to other Units give information on multi-professional teams and a range of settings.

Questions:

1. What does the term 'in need' mean?
2. How can you find out about organisations providing support to families in your own local area?

Learning Outcome 2

FOCUS ON...
how to build positive relationships with children and their families

This links with Assessment Criteria **2.1, 2.2, 2.3**

Range of challenges

The children and families that social care professionals work with may have experienced a broad range of challenges. These may include:

- Child abuse.
- Domestic violence.
- Abandonment (being left by parents/carers).
- Family breakdowns.
- Bereavement.
- Disability.
- Illness.
- Criminal involvement.
- Discrimination.
- Poverty/disadvantage.
- War.
- Becoming a refugee.

Valuing the role of the family

There's more information about this on page 286.

Children generally feel a deep sense of love and connection with their parents, carers and other close family members. It's your role as a childcarer to form partnerships with families based on this fact. You must always respect and value the important role family members play in their children's lives. You must always treat family members with courtesy and respect.

Families generally remain important to children despite the challenges a family may face or the difficult circumstances they may live in. Because the bonds between children and their families are so strong, social workers will arrange support services to enable children to keep living with their families whenever appropriate and possible.

This can include instances when abuse has occurred (see page 142).

When working in social care situations, it's important not to make judgements about the circumstances of families, or the actions of family members. It can sometimes be hard for someone who cares about children not to become upset or feel angry about the situation an individual child is in. But as a professional you will want to help the child by doing what's best for them. This involves building positive relationships with family members, and working in partnership with them. This is a key part of providing support to both children and families. If families feel they are not valued or respected, they may stop attending the setting or using the service altogether. This would have a negative impact on the child and the family as a whole. It would also mean you could no longer help the child.

Have a go!

There's detailed information about forming and maintaining effective relationships with families within Unit 7. You're advised to read (or re-read) that Unit as part of your study towards Unit 11.

Further information about communication and establishing relationships can be found on pages 225–230 and pages 286–292.

Communicating with children and families

Good communication is the key to establishing and maintaining positive relationships with both children and adults.

How to interact and respond

You will need to draw on strong communication skills to work effectively within social care settings, where you may often have to handle sensitive situations positively.

Everything you've learnt about how to interact and respond with children and families will be valuable to you in a social care situation. But it's also important that you understand the aims of the setting you're working in and your own role within a multi-professional team. These things will affect the way in which you should interact and respond with children and families.

For instance, some social care play settings may observe and gather information about the relationship and interaction that takes place naturally between a child and a parent. In this case, you may need to work as unobtrusively (discreetly) as possible when providing play experiences. In another instance, childcarers may be required to actively model good interaction with children for parents, to help them develop their parenting skills.

Sharing information when requested

An example of this was given in the case study on page 230.

It's important that you know how to share information when requested with both families and other professionals as part of a multi-professional team.

Information about this can be found on page 250 and 290. You must follow confidentiality guidelines at all times – see page 228–230.

Planning play activities and experiences

The play activities and experiences you provide should meet the individual needs of children and their families. Children should of course have the usual opportunities to participate in a wide range of play and learning activities, suitable for their age and stage of development. These should promote any curriculum frameworks that apply

See Unit 10.

But in addition, children may have individual play plans. These may detail particular experiences or activities that are recommended for a child. Individual play plans may be devised for a number of reasons. A child may have had limited previous experiences for instance, or it may be for therapeutic (therapy) reasons. Children who have experienced challenges in their lives are likely to benefit from plenty of opportunities to express themselves. Creative experiences such as imaginary play and art and craft work can be provided.

Activities for children and parents/carers to engage in play together may be required. In this case, experiences such as modelling with clay or making greeting cards can be useful. This is because adults and children can participate alongside each other, operating on their own levels. (In in other words, making cards and pottery are activities that you'd expect both adults and children to engage in, although in their own distinct ways. The activities are not seen as just 'for children' in the same way as hand printing is.) This is especially useful when adults are not used to playing with a child, because it helps them to feel less self-conscious. It can also be helpful when an adult and child are in the early stages of getting to know each other.

Information about meeting additional needs is provided in Unit 9. Information about planning activities and experiences is provided on pages 200, 327 and 385.

Allowing children to express themselves

As you've learnt, activities and experiences that encourage children to express themselves can be especially valuable within social care settings. Suggestions for these types of activities are given in the diagram below.

Professionals will develop strategies to help children cope with these emotions. The strategies will depend on the

individual child's age, abilities, temperament, personality and life experiences. The best advice is to pay attention to the approach of experienced staff and to ask for guidance and assistance whenever you need it. There's never any need to feel out of your depth. Your colleagues and managers are there to support you.

Activities that encourage expression ▶

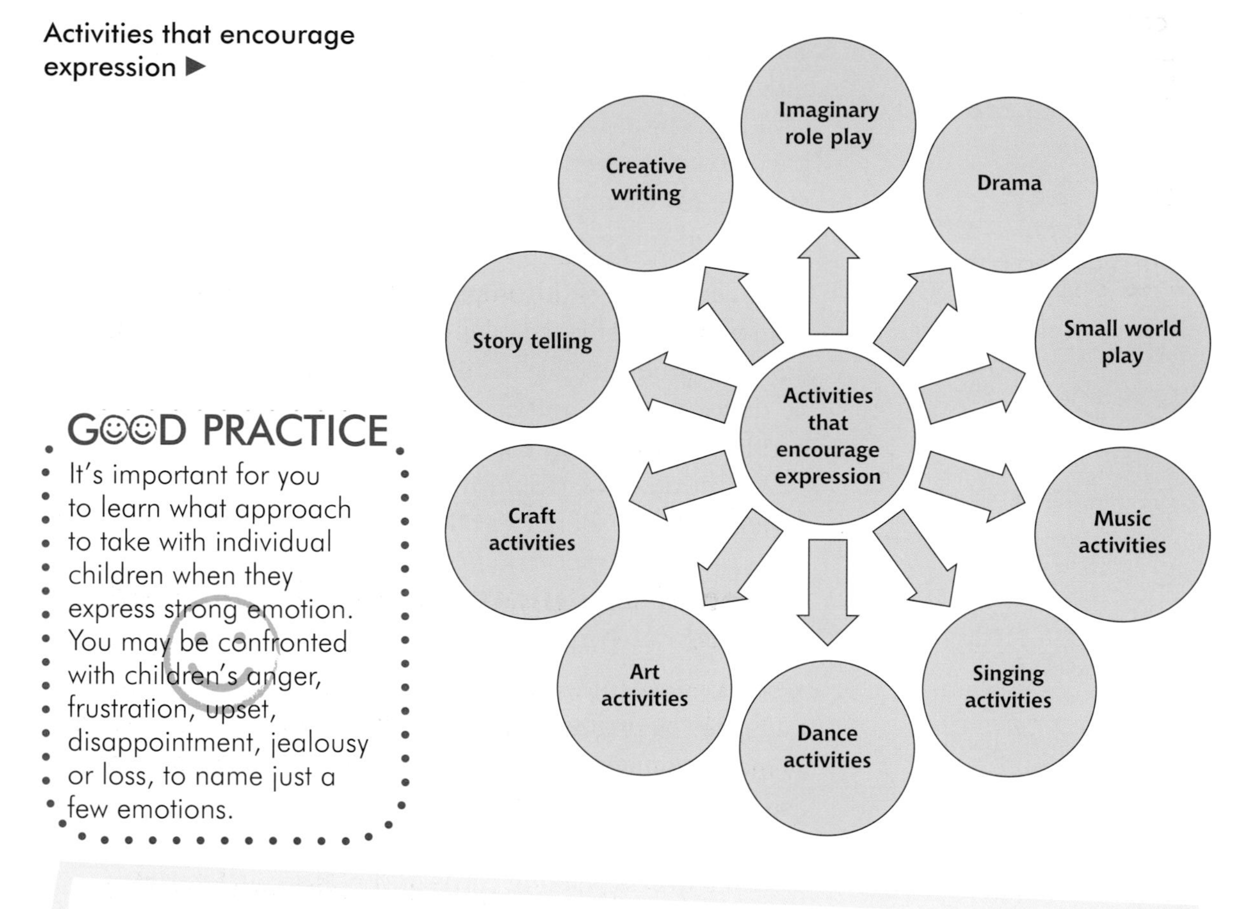

GOOD PRACTICE

It's important for you to learn what approach to take with individual children when they express strong emotion. You may be confronted with children's anger, frustration, upset, disappointment, jealousy or loss, to name just a few emotions.

FOCUS ON... your learning

In this section you've learnt how to communicate, treat and interact with families appropriately and the importance of recognising their role. You've also learnt about the range of challenges that may be experienced by children and families, and how to provide activities to meet their needs. Links to other Units give information on communication, relationships and meeting individual needs.

Questions:

1 Give four examples of the range of challenges that may be experienced by children and families.

2 Why is the role of families within their children's lives so important?

Learning Outcome 3

FOCUS ON...

the role of the adult when supporting children and their families in a social care setting.

This links with Assessment Criteria **3.1, 3.2, 3.3**

Working in teams

Details about working well with colleagues are included on pages 328–329. Information about working within multi-professional teams is included within Unit 7. You'll find details about sharing information and giving and receiving feedback on pages 228 and 234.

As you've learnt, multi-professional teams work within social care settings. It's important that you develop effective team-working skills in order to provide the best possible co-ordinated service for children and their families.

Confidentiality

See page 404 for details.

You must always work in line with confidentiality guidelines.

Supporting children's individual needs

Information about this is included on pages 68–82. Information about meeting children's additional needs is provided in Unit 9.

In Learning Outcome 2, you learnt about the importance of meeting the individual needs of children and families when you're providing play activities and experiences. You must also meet the care needs of children, as appropriate to their age and abilities.

Your role and responsibility within the setting

See page 404.

As outlined in Learning Outcome 2, it's important that you understand the purpose and aims of the social care setting and your own role within it. This information should be given to you when you first start a work placement at a setting, or when you apply for employment

(see page 12).

Always ask senior staff for guidance if you're at all unsure about the extent and limits of your role. You can't do a good job if you're not sure exactly what your responsibilities are. It's important to take your responsibilities seriously and to always be professional.

There are websites that give information and advice about careers in social care. They include details about professional roles as well as social care settings. Website addresses are given at the end of the Unit.

GOOD PRACTICE

You should approach your work with a positive attitude, and behave consistently, as outlined on page 000. It's important to respond to the way children behave, the things they say and the emotions they show as appropriate to the situation (see page 000). For example, you would show empathy and concern if a child is upset, and you would share their happiness when they're joyful.

Guidelines on what to do if you suspect child abuse or if a child makes a disclosure to you are given in Unit 3.

How to deal with sensitive situations positively

In Learning Outcome 2 you learnt that the children and families that social care professionals work with may have experienced a broad range of challenges. You also learnt about some of the strong emotions that children may express. In addition, adult family members may be going through situations they find stressful, intense or overwhelming. This means that you're likely to be exposed to sensitive situations when working in a social care setting.

It's important for you to learn to handle sensitive situations positively. Social care settings work with children and families through or following challenging circumstances. But they aim to be positive places where families get the support and services they need to help them move forward.

As you learnt in Learning Outcome 2, the best advice is to pay attention to the approach of experienced staff and to ask for guidance and assistance if you're unsure how to handle a sensitive issue you become involved in.

FOCUS ON...
your learning

You've learnt about the importance of working effectively within a team and maintaining confidentiality. You've learnt about your role and responsibilities within the setting. You've also learnt about dealing with sensitive situations in a positive way. There are links to Units 1 and 3.

Questions

1 Why is it so important to have a good understanding of your role and responsibilities?

2 Explain what you can do to deal with sensitive situations in positive ways.

RAPID RECAP

Learning Outcome 1

Social services work with families facing a range of challenges, including children who: have been identified as being 'in need', are 'looked after' by their local authority, who are placed for adoption, may have experienced or may be experiencing 'significant harm'. Multi-agency works takes place in a variety of settings, e.g. family centres, Children's Trusts, etc. National and local support is available to families via statutory, private and voluntary organisations. Links to other Units give information on multi-professional teams and a range of settings.

Learning Outcome 2

The children and families that social care professionals work with may have experienced a broad range of challenges. These may include: child abuse, domestic violence, family breakdowns, bereavement, disadvantage, disability, etc. You must communicate, treat and interact with families with respect and courtesy, recognising the importance of their role in their children's lives. You must provide activities to meet the needs of children and families. You're advised to read (or re-read) Unit 7 of this book as part of your study towards Unit 11.

Learning Outcome 3

You must work effectively within a team, and follow confidentiality procedures. You must have a good understanding of your role and responsibilities within the setting, or you will not be able to do a good job. You're likely to come across sensitive situations within care settings. It's important to deal with these in a positive way. There are links to Units 3 and 9.

FAQ

Q **How will I be assessed on this Unit?**

A *You'll complete an assignment task. CACHE publishes a task for each optional unit every year.*

Q **What will I have to do?**

A *Your tutor or Centre will help you to understand the task. See Unit 1 Learning Outcome 5 for more information on study skills.*

Weblinks

You may like to visit the following websites:

- www.scie-socialcareonline.org.uk
  Social Care Online has database of social care information, which is updated daily.
- www.socialworkandcare.co.uk
  The Department of Health's social care site. Includes career information.
- www.csci.org.uk/about_us/what_is_social_care.aspx
  Home of the Commission for Social Care Inspection. Explains a range of social care roles and settings
- www.scie.org.uk/
  Home of the Social Care Institute for Excellence (SCIE). Includes information about good practice.

Follow up

The following books will help you to plan activities:

A Practical Guide to Activities for Young Children, 2nd edition,
Christine Hobart and Jill Frankel (2005) Nelson Thornes

This book features activities for children aged 0–11 years

A Practical Guide to Activities for Older Children,
Miranda Walker (2007) Nelson Thornes

This book features 15 themes and linked play activities for children aged 4-16 years.

The following book will help you with your observational skills:

A Practical Guide to Observation and Assessment, 3rd edition,
Christine Hobart and Jill Frankel (2004) Nelson Thornes

This book provides clear coverrage of a range of observation techniques, their strengths and weaknesses and how the results can be used.

The following book will help you when you are seeking employment:

A Practical Guide to Child Care Employment,
Christine Hobart and Jill Frankel, Nelson Thornes (1996)

This book contains information on different types of employment, the job search, writing an application and interview techniques.

The following book will also be helpful if you are looking for information on the issues of race, gender and disa bility in the childcare setting:

A Practical Guide to Equal Opportunities,
Hyacinth Malik, (1998) Nelson Thornes

This book gives a clear introduction to the issues of discrimination and stereotyping in a straightforward and user-friendly way.

IMPORTANT INFORMATION ABOUT NEW LEGISLATION

Every Child Matters

Every Child Matters is a major government initiative which focuses on bringing together services to support children and families. It sets out five major outcomes for children:

- staying safe
- enjoying and achieving
- making a positive contribution
- economic well-being
- being healthy

Turn to pages 338 and 368 to find out more (Author note: Unit 10).

The Early Years Foundation Stage (EYFS)

As part of the Every Child Matters initiative, the EYFS (a framework for learning) will be mandatory from September 2008 for:

- schools
- early years providers in Ofsted registered settings

It will apply to children from birth to the end of the academic year in which the child has their fifth birthday. The EYFS brings together and replaces the *Curriculum Guidance for the Foundation Stage*, *Birth to Three Matters* and the *National Standards for Under 8s Day Care and Childminding*, which will no longer apply from September 2008.

Turn to page 368 to find out more about The Early Years Foundation Stage.

Glossary

ABC of behaviour – the pattern of all behaviour: antecedent – what happens before the behavior occurs; behaviour – the resulting behavior, acceptable or unacceptable; consequence – the result of the behavior: positive or negative.

Accessible – a facility that a disabled person is able to access, i.e. an accessible toilet, parking space, building.

Accident book – legal documentation of all accidents and injuries occurring in any establishment.

Anti-discriminatory practice – practice that encourages a positive view of difference and opposes negative attitudes and practices that lead to unfavourable treatment of people.

Appraisal – a review of an employee's work and effectiveness with their line manager.

Attachment – an affectionate two-way relationship that develops between an infant and an adult.

Auditory learners – people who prefer to learn by hearing.

Baseline or formative assessment – the first assessment of a child's current stage of development.

Behavior – all that we say and do, the way that we act and react towards others.

Behavior modification – a framework for managing children's behavior.

behaviour management policy – procedure for dealing with inappropriate behaviour

Bias – having a preference for one particular view or perspective over others.

Child protection – protecting children from physical, emotional or sexual abuse or neglect.

Children in need – a child is 'in need' if they are unlikely to achieve or maintain a reasonable standard of development without the provision of services, or if they are disabled.

Children with additional needs – all children have needs that must be met. But this term refers to children who have extra needs due to an impairment. Some people use the term 'special needs', but there's some disagreement about this. Some people don't like this term because they feel all children are special. Some disabled people think it's inappropriate as there's nothing 'special' about being disabled. Others think that 'special' is just another way of labelling disabled children as different from their peers. But families of young disabled children often feel more accepting of the term 'special'. Generally, if this term is used by a family, then practitioners will use it when working with them. The term 'disabled' may also be used to mean the same thing.

Children's Centres – places where children under five years old and their families can receive seamless integrated services and information and where they can access help from multi-disciplinary teams of professionals. The Government is committed to delivering a Sure Start Children's Centre for every community by 2010.

Children's Information Service – Each council has a CIS which provides information on childcare and related services for children aged from birth to 14 (up to aged 16 for children with special needs).

Code of practice – a description of how to respond/behave/a process to follow under particular circumstances.

Concentration span – the period of time someone is able to focus completely on one activity or task.

Consolidate learning – term used to describe the process of learning becoming strengthened and fixed in children's minds over time.

Content of play – what children want to do in their play and how they want to do it.

Creative play – play expressing creative ideas through manipulating materials e.g. painting.

Creativity – a mental process involving the generation of new ideas and concepts or new associations between existing ideas and concepts.

Curriculum vitae (CV) – a specification of personal details, education and employment history to provide information for potential employers.

Development – can be measured through social, physical and cognitive milestones.

Discrimination – choosing certain qualities as desirable and others as undesirable and rejecting those that have the undesirable qualities. Behavior based on prejudice, which results in someone being treated unfairly.

Diversity – a range including differences.

Emergent writing – marks made by a child when they first attempt to write. Symbols drawn in a line are often mingled with real letters.

Equal opportunities – all people participating in society to the best of their abilities, regardless of race, religion, disability, gender or social background.

Equal opportunities policy – the practice of offering equal opportunities to those that may be at risk of discrimination.

Expected pattern of development – when children are generally expected to achieve key development milestones

Family diversity – a range of family structures, beliefs, attitudes and ways of raising children.

Fine motor skills – small manipulative movements made with fingers.

Formula feeding – bottle feeding.

Germs – organisms such as bacteria and viruses that cause disease.

Gross motor development – development of the whole body and limb movements, co-ordination and balance.

Gross motor skills – whole body movements such as walking.

Hand/eye co-ordination – when vision and fine motor skills are used together on tasks such as threading.

Heuristic play – play with a range of diverse objects, often provided in a treasure basket for babies and toddlers.

Hygiene – things we do to ensure good health and cleanliness.

Imaginative play – involves activities and experiences that stimulate children to use their imagination.

Impairment – term used to identify an individual's child's disability, i.e. a visual impairment, hearing impairment, speech impairment, physical impairment, etc. A child may have more than one impairment, i.e. a learning difficulty and a visual impairment. The word 'disability' or 'difficulty' may be used to mean the same thing.

Inappropriate behaviour – when the well being of an individual or group are affected by the behaviour.

Inclusion – occurs when a child with additional needs is included within a setting/activity.

Inclusive – an inclusive setting includes children with additional needs. Mainstream settings are required to be inclusive.

Inclusive approach – an approach that enables all to take a full and active part; meeting the needs of all children.

Independent Schools – run independently of the government and do not receive government funding, sometimes referred to as 'private schools'.

Individual needs/specific needs – terms used to describe how an impairment impacts on the needs of an individual child. This will be specific to them. i.e. Emily, a wheelchair user, needs assistance with toileting and dressing. Nina, also a wheelchair user, does not.

Infection – when germs such as bacteria infect the body.

Institutionalised discrimination – occurs when a group of workers jointly discriminate.

Intellectual development – the development of thinking and understanding.

Intent of play – the purpose or reason for play.

Interpretation – the process of assessing and evaluating an observation or series of observations.

Job description – list of general tasks or functions and responsibilities of a job.

Key attachment – the special emotional bond that forms between a child and her closest carers.

Key worker – a childcarer appointed to form a key attachment with a child and to take a special interest in her welfare and development.

Kinaesthetic learners – people who prefer to learn through doing, movement and action.

Legislation – laws that have been made.

Low socio-economic group – families with low income

Mainstream setting – a setting that is not just for children with additional needs/SEN, i.e. most schools, nurseries, etc.

Making restitution – saying sorry; making things up to someone who has been hurt.

Manipulative play – enables children to practice and refine their motor skills.

Milestones – the different levels of accomplishment children make during different stages of their life.

Multicultural society – a society whose members have a variety of cultural and ethnic backgrounds.

Multidisciplinary team – team including workers from a number of professional groups, i.e. childcarers, teachers, social workers, etc.

National Curriculum – a course of study, laid down by government, that all children between five and 16 in state schools in the UK must follow.

Nature – describes the way children are genetically programmed from birth to be able to do certain things at certain times.

Need-to-know basis – term used to refer to only revealing confidential information to those who need to know.

Neonate – this term means 'newly born'. It's often used to describe a baby under one month old, especially when talking about development.

Non-judgemental – not taking a fixed stand on an issue.

Non-participant observer – an observer who doesn't interact with the child being observed

Nurture – describes the development that happens in response to the experiences that individual children have from the time they are born onwards.

Nutrition – ensuring you eat the right foods for a healthy and well balanced diet.

Observation – noting and recording events using one or more of our senses to determine what is happening.

Ofsted – The Office for Standards in Education, Children's Services and Skills which inspects and regulates care and education for children and young people.

Over-sexualised behaviour – when children act in sexual ways that are inappropriate for their age – they may say or know things you would not expect, or role play or act out sexual situations.

Participant observer – an observer who does interact with the child being observed.

Partnership with parents – a way of working with parents that recognises their needs and their entitlement to be involved in decisions affecting their children.

Person specification – profile of the type of person needed to do a job – their qualifications, required experience and personality type – usually produced alongside a job description.

Play – Physical or mental activity that has no objective other than for enjoyment or amusement.

Play agenda – what a child wants to achieve in their play.

Play cue – a signal that a child gives to show that they want to play.

Play return – a signal someone gives to show that they're willing to play. This is given in response to a play cue.

Play theory – someone's idea about why and/or how children play

Playwork – name given to the sector that works with children of school age in their leisure time, within play settings.

Playworker – people who work within playwork settings.

Poverty – having little money and few material possessions.

Prejudice – preconceived preference or idea, often based on incomplete facts.

Primary socialisation – when children learn how to behave within the family/home from parents or primary carers.

Primitive reflex – reflexes that are characteristic of newborn babies such as: grasping reflex, rooting reflex, hand to mouth reflex, walking reflex, placing reflex, startle reflex and sucking reflex.

Private provision– owned by an individual person or a company, and aims to make a profit.

Professional conduct – behaving in a way that is appropriate in the workplace.

Professional development – improvement in skills, knowledge and practice.

Professionalism – a professional approach to work.

Prone – the word used to describe the position of a baby lying on her front.

Racism – animosity and negative attitudes shown to people from ethnic minorities.

Respite care – temporary care that is provided for a short period to give families a brief break, or to support them in a difficult period (i.e. if a main carer has to go into hospital). This is usually provided outside of the family home.

Responsive care – the term used to describe how childcarers identify and respond to the care needs of children.

Role model – person who serves as an example.

Secondary socialisation – when children learn how to behave in society from people outside of the family or home.

Self-esteem – liking and valuing oneself; also referred to as self-respect.

Self-image (or self-concept) – the image that we have of ourselves and the way that we think that other people see us.

Separation distress – infants becoming distressed when separated from the person to whom they are attached.

Socialising – practicing social skills such as making conversation, sharing ideas, active listening and reading body language.

Socio-economic group – grouping of people according to their status in society, based on their occupation, which is closely related to their wealth/income.

Special educational needs (SEN) – Children with SEN learn differently from most children of the same age and may need extra or different help to learn. Not all disabled children need extra or different help to learn. It depends on their individuals needs. The term SEN is used by national and local education departments.

Special setting – a setting just for children with additional needs/SEN, i.e. special school, special youth club.

Staff appraisal – a regular meeting with supervisors to discuss your work performance.

Staff deployment – how, when and where staff work.

Statutory service – exists because parliament has passed a law to say that the service either must or can be provided.

Stereotyping – when people think that all the individual members of a group have the same characteristics as each other; often applied on the basis of race, gender or disability.

Supine – the word used to describe the position of a baby lying on her back.

Symbolic play – using one thing to represent another, e.g. a doll to represent a baby.

Terms of employment – contract between the employer and the employee, which usually includes details for holiday pay, sickness benefit, pension provision and details of any probation or notice period.

Theorist – name used for people who come up with theories

Transitions – periods of change.

Unconscious – showing no response to external stimulation.

Value – something that is believed to be important and worthwhile.

Visual learners – people who prefer to learn by seeing.

Vocabulary – the term given to refer to all the words someone knows.

Voluntary provision – run by organisations such as charities and committees, does not make a profit.

Weaning – the transition from milk feeds to solid foods.

Welfare – well being.

Welfare state – the combination of services provided by the state for all citizens, based upon legislation passed in the 1940s with the aim of protecting their health and providing financial resources from birth to death.

Index

▶ CONTENTS

Part 3: Managing infertility in secondary care 31

Part 4: The wider aspects of fertility treatment 73

▶ PREFACE

Patients want simple, clear information about the options, risks and implications of infertility treatment when they are feeling emotional at a vulnerable stage of their lives. They often ask their doctors for explanations and advice about their feelings and experiences of treatment. GPs and hospital doctors in turn need clear unambiguous information about best practice in a complex field, to be able to explain and discuss the complicated medical management and ethical dilemmas that face their patients who are seeking assistance for their infertility.

The book was 'conceived' by Ruth Chambers during her recent term as a member of the Human Fertilisation and Embryology Authority. Having been a GP for 18 years and caring for many patients with infertility problems, she is aware of how difficult it is for patients and doctors to keep abreast of all the new and complex developments in fertility treatment. Patients need to understand and think through the issues to be able to fully participate in the decisions made about their care.

It is really important for the welfare of the child-to-be and the would-be parents, that general practitioners work closely with fertility experts to provide seamless care for infertile couples. Some GPs shy away from the seeming complexities of fertility treatments and are reluctant to contribute to the assessment of couples' suitability as prospective parents. Clear and specific information should enable health professionals and patients alike to understand the complicated medical and ethical situations that are integral to the management of those with infertility and participate more fully in decisions about their care.

This book seeks to describe current thinking and best practice in the management of infertility in such a way that those doctors, other health professionals or patients who are new to the field can appreciate the key issues and concerns. It draws heavily on the publications from the Human Fertilisation and

Embryology Authority and the evidence-based clinical guidelines on the management of infertility recently published by the Royal College of Obstetricians and Gynaecologists which were supported by the clinical effectiveness programme of the NHS Executive.

Guidelines are raining down on GPs' heads from all directions, some offering conflicting advice, others complicated instructions. The Royal College of Obstetricians and Gynaecologists' guidelines[1,2] give the evidence for best practice in managing infertility in primary and secondary care settings. They have been developed by a multidisciplinary group including GPs, nurses and users as well as fertility experts, overseeing a dedicated research team undertaking systematic reviews of the literature on the topic. The draft guidelines were peer reviewed by a variety of health professionals and patients, and amended accordingly. The resulting national guidelines are intended to be adapted to local circumstances and used for commissioning high quality infertility care. For simplicity the main guidelines, reviews and reports will be referred to in support of the information given here, rather than the references being given to the hundreds of individual published research papers that they considered. The guidelines[1,2] themselves are graded according to how robust the evidence cited is, and whether statements are scientifically proven, are backed by good research or are the opinion of experts in the field.

We know that GPs who use infertility guidelines are more likely to undertake a more comprehensive work-up prior to referral including seeing and examining both partners, initiating basic investigations and speeding up the referral process.[3]

Ruth Chambers
April 1999

References

1 Royal College of Obstetricians and Gynaecologists (1998) *The initial investigation and management of the infertile couple. Evidence-based clinical guidelines. No. 2.* Royal College of Obstetricians and Gynaecologists, London (0171 772 6275).

2 Royal College of Obstetricians and Gynaecologists (1998) *The management of infertility in secondary care. Evidence-based clinical guidelines. No. 3.* Royal College of Obstetricians and Gynaecologists, London (0171 772 6275).

3 Emslie C, Grimshaw J and Templeton A (1993) Do clinical guidelines improve general practice management and referral of infertile couples? *BMJ*. **306**: 1728–31.

► ACKNOWLEDGEMENTS

I am very grateful to Suzanne McCarthy, the Chief Executive of the Human Fertilisation and Embryology Authority (HFEA) and her colleagues for their detailed feedback on the book as it was compiled. Much of the material in the book has been informed by the extensive working papers and documents produced by the HFEA which anticipate and address medical and ethical issues arising from assisted reproduction. I should also like to acknowledge the contribution that the *Guidelines* on the management of infertility published by the Royal College of Obstetricians and Gynaecologists have made to this book and will make to those working in primary care and hospital settings.

► PART 1

Introduction to the problem of infertility

▶ CHAPTER 1

An overview of infertility

How common is infertility?

Around one in six or seven couples experience difficulties conceiving a child[1–3] and need specialist help at some time in their lives. The increased numbers of people presenting for help with infertility may have given a false impression that infertility is becoming more common, when there has probably been little change in prevalence over recent years.[1] It is widely held

One in seven couples have trouble conceiving.

▼

that sperm counts are falling dramatically, but recent reviews[4,5] have shown that the findings of published surveys may have been wrongly interpreted, as far as countries other than the USA are concerned.

The numbers of births in the UK are dropping. The fall in the General Fertility Rate (GFR), which is the number of births per 1000 women aged 15–44 years, is mainly due to a reduction in babies born to women in the 16–34 age group. There has been a slight increase in the number of births to women aged 35 years and over. Natural fertility in women declines after the age of 32 years, and particularly after the age of 40 years. The frequency of other medical problems such as endometriosis, fibroids or tubal damage increases as a woman ages when miscarriages are more common too.

About half of couples having regular unprotected intercourse will have conceived within three months, two thirds by six months and 90% by 12 months.[6] The definition of 'subfertility' is 'failure to conceive within one year of unprotected intercourse'.[6] All types of subfertility are grouped under the general term 'infertility'.

The main factors that predict the chances of a successful pregnancy in infertile couples undergoing assisted conception, are the female partner's age, the length of time the couple have been trying to have a family, previous ability to conceive, and the quality of the sperm. The conception rate decreases by 16% for every year of infertility after one year of trying, and by 2.7% per additional year of the wife's age after the age of 19 years. If a couple have not conceived within three years of stopping contraception then the chances of a spontaneous pregnancy in the next year is not more than one chance in four, irrespective of the results of the sperm analysis.[7]

Causes of infertility

There is a huge spectrum of causes of infertility. These include failure to ovulate, failure to produce or deliver adequate numbers of healthy sperm to the fallopian tubes, obstruction in the fallopian tubes, endometriosis or adhesions involving the ovaries or fallopian tubes, previous or current infections in the reproductive tracts of male or female, poor timing or technique of sexual intercourse, an unreceptive lining in the uterus repelling implantation, immunological barriers to fertilisation or implantation, genetic factors, chemotherapy or other drugs, secondarily caused by physiological factors such as weight loss or excessive exercise, or from other causes of gonadotrophin disorder connected for example with hyperprolactinaemia, a pituitary tumour or polycystic ovary syndrome.

Causes of subfertility vary according to socio-economic and geographic factors. A minor cause of subfertility in both the male and female partners can combine to a more major problem of subfertility as a couple. The cause of subfertility is unexplained in about a third of cases.[2,6] In developed countries one fifth of infertility may be caused by purely male factors, and in another fifth of cases both male and female factors contribute to the two partners being infertile as a couple.[1,2] Tubal factor infertility in the woman partner occurs in 12–33% of infertile couples, mainly caused by previous episodes of pelvic inflammatory disease.[8] Polycystic ovary syndrome is more common than used to be thought and may be associated with lowered fertility in some cases.

One study of infertile couples presenting for treatment[2] found that 21% of infertility was classified as being caused by ovulatory failure, 14% due to tubal damage, 6% secondary to endometriosis, 26% due to male factor infertility, 6% attributed to suspected coital failure and 33% was unexplained or due to other causes. Eleven per cent of the women seen had had a previous termination of pregnancy, and it was more common for a woman with tubal damage to have had a termination.

Genital tract infection with *Chlamydia trachomatis* is a major risk factor for subsequent tubal infertility.[9] Unfortunately tubal infection with *Chlamydia* can be asymptomatic, and those with symptoms are often a small proportion of those affected.[9] The feasibility of general practice-based opportunistic screening, in sexually active women under 25 years and high risk older women, is currently being piloted. The numbers of cases of *Chlamydia* infection are soaring in the UK, with 75 408 cases

Who me infertile!
I don't think so!!

of *Chlamydia* infection being reported by laboratories and genitourinary clinics to the Communicable Disease Surveillance Centre in 1997. The rise in numbers of *Chlamydia* infection is probably due as much to increased detection by GPs and other clinicians who have become increasingly aware of the possibility of *Chlamydia* infection being present and tested for it accordingly, rather than increased prevalence.

Box 1.1: Causes of female infertility

- Tubal damage: from sexually transmitted diseases, complications of coil, any sepsis
- Primary ovarian failure
- Secondary ovarian failure – effects of age, premature menopause
- Polycystic ovarian syndrome
- Hypogonadotrophic hypogonadism – deficiency of follicle-stimulating hormone (FSH) and luteinising hormone (LH)
- Hyperprolactinaemia, from pituitary adenoma
- Endometriosis
- Intrauterine fibroids, polyps
- Significant systemic illness
- Previous sterilisation

Box 1.2: Causes of male infertility

- Deficient spermatogenesis – congenital (e.g. Klinefelter's syndrome) or acquired (for example chemotherapy)
- Previous vasectomy
- Antisperm antibodies
- Hypogonadotrophic hypogonadism – deficiency of FSH and LH
- Hyperprolactinaemia, from pituitary adenoma
- Ejaculation disorders, for example retrograde ejaculation, impotence
- Obstruction to outflow of sperm
- Significant systemic illness

Licensed and unlicensed treatment options

The range of treatment options for reversing infertility includes the use of fertility drugs in men and women to induce ovulation or improve hormone or sperm production, surgery to the male or female reproductive tracts to remove blockages or abnormalities, insemination of sperm, and assisted reproduction – most commonly, *in vitro* fertilisation (IVF) and intra-cytoplasmic sperm injection (ICSI). Surrogacy or third party reproduction for women without a uterus is also a possibility.

Some fertility treatment requires a licence, in accordance with the legal directions in the Human Fertilisation and Embryology Act (HF&E Act), passed in 1990. Any treatment that involves the creation, keeping and using of human embryos outside the body, or the storage or donation of human eggs and sperm, is a licensable activity. Insemination of a woman with her husband's or partner's sperm while he is alive is not regulated by the HF&E Act because insemination and fertilisation occur inside the woman's body and the man and woman are being treated together. That is why GIFT (gamete intra-fallopian transfer) using the partner's sperm does not require a licence whilst IVF (*in vitro* fertilisation) does. Unlike IVF, GIFT does not involve handling gametes and creating embryos in a laboratory outside the human body. So GIFT can be offered by District General Hospital Trusts that do not have a specialised fertility treatment service. There is controversy about the fact that GIFT is not covered by the HF&E Act despite the procedure incurring similar medical, social and ethical risks to IVF.

These licensed fertility treatments are invasive and it is all too easy for couples longing for a baby to want to rush for the ultimate assisted conception technology rather than wait a little longer for spontaneous conception to occur or try simpler treatments first.

The Human Fertilisation and Embryology Authority (HFEA)

The Human Fertilisation and Embryology Authority was set up to regulate and license infertility treatment in accordance with the HF&E Act in 1990, following the recommendations of the Warnock report in 1984. It grants licences to fertility clinics for treatment and storage of eggs, sperm and embryos, monitors and encourages good practice, maintains a database of treatments given, publishes information and describes centres' success rates, regulates research on embryos and regularly reports to, and advises, the Secretary of State for Health.

Besides licensing any assisted conception techniques involving donated eggs or sperm, the HFEA also licenses the storage of human eggs, sperm or embryos for treatment or research.

Research is limited to embryos up to 14 days after fertilisation has occurred. The HFEA Licence committees scrutinise research applications to ensure that the use of human embryos is essential for the purposes of research. This means that the numbers of embryos used should be kept to a minimum in any research protocol and that the proposed studies do not duplicate other published work unnecessarily.

The HFEA runs a web site and publishes a variety of information leaflets, reports and consultation documents for the public. Videos on IVF and donor insemination (DI) are available for educational purposes. Further details about titles and availability are given at the back of the book.

The HFEA does not license all fertility treatment and does not play any part in resource allocation and the differential NHS funding of fertility treatments around the UK. Although the HFEA likes to hear about patients' complaints, it does not act as an ombudsman and have any official role.

The over-riding importance of the welfare of the child

Clinicians considering whether to provide couples with licensed fertility treatment are required to take account of 'the welfare of any child who may be born as a result of treatment (including the need of that child for a father) and of any other child who may be affected by the birth' [Section 13 (5) of the Human Fertilisation and Embryology Act, 1990]. The child or children who 'may be affected' are any others within the potential child's household or family. The legal requirement to consider the welfare of the prospective child applies to all licensed fertility treatments and all unlicensed treatments at licensed fertility centres, and is good practice for all fertility treatment. In practice this means that all licensed fertility clinics must be able to demonstrate that they are adhering to their written protocols for assessing the welfare of any potential children. They should check who will be legally responsible for the child and the suitability of those intending to bring the child up, to be sure that there is a stable and supportive environment awaiting any child born as a result of fertility treatment (*see* Box 1.3 for more details).

Licensed clinics are required to check out past medical and social histories of the intending parents with their general practitioner(s) to make sure that there are no pre-existing reasons why they would not make suitable parents and that they are physically healthy and fit enough for a pregnancy. Some GPs resent these enquiries feeling that making such judgements is discriminatory against the infertile as society does not assess the suitability of parents who conceive naturally and that doctors are not in a position to judge other people's suitability as prospective parents (*see* Box 1.4, p. 12).

Clinicians considering treating older couples 'must bear in mind the welfare of the potential child when deciding whether or not to provide treatment. This includes both the parents' ages and their likely ability to look after and provide for a child in the future, the need of a child for a father, and the

Box 1.3: Factors to be considered about prospective parents and the welfare of the child, of which centres should be aware where people are seeking licensed treatment (HFEA Code of Practice[10]):

- their commitment to bringing up a child or children
- their ability to provide a stable and supportive environment for any child produced as a result of treatment
- their medical histories and the medical histories of their families
- their health and consequent future ability to look after or provide for a child's needs
- their ability to meet the needs of any child or children who may be born as a result of treatment, including the implications of any possible multiple births
- any risk of harm to the child or children who may be born, including the risk of inherited disorders or transmissible diseases, problems during pregnancy and of neglect or abuse
- the effect of a new baby or babies upon any existing child of the family.

Reproduced from the HFEA's Code of Practice, 1998, with their permission.

possible attitudes of other members of the family towards the child'.[11]

Most clinics treat women up until the age they might naturally be able to give birth. Some clinics interpret this upper age as being 50 years, but there are instances of women of up to 55 years being assisted with conception. In one survey, 12 clinics confirmed that their upper age limit for treatment for women was aged 50 years.[12] The HFEA 'would routinely investigate any clinic that appeared to be routinely treating women in their fifties and has done so in the past. But (the HFEA's) concern

Box 1.4: An exchange of correspondence describing one GP's perspective of a routine enquiry as to a patient's suitability to be a parent and the response:

'I don't feel able or willing to sign a form that, in essence, asks for a judgement from me on the suitability of a woman to become a mother. No such permission is required for natural conception, and who am I to say that someone is or is not 'suitable' to become a mother? Hitler I think would argue differently which is the whole point.'

And the reply:

'…Although there is no legal requirement for GPs to respond to these requests, the provision of information by a GP greatly assists the clinician offering treatment to come to a decision. However as you will see from Section 3 of the HFEA's Code of Practice[10] ["Centres should seek to satisfy themselves that the GP of each prospective parent knows of no reason why either of them might not be suitable for the treatment to be offered. This would include anything which might adversely affect the welfare of any resulting child."] the response that you give only forms part of the clinician's assessment. You and your GP colleagues are not absolutely "vouching" for a couple's suitability. It is the clinician at the licensed centre who must take responsibility for the decision to offer treatment.'

has always been with the process by which clinics reach their decisions rather than on the individual decisions themselves'.[11] Only a small proportion of women who receive licensed fertility treatment are in the older age groups – only 62 cycles of DI, 32 micromanipulation cycles and 202 cycles of IVF treatments were carried out on women aged 45 years and over, in the UK over a 12-month period to March 1997, which is less than 1% of all licensed fertility treatment.[13] The oldest woman to have been treated by IVF was 60 years of age according to the HFEA's register of details; the patient gave birth at 61 years old, having reportedly misled the fertility clinic about her real age.

The HF&E Act (1990) does not exclude any particular category of woman from receiving licensed treatment. The case of a single woman seeking treatment should be considered on its own merits, and the final decision as to whether to provide treatment will rest with the clinician concerned, taking into account the HFEA's Code of Practice.[11] Where there is no father, fertility clinics should assess the prospective mother's ability to meet the child's needs throughout childhood, and what other family and friends will be involved in bringing the child up. That means that it is possible for single women or one partner of a lesbian couple to undergo assisted conception if they fulfil these conditions. However, in practice, the HFEA records show that the treatment of single women is uncommon, with there being no male partner recorded for less than 1% of all treatment cycles undertaken by UK fertility clinics.

References

1 Royal College of Obstetricians and Gynaecologists (1998) *The initial investigation and management of the infertile couple. Evidence-based clinical guidelines. No. 2.* Royal College of Obstetricians and Gynaecologists, London (0171 772 6275).

2 Hull M, Glazener C, Kelly N, *et al.* (1985) Population study of causes, treatment, and outcome of infertility *BMJ.* **291**: 1693–97.

3 Braude P, Ledger W (1998) *Infertility into the Millennium.* National Infertility Awareness Campaign, London.

4 Becker S, Birhane K (1997) A meta-analysis of 61 sperm count studies revisited. *Fertility and Sterility.* **67**: 1103–8.

5 Bandolier (1998) Tight underpants. *Bandolier.* **5**: issue 9.

6 Johnson M, Everitt B (1997) *Essential Reproduction.* Blackwell, Oxford.

7 Hargreave T, Mills J (1998) Investigating and managing infertility in general practice. *BMJ*. **316**: 1438–41.

8 Royal College of Obstetricians and Gynaecologists (1998) *The management of infertility in secondary care. Evidence-based clinical guidelines. No. 3*. Royal College of Obstetricians and Gynaecologists, London (0171 772 6275).

9 Winter A, Ahmad S (1998) Managing infertility in general practice must include screening for sexual infections. *BMJ*. **317**: 1526 (letter).

10 Human Fertilisation and Embryology Authority (1998) *Code of Practice*. HFEA, London.

11 Press release, 11 September 1998. HFEA, London.

12 Furse A (1997) *Infertility Companion: A user's guide to tests, technologies and therapies*. Thorsons, London.

13 Human Fertilisation and Embryology Authority (1998) *Annual Report 1998*. HFEA, London.

PART 2

Managing infertility in general practice

▶ CHAPTER 2

The GP eye view of the symptoms and signs

Examine both male and female partners of the couple presenting with subfertility.

In the woman

In the woman **ask about:** personal and lifestyle details – age, the extent of stress in her life, whether she takes strenuous exercise, her smoking status, her usual alcohol intake, current and recent occupations, the frequency of sexual intercourse and the length of unprotected intercourse.

Medical details: menstrual history – that is amenorrhoea (absent periods) or oligomenorrhoea (irregular periods) and whether any previous pregnancies were with the same or other partners, previous abdominal or pelvic surgery, previous sexually transmitted disease or pelvic inflammatory disease (PID), previous abnormal tests such as a cervical smear, rubella status, her current medication including recreational drugs, and any systemic or debilitating illnesses including anorexia nervosa. The drug compounds that have been associated with adverse effects on fertility or sexual function[1] are: non-steroidal anti-inflammatory drugs, some chemotherapeutic agents and cannabis.

Look for: obesity (e.g. Body Mass Index >30) or abnormalities in the pelvic examination to give clues to the cause of subfertility, such as vaginal infection or pain indicating endometriosis or pelvic inflammatory disease. Previous treatment for abnormal smears may have caused cervical stenosis. Bimanual examination may reveal an ovarian cyst or fibroids. Hirsuitism and/or acne may be the clue to the presence of polycystic ovarian syndrome. Galactorrhoea will suggest the probability of hyperprolactinaemia.

In the man

In the man **ask about:** personal and lifestyle details – age, his smoking status, his usual alcohol intake, current and recent occupations, the frequency of sexual intercourse and the length of unprotected intercourse. Relevant occupational histories that are important to elicit are exposure to agricultural chemicals such as pesticides, X-rays, and chemicals used in the preparation of solvents and heavy metals, which have been shown to adversely effect sperm quality and/or quantity. Evidence suggests that an increased testicular temperature may decrease sperm count and quality, and occupational and social circumstances such as working as a welder, sitting in a wheelchair or wearing tight trousers, may be relevant to a history of male subfertility.[1] Showers and saunas do not increase the intrascrotal temperature, but soaking in a hot bath might do so.[2]

Medical details: any previous sexually transmitted diseases, any previous (uro)genital pathology or treatment, any systemic or debilitating illnesses, and whether there have been previous pregnancies with the same or other partners. Record drug history – the drug compounds that have been associated with adverse effects on male fertility or sexual function are:[1] sulphasalazine, nitrofurantoin, tetracyclines, ketoconazole, cimetidine, allopurinol, adrenoreceptor blocking agents, tricyclic antidepressants, monoamine oxidase inhibitors, phenthiazines, the beta blocker propanolol, cannabis, cocaine, anabolic steroids and some chemotherapeutic agents. There is an association between male infertility and the use of anabolic steroids by body builders.[3]

Look for: any genital abnormality such as small soft testes, a lump within the testis which might be testicular cancer, or

When the doctor said for us to 'cool it' – what made you think he meant my testes?
ICE

an undescended testis; assess secondary sex characteristics. About 25% of those seeking assessment for infertility have a varicocele,[3] and there is evidence that sperm quality may improve in men with a sperm concentration of less than 20 million per ml after surgical treatment of a clinically apparent varicocele.[4]

References

1 Royal College of Obstetricians and Gynaecologists (1998) *The initial investigation and management of the infertile couple. Evidence-based clinical guidelines. No. 2*. Royal College of Obstetricians and Gynaecologists, London (0171 772 6275).

2 Brindley GS (1982) Deep scrotal temperature and the effect on it of clothing, air temperature, activity, posture and paraplegia. *B J Urol*. **54**: 49–55.

3 Hargreave T, Mills J (1998) Investigating and managing infertility in general practice. *BMJ*. **316**: 1438–41.

4 Cooke I (1998) Putting new infertility guidelines into practice. *Pulse*. **14 November**.

▶ CHAPTER 3

Initial management by the GP

Figure 3.1 shows the key stages in investigating and managing the infertile couple in primary care, from taking a history at initial presentation, to examining both partners and carrying out a few simple tests and then deciding whether and when it is appropriate to refer them to a fertility specialist.

Advice and checks

- Check the rubella status in the woman. Seronegative women should have a rubella vaccination and avoid pregnancy by using effective contraception for one month after immunisation.
- Advise women who are trying to conceive to take folic acid as a dietary supplement, which should be continued until 12 weeks of any pregnancy. The recommended dose is normally 0.4 mg a day, or 4 mg daily in those women who have previously had a child with a neural tube defect or are taking anti-epileptic medication.[1]
- Provide details of organisations to which the infertile couple may apply for information about infertility, different types of treatment and the relative advantages of different clinics and centres (*see* Appendix 1).
- Advise both partners to stop smoking if either or both are smokers. Stopping smoking improves the woman's fertility and reduces the chances of a miscarriage if she does conceive.[1]

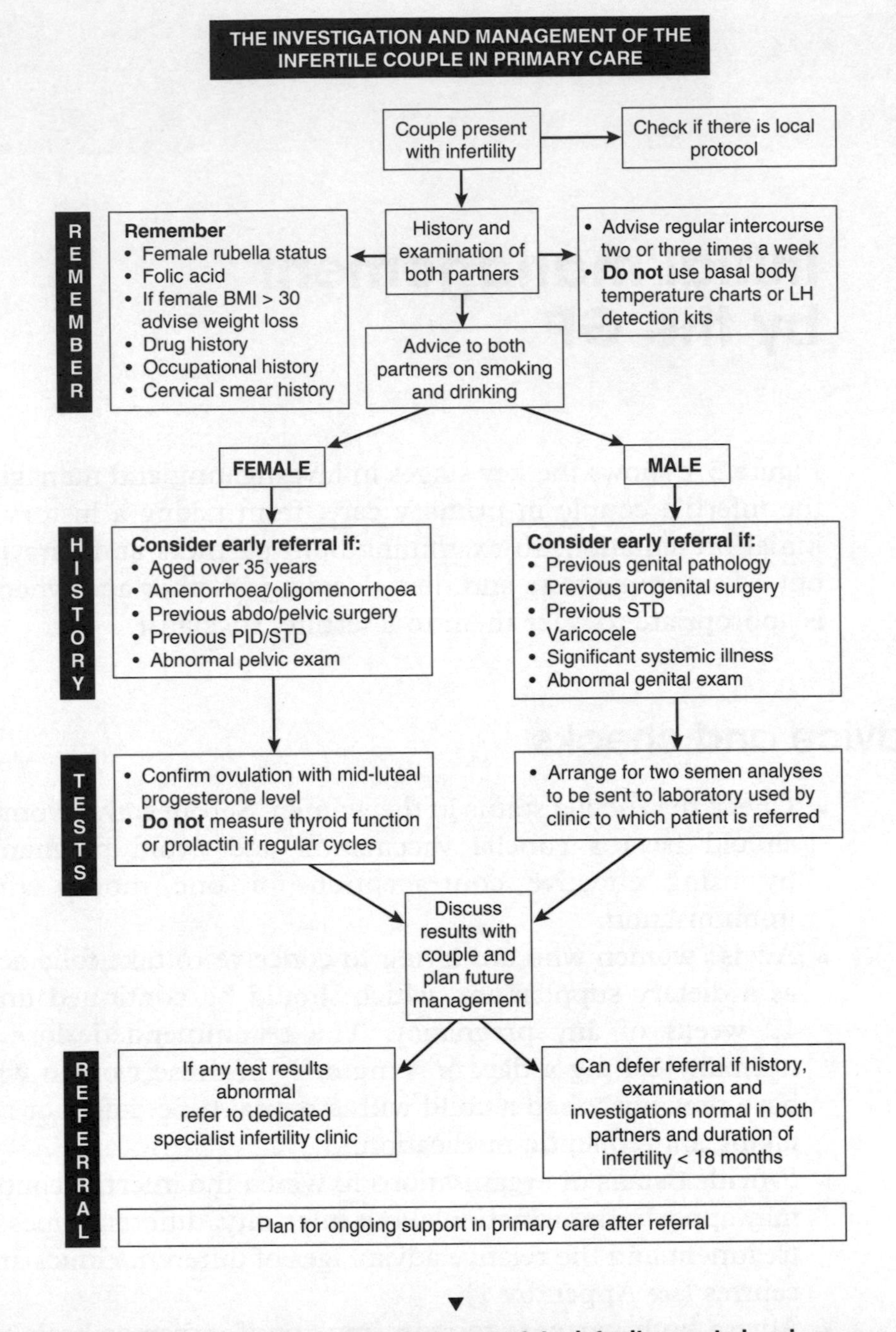

Figure 3.1: The investigation and management of the infertile couple in primary care. (Reprinted with permission from the Royal College of Obstetricians and Gynaecologists (1998) *Evidence-based Clinical Guidelines No. 2*. RCOG, London.)

Smoking in men is known to affect sperm quality in that smokers' sperm concentration is on average 13–17% lower than that of non-smokers[1] which may be particularly important in subfertile men with lowish sperm concentrations.

- Recommend women to limit their alcohol intake to no more than one unit of alcohol a day and preferably one or two units once or twice a week, whilst trying to conceive.[1,2] Until there is more evidence about the link between alcohol and female infertility and fetal development this is the advice advocated by the Royal College of Obstetricians and Gynaecologists and the Health Education Authority.[3] Similarly for men, evidence linking excess alcohol and male infertility is inconclusive and the experts' advice is to moderate drinking to three or four units or less of alcohol a day.[1]
- Encourage women who are obese, weighing in with Body Mass Indices of 30 or more, to lose weight. Moderate weight loss may restore ovulation, and improve pregnancy rates.[1] One study of 67 overweight women with infertility problems showed that fertility improved after they had lost an average of ten kilograms of weight. Obesity in men has not been shown to be linked with subfertility.[1]
- Urge couples to continue to have regular sexual intercourse rather than strictly timing intercourse around the woman's periods.
- Look for clues of any underlying psychosexual problems. Associated problems are common in the presentation of any gynaecological problem.
- Explore and address the couple's fears and anxieties about their infertility and remember that they will still need support whilst under specialist infertility care. There are a lot of myths around about infertility and even the most intelligent patients can have seemingly illogical beliefs about the causes or effects of their infertility. A survey of patient satisfaction of patients attending outpatient fertility clinics found that half of the respondents reported that they had not been given a clear plan for the future, and a quarter had received little or no information about their drug treatment or its side-effects.[4]

There are many causes of
infertility; losing weight may
help in more ways than one!

▼

▼

Is it true that?

- Stress causes difficulties in conceiving? Yes, the hypothalamus regulates ovarian function via the pituitary.[5]
- Taking the woman's temperature first thing in the morning and using temperature charts to detect ovulation can be counter-productive? Yes – basal body temperature charts are not good at predicting ovulation and trying to time intercourse can be emotionally stressful.[1]
- There is no need to measure thyroid function or prolactin in women presenting with infertility? Yes – these tests are

only indicated in women with a regular menstrual cycle if the history of physical symptoms or examination suggests thyroid disease or galactorrhoea.[1]

> **Box 3.1**
>
> A biology teacher confidently informed the clinic nurse that she could only have boy babies in future as she had had what she assumed was the 'girl egg' ovary removed when she had had an oophorectomy a few years before, and had since given birth to a boy.

Initial tests by the GP

- Sperm samples are best produced after two to three days abstinence, by masturbation, and collected in a wide mouthed sterile container rather than a condom or plastic bag. Sperm specimens should be examined in the laboratory of the licensed or unlicensed fertility clinic to which the couple are likely to be referred. Sperm analysis should be carried out as soon as possible after production within an hour.[1] Two samples should be tested on two different occasions.[1] There is considerable variability in reference ranges between different laboratories for sperm counts and quality, and it is important to know the laboratory's normal ranges for your population and select a laboratory that operates according to WHO recommendations[6] with internal and external quality controls.
- Measure serum progesterone in the mid-luteal phase to confirm ovulation; levels above 16 nmol/l for a minimum of five days or a single value above 32 nmol/l indicate that ovulation has taken place[1] as given in Figure 3.2 (although the guidelines[1] point out that only recovery of an actual egg or a pregnancy are 100% guarantees that ovulation has occurred).
- Ovulation predictor kits that detect luteinising hormone (LH) in the urine are widely available and have generally

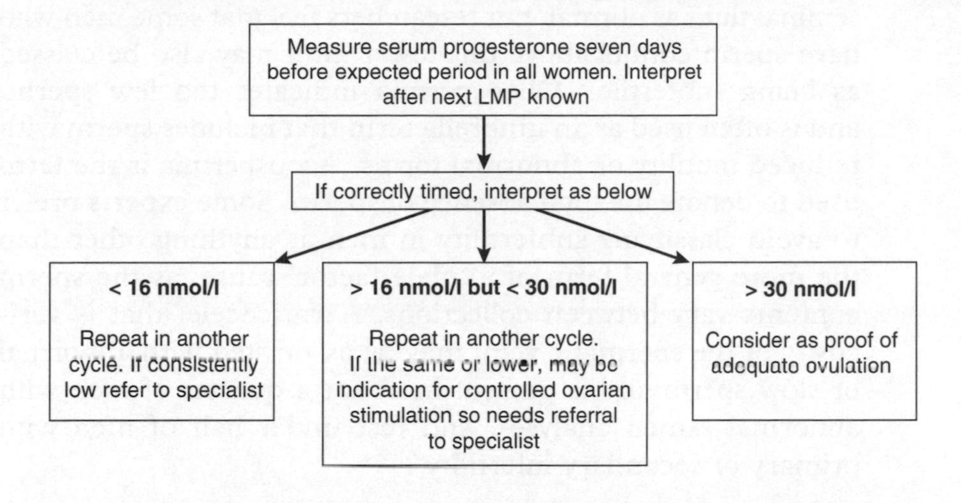

Figure 3.2: Measurement of serum progesterone. (Reprinted with permission from the Royal College of Obstetricians and Gynaecologists (1998) *Evidence-based Clinical Guidelines No. 2*. RCOG, London.)

replaced the use of temperature charts, but the kits are not generally recommended by those working in the field who feel that couples are best continuing with their normal sexual habit[7] rather than feeling that tests dictate when they must have intercourse.

Box 3.2: Sperm count

WHO normal values for semen[1,8]

Volume	2–5 ml
Liquefaction time	within 30 minutes
Concentration	>20 million/ml
Motility	>50% progressive motility
Morphology	>30% normal forms
White blood cells	<1 million/ml

WHO defines a sperm concentration above 20×10^6 per ml seminal fluid as normal, but researchers feel that some men who have sperm counts above this lower limit may also be classed as being subfertile.[9] Oligospermia indicates too few sperm, and is often used as an umbrella term that includes sperm with reduced motility or abnormal forms. Azoospermia is the term used to denote the total absence of sperm. Some experts prefer to avoid classifying subfertility in men as anything other than the more general term of a 'male factor' cause, as the sperm contents vary between collections. A varicocele, that is varicosity of the spermatic vein, may be associated with abnormal or slow sperm and is present in about a quarter of men with abnormal semen analyses, and just under half of men with primary or secondary infertility.[6]

References

1 Royal College of Obstetricians and Gynaecologists (1998) *The initial investigation and management of the infertile couple. Evidence-based clinical guidelines. No. 2.* Royal College of Obstetricians and Gynaecologists, London (0171 772 6275).

2 Jensen T, Hjollund NH, Henriksen TB, *et al.* (1998) Does moderate alcohol consumption affect fertility? Follow up study among couples planning first pregnancy. *BMJ.* **317**: 505–10.

3 Health Education Authority (1996) *Think About Drink – There's more to drink than you think.* HEA, London.

4 Souter V, Penney G, Hopton JL, Templeton A (1998) Patient satisfaction with the management of infertility. *Human Reproduction.* **13**: 1831–6.

5 Johnson M, Everitt B (1997) *Essential Reproduction.* Blackwell, Oxford.

6 Royal College of Obstetricians and Gynaecologists (1998) *The management of infertility in secondary care. Evidence-based clinical guidelines. No. 3.* Royal College of Obstetricians and Gynaecologists, London (0171 772 6275).

7 Hargreave T, Mills J (1998) Investigating and managing infertility in general practice. *BMJ*. **316**: 1438–41.

8 World Health Organization (1992) *WHO Laboratory Manual for the Examination of Human Semen and Sperm–cervical Mucus Interaction*. Cambridge University Press, Cambridge.

9 Bonde JP, Ernst E, Jensen TK, *et al.* (1998) Relation between semen quality and fertility: a population-based study of 430 first-pregnancy planners. *The Lancet* **352**: 1172–7.

Managing infertility in secondary care

▶ CHAPTER 4

Referring the infertile couple for specialist help

Box 4.1: What to put in the referral letter about the couple

- Patients' personal details – age, contact details
- Reproductive histories – previous pregnancies, length of time trying to conceive, previous contraception
- Results of all previous investigations
- Rubella immunity
- Any concerns about the welfare of any resulting child

About 70% of couples attending fertility clinics having been referred for fertility treatment eventually achieve a pregnancy, although this may take a long time.[1] Couples who have been attempting to conceive for more than a year should be referred early to a specialist clinic if the female partner is aged over 35 years.[2] Other reasons for early referral to a specialist are histories of amenorrhoea, gross menstrual irregularity or significant pelvic inflammatory disease (PID)[2] or any patients where the results from the initial investigations were abnormal. Otherwise if the history, examinations and investigations are normal in both partners, referral can be deferred until the couple have been trying to conceive for at least 18 months. Couples may prefer to be referred early though despite this advice if waiting times to be seen are unduly long and they want to claim their place in the queue.

Reasons for referring patients early

Women:

- over 35 years old and trying to conceive for a year
- amenorrhoea or oligo/amenorrhoea
- previous abdominal or pelvic surgery
- history of pelvic inflammatory disease (PID)
- history of sexually transmitted disease (STD)
- abnormal pelvic examination
- abnormal investigations.

Men:

- previous or current genital pathology or examination
- previous urogenital surgery
- history of sexually transmitted disease
- significant varicocele
- significant systemic illness
- low sperm count/poor sperm quality.

Couples with infertility problems should be referred together to clinics specialising in the management of infertility with easy access to other relevant specialists such as urologists[3] whenever possible rather than the woman being managed in a general gynaecology clinic and her male partner in a urology clinic. Licensed fertility clinics will offer a wider range of treatments than unlicensed centres, backed by well trained counsellors and appropriate laboratory facilities. There may be factors in both partners which are contributing to their infertile state, and simultaneous investigation and treatment of both is more likely to result in achieving a pregnancy. A urologist and fertility specialist both need to be involved for instance, if the reversal of a vasectomy and ovarian failure are parallel problems, when the freezing and storage of sperm retrieved at the operation may be used in future IVF cycles and for advanced microsurgical techniques such as intra-cytoplasmic sperm injection (ICSI) for men with low sperm counts. The only exception should be where there are obvious abnormalities of the genitalia, when the man is more appropriately referred to a urologist as well.

Choosing the fertility clinic

Fertility clinics have a 'threefold responsibility for:

- the patient's treatment – to get the highest live birth rate we can
- the potential child's welfare – to get the lowest multiple birth rate we can
- the community interest – to get the lowest number of live births because of the cost of healthcare for twins and triplets'.[4]

Most of the licensed clinics are in the private sector – it is estimated that only about 20% of fertility treatment is carried out by the NHS. The costs of treatment vary from clinic to clinic; the Department of Health estimates the range of costs for IVF as being between £2000 and £3000 per cycle.[5]

The *Infertility Companion*[6] gives information about costs and details of treatment at all licensed clinics at 1996 rates. The HFEA's Patients' Guide[7] is available to patients and health professionals free of charge and gives comprehensive information about the treatments of, and outcomes for, each licensed centre. Comparison of the clinics shows that there are many variations in what's on offer between them. There is not always an explicit upper age range for treatment. Clinic details[6] give a range between 35 and 50 years, with some clinics specifying different age limits for NHS and private treatment (for example 38 years versus 45 years old for NHS and private treatment respectively, Table 4.1), or for when a woman's own eggs or

Table 4.1: Survey of clinic's upper age limits for treating women*

Clinic's upper age limit (years)	*Number of clinics*
35–40	12
41–45	21
46–50	18
No declared upper age limit	36

*Adapted from Furse[6]

donated eggs are used in IVF (for example 45 years with own eggs and 50 years with donated eggs). Clinics vary as to whether they will treat single women and lesbian couples.

Box 4.2: Quote: from CHILD, the national infertility support network

'It is important that patients understand that they should contact a number of clinics asking the right questions to receive information that is relevant to their own personal circumstances.'

The HFEA's Patients' Guide[7] gives details about the number of treatment cycles undertaken in one year, and the outcomes in terms of pregnancy rates, percentage of multiple pregnancies and live birth rates for each licensed clinic. In the past, the media has tended to sensationalise the information about success rates by presenting them as a league table which may give a misleading impression. Some clinics may appear to have lower success rates than others because they have policies to minimise the risk of multiple births or treat an older age group of women. There are factors other than the live birth rate figures that couples intending to seek treatment should consider if they have a choice in selecting their clinic – such as the multiple pregnancy rate, the availability of a full range of fertility treatments, and the costs. The Guide encourages couples to make an informed choice about the centre they opt for and provides a checklist of criteria, summarised in Box 4.3.

The length of time waiting to be seen and the availability of NHS funded fertility treatment is obviously another critical factor in selecting the fertility clinic to which the couple are referred by their GP. In most clinics, there is no wait or a short waiting list of a few weeks for private treatment, whereas waiting times to be seen for NHS funded treatment are quoted as being up to five years.[6]

Box 4.3: Checklist of clinic details according to the HFEA's Patients' Guide[7]

- Location
- Services
- Special expertise
- Cost
- Restrictions on treatment
- Waiting list
- Information
- Live birth rate
- Multiple birth rate

References

1 Dowers A, Yates R (1998) New developments in infertility. *Pulse*. **4 April**.

2 Hargreave T, Mills J (1998) Investigating and managing infertility in general practice. *BMJ*. **316**: 1438–41.

3 Royal College of Obstetricians and Gynaecologists (1998) *The initial investigation and management of the infertile couple. Evidence-based clinical guidelines. No. 2*. Royal College of Obstetricians and Gynaecologists, London (0171 772 6275).

4 Lieberman B (1998) Workshop – multiple pregnancy and policy on number of embryos transferred. Report of the HFEA Annual Conference 1997. HFEA, London.

5 Hansard (1998) The cost of *in vitro* fertilisation. 6 July, col. 389.

6 Furse A (1997) *Infertility Companion: A user's guide to tests, technologies and therapies*. Thorsons, London.

7 Human Fertilisation and Embryology Authority (1998) *The Interim Patients' Guide, 1998*. HFEA, London.

▸ CHAPTER 5

Fertility treatments

The most important predictors of successful conception in infertile couples presenting for investigation and treatment is the woman's age, previous pregnancy history and duration of infertility, unless the male partner has azoospermia or extreme oligozoospermia.[1,2]

An overview of fertility treatments

Figure 5.1 describes the flow diagram guiding the sequence of investigation and management once the patient has presented to secondary care.

As far as the woman is concerned

- Are the tubes patent? A laparoscopy is the most reliable way to check that the tubes are patent or identify the cause(s) of a blockage. The information obtained from a hysterosalpingogram is limited to the internal state of the tubes and uterine cavity, whereas a laparoscopy visualises the rest of the pelvis, and therefore any adhesions, endometriosis, ovarian cysts or other pathology. However, an out-patient hysterosalpingogram is a cheaper and easier test to use than a laparoscopy which requires a general anaesthetic as an in-patient, so a hysterosalpingogram is often performed to confirm tubal patency in 'low risk' couples, that is for couples where

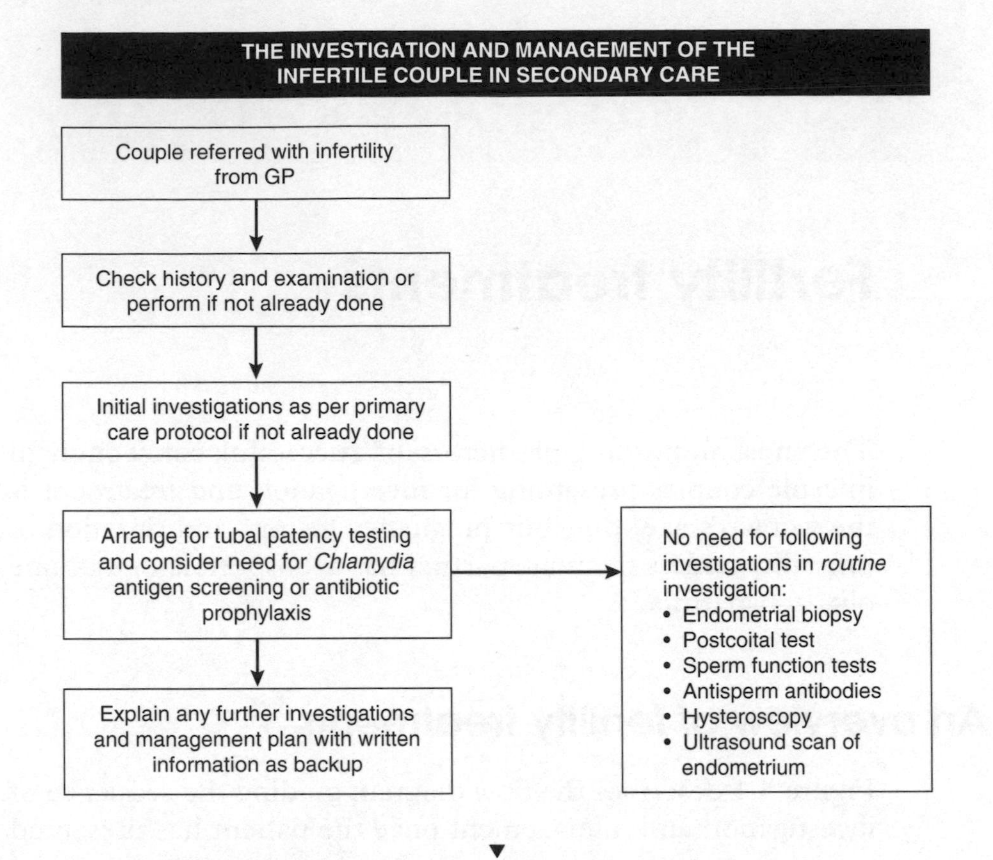

Figure 5.1: The initial investigation and management of the infertile couple in secondary care. (Reprinted with permission from the Royal College of Obstetricians and Gynaecologists (1998) *Evidence-based Clinical Guidelines No. 2.* RCOG, London.)

tubal blockage is not the expected cause of their infertility.[1] Women with risk factors for pelvic or tubal disease, an abnormal pelvic examination, or secondary infertility, should have a laparoscopy as the primary investigation as they are more likely to have pelvic pathology that could not be picked up by a prior hysterosalpingogram.[1] The test of hysterosalpingo-contrast-sonography is being evaluated as a potential technique for screening for tubal patency in the future.

- What is the *Chlamydia* status? *Chlamydia* screening should be carried out before uterine instrumentation is undertaken at the start of infertility investigations, to reduce the risk of carrying pre-existent, asymptomatic infection into the upper genital tract from the cervix. *Chlamydia* infection is an important cause of female infertility in that the likelihood of infertility is proportional to the number of episodes of pelvic inflammatory disease (PID) the woman has previously suffered; three episodes of PID gives a 50% chance of tubal blockage that is five times the risk of a single episode of PID.[1] Doxycycline or azithromycin are the drugs of choice for treating *Chlamydia* infection. *Chlamydia* is also thought to be a cause of male infertility.[1] The sexual partners of people proven to have *Chlamydia* should be traced, notified and treated.

As far as the man is concerned

- Physical examination as above if it has not already been done.
- Assessment of the sperm – review of the results of the investigations done before referral or arranging investigations as above if not done or undertaken in a general laboratory.
- More detailed examination of men whose sperm is abnormal. These include microbiological examination and culture of the semen of men with a history of orchitis, epididymitis or prostatitis and in the male partners of women with tubal disease; and subsequent treatment with antibiotics as appropriate, although there is no evidence that treating infection will improve fertility.[2] Endocrine tests should be undertaken on men to investigate hypogonadism or help differentiate between an obstructive cause and spermatogenic failure in men with azoospermia or oligozoospermia.[2] Imaging with contact thermography, Doppler sonography, or angiography are used as alternative investigations in different centres for looking at the testes in more depth.[2]

Tests that should only be carried out if they can be justified; not routinely or as a first line

- An endometrial biopsy. This has traditionally been used to investigate the response of the endometrium to progesterone and its state of readiness for implantation. A 'luteal phase deficiency' or 'defect' has been thought to indicate that too little progesterone has been secreted by the corpus luteum, but now the reliability of the test and its interpretation are in doubt, and recent guidance is that the luteal phase should not be evaluated by a routine endometrial biopsy, and its usefulness in the investigation of unexplained infertility remains to be evaluated.[1]
- Postcoital test. This test is falling out of favour because of the poor reproducibility of the test as there is wide variation in the way different observers rate identical slides.[1] It is a controversial test that is still used in the investigation of infertility.[1]
- Sperm function tests. There are a variety of methods of semen analyses which have been developed to try and determine particular defects and the severity of the associated male factor infertility. None of the tests seems to be overly helpful in isolation, but experimenting with a combination of tests may give a deeper understanding about the causes of male infertility and more predictive information in future.[1]
- Sperm antibody testing. This may be helpful in couples with unexplained infertility, but there are still a great number of methodological issues and conflicting evidence for their useful application to be resolved, before routine testing for antisperm antibodies in semen can be recommended.[1]
- Hysteroscopy. As this test involves looking directly at the uterine cavity it can detect uterine abnormalities which are associated with infertility, such as congenital abnormalities, endometrial polyps, and submucosal fibroids. However, because there is not yet any evidence that fertility is improved by treating such uterine abnormalities, hysteroscopy

cannot be recommended as a routine test for all infertile women.[1]

- Ultrasound examination of the endometrium. There is conflicting evidence about the value of ultrasonographic examination of the endometrium for managing infertility and the extent to which the measured endometrial thickness indicates endometrial function or the likelihood of conception. The examination can also be used to assess endometrial texture; this involves a subjective judgement, which may be more meaningful if carried out by a transvaginal as opposed to a transabdominal approach.[1] Such transvaginal imaging gives a more accurate picture of pelvic pathology and may pick up such cases as polycystic ovaries which would not be detected by bimanual pelvic examination. The guidelines recommend a transvaginal ultrasound scan of the ovaries in conjunction with a thorough physical examination before assisted conception is started or hormones to induce ovulation are prescribed.[1]
- Testicular biopsy. This requires microsurgical skills and equipment by appropriately trained staff in specialised centres, and should not be undertaken as a diagnostic test as the damage done by the procedure may reduce the chances of a successful conception in the future still further. It may be used in specialised centres where there are facilities for recovering sperm to be used straightaway for intra-cytoplasmic injection (ICSI) therapy or kept for use at a later date by freezing and storage (cryostorage).
- Chromosomal analysis. But analysis is required for women with premature ovarian failure before starting ovulation induction.[2] Chromosomal analysis should be undertaken in men with poor sperm counts of less than a million sperm in the ejaculate, because chromosome abnormalities are associated with low sperm counts.
- Genetic testing for cystic fibrosis. This is indicated in men with congenital absence of a vas deferens and their female partners if the male is carrying the gene for cystic fibrosis.

.....Some tests should only be carried out if they can be justified!

▼

Range of fertility treatments

For the infertile woman

- Tubal surgery: for patients who are well selected for likelihood of success, by experienced surgeons trained in microsurgical techniques. Tubal surgery can be as or more effective than IVF for selected cases of mild distal or proximal tubal obstruction and occlusion. Tubal surgery is unlikely to be successful if both the distal and proximal ends of the tubes are obstructed. IVF might be considered if pregnancy has not resulted within 12 months of tubal surgery that has rendered the tubes patent.[2]

- Tubal catheterisation: is recommended by the American Fertility Society for patients with proximal tubal obstruction as a minimally invasive alternative to tubal surgery.[2,3]
- IVF: should be considered as the first choice of treatment for moderate to severe distal tube disease.[2] Other factors that will influence the decision as to whether or not to embark on IVF are the age of the woman, the relative importance of other infertility factors, and the risks of ovarian hyperstimulation (OHSS) and multiple pregnancy.
- Reversal of sterilisation by tubal reanastomosis: operative success rates in women who are still ovulating and have fertile male partners are high with pregnancy rates described as being in the region of 44–92%.[2] Half of the women aged 40 years and over are reported to become pregnant after their sterilisation is reversed.[2] Surgery should be carried out only in centres with the expertise and facilities to undertake microsurgery.
- Induction of ovulation. There are many different reasons for ovarian failure; there may be a genetic cause, an autoimmune disorder, recent weight loss, concurrent drugs or medication suppressing ovarian function, too much exercise, a pituitary tumour causing gonadotrophin deficiency, or polycystic ovarian syndrome. The guidelines[2] recommend that investigations to determine the cause and the most appropriate treatment are carried out in a specialist centre with specialist endocrine testing, chromosomal analysis and skilled ultrasonography available. Ovarian induction should only be tried if any male factor subfertility is mild with at least five million sperm per ejaculate, and be limited to six cycles if ovulation occurs but pregnancy does not, before confirming that the fallopian tubes are patent and endometriosis is not a significant problem. The lowest effective doses of clomiphene and gonadotrophins should be used

with careful timing of stimulation at specific points in the cycle to minimise OHSS.[2]

- Bromocriptine suppresses prolactin secretion in patients with hyperprolactinaemia, but the patient may be plagued with side-effects such as nausea, vomiting, vertigo and headaches. Cabergoline and quinagolide are more effective and better tolerated than bromocriptine and need to be taken only once or twice weekly.[2] Neither bromocriptine nor danazol are effective treatments for unexplained infertility.
- Ablation of endometriosis: results so far suggest that surgical ablation of mild or moderate endometriosis improves fertility in subfertile women and is more effective than treatment with danazol[2] which improves the symptoms but not the pregnancy rate. The diagnosis should be proved laparoscopically. IVF or GIFT may be tried if surgery is unsuccessful.[2]
- Intra-uterine insemination (IUI) and ovarian stimulation is an effective combination for patients with unexplained infertility tried prior to undergoing IVF.[2] In the absence of tubal blockage or a severe male factor problem, the use of IUI or super-ovulation IUI is more cost-effective than IVF.[4]
- GIFT is an effective treatment for patients with unexplained infertility.[2]

For the infertile man

- Reversal of vasectomy: success rates following reversal are quoted as ranging from 17% to over 82%.[2] The chances of success depend on the time since the vasectomy was carried out, the type of the original vasectomy procedure, the existence of other genital pathology, and the technical skill of the surgeon attempting the reversal.[2] Successful reversal of vasectomy is not clear cut, for pregnancy rates are only a half or two-thirds of the patency rates of the vas deferens after the reversal operation. For example, patency and pregnancy rates are cited as being 97% and 76% respectively for a reversal operation carried out within three years of the original vasectomy being done.[2]

- Gonadotrophin drugs: given for months or years in hypogonadotropic hypogonadism, gonadotrophin drugs can stimulate spermatogenesis and achieve normal sperm counts. Gonadotrophin-releasing hormone is as effective as gonadotrophin drugs but needs to be given by an infusion pump for about a year.[2]
- Bromocriptine: is an effective treatment for men with hyperprolactinaemia and also helps reverse their associated loss of libido and impotence.[2] It is ineffective as an empirical treatment for ozoospermia or poor sperm quality of no known cause, as are anti-oestrogen (such as tamoxifen or clomiphene) or androgen (such as testosterone) drugs, which have been used in the past.[2]
- Varicocele treatment by ligation or embolisation: treatment of a man with oligozoospermia appears to improve sperm quality and subsequent fertility, whereas such treatment on an infertile man with normozoospermia has not been found to be beneficial.[2]

Ways of assisting conception

If investigations are normal, but there has been more than three years' infertility, assisted conception should be considered.

1 Clomiphene

Clomiphene is the most frequently prescribed fertility drug in America.[2] In the UK it is used by general practitioners as well as hospital specialists as the initial treatment for amenorrhoea or oligoamenorrhoea. The guidelines[2] recommend that treatment with clomiphene is tried for women who ovulate with clomiphene and have no other infertility factors, before embarking on more complex or invasive therapy. However, the guidelines[2] highlight the advice from the Committee on Safety of Medicines to limit treatment with clomiphene to six cycles to guard against increasing the treated woman's potential risk of ovarian cancer.

Clomiphene works by increasing the secretion of follicle stimulating hormone (FSH) which in turn stimulates ovarian follicular development. Usually a course lasts five days and starts on the second day of the menstrual cycle. If the initial dose produces ovulation, the same dose is repeated in subsequent cycles. If ovulation does not occur, the subsequent dose is increased. The lowest effective dose should be used, as one of the side-effects is to thicken the cervical mucous making it more impenetratable to sperm. Clomiphene may be successful in up to 50% of women who are not ovulating properly.[5]

The guidelines stress the importance of ultrasonic monitoring of at least the first cycle where clomiphene is prescribed, to titrate the drug to an appropriate dose and reduce the likelihood of a multiple pregnancy.[2] The risks of multiple pregnancy with clomiphene treatment are reported as being between 2 and 13% of clomiphene-induced cycles according to the results of different studies.[2] This recommendation will outlaw many GPs from initiating clomiphene, limiting their role to continuing to prescribe and monitor the drug under a shared-care arrangement with a hospital specialist who does have ready access to such ultrasonic monitoring equipment. This is likely to be a contentious issue for GPs who are used to initiating clomiphene therapy and who may not be aware of the importance of determining the lowest effective dose of clomiphene to minimise the risks of multiple pregnancy.

Clomiphene should not be given to women with unexplained infertility as current evidence suggests that it is ineffective, although trials are still proceeding to provide more information of currently unrecognised potential benefits. Clomiphene, danazol and bromocriptine should not be used where investigations show that ovulation is occurring normally, as they will be ineffective and may increase the risks of creating multiple pregnancies.

Recombinant FSH or ovarian diathermy are alternative treatments which may now be tried in women with clomiphene-resistant polycystic ovary syndrome.

2 *Intra-uterine insemination (IUI)*

This is the process by which sperm is placed in the woman's uterus by a fine plastic tube, timed to coincide with ovulation. The success rates are far higher for IUI than when sperm are placed in the cervix. IUI is used for women with patent fallopian tubes and overcomes barriers to sperm such as cervical mucous problems, where there are high levels of antibodies to sperm or male fertility problems. It is worth trying in cases of unexplained infertility. The sperm used may be that from the male partner or from an anonymous donor, depending on the nature and quality of the male partner's sperm. If donor sperm is used, the clinic carrying out the procedure must be licensed by the HFEA. If the partner's sperm is frozen rather than freshly produced for the IUI procedure, the storage of that sperm needs a licence too.

Ovulation is timed by monitoring with ultrasonic scans and measuring levels of luteinising hormone (LH) in the urine. Human chorionic gonadotrophin (hCG) may be given by injection to stimulate ovulation by triggering a surge of LH, and boost the chances of pregnancy occurring.

Sometimes low doses of the ovarian stimulating hormones clomiphene or gonadotrophins are used in conjunction with IUI. This runs the risk of a multiple pregnancy if more than one egg is released and fertilised, but is sometimes thought to be necessary if a woman has irregular cycles and timing ovulation is difficult. If prior scans show too many eggs have been stimulated, the cycle should be abandoned. The process might be repeated on another month, or another method such as IVF considered.

The probability of pregnancy with IUI is most likely within the first four attempts, and the likelihood of success is even less after the ninth attempt. If IUI does not work, patients may move on to try IVF, or intra-cytoplasmic sperm injection if the infertility is due to a male factor problem.

3 Donor insemination (DI)

Donor insemination is the insemination of sperm from a donor into a woman, via her vagina, through the cervical opening into the cervical canal or into the uterus itself (IUI). The treatment is licensed by the HFEA because it involves insemination by sperm from a donor and not by the male partner's own sperm. The donor does not have to be, but usually is, anonymous. Sometimes it is carried out in parallel with the giving of clomiphene or gonadotrophins to the woman to stimulate her ovaries to produce more eggs than usual (stimulated DI). The degree of ovarian stimulation needed is generally far less than for IVF.

Box 5.1: Factors that have a significant effect on the outcome of treatment by donor insemination (DI)

Negative effects

- Age
- Previous DI treatment cycles not resulting in a pregnancy
- Unstimulated treatment cycle (as opposed to stimulated cycle)

Positive effect

- Previous live birth

The number of donor insemination treatment cycles using donated sperm dropped by over a third in the 1990s, from 25 623 cycles of DI in a 12-month period in 1992/93 to 14 333 cycles of DI in 1996/97.[6] This has mainly been due to the rise in numbers of intra-cytoplasmic sperm injection (ICSI) treatments being carried out whereby even men with very low sperm counts can be enabled to achieve a pregnancy with their own sperm.

DI tends to be used where the man has no or very few sperm, has had a vasectomy and reversal has failed or not been tried, or where the man carries an inherited disease.

HFEA figures for success with DI or GIFT using donated gametes, give the overall live birth rate per treatment cycle started at UK fertility clinics as being 9.6% from treating 5419 patients of which just under half involved parallel treatment of the woman with fertility drugs to 'stimulate' her ovaries to produce more eggs.[6] The relative lack of success with DI compared to other assisted conception methods such as IVF or micromanipulation by ICSI can be seen by the figures given in Table 5.1 on p. 54 which gives comparative information about the live and multiple pregnancy rates for DI, IVF and ICSI techniques. Just over a quarter of patients receiving DI became pregnant with one or more treatment cycles. Multiple births are far more common with stimulated DI compared to unstimulated treatment; two quadruplets, 13 triplets, 68 sets of twins and 635 singleton babies were born after stimulated DI in 1996/97, compared to no triplets or quads, only 15 sets of twins and 896 singleton babies with unstimulated DI.[6]

DI may be requested by lesbian couples or single women. GPs and fertility specialists are advised by defence societies to make a clinically based decision, taking the mother's right to self-determination and the unborn child's rights and welfare, into account. The General Medical Council advises doctors not to allow their 'views about a patient's lifestyle, culture, beliefs, race, colour, gender, sexuality … to prejudice the treatment you provide or arrange'.[7] Catholic, Jewish and Muslim faiths believe artificial insemination by a donor outside marriage to be immoral.

The HF&E Act 1990 prohibits the HFEA from giving out identifying information about donors. The public reportedly want donor insemination to remain anonymous.[7] But a growing number of those using donor insemination seem to feel able to tell their children about the mode of their conception. In one study,[8] one third of recipients followed up had told their children about their origins, or intended to do so soon when they were old enough to understand. Two thirds of those receiving DI had told other people that they had used donor sperm to conceive. Most potential donors of sperm were in favour of the resulting children being told of their origins. Just under half of sperm donors in this study indicated that they would be prepared to be identified to the resulting offspring when they reached adulthood. Allowing people the right to trace their genetic parents is a contentious issue; those who donated sperm as they thought anonymously in the past, may be distraught if up to ten offspring conceived after donor insemination were able to turn up at their door unexpectedly in the future.

4 In vitro fertilisation (IVF)

IVF has been popularly termed the 'test tube baby' technique. Essentially the process starts with the collection of eggs after priming the ovaries with stimulating hormones. The hormones used for controlling ovarian function are buserelin or goserelin given to desensitise the ovary about a week or so before menstruation. The ovaries are then stimulated with FSH or human menopausal gonadotrophin (hMG) injections, started about 12 days after the daily subcutaneous injections of buserelin or single injection of goserelin was initiated. An alternative regime is to give booster doses of buserelin and then FSH or hMG for a shorter duration. The shorter regime is given to women with raised FSH levels or who have responded poorly to a previous longer course of treatment.

The levels of oestrogen produced by the follicles are measured intermittently to indicate the level of response to FSH or hMG

Box 5.2: Factors that have a significant effect on the outcome of *in vitro* fertilisation (IVF) treatment

Negative effects

- Age
- Longer duration of infertility
- Two or more IVF treatment cycles not resulting in a pregnancy
- Fewer than three eggs fertilised
- Complicating male factor causing infertility
- Multiple female factors causing infertility

Positive effects

- Previous IVF pregnancy
- Previous live birth

and to watch for OHSS. Ultrasound scanning is carried out intravaginally using a vaginal probe; subsequent monitoring assesses the number and size of follicles and shows when the eggs are ready for retrieval. An injection of hCG is given 34–36 hours before egg recovery. Eggs are removed from the follicles by ultrasound or laparoscopy under general anaesthetic.

Eggs are fertilised by sperm in a glass dish or test tube in a laboratory. In standard IVF about 200 000 sperm are placed with each egg, and incubated overnight.

Three or less embryos resulting from the procedure are transferred into the woman's uterus. Preferably two embryos are used to reduce the risk of multiple pregnancy, but up to three are permitted by the HFEA. Any remaining embryos may be frozen for future use. About two-thirds of the frozen embryos will usually survive the freeze–thaw process and be suitable for replacement in the woman's uterus on a future occasion, if the first cycle of IVF using fresh embryos is unsuccessful. The placement of thawed embryos in a woman's uterus can either be carried out in a natural cycle or in a hormonally controlled cycle when buserelin or goserelin may be used, followed by oestrogen tablets and progesterone vaginal pessaries. As many as a third of the pregnancies that are created by IVF may miscarry.

During a 12-month period in 1996/7, approximately 25 500 patients received IVF treatment in the UK. A total of 33 520 cycles were started which included frozen embryo replacements, and 27 981 reached the stage at which embryos were transferred. There were 6755 clinical pregnancies created, which led to 5601 births, that is, 16.7% of all the treatments started led to live babies.[6] The average live birth rate per treatment cycle of IVF was 15.5% compared to a rate of 21.6% per treatment cycle in which the embryo was created by another technique, micromanipulation (mainly the ICSI technique)[6] as Table 5.1 shows. The live birth rate for ICSI is higher than for IVF because the female partner is usually fertile and likely to be younger than those women undergoing IVF.

Table 5.1: Live and multiple birth rates for *in vitro* fertilisation, micromanipulation and donor insemination in licensed clinics in the UK during the 12-month period 1996–97*

	Number of treatment cycles	*Live birth rate per treatment cycle (%)*	*Multiple birth rate per live birth event (%)*
IVF**	26 868	15.5	26.8
Micromanipulation	6652	21.6	29.1
DI***	14 333	9.6	6.5

*Adapted from data in Human Fertilisation and Embryology Authority's Annual Report 1998.[6]
**The data for IVF given here does not include cycles involving micromanipulation; it does include transfers with frozen embryos.
***The data for DI includes GIFT using donor gametes and IUI.

The age of the woman is the most important factor in predicting success with IVF. The live birth rate for women using their own eggs undergoing IVF is highest for women in the 29–30-year old age group at 20.1% per treatment cycle, falling to 2.7% per treatment cycle in women aged 43–44 years old, as Table 5.2 shows.

Table 5.2: Live birth rate per cycle for examples of different age groups for women undergoing IVF using their own eggs*

	Age of woman (years)				
	Under 27	*29–30*	*35–36*	*43–44*	*≥45*
Number of cycles	1149	2833	4030	482	202
Live birth rate (%)	18.0	20.1	14.4	2.7	1

*Adapted from data in Human Fertilisation and Embryology Authority's Annual Report 1998.[6]

Women who have been pregnant before are more likely to conceive again with IVF. The live birth rate with IVF is at its highest at the first cycle, being about 17.4% for fresh embryo transfers compared to a 12.6% live birth rate at the fifth cycle and 8.6% by the 11th attempt, as shown in Table 5.3. As the numbers of attempts increases, those who have still not

Table 5.3: Percentage live birth rates per cycle by numbers of attempts for *in vitro* fertilisation, micromanipulation and donor insemination in licensed clinics in the UK during the 12-month period 1996–97*

Number of attempts IVF	1	2	3	4	5	6	7–10	11+
Live birth rate per cycle (%)**	17.4	16.1	16.3	16.5	14.4	12.6	13.8	8.6

Number of attempts Micromanipulation	1	2	3	4	5–8	9+
Live birth rate per cycle (%)	24.1	21.3	19.2	17.1	18.5	15.0

Number of attempts DI	1	2	3	4	5	6–8	9–11	12+
Live birth rate per cycle (%)	11.2	10.3	10.5	9.4	8.6	9.4	9.6	7.4

*Adapted from data in Human Fertilisation and Embryology Authority's Annual Report 1998.[6]
**The data for IVF given here does not include cycles involving micromanipulation; it does include transfers with frozen embryos.

conceived have infertility problems that are more resistant to treatment. About two-fifths of infertile women eventually conceive with a course of IVF involving up to three treatment cycles: the first cycle involving the transfer of fresh embryos and subsequent two cycles transfer of thawed, frozen embryos into the woman's uterus. This 40% success rate is termed the cumulative live birth rate.

Fresh embryos are more likely to be successful in achieving pregnancies than frozen embryos; the overall live birth for IVF using frozen embryos was only 11.6% per cycle in 1996/97.[6] This is probably because only the right numbers of frozen embryos intended to be used are thawed out for transfer in the IVF process and there is no choice about which ones are transferred, whereas in fresh cycles there is often a choice and the best embryos can be selected for use.

Slightly more boys than girls are born after IVF (51.4% boys compared to 48.6% girls[6]).

5 Gamete intra-fallopian transfer (GIFT)

The first birth following GIFT took place in 1985. A maximum of three eggs and sperm are surgically transferred into the fallopian tube using the GIFT technique, so that fertilisation occurs in the tube. GIFT is only possible if the woman partner has normal patent fallopian tubes and the sperm quality is reasonably good.

The risk of ectopic pregnancy is around 4%. As many as a third of pregnancies may miscarry.

GIFT does not need to be licensed by the HFEA because fertilisation takes place within the woman's body and the egg and sperm are produced by the couple being treated.

A few clinics use GIFT and IVF in the same treatment cycle, which is a licensable activity. The total number of eggs and embryos transferred cannot exceed three in the same way that no more than three embryos can be transferred in conventional IVF, in accordance with the HFEA guidelines.

▼

6 Micromanipulation sperm techniques – usually intra-cytoplasmic sperm injection (ICSI)

ICSI is a relatively new technique and it may be worth re-referring men with very low sperm counts back to a specialist clinic, if they have been told in the past that they could not be helped. The first birth following ICSI took place in 1992. Since then ICSI has become widely used throughout the world as it enables men to father children of their own rather than use sperm donated by another man.

ICSI is a technique where an individual sperm is injected directly into the cytoplasm of an egg with a fine glass needle, to bypass natural barriers that previously prevented the sperm penetrating the egg. ICSI is used for couples who have failed to achieve successful fertilisation with IVF techniques or where the quality of the sperm is too poor for normal IVF to be likely to succeed. Typical sperm problems are low sperm numbers, poor sperm motility, where there are high levels of anti-sperm antibody, where the vas deferens is absent, where vasectomy reversal has failed or where there is an obstruction in the testis or epididymis to the outflow of sperm. Men with low sperm counts are more likely to have sperm abnormalities, such as microdeletions on the long arm of the Y chromosome. It is likely that these may be passed on to any sons born as a result of this method of assisted conception who may in turn have impaired fertility.[2] So far ICSI seems to be a safe technique, in that a review of data from 101 centres worldwide has not demonstrated any more congenital malformations in children born after ICSI treatment using ejaculated, epididymal or testicular sperm, than would be expected to occur in the general population.[6] The HFEA is continuing to monitor information about the safety of the technique and keeping the licensing of ICSI under review.

ICSI can use fresh or frozen sperm or a biopsy of tissue from the testis. The surgical retrieval of sperm from the epididymis or testis can be done under a local or a general anaesthetic and takes about 30 minutes. Men can go home after about two hours. The eggs are collected in the same way as for IVF after stimulating the woman with ovarian hormones. Sperm are injected into several healthy and mature looking eggs. The injected eggs are observed *in vitro* for 48 hours to check that fertilisation has occurred, whereupon up to three embryos are transferred to the woman's uterus. Spare embryos can be frozen for future use, which will make repeating the exercise easier and cheaper without having to collect eggs and sperm first.

An increasing number of fertility clinics are offering ICSI. The HFEA's Patients' Guide[9] lists 56 of the 103 licensed fertility clinics as offering ICSI. A total of 5828 patients were treated by micromanipulation in 1996/97 and 6652 cycles of treatment were provided by licensed fertility clinics in the UK. Ten terminations, 229 miscarriages, 18 ectopic pregnancies and 1896 live babies resulted. Most of these were using the ICSI technique, but a very small number were by Sub Zonal Insemination (SUZI) or Partial Zona Dissection (PZD). SUZI is a variation of IVF treatment whereby a single sperm is deposited into the zona pellucida, the space between the egg and its protein shell. PZD is a treatment in which a small hole is made in the outer membrane of the egg so that sperm placed near the egg can move into the egg without further aid. ICSI yields higher numbers of embryos than SUZI and has largely replaced the other micromanipulative techniques.

The overall live birth rate per treatment cycle for micromanipulation in UK fertility clinics was 21.6% in 1996/97.[6] Pregnancy rates are around 30–35% per cycle for sperm obtained from the ejaculate of semen or directly from the epididymis, and about 20% when carried out using testicular sperm.[10] Women in the 29–30-year-old age group have the best chance of getting pregnant, as for IVF with 28.1% live birth rates per cycle of treatment compared with a 3.1% chance of a live birth per cycle in over 45-year-old women.

A new development is the mixing of ICSI and IVF embryos in a treatment cycle which a few clinics are undertaking. The HFEA is currently reviewing the implications of this procedure.

7 Spermatids

These are immature precursors of spermatozoa. They carry the same genetic information as sperm but have not yet finished maturing. Their use is confined to research purposes in the UK and the HFEA has not issued any clinics with a licence to use spermatids in treatment. There is debate about the potential of using round spermatids which are very immature, as opposed to the more mature version, elongated spermatids, in treating patients. It is thought that spermatids may be useful for fertility treatment in the future in men where it proves impossible to retrieve mature sperm for use in ICSI. There is concern about the difficulty of distinguishing between a spermatid and an immature spermatazoon from the testis that has still to complete spermatogenesis and journey through the epididymis[11] and that spermatids may inadvertently be used in some micromanipulation treatment processes.

The HFEA will consider whether to license spermatids for treatment once there is sufficient evidence about the safety and efficacy of the use of spermatids in ICSI. Such evidence will be accumulated from animal studies and human embryo research. Spermatids are used to treat infertility in some overseas fertility centres by their direct injection into eggs using the ICSI technique. Success rates in creating pregnancies have so far been very low.

References

1 Royal College of Obstetricians and Gynaecologists (1998) *The initial investigation and management of the infertile couple. Evidence-based clinical guidelines. No. 2*. Royal College of Obstetricians and Gynaecologists, London (0171 772 6275).

2 Royal College of Obstetricians and Gynaecologists (1998) *The management of infertility in secondary care. Evidence-based clinical guidelines. No. 3*. Royal College of Obstetricians and Gynaecologists, London (0171 772 6275).

3 American Fertility Society (1993) *Guideline for Practice. Tubal disease*. American Fertility Society, Birmingham, Alabama.

4 Van Voorhis BJ, Stovall DW, Allen BD, Syrop CH (1998) Cost-effective treatment of the infertile couple. *Fertility and Sterility*. **70**(6): 995–1034.

5 Dowers A, Yates R (1998) New developments in infertility. *Pulse*. **4 April**.

6 Human Fertilisation and Embryology Authority (1998) *Annual Report 1998*. HFEA, London.

7 General Medical Council (1995) *Good Medical Practice*. GMC, London.

8 Shepherd ST (1998) *Donor Insemination. Payment, anonymity, secrecy and disclosure*. Infertility Research Trust, Jessop Hospital, Sheffield.

9 Human Fertilisation and Embryology Authority (1998) *Interim Patients' Guide 1998*. HFEA, London.

10 Ndukwe G (1997) New treatment for male infertility. *GP News*. **7 November**.

11 Lewis S, McClure N (1998) Difficulties in distinguishing between a mature spermatid and a testicular spermatozoon. *Human Reproduction*. **13**: 2979 (letter).

▶ CHAPTER 6

Risks of fertility treatments

Multiple pregnancy

Multiple pregnancy is a common outcome from using fertility drugs due to the ovaries being stimulated to produce several eggs at a time, or more than one embryo being transferred to the uterus in IVF, or more than one egg being replaced in GIFT. Two-thirds of triplets and higher order pregnancies are due to ovarian induction with clomiphene and gonadotrophin drugs.[1]

Clinics balance the risks of multiple pregnancy against gaining an acceptable pregnancy rate. The number of embryos that can be transferred after IVF is limited to three by the HFEA, and of course there is a further chance that a single embryo could sub-divide to give an identical set of twins or triplets. Respected authorities[2–5] are pushing for a policy whereby a maximum of two embryos are transferred when more than three have been created. Three embryos were intentionally replaced in more than half of the cycles of IVF carried out in the UK in 1995/96. This approach has led to the high overall multiple birth rate in the UK. Forty-seven per cent of individual babies born from all types of IVF came from a multiple pregnancy in 1996/97.[6] This compares with a spontaneous conception rate of less than one multiple pregnancy in a hundred, in normal couples not receiving any infertility treatment.

Reducing the multiple pregnancy rate will require a substantial change in professional practice and patient outlook. Table 6.1 shows the comparative miscarriage and still birth/

Table 6.1: Single and multiple clinical pregnancy outcomes after IVF or frozen embryo transfers in the 12-month period 1996–97*

Number of babies	*Outcome of pregnancy*		
	Live births	*Miscarriages*	*Still birth and neonatal deaths (per 1000 births)*
Singleton	3867	674	9.6
Twin	1502	218	44.6
Triplet	230	59	87.0
Quadruplet	2	–	500.0

*Adapted from HFEA Annual Report 1998.[6]

neonatal death rates for single and multiple pregnancies resulting from IVF, with more than four times as many twins and more than ten times the numbers of triplets compared to single births.[6] Most multiple pregnancies are delivered before full term and about one-third of twins will be delivered pre-term before 37 weeks' gestation. The average length of pregnancy for triplets is 34 weeks and that for quadruplets is 32.5 weeks. Premature babies are more likely to be of low birth weight. The average birth weight of a single baby is 3.3 kg compared to that of twins being 2.5 kg and triplets 1.8 kg. Babies born very prematurely are more likely to have a disability such as cerebral palsy; 38% of infant survivors born at 24 weeks and 24% of survivors born at 26 weeks are handicapped.[7] Maternal obstetric complications are more likely in multiple pregnancies than in women bearing singleton babies. The majority of triplets and quadruplets are delivered by Caesarean section.

Even though most patients know and seem to understand the risks of multiple pregnancy, many still choose to have three embryos replaced. The prospect of twins or triplets can seem attractive to infertile couples who are desperate to conceive. They think that a multiple birth will save them from having to repeat the fertility treatment procedures to become pregnant again in the future, saving them hassle and money. Such couples need to be well informed about the serious risks and consequences of multiple births. New parents can find multiple births far more of a strain than they had anticipated – financially, practically and emotionally – and even seriously regret having the much longed-for babies. Women who had hoped to return to work may find that the child care costs are far more than for one baby and make it difficult financially for both parents to return to work.

Happy families?

▼

Clinics give patients different advice on the numbers of embryos that should be transferred. Some base that advice on whether the woman is over 37 years old and consequently recommend the transfer of three rather than two embryos as she is less likely to become pregnant. However, the evidence is that there is as much chance of a live birth if the best two of four or more fertilised eggs available for transfer are replaced than if three embryos are replaced in a woman's uterus.[5] Replacing a maximum of two embryos reduces the chances of a multiple birth[5] and makes the creation of triplets extremely unlikely. The latest figures from the HFEA show that there is an encouraging trend for clinics to be replacing two rather than three embryos.[6]

Fetal reduction may be carried out as a planned procedure to terminate the life of one or more fetuses in a multiple pregnancy. The procedure is usually carried out between 8 and 14 weeks' gestation. Usually the operative reduction is carried out so that two fetuses remain who have an improved chance of developing normally into healthy babies; and the mother is less likely to have obstetric complications. A particular fetus might be selected for termination if it appears weaker than the others or alternatively the fetus to be sacrificed may be picked at random. The risks from fetal reduction have to be carefully balanced: carrying out embryo reduction on triplets to achieve twins can increase the probability of the pregnancies being carried to more than 32 weeks' gestation, but also increases the risks of miscarriage with a 15–17% risk resulting from the procedure.[4] The decision to opt for fetal reduction is a very difficult emotional dilemma for parents who will require much time and support before and after the operation.

Ovarian hyperstimulation syndrome (OHSS)

The condition occurs in about 4% of women receiving ovarian stimulating drugs,[8] and is severe in 0.5–2% of all IVF cycles.[8] Its occurrence is not predictable, and all women undergoing ovarian stimulation with hormones should be warned of the signs and symptoms of OHSS and have emergency contact numbers to hand for obtaining immediate advice and help from the specialist fertility centre.

Cases may present with lower abdominal discomfort or pain, abdominal swelling, nausea and later vomiting, and in more severe conditions ascites, pleural effusion and venous thrombosis requiring hospitalisation. The ovarian stimulating treatment should be immediately discontinued and any fertilised eggs frozen for use on another occasion.

The risk of OHSS is reduced by close monitoring of the number and size of the developing follicles during ovulation induction cycles by measuring the serum oestrogen and ultrasound scanning. If the ovaries are over-active, the dosages of fertility drugs can be reduced appropriately or the cycle of treatment abandoned if the numbers of mature follicles are too great, which also avoids multiple pregnancies.

Medical complications

The overall medical complication rate from assisted reproduction techniques was 8.3% in one report describing the incidence of complications arising during 3500 treatment cycles in couples undergoing conventional IVF or ICSI using either ejaculated or surgically retrieved sperm.[9] OHSS occurred[9] in a moderate form in 6% and in a severe form in 2% of cycles. Other complications were relatively uncommon: vaginal bleeding in three patients, deep vein thrombosis in four, hemiparesis in two patients, an acute abdomen that necessitated laparotomy in three patients (two for ruptured heterotropic pregnancies and one for torsion of an adnexal cyst) and anaesthetic complications in two patients.[9] Four men had testicular infections following 575 surgical retrievals of sperm. The one patient who died due to liver failure following OHSS had withheld information, about her previous liver damage from hepatitis C, from the clinicians treating her.

The emotional rollercoaster of fertility treatment

The state of infertility is very difficult for many couples to come to terms with. Typically the couple decide it is time to start their family and stop using contraception. The woman confidently expects to become pregnant almost straight away having spent the last few years trying hard to remember to use contraception and not take any chances with unprotected intercourse and pregnancy. After the first few periods arrive with one or two false hopes as they start a little later than expected, she and her partner become progressively more despondent and very emotional at the first sign of menstrual loss. Men may tend to assume that the blame for the couple's infertility is more likely to lie with the female partner, especially if they associate infertility with being less 'manly'. If the woman has had a previous termination she could well be feeling very guilty about her past, especially if she has not told her partner about the termination(s).

The couple will have invested a lot of emotion in their first visit to the GP to discuss the delay in their conceiving. It may be the first time they have talked publicly about their problem. They may be disappointed to realise that there will be no instant solution to their delay in conceiving and that they are expected to wait longer for spontaneous conception to occur. Then they may become progressively more frustrated by waiting for test results at the practice, or maybe a long wait to be seen by an NHS specialist at a fertility clinic.

The infertile couple need as much good information at this stage as possible. They need to be able to understand their situation, assess their options and discard the myths about the causes and circumstances of infertility that others may tell them. If the couple are not well informed they might press for treatment that is inappropriate, such as a quicker referral to a urology or gynaecology clinic rather than wait to be seen at a fertility clinic.

Those who undergo the sequence of specialised fertility investigations and assisted conception treatments describe the emotional rollercoaster of the highs and lows in the different stages of their treatment. Their expectations may be fuelled by embarking on new treatments only to be dashed when eggs and sperm fail to fertilise, or treatment has to be abandoned because of complications, or when a miscarriage, or worse still a stillbirth, occurs. The quotes from some infertile couples recently surveyed[10] describe some of these feelings.

The many intertwined emotional and ethical decisions taken by infertile couples in the course of treatment can be distressing. Being involved in weighing the balance between achieving a successful pregnancy and the risks of creating a multiple pregnancy, is one of the most fundamental dilemmas. It is asking a lot for an infertile couple to make a rational decision when they are desperately longing for a baby and do not fully appreciate

Box 6.1: Selection of comments by men and women who responded to the National Infertility Awareness Campaign's survey[10]

'The strongest feeling was one of total and utter failure.'

'Our relationship has experienced extremes of despair and then strength. Only we understand, like other infertile couples, the pain.'

'Infertility not only had a marked effect on my relationship with my partner but also with friends, family and complete strangers. The pressure to be "normal" in today's society is extreme and the lack of government support via funding and inadequate diagnosis makes infertility an abnormality.'

'The area of infertility is a very traumatic one – filled with obstacles and difficulties that you can never imagine when you first start out.'

'…there was no support for people in our situation in this area, in fact there is an overwhelming feeling of hitting a brick wall as we cannot afford private treatment.'

the increased chances of abnormalities and complications from multiple pregnancies, nor the financial, practical and emotional hardships of caring for twins, triplets or more babies.

The potential risk of ovarian cancer

It is still unclear whether there is a causative link between drugs given for infertility treatment and subsequent ovarian cancer. Several studies from overseas have suggested a link between infertility drug treatment and ovarian cancer, but others have pointed out that even if there were such an association, fertility drugs may not be the cause of the cancer, and that whatever caused the original problem of infertility might be the real link to the later development of ovarian cancer. Another theory propounded is that those with an increased risk of developing ovarian cancer are more susceptible to any cancer-provoking properties of infertility drugs. At present the guidelines[11] describe the evidence as suggesting that clomiphene is not associated with any increased risk of ovarian cancer if used for less than 12 cycles. Until more is known from the ongoing follow-up trials, all infertility drugs should be used at the lowest effective doses possible, to minimise any potential risks of ovarian cancer.

References

1 Levene MI, Wild J, Steer P (1992) Higher multiple births and the modern management of infertility in Britain. *The British Association of Perinatal Medicine. British Journal of Obstetrics and Gynaecology.* **99**: 607–13.

2 Coetsier T, Dhont M (1998) Avoiding multiple pregnancies in *in-vitro* fertilisation; who's afraid of single embryo transfer? *Human Reproduction.* **13**(10): 2663–4.

3 Lieberman B (1998) An embryo too many? *Human Reproduction.* **13**(10): 2664–6.

4 Murdoch A (1998) How many embryos should be transferred? *Human Reproduction*. **13**(10): 2666–70.

5 Templeton A, Morris J (1998) Reducing the risk of multiple births by transfer of two embryos after *in vitro* fertilisation. *NEJM*. **339**(9): 573–7.

6 Human Fertilisation and Embryology Authority (1998) *Annual Report 1998*. HFEA, London.

7 Rennie J (1996) Perinatal management at the lower margin of viability. *Archives of Diseases in Childhood*. **74**: 214–8.

8 Royal College of Obstetricians and Gynaecologists (1998) The management of infertility in secondary care. Evidence-based clinical guidelines. No. 3. Royal College of Obstetricians and Gynaecologists, London (0171 772 6275).

9 Serour G, Aboulghar M, Mansour R, *et al.* (1998) Complications of medically assisted conception in 3,500 cycles. *Fertility and Sterility*. **70**(4): 638–42.

10 Braude P, Ledger W (1998) *Infertility into the Millennium*. National Infertility Awareness Campaign, London.

11 Royal College of Obstetricians and Gynaecologists (1998) *The initial investigation and management of the infertile couple. Evidence-based clinical guidelines. No. 2*. Royal College of Obstetricians and Gynaecologists, London (0171 772 6275).

PART 4

The wider aspects of fertility treatment

▶ CHAPTER 7

The wider aspects of fertility treatment

Cryopreservation therapy

Cryopreservation is the freezing of sperm or embryos and their storage in liquid nitrogen, for thawing and transfer at a later date. The process is now available in most clinics. The use of frozen human eggs is still experimental as there is insufficient information about safety; research is continuing in this field. The HFEA does not allow frozen eggs to be used for treatment. Some embryos do not survive being frozen, but the suggestion that abnormal embryos are more likely to be killed by freezing has yet to be proven.

Sperm donors are screened for HIV, hepatitis B and C, and syphilis. The gametes are stored for 180 days and a second HIV antibody test is undertaken to exclude the possibility that the male donor was infected with HIV but had not yet developed antibodies in his blood. Such comprehensive screening is not necessarily adopted for people wishing to store gametes and embryos for their own use, such as people about to undergo oncology or radiotherapy treatment, or a woman suffering from OHSS who wishes to freeze her embryos for future use.

Pregnancy rates with frozen as opposed to fresh embryos are lower (12% of 4908 transfers of frozen embryos resulted in live births as opposed to 18% per fresh embryo transfer for 23 153 patients treated by IVF[1]). There appears to be no increased risks of miscarriage or congenital abnormality and the cryopreservation process does not appear to adversely affect the growth or health of children during infancy and early childhood, although more follow-up studies are yet needed to be sure.[2] There is no increase in obstetric or perinatal complications in pregnancies resulting from the transfer of frozen embryos, nor is there any evidence of genetic damage to embryos according to research studies on animals.[3]

There has been no recorded incident of cross contamination with stored gametes and embryos intended for treatment, such as from microbial or viral infection. The good laboratory practices that licensed clinics have established minimise such risks.

The media recently reported that a couple were exploring the possibility of storing their frozen embryos to allow them to time conceiving their children at convenient stages in their lives. The 32-year-old would-be mother apparently wanted to delay motherhood until she was 40 years old and reduce the chances of infertility or congenital abnormalities occurring then.[4] Such an arrangement would be legal so long as the length of storage was less than the five year maximum statutory period. However, the assisted conception techniques involved in creating the embryo and transferring it to the prospective mother's receptive uterus is invasive and expensive, and less likely to succeed than natural conception. The story has provoked a new ethical debate over the relative justification of freezing embryos for social reasons as opposed to medical reasons, and why if frozen embryos are stored for an infertile couple it is wrong not to extrapolate that facility to fertile couples too. If the couple later split up the embryos could not be used without both partners' agreement.

The removal and storage of testicular or ovarian tissue

Testicular or ovarian tissue containing gametes can only be stored on licensed premises with the patient's written consent; pre-pubertal tissue that does not contain gametes can be stored on unlicensed premises. If immature gametes are taken from the tissue and matured *in vitro*, then the HF&E Act applies and subsequent storage, treatment or research with those gametes must be licensed and the appropriate consent obtained.

Anyone who has attained the age of 16 years and is of sound mind may give legal consent to surgical or medical treatment or procedures. The issues for children under the age of 16 years are discussed later in the book in the section on 'Consent'.

The maximum statutory storage period for embryos was extended in 1996 from five to ten years. In some cases consent can be renewed and storage take place up until an individual partner is 55 years of age. Once the permitted storage period has expired, the embryos must be allowed to perish.

Little is known about the long-term effects of prolonged storage on frozen embryos, but it is said that there is no evidence that the length of storage will increase abnormalities in frozen embryos later used for creating pregnancies.

Donation of gametes

There is a legal limit of ten offspring per male or female donor because of public unease. The upper age limit for sperm donors is 55 years old whereas that for egg donors is 35 years old. The restrictions on age and number apply to donated sperm or eggs, not those recovered from either partner for their own use. The HFEA makes exceptions where a couple want to have another child using the same donor who provided gametes used in conceiving a previous child.

Gametes can be imported from overseas to a specific licensed clinic under a special direction by the HFEA, who will require satisfactory information about the sender, whether the donor gave consent to the export of the gametes, the purpose of the import, reassurance that the donor was appropriately screened, and the nature of material being imported. There is a problem where gametes originate from overseas in that some overseas centres will not provide the names of donors because of preserving confidentiality about their identity. Treating centres in the UK have to rely on the overseas centre's assurances that consent has been properly obtained from the person donating the gametes or whose gametes were used to bring about the creation of the embryo in question.

Embryos can only be exported overseas with the written consent of the provider of those gametes under a special direction from the HFEA and similar information as for the import of gametes or embryos.

1 Anonymity

The HF&E Act (1990) makes it an offence for licensed clinics or the HFEA to disclose the identity of donors. The only exception where the HFEA may disclose identifying information is if a child that was born with a disability as a result of the donor's failure to disclose an inherited disease was to sue a clinic for damages. If this were to occur a court might require the HFEA to disclose the donor's identity under the Congenital Disabilities (Civil Liabilities) Act 1976. Whether individuals have a right to know their genetic background continues to be a matter of public debate. The Department of Health is looking at this issue at the present time so that there is a possibility that those conceived from donor eggs or sperm could trace their genetic parents in the future, but a change in primary legislation would be required, and the strength of public feeling on the topic makes it unlikely that any such change in the law would be applied retrospectively.[5]

2 Paternity

The birth mother is the legal mother of any child born from licensed assisted conception treatments. Thus an egg donor does not have any legal rights over, or responsibilities for, any child resulting from treatment with her eggs. Similarly a sperm donor is not the legal father of any child who results from treatment with his sperm. The resulting child's birth certificate will not have any indication that either a sperm or egg donor was involved in the conception. Where a single woman is treated with donor sperm, there will be no entry under the section for 'father' on the birth certificate.

Payments to donors and 'egg sharing' in IVF

Egg and sperm donors can receive payments of up to £15. The HFEA would prefer that sperm and eggs were donated as a voluntary gift and are looking for ways to promote a culture of altruism.

Egg donors have to undergo extensive medical screening, and then be primed with hormones to stimulate their ovaries to produce plenty of eggs. This means that they are subject to the side-effects of powerful hormones before having an operation under general anaesthetic to retrieve the eggs through the vagina, after which they need time to convalesce. Some clinics encourage women needing egg donation to find and recruit egg donors to donate to them or anonymously to other women in return for which the clinic will expedite their own IVF treatments.

Some women going through IVF may choose to share surplus eggs with someone else, but usually they agree to this arrangement in return for free or subsidised IVF treatment. As donated eggs are in short supply, this arrangement allows women who have no eggs but who can afford to pay for private treatment to receive IVF, and those who are unable or unwilling to pay for private treatment to receive IVF. Eggs can be shared disproportionately between the donor and recipient so that the donor retains more, to balance the donor's chances of conceiving from a particular batch of eggs. Otherwise, the woman donating eggs in this way is less likely than the woman receiving her eggs to become pregnant because of the differing reasons for the causes of their infertility in the first place. It is the egg donor who takes most of the risks of treatment from the ovarian stimulation, compared with the recipient, and if a woman gives away a proportion of her eggs to another rather than going on to freeze embryos for her own future use, she will have to repeat the ovarian stimulation procedures if she does not become pregnant and wants to try IVF again, which she might have avoided by keeping her own eggs. The HFEA will be developing specific guidelines to regulate egg sharing for the next edition of its Code of Practice, following a public consultation exercise which supported the continuation of egg sharing as an option.

It seems that few women who have donated eggs in return for IVF treatment have regrets about sharing their eggs with another infertile woman.[6,7] They seem to have been genuinely glad to have helped other women like themselves to have become pregnant using their eggs, and if they failed to become pregnant themselves and their egg sharers did, seem pleased that their efforts were not in vain. One study concluded[7] that 'as long as egg donation is not covered by the NHS, it is fairer to offer egg sharing than to refuse treatment to those unable to pay'.

Box 7.1

'Egg sharing is a loving anonymous donation in just the same way as altruistic egg donation. Some would say more so because it is a gift from one woman who has suffered the pain of infertility to another who has gone through a similar experience.'[8]

The more that independent counsellors and GPs are involved in discussions with potential egg or sperm donors, and can explain the ethical and practical implications of donation, the better informed such donors can be about their choices.

The welfare of the potential child created by donated gametes should be of paramount concern, but even the welfare of the child is regarded in alternative ways by those for and against banning payments to donors and used to justify their arguments and platforms. On the one hand supporters of banning payments think that the resulting children might have their sense of self-worth undermined by thinking that their birth parents had purchased their genes, whilst those who support egg sharing or the reimbursement of 'reasonable expenses' argue that the children might be grateful for their birth parents taking such trouble to procreate them.

Pre-implantation genetic diagnosis

Pre-implantation genetic diagnosis (PGD) is a technique used to detect inherited genetic disorders in embryos before they are transferred to the uterus. There are two types of PGD: tests for particular disorders and tests for a sex-linked disorder. This entails the removal of one or two cells from an embryo for genetic analysis, usually at two to three days after fertilisation when the embryo consists of 8–16 cells. Studying two cells gives a better picture and more chance that the material is representative of the whole embryo as cells vary considerably; it is not possible to take more than two cells for analysis at this stage. In this way, affected embryos might be identified and only healthy embryos without the genetic defect are transferred as part of an IVF procedure. Such early diagnosis will avoid termination in mid-pregnancy after pre-natal diagnosis has been carried out by chorionic villus sampling or amniocentesis with an associated 1–2% risk of subsequent miscarriage.

A few hospitals have been licensed to offer PGD for specific disorders – the X-linked Duchennes disease, cystic fibrosis, Tay Sachs, spinal muscular atrophy, β-thalassaemia, and Huntington's chorea. Following a public consultation exercise in 1993, the HFEA decided that sex selection by PGD should not be used for social reasons but be confined to identifying sex-linked disorders with 'serious or life threatening diseases and disorders' such as the reduced life expectancy or quality of life of affected individuals. The HFEA is working with the recently constituted Advisory Committee on Genetic Testing to develop licensing parameters for PGD in the future.

Reports do filter through of experiments in sex selection occurring abroad;[9] the particular method cited has triggered concerns about the potential risks of sperm being stained with dye and exposed to ultraviolet light to aid separation of XX and XY chromosomes. The procedure exploits the size difference between X and Y chromosomes by sorting sperm through the disproportionate uptake of fluorescent dye by X-bearing sperm containing more DNA than Y-bearing sperm. X and Y sperm are then sorted to increase the chances of achieving a baby of the desired gender through IVF or IUI procedures. However, the process is imprecise and only capable of sorting sperm up to about 85% of X-bearing sperm or 65% of Y-bearing sperm, compared to the usual 50–50 mixture of untreated sperm.

Counselling

Patients should be as well informed as possible about the ethical and practical implications of treatment as well as know full details of the range and success of different methods of assisted conception. Easy access to an independent infertility counsellor is an important option for those undergoing investigations and treatment. Patients may want to discuss whether and when they should embark on alternative treatments or stop treatment, with someone with another perspective than that of the treating team away from the clinic setting.

There are three different aspects to the counselling that should be available to infertile couples:

- therapeutic counselling about the nature and implications of treatment and advice about the consequences of the infertile condition itself, the investigations and treatment;
- emotional support about the pyschological and social issues related to infertility and reproductive health care during their attendance at the infertility clinic and coping with the couple's feelings if they fail to conceive;
- counselling about the ethical and legal issues of assisted conception to gain an increased understanding of the implications

of the proposed infertility measures as far as the couple, their family or resulting children are concerned.

Counsellors should also be able to help infertile couples decide when to cease treatment and come to terms with their continued childlessness, which really comes under the umbrella of bereavement counselling. Local and national patient support groups also offer practical and emotional support.

Infertility counsellors often come from nursing, social work or psychology backgrounds. The British Infertility Counselling Association and British Fertility Society accredit infertility counselling qualifications. Those with the Diploma in infertility counselling will know about the causes of sub-fertility and sterility, the type and reason for various medical investigations, and have an in-depth knowledge of alternative treatments and the drugs used. They will be aware of the physical, psychological and social effects of infertility treatment, the issues surrounding the welfare of any future children and the roles and responsibilities of other health professionals involved in delivering fertility care. Training as an accredited counsellor involves practical supervision by another qualified counsellor, to ensure that the new counsellor can apply their theoretical knowledge in the clinical setting.

There are many ethical and legal considerations in reproductive health care, for the donor, the recipient, the partner, existing and potential children. As techniques become more sophisticated and new developments make conceptions possible in specific circumstances for the first time, counsellors have to keep abreast of new ethical dilemmas as they unfold.

Each licensed fertility centre should offer couples the opportunity of seeing a well-qualified counsellor who is independent of the centre as well as making counselling available from staff at the centre. Such an independent counsellor may reassure the consulting infertile couple that there are no commercial considerations involved in the advice they are given about treatment options.

A new area where counselling is needed is when genetic testing on donated gametes reveals a genetic defect of which the donor was previously unaware. Pre-test information and counselling must be offered with subsequent advice and support for those donors who turn out to be carriers. The couple need to be informed and counselled of the risks where such screening has not been done; and to receive reliable and comprehensive information about the meaning and the limitations of screening when it is carried out.

Ethics committees

It is not obligatory for licensed fertility clinics to have ethics committees, but is accepted good practice. Most but not all clinics have ethics committees who advise the clinic on ethical matters of policy or issues relating to the provision of assisted conception. Members do not consider specialist medical matters in the way that district medical ethics committees consider general health-related research submissions. Their remit is wide and they consider and advise on such issues as the ethnic factors that affect ethical decisions about fertility treatment, the appropriateness of treating unconventional couples such as lesbians, and should act as a check on 'over-enthusiastic social engineering'.

Genetic testing

Genetic disorders affect about 1% of the population at birth. Genetic testing detects the presence of, or a change in, a particular gene. Genetic disorders may be recessive or dominant. In an autosomal recessive disorder such as cystic fibrosis or sickle cell disease, a defective gene has to be inherited from both parents, and a person carrying one gene (a heterozygote) is usually unaffected by the disorder. Only males are affected by X-linked recessive genetic disorders such as Duchenne muscular dystrophy and all daughters of affected males are carriers. In an autosomal dominant disorder, such as Huntington's chorea or polycystic kidney disease, inheriting one defective gene from one parent is sufficient for the person to be affected by the disorder. Those with an autosomal dominant condition have a one in two chance of passing it on to their children. Genetic test results need to be interpreted in the light of medical and family histories, and genetic counselling should be seen as a complex specialism as there are so many multi-factorial disorders.

Cystic fibrosis is the commonest genetic disorder amongst the Caucasian population in the UK whereby a recessive disorder involving a single gene can cause serious disease. About one in 25 healthy adults carry the defective gene; one in 2500 children are affected by cystic fibrosis when they inherit two defective genes, one from each parent.

Genetic testing can diagnose people who are suffering symptoms of a condition or detect people who will develop a particular disorder later in life, or are carriers of a disease. Genetic tests for susceptibility to diseases such as cancer, heart disease and diabetes have been developed. Testing is undertaken by blood or urine samples or cells from inside the mouth.

Fertility clinics should take 'all reasonable steps to prevent transmission of a serious genetic disorder ... Genetic testing should be limited to the determination of carrier status for inherited recessive disorders'.[10] Although screening for cystic fibrosis is not mandatory it is strongly recommended;[10] specific diseases mentioned for which egg and sperm donors should be screened are cystic fibrosis, and Tay-Sachs, β-thalassaemia and sickle cell anaemia where appropriate for specific population groups.

All those donating gametes should be screened for HIV and other sexual diseases, and common genetic diseases such as cystic fibrosis, but it is not feasible to screen everyone who is being treated with their own eggs or sperm. Some clinics screen *all* gametes that are being cryopreserved to reduce the chances of cross-contamination, although with good laboratory practices this should not be an issue. Many clinics screen men undergoing intra-cytoplasmic sperm injection

(ICSI) too, because in general, poor sperm quality is associated with an increased incidence of sex chromosome abnormalities.

Issues of consent

Informed consent involves knowing about:[11]

- the nature and purpose of the intervention
- the intended effects and unintended side-effects
- the risks, harms and hoped for benefits
- any reasonable alternatives.

No licensed treatment should be given to any person without their written consent to all the stages of the particular treatment. The only exception would be in a case where someone's life was at risk if emergency treatment was not given and he or she was incapable of giving consent, as for any other life-threatening condition.

Consent to treatment or storage should be informed and voluntary. There should be no coercion or fraud or constraint applied to any person giving consent in a healthcare context. The consenting person has a right to refuse or withdraw from the situation without prejudicing their future healthcare. The person has a right to ask questions and to negotiate aspects of their treatment.[12] People giving consent to the use to which their gametes or embryos may be put or how they will be stored, may vary or withdraw their consent at any time before the gametes or embryos are used.[10] Gametes must not be taken from anyone who is not capable of giving valid consent.

The long-term partner or spouse of a person receiving or donating gametes does not have to consent to the treatment or donation of eggs or sperm for treating infertile couples[10] but it is good practice to encourage any such partner to give their written consent too and may avoid legal disputes about paternity in the future if the couple are unmarried. A woman's husband will be the legal father of a child born after treatment with donated sperm unless they are legally separated or there is evidence that he did not consent to treatment. Where the couple are unmarried when the treatment is carried out, the male partner will acquire 'legal paternity' of the child who is born provided that:

- the couple received treatment together
- the male partner consented to the treatment.

However, there is a legal distinction between 'parental responsibility' and 'legal paternity', and 'parental responsibility' is not automatically granted to unmarried men who become fathers as a result of receiving treatment together at a licensed fertility clinic. Unmarried couples who may be affected may be best seeking advice from a legal adviser about their own circumstances.

Any donor of eggs or sperm must give written consent about the specific use for which the gametes are intended, which might be for the treatment of themselves, for themselves and a named partner, to provide treatment for others, or for research. People must give consent to their gametes being stored, stating what should be done with the gametes or embryos if they die or become incapable of varying or revoking their consent. Several instances of sperm donation from a brain dead patient and the use of stored sperm after men have died has provoked public debate about the ethics and morality of creating children whose fathers died a considerable time before they were conceived. Posthumous storage or use of sperm or eggs without effective consent is unlawful in the UK in all cases. Ideally anyone intending to donate organs or tissues after their death should have their written consent witnessed by others.

The law does not specify at what age a child is considered able enough to give consent. A child who understands what the medical treatment is, its purpose, why it is proposed and any risks, and the consequences of not receiving the proposed treatment can consent to treatment. He or she is regarded as being 'Gillick competent', following the guidance that emerged in the Gillick case.[13] The judge in this case instructed that a child under the age of 16 years would have the capacity to consent to prescribed contraception if she was of sufficient maturity to understand the nature and consequences of that consent. The kind of situation in which consent to treatment by under 16-year-olds becomes important is where they are about to undergo chemotherapy which may threaten their fertility and it is logical to store testicular or ovarian tissue in case they are infertile in the future. Whilst parents can consent to a child's examination and treatment, the child's consent is needed for storage of their gametes if they have reached puberty.

Surrogacy

Surrogacy describes the arrangement by which a woman acting as a surrogate mother 'agrees to bear a child for another woman or a couple (the intended parents) and surrender it at birth'.[14] Surrogacy should only be arranged where it is medically impossible or undesirable for a woman to carry a child such as after a hysterectomy, and not for purely social reasons, such as avoiding pregnancy disrupting a woman's career. However, such good practice is not enforceable as it is possible for surrogacy to be carried out on a do-it-yourself basis where health professionals are not involved.

In partial surrogacy, the child is genetically linked to the surrogate mother and the male of the commissioning couple (the intending parents) by the prospective father's sperm being placed in the surrogate mother's vagina and fertilising the surrogate mother's egg. This may be performed by self-insemination at home, away from any health service clinic, or by a health professional in a licensed fertility clinic. In full surrogacy the resulting child has no genetic link with the surrogate mother and the embryo is usually created from the eggs and sperm of one or both of the commissioning couple using the IVF technique. If one or both of the intending parents are unable to produce eggs or sperm themselves, donated sperm or eggs can be used in the IVF procedure. About 60 couples per year use IVF surrogacy.[15]

Surrogacy is not illegal, but the commissioning couple cannot legally force the surrogate mother to give them the child once it is born. Trouble may arise if the child is born with a disability or the commissioning couple change their minds about being parents for any other reason, or if the surrogate mother decides to keep the child once it is born. The HF&E Act (1990) states that 'no surrogacy arrangement is enforceable by or against any persons making it'. When the child is born the surrogate mother is the legal parent. So long as one of the intending parents is genetically linked to the child and the surrogate mother consents, the commissioning couple can apply for a parental order within six months of the birth of the child; otherwise they have to follow formal adoption procedures. If the surrogate mother has a partner, he is the legal father of the resulting child even though the sperm of the intending father was used to create the embryo. Surrogacy can be arranged by individuals or agencies so long as they are not profit making; surrogate mothers can be paid expenses by the commissioning couple, but not wages to reward their time or effort.

Surrogacy obviously has many emotional risks for the commissioning couple, the surrogate mother and her partner, not to mention the physical risks to the surrogate mother if the intending father is not screened for sexual diseases in a do-it-yourself arrangement, or there are problems in pregnancy. There are also implications for the siblings and other relatives of the child too, who may grieve for the baby being taken away after birth to live with the commissioning couple.

Surrogacy regulations are being tightened up to prevent women acting as professional surrogates and taking up surrogacy as an alternative to paid employment outside the home. Reports are starting to circulate of women renting out their wombs for up to £15 000 per baby.[16] If loss of earnings is taken into account when reimbursing expenses, such a sum might easily be justifiable.

Cloning

Cloning is not envisaged as ever being permitted as a method of artificial human reproduction of whole human beings, but this section is included in the book for information about its potential for developing new treatments and furthering knowledge through research on ageing, cancer, infertility, congenital disease and miscarriage.

Cloning is performed by either artificially dividing a single embryo into two parts to produce identical twins, or by nuclear replacement where foreign genetic material is introduced into the cytoplasm of an unfertilised egg or embryo whose own genetic material has been previously removed. An entire animal is produced from a single cell in 'reproductive cloning', in the same way that Dolly the sheep was created by the nuclear replacement of an egg.[17] Dolly was generated by transferring the nucleus of an udder cell taken from a six-year-old sheep into an unfertilised egg which had its own nucleus removed. Since then other scientists in America have proved that cloning Dolly was not a fluke as they have managed to clone several generations of mice. Animal reproductive cloning research is aimed at improving the genetic make-up of livestock.

Reproductive cloning is the creation of a fetus, baby or adult who is genetically identical to another fetus, baby or adult, whether alive or dead.[18] The HFEA bans any research which has human reproductive cloning as its aim.

Therapeutic or non-reproductive cloning is any use of a cloning technique undertaken for medical purposes, 'which does not result in the production of genetically identical fetuses or babies'.[18] The term 'cell nucleus replacement' has been coined to describe the process of cloning. The process involves removing the genes from an egg with a fine needle. Stem cells are extracted from the tissue to be cloned and fused with the empty egg using an electric current. Researchers expect that using cloned tissue in this way to repair damaged tissue will avoid rejection of transplanted tissue. Possible examples cited as benefiting from developments in therapeutic cloning might be the cultivation of brain cells to replace cells damaged by Alzheimer's or Parkinson's diseases.

A person's identity is not only determined by their genetic make-up, as environmental and social influences also affect an individual's development – so that it is impossible to produce an exact replica of a person by cloning. Some of the grave concerns about cloning include the reasons why the cloning of a particular person should be wanted in the first place – such as the desire to replace a loved person who has died. A child resulting from such an origin would be unlikely to be allowed to function in their own right, and would be unfairly expected to replicate their predecessor's behaviour and feelings.

There is a great deal of public disquiet about the growth of the biotechnological industry and developments in cloning techniques. The distinction between the research and developments allowed under the umbrella of therapeutic cloning and the disallowing of any stages in reproductive cloning will need to be made explicit.[17,18]

Research involving human embryos

All research studies need to be licensed by the HFEA as well as gaining approval by the researchers' own local ethics committees. Spare unwanted embryos generated by treatment may be used for research purposes with the parents' written consent. Research is limited to the first 14 days of an embryo's life after fertilisation has occurred.

The purpose of any research on embryos must be confined to promoting advances in the treatment of infertility, increasing knowledge about the causes of congenital disease or miscarriages, developing more effective techniques of contraception or detecting the presence of gene or chromosome abnormalities in embryos.[10]

References

1 Human Fertilisation and Embryology Authority (1997) *Patients' Guide 1997*. HFEA, London.

2 Wennerholm UB, Albertsson-Wikland K, Bergh C (1998) Postnatal growth and health in children born after cryopreservation as embryos. *The Lancet*. **351**: 1085–90.

3 Wood MJ (1997) Embryo freezing: is it safe? *Human Reproduction*. **12**, national supplement: 32–7.

4 Brennan Z (1998) Woman freezes embryo for sake of her career. *Sunday Times*, 16 August.

5 Human Fertilisation and Embryology Authority (1998) *Update August 1998*. HFEA, London.

6 Ahuja K, Simons E, Fiamanya W, *et al.* (1996) Egg-sharing in assisted conception: ethical and practical considerations. *Human Reproduction.* **11**(5): 1126–31.

7 Ahuja K, Mostyn B, Simons E (1997) Egg sharing and egg donation: attitudes of British egg donors and recipients. *Human Reproduction.* **12**(12): 2845–52.

8 Ballantyne A (1998) Watchdog may end women's shared hope. *Times*, 23 November.

9 Bendall K (1998) Sex aid for conception control. *Financial Times*, 21 November.

10 Human Fertilisation and Embryology Authority (1998) *Code of Practice 1998.* HFEA, London.

11 World Medical Association (1989) Declaration of Helsinki. In: *World Medical Association Handbook of Declarations*. Ferney Voltaire, World Medical Association.

12 Alderson P, Goodey C (1998) Theories of consent. *BMJ*. **317**: 1313–5.

13 Gillick versus West Norfolk and Wisbech Area Health Authority (1985) 3 All ER 402.

14 British Medical Association (1996) *Changing Conceptions of Motherhood. The practice of surrogacy in Britain*. BMA, London.

15 Department of Health (1998) *Surrogacy Review*. Stationery Office, London.

16 Murray I (1998) Rent-a-womb surrogates face ban. *The Times*, 15 October (editorial).

17 Wellcome Trust (1998) *Public Perspectives on Human Cloning*. Wellcome Trust, London.

18 Human Genetics Advisory Commission and Human Fertilisation and Embryology Authority (1998) *Cloning Issues in Reproduction, Science and Medicine*. HFEA, London.

▶ CHAPTER 8

The costs and availability of fertility treatment

There is a great variation in the availability, accessibility and range of services of NHS-funded provision of fertility treatment. The varying selection criteria set by health authorities has the effect that the availability of NHS-funded fertility treatment depends on geographical location and social situation rather than patients' needs. Such selection criteria include: the woman's age, whether or not either one of the infertile couple have had a previous child, the length of the couple's stable relationship, or whether the woman has been previously sterilised. Waiting lists are long even if couples fulfil the selection criteria.

ICSI is more expensive than conventional IVF. Retrieving the sperm surgically is an additional cost. The relative costs of different treatments given by one clinic[1] are:

Conventional IVF per cycle	£1700
ICSI per cycle	£2650
ICSI with surgical retrieval of sperm per cycle	£3700
Initial consultation and investigations	£170
Ovarian stimulation drugs per cycle	£500–800

In addition there are the hidden costs of IVF associated with multiple pregnancies and pre-term deliveries.

Rationing and eligibility for fertility treatment

IVF was one of the first treatments to be explicitly rationed by the NHS. In 1993, the purchasing plans of six of 114 health authorities in the UK explicitly stated that they would not be buying any IVF or GIFT treatments for their populations. At the other end of the scale, some other authorities were investing heavily in purchasing more services for their localities.[2] The differences in outlook were based on diverse interpretations of the relative importance of factors considered in assessing the needs of their local populations. The presence of local champions, whether there was a local provider, and pressure from local GPs and the community appeared to be important influences on whether health authorities purchased fertility services. Local public health experts in different health authorities interpreted the evidence about cost effectiveness and assessed needs differently, for example whether infertility could be categorised as a health need. There were rough and ready assessments of the relative health gains of different treatments and authorities started devising qualifying criteria about how to allocate limited treatment resources. Some started querying whether there should be equity of access in the NHS across the UK, and if so whether there should be a national decision about how to ration fertility treatment on a fair basis.

Since the early 1990s, the geographical variation in the availability of NHS-funded fertility treatment has become more marked. There has been a rapid increase in the level of IVF treatment funded by the NHS overall, but an increasing division between health authorities willing to fund high levels of treatment and those funding no treatment at all.[3] The criteria health authorities are using to define eligibility for NHS treatment and limit access vary greatly. Some authorities limit funding for assisted conception but do not restrict funds for tubal surgery, which may mean that patients with severe tubal damage will be referred for tubal surgery if this is their only option, even though assisted conception is the most appropriate treatment. A survey of all health authorities and boards in the UK in 1997 found that on average they were purchasing about one-third of the number of IVF cycles per population of that recommended for the provision of a comprehensive subfertility service.[3,4]

Box 8.1: A patient's perspective:

'I feel strongly that there should be nationally agreed funding criteria, so that all patients are treated fairly ... the lottery patients currently face depends on their post-code, and whether the GP is sympathetic and willing to prescribe drugs for them which is completely unjust.'[5]

Only 6% of responding health authorities or boards do not use eligibility criteria when deciding to fund IVF Ninety-nine per cent put limits on the woman's age, 30% on the man's age, 94% on the number of previous children, 49% on the length of the couple's relationship, and 67% on the number of previous cycles of assisted conception. Eighty-eight per cent of health authorities or boards limited the number of treatment cycles they were prepared to fund.[3] The maximum age limits for infertile women seeking IVF ranged from 34 years (3% of health authorities or boards) to 43 years (1%) with the median age being 38 years. One quarter of health authorities or boards who purchased assisted conception did not fund the drugs too. There was a variation in waiting time for assisted conception treatment from up to a year after referral (14 authorities) to more than four years after referral (three authorities).

The National Infertility Awareness Campaign's call[5] for national guidelines should ensure that: 'eligibility criteria are based on clinical need, that the most appropriate treatment is given to an individual couple and that decisions to treat are based on the potential for a successful outcome'.

References

1 Ndukwe G (1997) New treatment for male infertility. *GP News*. **7 November**.

2 Redmayne S, Klein R (1993) Rationing in practice: the case of *in vitro* fertilisation. *BMJ*. **306**: 1521–4.

3 College of Health (1997) Report of the fifth national survey of the funding and provision of infertility services 1997. National Infertility Awareness Campaign, PO Box 2106, London W1A 3DZ.

4 *Effective Health Care Bulletin* (1992) *The management of subfertility*, Vol. 1, number 3. NHS Centre for Reviews and Dissemination, University of York.

5 Braude P, Ledger W (1998) *Infertility into the Millennium*. National Infertility Awareness Campaign, London.

▶ APPENDIX 1

Organisations

British Infertility Counselling Association (BICA), 69 Division Street, Sheffield S1 4GE, Tel. 0171 354 3930 – offers information to those seeking details of counsellors specialising in infertility.

CHILD (National infertility patients' support group), Suite 219, Charter House, 43 St Leonard's Road, Bexhill-on-Sea TN40 1JA, Tel. 01424 732361 – offers support, counselling and information about infertility.

DI Network, PO Box 265, Sheffield S3 7YX – provides contact and support for those who plan to conceive children or have conceived children, using donated sperm for donor insemination, or donated sperm or eggs in IVF.

Human Fertilisation and Embryology Authority (HFEA), Paxton House, 30 Artillery Lane, London E1 7LS, Tel. 0171 377 5077.

Issue, 509 Aldridge Road, Great Barr, Birmingham B44 8NA, Helpline 01922 722888, manned by professional infertility counsellors is available to the public on weekday evenings – offers information on all aspects of infertility; organisation works to improve the quality and delivery of infertility care.

Miscarriage Association, c/o Clayton Hospital, Northgate, Wakefield, West Yorkshire WF1 3JS, Tel. 01924 200799 – offers support and information on all aspects of pregnancy loss.

Multiple Births Foundation, Institute of Obstetrics and Gynaecology, Queen Charlotte's and Chelsea Hospital, Goldhawk Road, London W6 OXG, Tel. 0181 383 3519 – offers professional support and advice about all aspects of multiple births.

National Infertility Awareness Campaign, PO Box 2106, London W1A 3DZ – provides information and advice about the funding of infertility treatment within the NHS, and campaigns to publicise inadequate funding.

RELATE, local services (consult telephone directory) – offers help for couples with emotional, psychosexual and relationship problems.

► APPENDIX 2

Books/booklets

Brian K (1998) *In Pursuit of Parenthood.* Bloomsbury, London.

British Medical Association (1996) *Considering Surrogacy?* BMA, London.

British Medical Association (1996) *Changing Conceptions of Motherhood. The practice of surrogacy in Britain.* BMA, London.

Family Planning Association (1998) *Infertility Tests and Treatment.* FPA, PO Box 1078, East Oxford DO, Oxfordshire OX4 5JE.

Furse A (1997) *Infertility Companion: A user's guide to tests, technologies and therapies.* Thorsons, London.

Hammer Burns L, Covington S (1998) *Infertility Counselling. A comprehensive handbook for clinicians.* Parthenon, London.

Human Fertilisation and Embryology Authority:
(i) Information leaflets

- Consent to the use and storage of gametes and embryos
- Donor insemination
- Egg donation
- Embryo storage
- *In vitro* fertilisation
- The role of the HFEA
- Sperm and egg donors and the law
- Treatment clinics: questions to ask

(ii) Interim Patients' Guide to DI and IVF clinics 1998 (free from the HFEA)
(iii) Code of Practice 1998
(iv) Annual Report 1998
(v) Videos: *In vitro* fertilisation and Donor insemination
(vi) Web site: www.hfea.gov.uk

Johnson M, Everitt BJ (1995) *Essential Reproduction*. Blackwell Science, Oxford.

Mack S, Tucker J (1996) *Fertility Counselling*. Baillière Tindall, London.

Royal College of Obstetricians and Gynaecologists (1998) *The initial investigation and management of the infertile couple. Evidence-based clinical guidelines. No. 2.* Royal College of Obstetricians and Gynaecologists, London (0171 772 6275).

Royal College of Obstetricians and Gynaecologists (1998) *The management of infertility in secondary care. Evidence-based clinical guidelines. No. 3.* Royal College of Obstetricians and Gynaecologists, London (0171 772 6275).

Tan SL, Jacobs HS (1991) *Infertility: Your questions answered.* McGraw-Hill, London.

Winson R (1994) *Infertility: A sympathetic approach*. Vermilion, London.

▶ GLOSSARY

- **Consent**: a person donating his or her genetic material or a patient undergoing infertility treatment must consent to the procedure in the same way as for any other medical treatment. The consent must be valid and informed. The storage and use of genetic material requires written effective consent.
- **Cryopreservation**: the freezing of sperm or embryos and their storage in liquid nitrogen, for thawing and transfer at a later date.
- **Donor insemination (DI)**: sperm from a donor is placed into the vagina, cervix or uterus.
- **Embryo**: a fertilised egg up to eight weeks of development.
- **Fetus**: the term used for an embryo after the eighth week of development until birth.
- **Follicle**: a small sac in the ovary in which the egg develops.
- **Gamete**: a reproductive cell such as an ovum or a spermatozoon which has a haploid set of chromosomes and which is able to take part in fertilisation with another of the opposite sex to form a zygote.
- **Gamete intra-fallopian transfer (GIFT)**: a procedure in which eggs are retrieved from the woman, mixed with sperm, and then immediately replaced in one of the fallopian tubes so that fertilisation occurs inside her body (*in vivo*).
- **Intra-cytoplasmic sperm injection (ICSI)**: is a variant of IVF whereby micromanipulation is used to inject a single sperm into an egg so that fertilisation occurs; the resulting embryo is transferred into the woman's uterus.
- **Intra-uterine insemination (IUI)**: the process by which sperm are placed in the woman's uterus by a fine plastic tube, timed to coincide with ovulation.
- ***In vitro* fertilisation (IVF)**: a method of assisted conception whereby eggs and her partner's or a donor's sperm

are collected and placed together so that fertilisation occurs outside the body in laboratory conditions (*in vitro*); the resulting embryo is transferred to the woman's uterus up to 48 hours later.

- **Licensed treatment**: any fertilisation treatment which involves the use of donated eggs or sperm (e.g. donor insemination) or where embryos are created outside of the body (e.g. *in vitro* fertilisation).
- **Live birth rate**: the number of live births achieved with 100 treatment cycles.
- **Ovulation induction**: fertility drugs given to women whose ovaries are not producing eggs in normal cycles.
- **Pre-implantation diagnosis (PGD)**: a technique to detect inherited genetic disorders in embryos *in vitro* before transfer to the uterus; the procedure entails removing one or more cells from an embryo for genetic analysis, usually at about two to three days after fertilisation when the embryo consists of 8–16 cells.
- **Spermatid**: an immature precursor of spermatozoa.

▶ INDEX